THE PARTY AND THE PEOPLE

THE PARTY AND THE PEOPLE

Chinese Politics in the 21st Century

BRUCE J. DICKSON

PRINCETON UNIVERSITY PRESS

PRINCETON & OXFORD

Published by Princeton University Press
41 William Street, Princeton, New Jersey 08540
6 Oxford Street, Woodstock, Oxfordshire OX20 1TR

press.princeton.edu

Library of Congress Cataloging-in-Publication Data

Names: Dickson, Bruce J., author.
Title: The party and the people : Chinese politics in the 21st century /
    Bruce J. Dickson.
Description: Princeton : Princeton University Press, [2021] |
    Includes bibliographical references and index.
Identifiers: LCCN 2020032357 (print) | LCCN 2020032358 (ebook) |
    ISBN 9780691186641 (hardback) | ISBN 9780691216966 (ebook)
Subjects: LCSH: Zhongguo gong chan dang. | Political parties—China—
    History. | Political leadership—China. | Political planning—China. |
    China—Politics and government—1949–
Classification: LCC JQ1519.A5 D5297 2021 (print) | LCC JQ1519.A5 (ebook) |
    DDC 324.251/075—dc23
LC record available at https://lccn.loc.gov/2020032357
LC ebook record available at https://lccn.loc.gov/2020032358

British Library Cataloging-in-Publication Data is available

Editorial: Bridget Flannery-McCoy and Alena Chekanov
Production Editorial: Natalie Baan
Text Design: Karl Spurzem
Jacket Design: Layla Mac Rory
Production: Erin Suydam
Publicity: James Schneider and Kathryn Stevens
Copyeditors: Kellye McBride and Anne Cherry

Jacket image: Honor guard at Tiananmen Square.
Photo: Tony Vingerhoets / Alamy Stock Photo

This book has been composed in Arno

Printed on acid-free paper. ∞

Printed in the United States of America

10 9 8 7 6 5 4 3 2 1

For Benita, Andrew, and Caitlin

CONTENTS

ACKNOWLEDGMENTS

This book was not my idea. I would not have written it were it not for Eric Crahan, then the political science editor at Princeton University Press. He pitched the idea of a book about the big questions in Chinese politics. His enthusiasm for the book and the potential scope of its audience eventually hooked me in. After he was promoted, Bridget Flannery-McCoy took over the project. She read multiple drafts of the manuscript and made wise suggestions on all aspects of the book, including the framing of the argument, the sequence of topics, and the need for ever more examples to illustrate the conceptual issues throughout the book. It was a joy to work with her, and she made the book unquestionably better with her careful eye for detail and insights on what readers would want to know.

The production team at Princeton kept the process moving on schedule. I would like to thank Natalie Baan, Theresa Liu, and especially Alena Chekanov, for their quick responses to multiple questions. Kellye McBride and Anne Cherry provided judicious copy editing.

Several people made very useful comments on the manuscript, saving me from making unforced errors of facts and interpretations. Martin Dimitrov and three other still anonymous reviewers read the entire manuscript and offered many helpful comments that improved the book immensely (if the shy reviewers ever make themselves known, I owe them a dinner). Others answered questions about specific chapters: I would like to thank Steve Balla, Joe Fewsmith, Iain Johnston, John Kennedy, André LaLiberté, Marie-Eve Reny, Shawn Shieh, Jessica Teets, and Carsten Vala. And still others helped me through our conversations over the years to understand the topics covered in the book, including Chunhua Chen, Mary Gallagher, Enze Han, Pierre Landry,

Lianjiang Li, Melanie Manion, Minxin Pei, Shen Mingming, Victor Shih, Yuhua Wang, and Dan Wright.

I had the good fortune to work with several talented young scholars while writing this book. For their invaluable research assistance, I thank Eleanor Albert, Kendrick Kuo, and Marx Wang. They helped me make sense of a vast amount of the scholarly literature on Chinese politics and to compile several of the case studies.

As always, I want to thank my family—my wife, Benita, and our kids, Andrew and Caitlin—for indulging me during the research and writing process. This book did not involve extended stays in China while they remained at home. Still, research and writing can be a solitary endeavor, and I disappeared frequently into my cone of silence. I hope the end results compensate for being so often away even while I remained at home. This book is lovingly dedicated to them.

THE PARTY AND THE PEOPLE

INTRODUCTION

In September 2011, the people of Wukan—a village in southeastern China—rose up in protest. Their elected leaders, they alleged, had sold land to developers without adequate payment to those who had made their livelihoods farming it. They marched on the government headquarters in nearby Lufeng city, demanding both compensation and the right to new elections.

The leaders of Lufeng did not accede to their demands. Instead they sent riot police to Wukan to shut down the protests and occupy the village. Over the course of several months, the village endured a standoff with police, and a handful of protesters were arrested and charged with attacking officers. One of the protesters, Xue Jinbo, died in custody. According to Xue's family, the body showed signs of torture, but the official cause of death was cardiac arrest. Tensions between police and the villagers escalated.

Situations like this are all too common in China: leaders ignore the legitimate demands of the people, and punish those who dare to push back against the unpopular and often illegal actions of leaders at all levels of the political system.

And then something extraordinary happened: the provincial leaders stepped in and agreed to the protesters' demands. They offered to investigate the compensation the Wukan farmers had received, and they fired the Wukan leaders who sold the land, arranging for new elections to replace them. One of the leaders of the protest, Lu Zuluan, was elected the new village chief.

The protests and their resolution were hailed as a potentially new model of grassroots democracy in China. Provincial party chief Wang Yang, soon to be elevated to the Politburo in Beijing, said he intended to use his peaceful "Wukan approach" to reform local politics across the province.

But, as is so often the case in Chinese politics, there was more to the story than this. Like the deposed village chief, the newly elected leader was a party member. He had been approved by the provincial party committee, which had intervened to prevent the protests from escalating. The Wukan protests did not spread to other communities, in part because of a blackout on media coverage of the protests, and in part because of fear of arrest. What looked to be a prodemocratic triumph was actually the Chinese Communist Party (CCP) reimposing its authority.

Lu, the new village chief, was himself charged with corruption several years later. Was this delayed retaliation for leading the original protest? Or a reminder that even protest leaders may fall prey to the same bad behaviors as those they once protested against? It's hard to say, because the domestic media blackout continued, and the people of Wukan were warned against speaking to foreign media. What originally seemed like the start of something big turned out to be just one more small-scale event that—while it did break out into global news—went unnoticed by most people in China. In the end, the "Wukan approach" did not spread.

This episode illustrates well many of the themes familiar to students of Chinese politics. The imperative from the CCP to create economic growth—by, for instance, converting farmland for industrial and commercial purposes—creates tensions between state and society, as local leaders take actions that align with the party but infuriate local citizens. With stability as another policy imperative, higher level officials are often tacit allies of local citizens when tensions boil over, willing to remove local leaders to defuse conflict. In these instances, the CCP is responsive to public opinion—but will not tolerate demands that would challenge its monopoly on power.

To understand China in the twenty-first century, we must begin with one basic fact: all political activity centers on the CCP. How the party has approached economic, political, and social reforms over the past few decades—and the reversal of many of these reforms under the current leadership—shaped not only the political system but also the party's relationship with the people.

* * *

In the decades after Mao's rule ended, major reforms transformed economic and social life in China. The private sector greatly expanded and the country opened up to connect to the global economy; as it did, incomes rose, mobility increased, and Chinese people began to move from the countryside to the cities. All of this change created expectations among foreign observers that China's political system would have to change as well.

These expectations of political change were influenced by modernization theory, which is based on one of the most well-established relationships in the social sciences: the more prosperous a country is, the more likely it is to be a democracy. According to this theory, an increasingly modernized economy is ultimately incompatible with an authoritarian regime, as economic modernization triggers social changes—urbanization, higher levels of education, the decline of agriculture in favor of industry and commerce, the emergence of a middle class—that change political values, and these new values in turn produce demands for a more open political system. This is what happened in the Western world in the eighteenth and nineteenth centuries and in East Asia and Latin America in the late twentieth century.

However, China's leaders had a different expectation. Going back to Deng Xiaoping and continuing under Xi Jinping, the CCP expected that economic modernization, if handled properly, would produce popular support and solidify its hold on power. Greater prosperity was intended to enhance the CCP's legitimacy, not threaten its survival. They wanted to preserve the essential elements of the one-party regime they established in 1949, with the CCP firmly in command of the policy goals, of who would be allowed to participate in the political system, and of the ideas and interests that would be allowed or—alternatively—suppressed. Unlike democratic regimes, the legitimacy of the regime would be based not on the consent of the governed but on its ability to modernize the country.

To a large degree China's leaders have achieved their goals. There are certainly democracy advocates in China, but they find little support among their fellow citizens, who place a higher value on economic growth, social stability, and national unity—the same priorities as the party's—than on the political rights and freedoms that democracy promises. China's leaders have been determined to avoid political liberalization that would weaken party rule, even if it yielded better economic results. They were willing to settle for poorer economic results, if necessary, to maintain the party's supremacy, and have resisted and repressed all efforts to promote political reform leading to democratization.

But with the international financial crisis in 2008, after fifteen years of double-digit growth, China entered a new phase. Slower economic growth—6.1 percent in 2019—has become the new normal. (The economy even shrank by 6.8 percent in the first quarter of 2020, but that was an aberration due to the COVID-19 epidemic.) Under President Xi Jinping, China is turning away from the "reform and opening" policies championed by his predecessor Deng Xiaoping and toward a still ill-defined "socialism with Chinese characteristics for a new era."

China's contemporary political system is best described as "responsiveness without accountability." Just as it was in Wukan, the party is often responsive to public opinion on strictly material issues. When new initiatives spark public opposition, the party has agreed to cancel the building of hydroelectric dams, petrochemical plants, and high-speed rail lines. After public outrage about the worsening air quality in major cities, it adopted stricter air pollution standards. Faced with a surge of protests and petitions about inadequate compensation for land seized for redevelopment, it adopted new policies on paying compensation to farmers and homeowners.

But the CCP is not responsive on political issues. And in China, almost anything can have political overtones: academic freedom; internet use; and the rights of women, migrant workers, the handicapped, ethnic minorities, and other disadvantaged groups all easily become politicized if the party deems them so.

And, while the party and government are responsive in some specific situations, they refuse to be accountable to the public at large. Officials are not elected by the people but appointed by those at higher levels of the party and government. With the exception of village leaders and local people's congresses (the CCP's name for legislatures), officials do not have to worry about garnering votes. Their public appearances are limited and usually scripted. While there are opportunities for individuals and groups to comment on pending laws and regulations, the government does not make these comments public (as occurs in the United States); it is impossible to know whether the comments led to changes in the final versions. A free media and a vigorous civil society can be important watchdogs on the government's performance, but the media is controlled by the state in China, investigative journalists are censored and occasionally imprisoned, and civil society groups that criticize the party's policies and its leaders are routinely suppressed. Protests against local officials often lead to concessions, but in order to prevent these cases from emboldening other potential protesters, some protest leaders are typically charged with endangering social order and are imprisoned—as happened in Wukan. Protests can be an effective means of challenging officials who do not implement policies properly, but harsh punishment serves as a warning to others not to try the same thing.

In short, the party may be responsive to the public, but selectively and on its own terms. It is not accountable to the people, which would require its officials or its laws to be endorsed by the public. There is no formal equivalent of initiative, referendum, and recall as in democracies around the world. The party does not even allow public opinion surveys to include approval ratings for its leaders, instead asking only if people support or trust party and government officials in general. To challenge officials they deem to be corrupt, malfeasant, or incompetent, Chinese citizens instead use online and public protests. These officials can be removed from office, but only by their superiors—making them accountable to their superiors, not directly to the people.

This responsive aspect of the Chinese political system is well known to specialists, but less familiar to others. Much of the research on contemporary Chinese politics is published in scholarly outlets that are not easily accessible to more general readers, and—like the study of political science more generally—it is increasingly quantitative and largely impenetrable to readers without advanced training in statistics. Therefore, few readers outside the academy understand what has now become the conventional wisdom on Chinese politics.

Much of the media—including excellent reporting by journalists—focuses on the repressive aspects of the political system, which are quite real, without similar coverage of the other tools used by China's leaders to govern the country, the informal understandings of both the party and the people that influence political activities, and the everyday practice of politics in twenty-first-century China.

* * *

The following chapters have three broad themes. First, they focus on issues of greatest salience to many political systems: how leaders are chosen, how policies are decided upon and implemented, and how the state interacts with society (whether in cooperation or in conflict). Second, they track the dramatic change in these practices over time as the party's prevailing priorities have evolved—with a particular focus on what has changed (and what has not) under Xi Jinping. In particular, Xi's approach is more repressive than responsive. Third, they identify where consensus exists among scholars, where debates continue, and where gaps in our knowledge remain. China's political system is more opaque than most. We need to recognize where reliable evidence does and does not exist. In the absence of good information, we should not substitute our own logic or fears for the vision of China's leaders.

Whether framed in terms of democracy, regime resilience, or regime vulnerabilities, most foreign observers are interested in what keeps the party in power. That is the question animating much of empirical research on China. It is therefore fitting to begin with this topic in chapter 1, where I compare the political and economic priorities of China's five generations of leaders, from Mao Zedong to Xi Jinping, and the resulting changes in the party's relationship with the people. This chapter also introduces the three main political institutions in China—the party, the government, and the legislature—and how the party controls the other two.

The regular replacement of leaders at all levels is a distinctive feature of China's authoritarian political system. Most authoritarian regimes replace their leaders in one of two ways: the death of the incumbent or his overthrow in a coup. Both methods of leadership change create a crisis for the regime. China has been an outlier in this regard. Over the past few decades it has devised a routine process for selecting, promoting, and replacing leaders. Chapter 2 will describe the process, mapping how local leaders compete with one another to demonstrate their capability: those that produce economic growth and greater tax revenue are more likely to be promoted and moved into higher levels of government—from villages to townships to counties to prefectures to provinces and ultimately to the central level in Beijing. After several rounds of this competition, all survivors have shown their competence. As a result, promotion to provincial and central posts relies instead on political connections and factional alliances. The importance of both competence and connections for those who make it to the top is apparent in the career paths of China's most recent top leaders: Jiang Zemin, Hu Jintao, and Xi Jinping.

Once leaders are in place, how do they advance their policy agendas? That is the topic of chapter 3. Studies of China's policy process reveal different patterns of decision making in different policy areas. Politically sensitive issues that pose an existential threat to the CCP—for example, internet censorship and developments in restive provinces like Tibet and Xinjiang—are made strictly within the top leadership. Areas of strategic importance, such as whether to stimulate the economy in order to produce short-term growth or to introduce structural reforms to achieve long-term goals, allow for extensive politicking within the state, both between different bureaucracies and between central and local officials. Policy options that are more technical in nature, such as the environment and health care, are more open to nonstate stakeholders and the public more generally. In short, the party is willing to be responsive in some policy areas but not others.

The role of civil society in both making and implementing policy is the topic of chapter 4. For much of the post-Mao period, China specialists have debated the existence of civil society in China and its potential to affect social and political change. This debate is based on the premise that a strong civil society is both a threat to authoritarian regimes and the basis for stable democracy. This chapter will distinguish between different realms of civil society: one that is engaged in politically oriented issues and strives to bring about democratization (what some refer to as the "real" civil society and which is in short supply in China), and another that is composed of nongovernmental organizations (NGOs) focused on social issues, such as adult literacy, job training, and poverty alleviation (these are much more numerous). The former group is critical of the state, and the state responds with often harsh repression; the latter group seeks to partner with the state in order to avoid being shut down and to obtain the resources it needs. This chapter will explore the remarkable variation in how the party treats different types of civil society groups, in different parts of the country, and at different points in time.

Chapter 5 will examine the sources of public protests and assess how much of a threat they pose to political stability in general and regime survival in particular. Are protests a sign of underlying resentments that could overwhelm the regime? Do they pose a danger or simply allow the public to vent and are harmless? Could they be beneficial to political leaders as a source of information about trends in public opinion and pockets of dissatisfaction? The politics of protest have been the subject of many academic studies; some focus on the motivations and strategies of protesters, others on the state's response. How the CCP handles protests reflects one of the dualities of Chinese politics noted above: it is often willing to meet the material demands of protesters (e.g., low or unpaid wages, inadequate compensation for seized property) while also punishing protest leaders and repressing any demands for political change. This chapter will synthesize what we know about protest in China as well as the limits of that knowledge.

The resurgence of religion is the focus of chapter 6. Much media attention has focused on the spread of Christianity and the state's efforts to control it, but the revival of traditional religions, especially Buddhism, has been just as rapid. In some cases, religious institutions in China have provided useful goods and services to local communities;

in other cases, they have been the source of violent conflict between state and society. In contrast to the popular perception that the Chinese state is determined to suppress religion, this chapter will emphasize the more varied expressions of religion, religious policy, and religious belief in China. This chapter also illustrates a recurring theme of the book: the more repressive atmosphere under Xi Jinping and the resulting pressure on unsanctioned but previously tolerated religious groups.

Nationalism has been a prominent feature in both China's domestic and foreign policies. The causes and consequences of Chinese nationalism are explored in chapter 7. On one hand, nationalist protests are one of the few types of dissent tolerated by the state in China. As a result, nationalist protests often become a proxy for other types of complaints. Chinese society is not necessarily more nationalistic than in the past, but nationalism is more permissible as a frame for protesters. On the other hand, the state uses patriotic education campaigns and official media to promote nationalism, and in turn popular support for the regime. However, promoting nationalism is risky business: it can help create public support for the state, but it can also turn against the state if the public believes the state is too slow or too weak in response to the actions and statements of other countries. The causes and consequences of Chinese nationalism are not simply an academic concern but are also of great interest to foreign observers. Will an increasingly nationalistic China take more aggressive actions toward its neighbors? Will it be a threat to foreign interests? This chapter will explore these questions by using public opinion survey data and case studies of nationalist protests, and by assessing the potential implications for China's foreign policy behavior.

This chapter will also look at the party's treatment of groups that do not share its vision of national identity. In Tibet and Xinjiang, religion and ethnic identity overlap in ways the party finds threatening, and the party has responded with both harsh repression and intensive patriotic education programs. In Hong Kong, a rising sense of Hong Kong identity, distinct from Chinese national identity, prompted prolonged protests in 2014 and 2019. These cases show how the party's notion of Chinese identity produces often violent conflict when it is not shared by local identities.

The book ends with a chapter assessing the prospects for democratization in China. In my experience as a teacher and public speaker, this is the question that interests American audiences the most—and yet it is really secondary to a more fundamental question about the potential for regime change. Without regime change, there can be no democratization—but even if the party does fall from power, democracy is not guaranteed. In recent decades, most cases of regime change did not result in democracy but in new forms of authoritarian rule. This has led many scholars to turn their attention to sources of regime stability, looking at the regime's frailties without exploring the prospects for democracy per se.

Still, throughout the post-Mao era of reform in China, the potential for China's democratization has driven debate among those in academia and beyond. Is democracy the inevitable consequence of economic modernization? Will economic reforms be stymied if not accompanied by political reform? Is Chinese society developing a preference for democracy, or does public opinion favor the continuation of authoritarian rule? Can an authoritarian government be responsive if it is not also accountable? This chapter will assess the ongoing debate and use the recent experiences of other countries to offer a comparative perspective on the likelihood of democratization, how it may happen, and what consequences may result.

The intent of this book is to share the rich research findings that have shaped the current academic understanding of Chinese politics. At a time when the political discourse about China has tilted toward demonization, this is more important than ever. For readers whose views of China are shaped by memories of the Cultural Revolution or the 1989 demonstrations in Tiananmen Square, by critiques from political leaders in the decades following, and by media coverage, this perspective may seem jarring. There is no question that the CCP uses repression against its perceived enemies, but it also uses other tools to create popular support: rising prosperity, nationalist pride, and even responsiveness to public opinion in varying degrees. It is my hope that readers will come away with a fuller understanding of China's political system, how it has arrived at this point, and where it may be heading.

1

WHAT KEEPS THE PARTY IN POWER?

The CCP has led China since 1949. During its seven decades in power, the party has faced elite conflict, economic calamity, and dramatic tensions with the Chinese people. And yet it has presided over the fastest economic growth in China's history and, with no significant organized opposition, appears secure in its status as China's ruling party. How has a party that has often seemed so fragile managed to survive for so long? And how much longer can it remain in power?

To understand the durability of China's political system, we must understand the CCP—and understanding the CCP means going back to the roots of communist thought.

Communism in theory is based on the ideas of Karl Marx, who provided the rationale for a worker-led revolution to overthrow the capitalist system of his day and for a vision of a communist utopia. But Marx had little to say about how the communist revolution would happen or what a communist government would look like. As a result, communism in practice relies on the ideas of Vladimir Lenin, who recognized that a "vanguard party" led by intellectuals like himself was necessary to organize the workers, to lead the revolution, and—once the revolution was over—to lead the new communist government. If Marx provided the ideology of communism, Lenin provided the organization.[1]

Leninism was the basis not only for leading a communist revolution but for leading the communist government once the revolution was over. Marx expected the communist state to eventually "wither away," but Lenin made sure it did not. In a Leninist political system, the party has a monopoly on political organization; it does not compete with other parties for power and influence, and it suppresses efforts to create new organizations autonomous from the party. It makes all important policy decisions and oversees the work of the government through the appointment of party members to all leading posts. Similarly, it puts party members in control of the military and security forces. Moreover, it creates party organizations known as "cells" throughout the government, military, workplaces, schools, and neighborhoods to monitor activities and to provide ideological education to party members working and living there. The party remains a vanguard party even after it becomes the ruling party: only a small percentage of the population become party members (in the former Soviet Union and Soviet Bloc countries, about 10 percent of the population were communist party members).

The CCP has survived as China's ruling party for more than seventy years because it was built on Leninist organizational principles and continues to abide by them. As a ruling Leninist party, the CCP sits atop the political system, controlling appointments to government and legislative posts, and ensuring that its policy priorities are enacted into law and implemented. It has a network of party cells throughout the government, workplaces, and neighborhoods to monitor and influence what happens in those places. The role of the CCP in day-to-day life has waxed and waned since it took power in 1949, but in recent years it has been increasingly dominant. As CCP General Secretary Xi Jinping said at the 19th Party Congress in 2017, "government, military, society, and schools—north, south, east, and west—*the party is leader of all.*"

Subsequent chapters will detail the different dimensions of the party's relationship with the people, but, to begin, it is important to have an understanding of the ebbs and flows of party rule in China and how the party controls the political system.

A Short Course on Communism in China

To follow the dramatic changes that have taken place in China after 1949, it is useful to think of five generations of leaders, each with distinctive leadership styles, policy priorities, and slogans that characterized their generation (see figure 1.1).[2] Two key trends are important to follow: first, the evolution of the party's economic development policies from a Soviet-style state-owned and centrally planned economy to Mao's radical leftist policies to an increasingly marketized and globalized economy, and second, the resulting impact on the party's relationship with the people.

Mao Zedong (1949–76): "It Is Right to Rebel"

Under Chairman Mao, the CCP alternated between periods of radical leftism, when it pursued the utopian goal of building a communist society, and periods of development, when the goal was economic growth and building an effective state. When Mao veered left, the party appointed ideologues (or "reds") to run political campaigns and implement policies with a mix of propaganda and coercion. When it switched to economic development, it appointed people with technical expertise and offered material incentives to achieve policy goals. These policy swings created conflict between reds and experts: reds appointed in leftist phases would be replaced by experts during developmental phases. Because policy priorities lurched between these competing goals and methods, neither officials nor members of society knew how long a policy would last or what was expected of them. Supporting a policy today could lead to punishment tomorrow when the policy changed.

The swings between leftist and developmental goals can be seen in the campaigns that characterized the Mao era. Upon taking power in 1949, the CCP embarked on a developmental period of rural and urban policies that were designed to restore the economy after several decades of civil war and the war against Japan. It undertook land reform in the countryside, taking property from landlords and redistributing it to the

FIGURE 1.1. Five "generations" of Chinese leaders (clockwise from top: Mao Zedong, Deng Xiaoping, Hu Jintao, Xi Jinping, and Jiang Zemin) (photo: courtesy of Matt Rivers / CNN)

farmers who actually worked the land. In the cities, it allowed the continuation of private ownership of industrial and commercial firms. To smooth the transition to communist rule, it allowed many of the bureaucrats from the old Nationalist regime to remain in their posts.

By the mid-1950s, the party replaced these development-oriented policies with more orthodox communist policies based on the Soviet model. It nationalized industry and commerce, although the former owners were often allowed to remain as managers of the new state-owned enterprises. The CCP took ownership of the land it had given to farmers a few years before in order to engage in collective farming. A central planning bureaucracy replaced markets as the basis for distributing goods and services. Thousands of Soviet advisers moved to China to supervise the development of an industrial base. For Mao, simply adopting the Soviet model was not enough. He grew frustrated with this planned and methodical approach to development and veered toward radical policies to yield more rapid economic growth. During the Great Leap Forward (1958–60), launched by Mao but opposed by most other CCP leaders, the CCP created rural communes for both agriculture and industry. Party propaganda replaced material interests as the motivation to work harder, and enthusiastic reds replaced industrial and agricultural experts. This proved disastrous: the combination of policy mistakes and bad weather led to a large-scale famine in which an estimated 30 million people died.

In the early 1960s, the CCP switched to developmental policies to restore the economy. Farmers were given financial incentives to produce more and were allowed to farm both the collective fields and their own small plots (these policies became the basis for the post-Mao reforms in agriculture in the late 1970s and early 1980s). Reds appointed to party and government posts during the Great Leap were replaced by experts to spur industrial and agricultural production. The result was a period of improved living standards and political calm.

Mao was unhappy with these growth-oriented policies, despite their success; he believed it was better to be poor and communist than rich and capitalist. In 1966, he began the Cultural Revolution to prioritize his utopian goals. The slogan that characterized this period was "It is right to rebel," encouraging groups of young people known as Red Guards to criticize and "seize power" from party and government leaders who were "taking the capitalist road" by relying on material incentives instead of mass mobilization to promote growth. Numerous leaders, including Deng Xiaoping, the architect of the developmental policies that provoked Mao's ire, were purged from their positions. Many of them were sent to prison or to work in the communes or factories.

Without a functioning party and government apparatus, China verged on the brink of civil war. Rival groups of Red Guards and other supporters of Mao faced off against each other in armed battles. By 1967, Mao grew disenchanted with the chaos he had unleashed and called in the People's Liberation Army to restore order. New revolutionary committees consisting of young radical leaders, local military commanders, and veteran officials were formed as temporary replacements for party and government organizations throughout the country. Beginning in 1970, party committees began gradually to reform, many of them staffed with the very people who had been ousted during the Red Guard phase of the Cultural Revolution.[3] After all the turmoil his Cultural Revolution had unleashed, it became apparent that Mao lacked an alternative vision for organizing political power. He simply rebuilt the previous party committees, often with the same people he had previously displaced.

The CCP now had to restore the economy once again. Leaders like Deng were rehabilitated and put back in their old positions, much to the resentment of the radicals who had risen to power during the Cultural Revolution. The radicals competed with the veteran officials for Mao's support, and Mao in turn swung between supporting one policy approach and then the other.

As Mao grew increasingly frail in his later years, the CCP was divided into rival camps: those like Deng Xiaoping who had been victims of the Cultural Revolution; those like Hua Guofeng (who became China's leader upon Mao's death) who had benefited from it; and the radical ideologues who had provided the ideas for it, above all the so-called Gang of Four, a group that included Mao's wife.[4] They convinced Mao to purge Deng a second time in April 1976 to prevent the continuation of his development-oriented economic policies. In September 1976, Mao died, and in October the Gang of Four were arrested by Hua and other senior leaders. This constant alternation between leftist and development policies, along with the resulting leadership strife, was dizzying; people did not know from one day to the next what was expected of them. By the time of Mao's death, both the state and society were exhausted from the policy swings and political turmoil.

Although Mao disliked the bureaucratic nature of his political system, by the time of his death the command economy had given the party control over society in three important ways.[5] First, with markets largely eliminated, people were dependent on the party for their jobs, housing, food, education for their children, and other life necessities. Housing was often linked to where you worked: workers who lost their jobs (which most often happened for political reasons, not for quality of work) also lost their housing, and their children could no longer attend their schools. There was no real estate market; a one-bedroom apartment that was appropriate for a newly married couple would become more and more crowded as the family grew. If workers wanted to move to another job or another city, they had to apply to the party for transfer, and their applications were usually denied. Desired consumer goods—bicycles, washing machines, clothing, even food—were strictly rationed. During leftist upheavals, not only markets were eliminated but money as well. People received monthly coupons for certain amounts of meat, grain, fabric, soap, and other daily necessities. These types of goods were in short supply because the centrally planned economy was geared toward heavy industry and not consumer goods. Those who ran out before the month was over had no way to restock their cupboards; they simply had to do without.

This dependence made it easy for the party to control society in a second way—by monitoring people's behavior. Each individual was registered to live in the place they were born, and moving was virtually impossible without the party's permission. This household registration system, known as the *hukou*, determined not only where people lived but also where they worked and what social services they were entitled to. In the countryside, most people were stuck in their villages and communes. Under these conditions, people were not free to come and go without being noticed. The party used its grassroots organizations in neighborhoods and workplaces to monitor what people said, what they did, and even the attitude with which they said and did things. During times of Maoist upheavals, such as the Cultural Revolution, the party also tried to control people's thoughts and leisure-time activities. Being able to monitor society gave the party tremendous control over even the most mundane parts of life. How people dressed, what they read, and what music they listened to suddenly took on political meaning. People could lose their jobs and even be imprisoned for politically incorrect speech and behavior.

As a consequence of this dependence and monitoring capability, the party had a third way to control society—by sanctioning individuals, rewarding certain behaviors with promotions, bonuses, and extra rations of desired consumer goods, and punishing unwanted behavior by cutting rations, demoting and firing workers, and even sending some to prison. With recurring political campaigns, party officials had frequent opportunities to punish their enemies and rivals, whether due to ideological apostasy or petty personal slights. But the repeated campaigns were also opportunities for payback, as the victors of one campaign became the victims of the next. In these three ways—dependence, monitoring, and sanctioning—the party had tremendous control over most members of society. In the post-Mao period, these three modes of control were weakened by Deng's economic reform policies but never fully disappeared.

Deng Xiaoping (1978–92): "To Get Rich Is Glorious"

After Mao's death in September 1976 and the arrest of the Gang of Four the next month, there was a brief interval of elite struggle before Deng emerged as victor. He remained de facto leader until his death in 1997, even though he was never the official head of the CCP or government (see chapter 2 for more details on leadership succession in the post-Mao era). The post-Mao reform era effectively began in December 1978, when the Central Committee officially declared the end of class struggle—the key tactic in Mao's leftist approach—and other types of political campaigns and adopted economic modernization as the main task of the CCP.

Deng championed "reform and opening" policies that included dismantling the communes in favor of family farms; encouraging a private sector that grew from mom-and-pop shops and restaurants to global conglomerates; and integrating with the global economy for trade, investment capital, and technology. In sharp contrast to the radicalism of the Cultural Revolution, citizens were now told that "to get rich is glorious." This reassured the people that they would not be labeled "capitalist roaders" and punished for pursuing greater wealth, as was common during the Maoist era.

Deng's policies found the middle ground between two opposing camps. Conservative ideologues wanted to restore the orthodox Soviet model and rely on Marxist ideology for policy making. In particular, they saw the central planning system of the mid-1950s, before the disastrous Great Leap Forward, as the golden era to which they wanted to return. In contrast, radical reformers wanted to abandon central planning altogether and move toward more market-oriented policies. Rather than immediately dismantle the planned economy (as in the "shock therapy" policies in post-Soviet Russia), party leaders agreed to experiment with markets and private ownership in a few isolated "special economic zones" while the rest of the economy was run under the central plan. Over time, the market economy was allowed gradually to outgrow the planned economy as private firms provided the lion's share of new jobs, foreign direct investment, increased tax revenue, and—above all—new economic growth.[6]

Deng set the model of economic liberalization without political liberalization: the CCP might reduce its control over the economy but would not compromise its monopoly on political organization. However, its new focus on economic modernization weakened each of the three pillars of party control. The reemergence of family farms and privately owned factories, shops, and restaurants gave people new opportunities for work and made them less dependent on the party for their livelihood. These new enterprises created new demand for workers, triggering a flood of young people migrating from the countryside into China's cities in search of better-paying jobs. The hukou system was still in place, which meant migrants were not eligible for state-provided health care and could not send their children to local schools—but they could find housing and food, thanks to the emergence of a private market. All of this was taking place outside the party's control—although often with the party's blessing, especially the growth of private enterprises. With the population suddenly mobile, the party was less able to monitor people's whereabouts or daily activities, much less their thoughts and attitudes. With a private sector providing jobs, housing, food, and clothing, the party was less able to reward or punish members of society who were no longer dependent on the party as provider of necessary goods and services.

By weakening these pillars of a traditional communist system, and by making the party less and less relevant in the daily lives of most people, the post-Mao reforms limited the party's power. In part, this direction was intentional: Deng Xiaoping and other reformers believed that the mistakes of the Maoist period came from too much power centralized in the party, and in Mao in particular. Taken to their extremes, however, the reforms threatened to tilt the balance of power away from the party toward society and the private sector, thereby threatening the CCP's authority.

A major test of the CCP's hold on power came in 1989 during protests in Tiananmen Square and throughout China. What began as protests against the side effects of the reform and opening policies—corruption, inflation, and job losses—soon morphed into calls for political reform and democracy. Party leaders were divided over how to respond, some encouraging dialogue and compromise, others—including Deng— favoring repression to avoid another political upheaval like the Cultural Revolution, which had nearly ruined their careers and almost destroyed the party.

In the end, hard-liners prevailed and the party reasserted its control. Martial law was imposed on June 4, and hundreds—perhaps thousands—died. With the crushing of peaceful protests, many in and out of China predicted the imminent demise of the CCP; the party had lost the "mandate of heaven" and therefore its right to rule. The use of force damaged the CCP's legitimacy but not Deng's commitment to economic reform. Moreover, the end of communism in the Soviet Union and Eastern Europe between 1989–91 provided a new warning: the CCP could fall from power if it failed to modernize China's economy and restore the party's authority. From the party's perspective, these other communist parties were overthrown after long periods of economic stagnation and bureaucratic ossification.[7] For the CCP to survive, it would have to chart its own course.

Jiang Zemin (1992–2002): "Achieve a Moderately Prosperous Society"

In the immediate aftermath of the June 4 crackdown, Deng and other CCP leaders elevated Jiang Zemin from leader of Shanghai to CCP general secretary. Deng's conservative colleagues wanted to roll back his reform and opening policies of the 1980s, which they blamed for the protests of 1989. However, Deng believed that economic reform was essential for restoring the party's legitimacy. China's rapid pace of sustained economic growth began in 1992, when Deng traveled to the special economic zones in southern China to publicize their success. After a period of waffling, Jiang jumped on Deng's bandwagon and promoted his model of "socialism with Chinese characteristics," which looked a lot like capitalism but with one-party rule. A key reason that Deng's reforms reached their full potential under Jiang: the conservative leaders who opposed Deng's reforms either passed away or were pushed into retirement. During Jiang's tenure, China's period of rapid economic development reached its peak, but Prime Minister Zhu Rongji was widely seen as the main architect of this period's economic policy.[8]

Jiang represented a shift in China's leaders. He was not part of the revolutionary generation, like Mao and Deng. He was the leader of the "Third Generation," those who rose to power after Deng and his peers. This third generation was made up primarily of technocrats, officials with backgrounds in science, technology, and engineering. Technocrats differed from the conservative leaders who wanted to stick to the orthodox Soviet-style, centrally planned economy. Technocrats had a more pragmatic approach to policy making and were not beholden to the writings of Marx, Lenin, and Mao. The technocrats were also unlike radical reformers who wanted to reinvent the system and were willing to jettison any part of the status quo that stood in their way. Instead technocrats were problem solvers, willing to tinker with the political and economic systems in order to make them work better but not seeking to reinvent them. When they deviated from party traditions, they provided an ideological rationale for doing so, but because Jiang and other leaders in the 1990s were not committed to a Marxist vision, they began to draw upon Chinese traditions as sources of ideological legitimacy. The key goal of this era was to "achieve a relatively prosperous society," they said (a phrase with Confucian origins).

The expansion of China's private sector posed a particular quandary for the CCP. Independent sources of wealth are a threat to any authoritarian regime[9]—even more so to communist regimes because capitalists are supposedly their class enemies. After the 1989 demonstrations, the CCP officially banned the recruitment of private entrepreneurs into the party as it tried to preempt new political challenges. This was consistent with tradition but inconsistent with the commitment to economic modernization. Capitalists were essential to the CCP because they were the main source of economic growth, the party's key task in the post-Mao era. Most of China's exports also came from the private sector.

The party also took steps to more closely monitor the private sector, relying on traditional Leninist techniques.[10] First, it created official business associations to which private firms had to belong. These business associations were under the supervision of the party's United Front Department, its link to noncommunist groups. Second, it created party cells in private firms to provide logistical support in marketing, finance, and human relations—and to monitor their activities. Third, it co-opted entrepreneurs into the party, local legislatures, and other honorary political positions, all of which could provide business advantages. This violated the party's official ban, but local leaders saw private entrepreneurs as essential to their mandate of promoting economic growth and went to great lengths to justify their relationship with the private sector—in some cases simply denying that a firm was privately owned. By labeling them collective enterprises or joint-stock companies, the party gave a politically correct label to an otherwise incongruous entity.[11] Many of the largest firms were owned and operated by "red capitalists"— private entrepreneurs who were also CCP members, often former party and government officials.

To make its ideology fit the prevailing practice, the CCP adopted the Three Represents theory, which stated that the CCP represents (1) the advanced productive forces (a euphemism for private entrepreneurs), (2) advanced culture, and (3) the fundamental interests of the overwhelming majority of the people of China. Traditionally, the CCP represented the "three revolutionary classes": workers, farmers, and soldiers. But in the reform era, when the CCP was promoting economic modernization, it needed to adapt. The Three Represents theory was added to the party's constitution in 2002 when Jiang retired.

Ideology may not have been the source of policy, but the party still found it necessary to provide an ideological rationale for its policies. In this way, the party continued to insist it was the unquestioned leader of China's political system despite the rapid diversification of the economy and society. Above all, it continued to maintain the essence of a Leninist system: the party's monopoly on political organization.

Hu Jintao (2002–12): "Achieve a Harmonious Society"

The economic model of the Jiang Zemin era was built on expanding the private sector, promoting foreign trade, and investing in infrastructure and real estate. This model produced double-digit growth but also a growing income gap. With inequality increasing at an alarming rate, Hu Jintao—a technocrat, like Jiang had been—tried to balance growth with equity. He described this idea as "scientific development." This effort to address the gap between rich and poor had limited success; while inequality plateaued in the late 2000s, it did not significantly decline thereafter.[12]

In addition to promoting equity, the CCP under Hu had a second goal: maintaining political stability. The number of public protests had grown sharply from 32,000 in 1999 to 87,000 in 2005. The CCP adopted another Confucian phrase, "harmonious society," as its euphemism for increased spending on public security and other measures to maintain stability. By 2011, spending on public security surpassed the official budget for national defense, reflecting the party's priority on maintaining order and suppressing any hint of opposition.

The global financial crisis that began in 2007 exposed the limits of the Western model of unregulated markets, especially financial markets. The crisis confirmed to China's leaders the benefits of China's statist approach to development. China's economy slowed in the wake of the global recession as demand for Chinese exports of consumer goods suddenly dropped in many Western countries, but China did not fall into recession as many other countries did. The CCP launched a large economic stimulus package to cope with the crisis, but the vast majority of the stimulus went to state-owned enterprises (SOEs), forcing many private enterprises to go out of business. This gave rise to the expression "advance of the state, retreat of the private" after years of party support for the private sector.

Not only did the economy slow, so too did momentum for further economic reform. China's leaders became deadlocked between those who wanted to further stimulate the economy and those who want to restructure it.[13] The argument for stimulus was straightforward: if economic growth was essential for the CCP's legitimacy, then keeping the economy growing was the most important and most immediate goal, even if cheap loans and infrastructure spending added to the growing debt burden.

In contrast, those who supported restructuring argued that the economic model that produced the explosive growth in the past had outlived its usefulness. The debt burden could not be ignored forever, they argued: China had enough roads, railroads, airports, port facilities, power grids, and other infrastructure; continuing to invest in these areas would be wasteful and redundant. The financial crisis had shown that reliance on exports was problematic, and some leaders and economists argued that China needed to begin restructuring its economy toward more domestic consumption as the engine of growth. That might reduce growth in the short run, but was necessary to produce smarter growth in the long run.

This debate between stimulating and restructuring the economy played out—mostly behind closed doors—for almost a decade without resolution. In the meantime, economic growth steadily declined, from over 14 percent in 2007 to just 6.1 percent in 2019, its lowest growth rate since 1990 (see figure 1.2).

The Hu Jintao era brought so little political reform that many in China referred to it as a "lost decade." But, as I will describe in more detail in subsequent chapters, these years saw greater informal cooperation between local party and government officials, on one hand, and a wide range of newly formed social organizations involved in social welfare services and religious groups on the other. The party became more responsive to public protests, often negotiating with protesters instead of simply suppressing them. Despite these informal types of

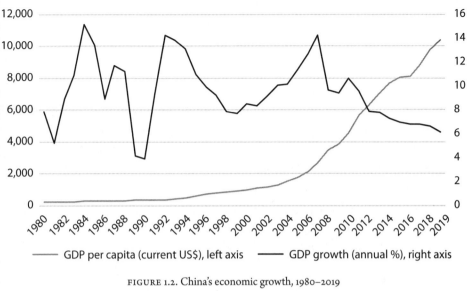

FIGURE 1.2. China's economic growth, 1980–2019
(source: World Bank, World Development Indicators)

responsiveness, the CCP still refused to be formally accountable to the people it governed.

Xi Jinping (2012–Present): The "China Dream"

Xi Jinping is the core of the CCP's fifth generation of leaders. His signature slogan, "China Dream," does not have Confucian origins but rather echoes the goal of achieving wealth and power that had motivated China's leaders since the mid-nineteenth century.[14]

Xi's tenure as CCP general secretary reversed a pattern in elite politics: the steady diminution of the top leader's power. Mao had nearly unquestioned power while he was chairman: he was able to launch one political campaign after another, even though many had devastating outcomes. Deng did not have that same kind of clout. Although his policy preferences usually prevailed, he had to work hard to get support for his reforms from his fellow leaders. Jiang was even less powerful than Deng. He was appointed as general secretary at a critical moment—the immediate aftermath of the 1989 demonstrations in Tiananmen Square and throughout the country—in part because he was not closely tied to any of the rival factions. Hu Jintao was the weakest in this string of leaders. He was outnumbered on the Politburo Standing Committee by Jiang's protégés and was generally seen only as first among equals in a collective leadership.

Xi Jinping reversed that trend. He launched an extensive and widely publicized anticorruption campaign that was seen as an effort not only to root out corruption among party and government officials, which threatened to undermine public support for the CCP, but also to unseat his political rivals. By 2017, more than 350,000 local party and government officials had been investigated for corruption.[15] It also targeted high-level officials who were not in Xi's camp, including former members of the Politburo and its Standing Committee, the chief lieutenants of Jiang Zemin and Hu Jintao, and even retired military leaders.[16] This broke an unwritten rule of elite politics: Politburo members (and their families) were off-limits in corruption campaigns. Opposition to Xi, whether in party, government, or military, was risky business.

Xi's dominance was seen in the revisions to the party and state constitutions. Such revisions recognized the prominence and guiding ideology of top leaders, typically after the leaders retired. In 1997, seven months after Deng died, the 15th Party Congress added "Deng Xiaoping Theory" to the list of Marxism, Leninism, and Mao Zedong Thought. When Jiang Zemin finished his tenure as the party's general secretary in 2002, the constitution was revised to include the "important thought of the Three Represents." Similarly, when Hu Jintao resigned after two terms as general secretary in 2012, the party constitution was revised to include his signature slogan—the scientific development concept—as a guiding ideology; however, it was said to be the "crystallization of the collective wisdom" of the CCP, not Hu's wisdom per se.[17]

Xi Jinping outdid each of them. After only one term as party leader, "Xi Jinping Thought on Socialism with Chinese Characteristics for a New Era" was enshrined in the constitution. Not only was Xi mentioned by name—like Mao and Deng, and unlike Xi's two predecessors—but his contribution was termed "thought," which in the CCP's lexicon is of higher significance than "theory." Xi Jinping Thought puts him on the same level, ideologically speaking, as Chairman Mao. Xi had usurped a phrase associated with Deng ("socialism with Chinese characteristics") by simply adding the words "for a new era," and he didn't have to wait until his terms were over to be added to the constitution. For those paying attention to these nuances, the constitutional revisions at the 19th Party Congress in 2017 signified Xi's unquestioned consolidation of power after only one term as general secretary.

Revisions to the state constitution in 2018 went beyond the symbolic: they removed term limits on the president and vice president. Limits of two five-year terms, a carefully constructed feature of political reforms begun under Deng and continued under later leaders, were designed to prevent the indefinite tenure of individual leaders, as occurred under Mao, and allow for a regular turnover of leaders (see chapter 2 for more details). By removing term limits from the constitution, Xi signaled his intention to remain as China's leader indefinitely.

To consolidate his power further, Xi became chair of an increasing number of commissions and leading groups with broad authority over domestic and foreign policy. Xi even usurped authority over the economy from Li Keqiang, who as prime minister would normally be in charge of economic policy, as was the case under Jiang Zemin and Hu Jintao. He revamped the military in order to enhance his control over it. It was a consolidation of power that few thought possible when he became general secretary in 2012.[18]

Xi is often compared to Mao in terms of his personal power and his dominance of the political system and the official news media.[19] Party members are required to study every speech by Xi (not just the major speeches and new policy documents, as was the case under his predecessors). There is even an app called "Study the Strong Country" (a pun in Chinese, as the word for study, *xuexi*, can also mean "study Xi") that lets users test their knowledge of Xi Jinping Thought. Government and private sector employees are encouraged (some say pressured) to use the app daily to win points for their departments or companies.[20]

But this focus on Xi's personal power overlooks an equally important development: he is reviving and strengthening Leninist aspects of the CCP that had atrophied during the reform era. The visibility of the CCP had steadily declined during the post-Mao years and for many Chinese it became increasingly less relevant to their lives. Under Xi, the CCP once again became front and center. Although local media had become bolder—and more popular—by exposing official corruption, misconduct, and policy failures,[21] Xi directed the media only to sing the praises of the party, not report on its shortcomings. He expanded party organizations in civil society groups, private firms, and even foreign-invested enterprises in order to monitor their activities more closely. He ordered professors to stick to the party's line on history and international affairs and not to encourage open debate or so-called Western ideas.

In addition to strengthening and expanding the role of the party, he also forced all types of activities into formal channels and undid the informal relationships that grew under Hu Jintao. As will be detailed in later chapters, NGOs now have to register with the government and cannot simply operate with the tacit knowledge of local officials (chapter 4); complaints about political, economic, and social problems are forced into the legal system, with less tolerance for public protests (chapter 5); religious groups have to affiliate with party-sanctioned organizations and cannot host unofficial religious activities (chapter 6). It is not clear whether the party can actually accomplish these ambitious and atavistic goals—but Xi has been determined to try.

The Primacy of the Party

As in all Leninist political systems, the party is the dominant actor in China's political system. The CCP oversees and is integrated with the government and legislature. There are no checks and balances; the government and legislature are not sources of opposition to the party's leadership, and they do not block the party's initiatives on policy or personnel matters. Instead, there is a division of labor between them. To greatly oversimplify this division, the CCP makes the key decisions on personnel and policy, which the legislature then ratifies and codifies, and the government implements them. The judiciary is not a separate branch, but part of the government and under the party's oversight.

Figure 1.3 shows the CCP's leading bodies and its relationships with other branches of the state.[22] The party's Central Committee is elected

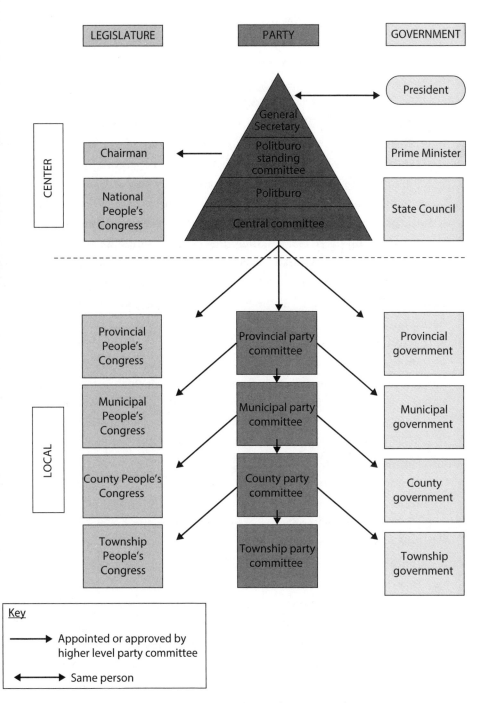

LEGISLATURE | PARTY | GOVERNMENT

CENTER

President

General Secretary

Chairman ← Politburo standing committee | Prime Minister

National People's Congress | Politburo | State Council

Central committee

LOCAL

Provincial People's Congress | Provincial party committee | Provincial government

Municipal People's Congress | Municipal party committee | Municipal government

County People's Congress | County party committee | County government

Township People's Congress | Township party committee | Township government

Key

→ Appointed or approved by higher level party committee

↔ Same person

FIGURE 1.3. China's political system (source: author)

by the National Party Congress, which brings together more than two thousand party leaders from all over the country every five years. Provinces, major cities, and professions (military, banks, SOEs, etc.) are given a quota of seats and party members in those jurisdictions and professions vote for delegates to attend the conference. These elections are not open to the public: only CCP members can vote, and all nominees are approved by higher-level party leaders.

Given its size, the National Party Congress is too large to hold actual deliberations or make decisions. Instead, its key task is to elect a new Central Committee, a body of more than two hundred party leaders that meets once or twice per year. Candidates for the Central Committee are decided by top party leaders, including both incumbents and retired leaders. In a nod to democratic consultation, the list of nominees exceeds the number of spots on the Central Committee, but by less than 10 percent. For example, at the 19th Party Congress in 2017, delegates selected 205 Central Committee members from a list of 222 nominees. This difference of 8 percent was hailed as an example of democratic centralism, which may seem silly from the vantage point of democratic countries, but is taken seriously by the CCP.[23] After electing the Central Committee, the National Party Congress is over until the next one, five years hence.

The Central Committee operates with a set agenda. At its first meeting immediately after the close of the Party Congress, it elects the party's leadership for the next five years: the Politburo, its Standing Committee, and the general secretary. Its second meeting occurs the following spring, when it makes final arrangements for the National People's Congress, described below. At subsequent meetings, the central committee focuses on specific policy issues: economic reform, legal reform, ideology and propaganda, and so on.

Being on the Central Committee does not give a person authority; rather, membership indicates the person already holds a position of influence. Many of the seats on the Central Committee are reserved for those in specific posts: central party and government leaders, provincial-level party secretaries and governors,[24] heads of prominent SOEs and banks, military leaders, and so on. While some Central Committee members live and work in Beijing, most hold leadership positions in other parts of the country. With more than two hundred members, the Central Committee is also not a venue for debate; it mostly ratifies decisions made by the top leadership.

The next level of the CCP's political hierarchy is the Politburo, a body of roughly two dozen party leaders that normally meets once a month. Most Politburo members are based in Beijing, but there are always a few local leaders to signify the strategic importance of their province or city; the Politburo elected in 2017 included the party secretaries of Shanghai, Beijing, Guangdong, Tianjin, Chongqing, and Xinjiang. Like so much about the CCP, the deliberations of the Politburo are shrouded in secrecy in order to prevent overt lobbying and to maintain a public façade of unanimity among CCP leaders. In the past, even the fact of meeting was treated as a state secret. Beginning in the Hu Jintao era, the media began to provide short reports on Politburo meetings: who attended, what was discussed, what the general secretary spoke about, and so on. These reports are not verbatim transcripts, but they do reflect a degree of greater openness about party deliberations.

Within the Politburo is its Standing Committee, the true inner circle of power in China. The size of the Politburo Standing Committee has varied between five and nine but is normally seven. There is always an odd number of members so that votes can never end in a tie—but as best we can tell, formal votes are rarely if ever taken.[25] If the Standing Committee members cannot reach a consensus, they defer a decision until further information (or further persuasion) can yield unanimous consent. The members of the Politburo Standing Committee are publicly ranked, making clear the pecking order at the apex of China's political system.

At the top of this pyramid is the general secretary, the top party leader and therefore the most powerful individual in China. The party retired the post of chairman after Mao died, and since 1982 the general secretary has been the top post. The general secretary is also chairman of the Central Military Commission, making him commander in chief, and since 1993 also simultaneously president, making him China's head of state. This third position is mostly symbolic: the presidency itself does not have much authority. With the fall of communist countries in the Soviet Union and Eastern Europe, having the same individual hold both positions puts him on par with other global leaders: he is not merely head of China's ruling party but also head of state.[26]

These are nested positions: the general secretary is a member of the Standing Committee, whose members are all on the full Politburo, whose members must be chosen from among Central Committee members. Although the formal mechanisms as described here may sound like a bottom-up process with one level electing the one above it, in reality the procedure is top-down: the top party leaders make the key personnel decisions in advance, and these are then ratified by the Party Congress and the Central Committee.

After the Central Committee has chosen the party leaders, next come the legislature and government. China's official legislature is the National People's Congress (not to be confused with the National Party Congress), or NPC. The NPC sits atop a hierarchy of local people's congresses. At the grassroots level (which includes rural townships, counties, small cities, and districts in larger cities), voters directly elect members of the local people's congress. Each level of the people's congress system then appoints members to the next higher people's congress: the county level people's congresses appoint people to the municipal people's congress, which appoints people to the provincial people's congress, which appoints people to the NPC, whose delegates serve a five-year term.

The full NPC meets annually in the spring. In addition to hearing reports on the work of various government ministries, passing laws, and revising the state constitution, the NPC also ratifies the CCP's nominees for government leaders.[27] This is largely a formality: the NPC has never rejected any of the CCP's nominations.[28]

On paper, the NPC looks like a typical parliamentary system: most NPC members belong to the CCP, as do the government officials they vote on; party departments and government ministries draft most of the laws presented to the NPC for approval; most bills presented to the NPC are eventually passed, although they may be returned to NPC committees and government ministries for revision before final approval. But this is not a parliamentary democracy: NPC delegates are not directly elected by the voters, but rather are appointed by lower-level people's congresses, and there are no opposition parties.[29]

The prime minister, vice prime ministers, state councilors, and ministers of the most important ministries and commissions form the State Council, the rough equivalent of a cabinet. There is normally at least one State Council minister who does not belong to the CCP, representing the fiction that China's political system is not a one-party dictatorship. But with Xi Jinping's renewed emphasis on the party's central role, that fiction has been dropped. All of the State Council ministers appointed in 2018 were CCP members, symbolizing again the party's leadership over the work of the government.

The CCP's dominance over the government and legislature is achieved in several ways. First, the heads of the government and the legislature—the prime minister and NPC chairman, respectively—are on the Politburo Standing Committee.[30] This is designed to prevent them from becoming sources of opposition to the party. Instead they do its bidding. Below the central level (that is, at the provincial level and below), the party secretary often chairs the local people's congress, further reinforcing the party's leading role.

Second, all key positions are held by party members. Any post of significance in the state, in SOEs, and in state-owned institutions like universities and hospitals, is held by a party member. Controlling the appointment of leading personnel is a key source of political authority for the party. It is based on the original Soviet *nomenklatura* system: central leaders appoint provincial leaders, who appoint municipal leaders, and so on.[31] This is designed to ensure that all leadership posts are held by people who are loyal to the party. So many government officials are party members that it can be difficult to determine where the party ends and the government begins. Even though they are separate institutions, the vast majority of government officials are party members, and throughout their careers individuals frequently transfer between party and government posts.

Third, the party has eyes and ears throughout the state (and increasingly throughout society) with a network of party cells, a hallmark of

Leninist parties. These small groups of party leaders within other agencies and organizations are rather secretive bodies, making the key decisions for the agencies in which they are embedded and monitoring their compliance with the party's directives. The party also organizes regular meetings of rank-and-file party members who work in these agencies and organizations in order to inform them of recent policy decisions and major speeches by party leaders.

Finally, the party is the leading political authority. At every level of the political system and in every office, the party is supreme: the general secretary outranks the prime minister, the provincial party secretary outranks the governor, the municipal party secretary outranks the mayor, and so on. This also holds true for banks, SOEs, universities, and other units: the party secretaries are the top leaders, even though they may not be the public face of the bank, company, or school.

The integration of the party with the government is so extensive that they are often referred to as a single party-state. They are separate formal institutions, but in practice they are blended together in the variety of ways described above. Throughout the book, I will specify either party or government when the distinction is called for, and refer to the state when the more collective identity of the party and the government is intended.

The CCP today is a party of more than 90 million members, which is larger than the populations of Germany and every other country in Europe. But, as a percentage of China's population, it remains a vanguard party: only 6.5 percent of the population are party members. The CCP is highly selective about whom it admits: fewer than one in ten applicants are accepted. Under Xi Jinping, the party has become even more selective. Whereas party membership grew close to 3 percent per year under Hu Jintao, it is growing only 1 percent per year under Xi. As a vanguard party, it is a party of elites that does not represent the population overall. College campuses are the main source of new recruits, and little if any recruitment is done in the countryside. Party membership is a necessity for jobs in a wide variety of sectors, including the government, education, health care, and management. Any position of consequence is typically held by a party member.

The CCP also has more than 4.6 million party cells throughout the government, SOEs, private enterprises, universities, hospitals, and neighborhoods. Wherever party members live and work, they are expected to belong to and participate in these party organizations. These party organizations give the CCP eyes and ears throughout the political, economic, and social arenas.

When you start with the recognition that China is ruled by a Leninist party, many aspects of the policy-making process, state-society interactions, even its political economy—a seeming mismatch between an increasingly marketized economy and a one-party authoritarian political system—begin to make sense. Subsequent chapters will detail how the party interacts with the people in the making and implementation of policy, religious life, and other types of political participation. While the party is best known for its repression of unwanted speech and behavior, that is but one option in the tool kit of party rule. It also encourages some types of participation and tolerates others. To understand China in the twenty-first century, it is necessary to understand all the tools the CCP uses to keep itself in power.

* * *

The CCP has been the dominant political actor in China since the establishment of the PRC in 1949, but its dominance has varied over time. Prominent in the Maoist era, it later abandoned radical leftism in favor of the more pragmatic task of economic reform, and in doing so came to play a less prominent role in personal and professional life. The presence of a market economy and the private sector meant that people did not have to be loyal supporters of the party and its leaders in order to have career options and full lives. And, though the party was still willing and able to use political repression against perceived threats (as was clear from its actions at Tiananmen Square), repression was more targeted than the political campaigns of the Maoist era. Local officials were not assigned a quota of "class enemies," for example, to uncover and punish, as in the past; instead they were directed to prevent protests, dissent, and opposition from emerging or spreading. As later chapters will detail, the party became more responsive to public opinion—but not at the expense of party authority.

The party's style of rule hardened in more recent years. Since 2008, when the international financial crisis began and Beijing hosted the Summer Olympics, and especially after 2012, when Xi Jinping became China's leader, China has been in a prolonged period of increasing political pressure against an ever-widening range of groups and individuals. Political controls have become more overt and the political system has become less liberal and more Leninist. Rather than continuing to adapt the party to China's changing economic and social conditions, the CCP under Xi is instead bringing the economy and society back into compliance with the party's priorities and its traditional Leninist practices. It seeks closer supervision over the government, tighter control over the media, greater scrutiny of civil society groups, and less tolerance for social diversity. While not necessarily the end of political and economic reform, this new era promises to be a retreat from the rapid privatization of the economy and the routinization of politics that China watchers and the Chinese themselves had gotten used to.[32]

With this overview of China's political system and the leading role of the party in mind, the next chapter will focus on one of the key distinctions between different types of political regimes: how leaders are selected. The criteria for leadership appointment, promotion, and removal provide incentives and constraints on what policies party and government leaders promote and how they manage relations with society, which I take up in the remainder of the book. To understand those issues, it is necessary first to understand how the party selects and supervises its leaders at various levels of the state.

2

HOW ARE LEADERS CHOSEN?

When Xi Jinping became China's leader in 2012, it was the last step of a long upward climb from a county-level official to a provincial leader and to eventually being identified as heir apparent in 2007 when he joined the CCP's top decision-making body, the Politburo Standing Committee. Such a smooth rise to the top is extremely unusual in authoritarian regimes, where leaders either die in office, are replaced in a coup, or get overthrown in a revolution. Even in the Mao era, leaders were replaced when they died or ran afoul of Mao, but they did not routinely retire.

Yet, since Mao, China has seen a regular transition of leaders every ten years (with a less thorough change every five years). Instead of these unpredictable and often violent transitions, the CCP has adopted a more routine process of selecting, promoting, and replacing its leaders, a process that includes age limits and term limits. Those who are being groomed for higher office work in a variety of local party and government posts as well as in Beijing, allowing them to gain valuable work experience, demonstrate their skills, and develop political ties. The regular and peaceful replacement of leaders at all levels is a distinctive feature of China's authoritarian political system.

Understanding the party's leadership selection process is key to understanding the Chinese political system. The ruling communist party is the only game in town. Every leader with political influence—whether in the party hierarchy, the government, the military, SOEs, even universities, banks, and hospitals—is a CCP member. There are no opposition parties and no open competition for high office.

This chapter will proceed from the bottom to the top of the Chinese political system. It will begin with village elections for village chiefs; move on to the appointment, evaluation, and promotion of local leaders (specifically party secretaries, mayors, and governors); and then consider the selection of central level party and government leaders. Finally, I will use the career paths of Jiang Zemin, Hu Jintao, and Xi Jinping to show two distinctive aspects of how the CCP selects and manages its leaders: circulation through local and central level assignments to gain experience before being appointed to the top; and norms of age limits and term limits that constrain how long leaders remain in their posts.

The peaceful, routine, and even institutionalized manner in which the CCP appoints and promotes its leaders has been a crucially important political reform in the post-Mao era and a key source of regime stability. But the benefits of this appointment and promotion process are now being undermined by Xi Jinping. Xi has not followed the norms set down by his predecessors: he has not designated his successor and has revised the state constitution to eliminate term limits on the presidency, one of his key posts. These steps indicate that he intends to remain in power indefinitely, and if he succeeds in this goal, he will unravel one of the signature features of the Chinese political system: the regular rotation of leaders.

Village Elections

Beginning in the 1980s, some villages began spontaneously electing their village chiefs and village committees in order to fill the administrative void left behind by the dismantling of rural communes. This was a grassroots initiative that later became national policy. As I explain in more detail in the next chapter, China frequently allows and even encourages local experimentation before rolling out reforms nationwide.

Village elections attracted a lot of enthusiasm at first, among Chinese leaders as a prominent political reform, among scholars as a research topic, and among villagers themselves.[1] Many of its proponents saw it as an experiment in grassroots democratization, with the hope that it would eventually rise to higher levels of the political system.[2] However, CCP leaders described it as village self-government, not democracy, and it was designed to improve relations between villagers and their leaders and thereby maintain political stability. Its leading sponsor in Beijing was senior party leader Peng Zhen, considered more of a hard-liner than a reformer and more concerned with law and order than re-sponsiveness to public opinion.

Village elections were more popular among central party leaders than local officials. Township party leaders worried that village elections would create a conflict between village leaders who had been popularly elected and the village party chief and township officials who had been appointed by and were accountable to higher levels. They feared that this popular mandate would make it difficult to implement unpopular policies like collecting taxes and implementing the one-child policy. Ironically, the opposite seemed to be true: elections actually made this task easier. Candidates could not run on a platform of changing these policies, but they could promise to implement them in a more transpar-ent way.[3] Township officials therefore frequently interfered with elec-tions by deciding which candidates would be allowed and nullifying election results when they were unhappy with the outcome.

To address this concern, in some villages the same person elected village chief is also the appointed party secretary. In some cases, villa-gers preferred this arrangement in order to make their elected chief more acceptable and therefore more influential with higher-level lead-ers. In others, this outcome was imposed by township officials in order to eliminate any potential for divided loyalties.

The procedures for nominating candidates and holding elections became increasingly codified over the years, first with a draft law in 1987, and then the final version in 1998: elections every three years, a secret ballot, more than one candidate per office, nominations to come from villagers, and provisions for proxy voting. However, these proce-dures are not always observed in practice, and the quality of elections varies considerably. As a result, the goal of improving relations be-tween villagers and their leaders was only realized when the electoral law was followed. In villages where election procedures were properly

FIGURE 2.1. Wukan village elections, 2012 (photo: Xinhua/Alamy Stock Photo)

implemented, the views of elected village leaders and villagers closely aligned. Implicitly, candidates were appealing for popular support, and elections three years hence kept them accountable to voters. But in villages with poor-quality elections—for example, where elections were less competitive because there were fewer candidates per posts to be filled—the views of elected leaders and villagers did not align because there was little need for the leaders to be responsive to public opinion.[4]

Village elections eventually lost steam, both as a reform initiative and as a research topic. They proved not to be a precursor of greater democratization to come, because the CCP had no intention of allowing elections at higher levels. When some local party officials experimented with township-level elections, they were immediately declared to be unconstitutional and stopped.[5] The complaint about township elections was similar to the complaint about village elections: the higher-level party committee would not be able to control popularly elected leaders. Appointing party and government leaders is the responsibility of the party's organization department at all levels of the political system, and it would not surrender this important power.

Village elections also lost their momentum because villages have been hollowed out in different ways. First of all, the migration of villagers to the cities in search of work meant that many villages were left with only the very young and very old. Few people of ambition and talent remained behind in the villages to provide effective leadership.[6] Villagers were also hollowed out because the townships and counties above them took direct control over village finances. Without access to village funds and less leeway for new initiatives, there was less incentive to be village chief.[7] And when township and county leaders intervened in nominations and results, the voters quickly learned that their votes counted for little.

Much of the attention given to village elections focused on the quality of the elections themselves; that is, how well they followed the procedural requirements mandated by the electoral law.[8] More difficult to assess has been the impact of elections on village governance. In fact, village elections have exacerbated the problem of corruption among village leaders, especially due to land sales, as in the Wukan example that opened the book. Depending on how large the difference is between what price developers pay for the rights to the land and what compensation farmers receive, village leaders are in a position to reap enormous financial wealth. This potential for personal gain has led to vote buying in many villages.[9] Instead of improving relations between villagers and their leaders, as its proponents first hoped in the 1980s, vote buying and land sales have become new sources of tension.

Although village elections continue to be held every three years, they do not receive the attention they attracted in the past.

Appointing and Promoting Local Leaders

In the post-Mao period, the CCP has devised a well-institutionalized process for appointing and promoting local leaders that is largely meritocratic, especially at lower levels of the political system, but also clientelistic. Appointments are determined by the next-higher level: central leaders appoint provincial leaders, who appoint municipal leaders, etc. This gives each level great autonomy in selecting and promoting subordinates.

The CCP's Organization Department is in charge of appointing officials and monitoring their performance. This makes the head of the Organization Department a very powerful individual, which is why the person in this position is usually a trusted lieutenant of the party leader. The party leader wants to be sure that his people get assigned to the most influential positions, and control of the Organization Department is essential to make this happen. This type of patronage is a key element of the party leader's power.

The people making appointments have two main criteria: they want to appoint people who are *competent* to carry out the regime's policy priorities, and they want to appoint people who are *loyal* to their superiors, thereby promoting regime stability. Ideally, potential appointees are both competent and loyal, but there is a tension between the two goals: those who are most competent may not be loyal, and those who are loyal may not be competent. This dilemma has confronted the CCP since the founding of the People's Republic in 1949. For much of the Maoist period, this dilemma was delineated as the reds versus experts debate: the reds were loyal supporters of Chairman Mao, but better known for their ideological zeal than for their ability to implement policy; in contrast, the experts had scientific or management skills necessary to implement policy, but their loyalty to the party's goals and Chairman Mao in particular was always in doubt. The tensions between these two goals—and Mao's wavering between them—led to repeated political campaigns in the 1950s and 1960s that removed some from office, alternating between reds and experts as CCP policy swung between leftist and developmental goals.

In the post-Mao era, the CCP has made economic modernization its key task and therefore made expertise a key criterion in the selection and promotion of officials. In contrast to officials left over from the late Cultural Revolution era,[10] Deng Xiaoping called for the "four transformations" of China's officials: they should be younger, better educated, more professional, and more revolutionary. The first three transformations have formed the basis for the CCP's personnel policies, but the fourth cannot be ignored. To be appointed, officials must have the proper credentials and record of achievement, but they will not rise very far if they do not have the political connections necessary to establish their loyalty to their superiors and the CCP as a whole. At a minimum, joining the CCP is a necessary prerequisite for anyone who wants to rise through the political hierarchy.

Unlike the practice of the Maoist era, officials no longer enjoy lifetime tenure. Since the early 1980s, leaders serve a fixed term of five years, although many are transferred or promoted before the end of their full term. In order to remain in office and be promoted, they have to meet expectations of policy performance set by higher levels. Officials sign contracts that specify the targets they are expected to meet. There are three types of targets: imperative targets, such as maintaining social stability and implementing the family planning policies (these are also known as "veto" targets, because if these goals are not met, the official will not be promoted and may be demoted or even fired); hard targets, such as fostering economic growth, generating tax revenue, and attracting foreign investment; and soft targets, such as reducing burdens on peasants, improving education, health care, and other types of public goods. These are good to achieve, but hard to measure and hard to accomplish in a short period of time. More significant is that by themselves they are unlikely to result in promotion unless the imperative and hard targets are also met. Given this set of incentives, local officials tend to focus primarily on meeting imperative and hard targets and make soft targets of secondary importance.[11]

Local officials are accountable to the higher levels who appoint and evaluate them, but not to the local citizens they govern. If they do not meet their performance targets, they can be transferred, demoted, or removed from office altogether. In particular, if they fail to provide minimal standards of governance—corruption, pollution, unemployment, etc.—they can trigger protests and petitions for higher levels to step in. In this sense, higher officials serve as proxies for local citizens, doing for them what they cannot do for themselves: remove corrupt, malfeasant, and incompetent officials. By installing a new local leader, higher-level officials can look responsive without being directly accountable. This can improve trust in the higher authorities, which in turn preempts public protests, the common alternative when the state seems unresponsive.[12]

What matters more in terms of getting promoted: competency, loyalty, or connections to higher-level leaders? Scholars have debated these questions for years with varying results: some find strong evidence for policy performance, others find that only political connections matter.[13] A large part of this discrepancy is based on what level of the political system people are focusing on, and how they try to measure competence and loyalty. Much of this research is very technical and very quantitative, and therefore not always easy for others to adjudicate. But, despite these differences—in fact, because of these differences—these numerous studies point to a two-part strategy in the CCP's policy for selecting and promoting cadres.

This strategy is best likened to a tournament in which different skills are needed at different levels. At the entry level, cadre policy is mostly meritocratic: people have to demonstrate their competence to be appointed in the first place and to qualify for promotions. Local leaders are placed in a contest to demonstrate their capability as leaders: those that produce economic growth (or, more specifically, tax revenue for higher-ups) are more likely to be promoted. Being able to deliver on its policy goals, especially economic and social development, is a key part of the CCP's legitimacy. Existing research indicates that economic growth is highly correlated with the promotions of party and government leaders: the faster the economy grows, the more tax revenue is generated; and the more foreign investment is attracted, the more likely leaders are to be promoted.[14] The imperative targets (family planning and maintaining political stability) are harder to measure in a systematic way. Except for a few examples of local officials being fired after large-scale protests, we do not have a good sense of how these imperative targets factor into the evaluations of their performance, and hence their prospects for promotion.[15] This competition is primarily between neighboring jurisdictions and not a nationwide tournament: cadres only have to outperform the local competition.[16] Officials in inland cities do not have to outdo those in economic and financial centers like Shanghai.

The competition for promotions to higher levels is intense because the political hierarchy is steep: there are approximately three thousand counties in China, about three hundred prefecture-level cities, and around thirty provincial-level units, including cities like Beijing and Shanghai and so-called autonomous regions like Tibet and Xinjiang.[17] Those who are not promoted early and often will not make it very far up the ladder.

Local officials do not have much time to show their competence: they typically move to a new post every three years or so. As a result, ambitious officials have to show results quickly. Many pump new money into the local economy, investing in roads, industrial parks, commercial developments, and real estate in order to inflate statistics on economic growth. This creates growing debt, but leaders are usually transferred to a new position and the debt problem is passed on to subsequent leaders. Remarkably, the long-term consequences of these short-term decisions do not seem to influence the officials' career prospects. If a project fails, the burden falls on the current incumbent, not the person who initiated the project. This is one reason for China's exploding local government debt: incumbent leaders reap the benefits of these short-term choices but do not suffer the consequences when their costs become apparent and burden their successors.

Age limits create incentives for local officials to demonstrate competence and develop connections early. They seek to be promoted before their full five-year term is completed, a practice known as "sprinting with small steps."[18] The longer they remain at one level, the less likely they are to make it to the next. If a county-level official is not promoted by the age of fifty, he or she will be stuck at that level or pushed into retirement.[19] Those who are near or above the retirement age at each level have less chance for promotion and may therefore turn to corruption to make the most of their remaining time in office, including nepotism, accepting bribes from developers and private entrepreneurs, buying and selling official posts (where the price of a post is equivalent to the amount of bribes the incumbent can expect to receive), and securing a job once they retire from their party or government posts.[20]

Economic performance is not the only indicator of competence. Officials are increasingly expected to have college and even graduate degrees, although many are of suspect credibility because they come from part-time programs, the party's own schools, correspondence classes, and other types of diploma mills. Previous work experience can be a proxy for competence. For example, officials who have worked in China's universities are often promoted even if they are not economic high achievers.[21] It is assumed they have other attributes of competence, such as research and administrative skills. However, officials who previously worked in state-owned enterprises do not get a pass on economic results. Given their SOE experience, they are expected to have advantages in meeting their economic targets and therefore have to demonstrate their competence.

After several rounds of this tournament, all survivors have shown their competence. Meeting the targets set by higher levels is a necessary element of surviving the early rounds of competition for promotion and career advancement, but in order to reach the top, it is not sufficient. For one thing, it is harder for provincial officials than for local officials to make their personal mark on the economy. For another, all of them showed their competence at lower levels and as a result there is less variation in the capabilities of cadres at higher levels. In later rounds of the tournament, promotion to provincial and central posts requires political connections and factional alliances. Competence is necessary to make it out of the early rounds, but then the importance of connections becomes primary.

How do cadres develop political connections? First of all, by joining the CCP. There is a definite glass ceiling for those who are not party members, and the ceiling is very low. As noted above, virtually every influential position in China is held by a party member. The exceptions are private enterprises and nongovernment organizations, but many private entrepreneurs and NGO leaders are party members or develop ties to local officials to signal their loyalty to the party (the party's relationship with NGOs will be examined in chapter 4).

Another way to develop connections necessary to rise to high-level posts is by attending party schools. In addition to the Central Party School in Beijing, there are numerous party schools around the country run by provincial, prefectural, and lower-level party committees.[22] The curriculum includes politics and ideology, but these schools also teach administrative and management skills, public relations, and international negotiation. Attendance at party schools also provides a great opportunity for networking with officials from other areas. This is important in a largely vertical political system where cultivating horizontal ties is regarded with a suspicion that it might be designed to create cooperation among one level against a higher level. But these ties are essential in climbing the bureaucratic ladder later on.

Above all, the most important means of developing connections is by forging personal relations with higher-level leaders. Understanding how these patron-client ties emerge, develop, and are acted upon is difficult. This is where we reach the limits of what we know about elite politics in China. CCP leaders do not divulge what faction they belong to or who their patrons and clients are. Efforts to determine factional alliances are dicey. They are often based on assumptions that people who come from the same province, went to the same colleges, and worked in the same departments necessarily belong to the same factions. This produces a lot of "false positives," that is, predictions of factional ties when they do not really exist. However, in the absence of formal factional affiliations (which are formally banned in the CCP but nevertheless operate informally[23]), making predictions based on personal backgrounds and career experiences is often the best we can do.[24] In short, the black box of Chinese politics makes it difficult to see exactly how political connections factor into promotions, yet we know they definitely do.

Selecting Central Leaders

The formal process for selecting central leaders mimics democratic procedures but does not allow for true representation. What seems like a bottom-up process, with one level formally electing the next higher level, in practice is top-down: incumbent and retired leaders (essentially current and past members of the Politburo) negotiate over who will be appointed and to what positions in order to maintain a balance of power among key leaders and their factions. These negotiations begin more than a year before leadership transitions occur, and the process is shrouded in secrecy. The CCP wants to present a united public façade on matters of policy and personnel. Like the political conventions that occur every four years in the United States, the meetings where Chinese leaders are formally elected produce few surprises. The arrangements are finalized in advance and held in secret until the formal votes occur. The real decision-making on personnel changes occurs behind closed doors. We learn the outcome, but not the politics of the process.

Since 1992, the CCP has followed a routinized process for selecting and replacing top party leaders. Every five years, the National Party Congress convenes to elect the Central Committee, which in turn elects the Politburo, its Standing Committee, and the general secretary. This routinized selection of top leaders was constrained by two types of limits, on age and term. These innovations were designed to institutionalize personnel appointments and to prevent the ossification of party leadership that is inevitable when there is no retirement system for senior leaders. Regular turnover of top leaders also allows a more predictable upward mobility for ambitious younger officials. For government leaders, these limits were formal and binding, but for top party leaders they were informal norms in place since the early 1990s. And because a full-scale leadership transition happens only once every ten years, there have been few tests of how strong the norms are. As will be shown below, the norms of leadership transition are strong only when the leader is weak.

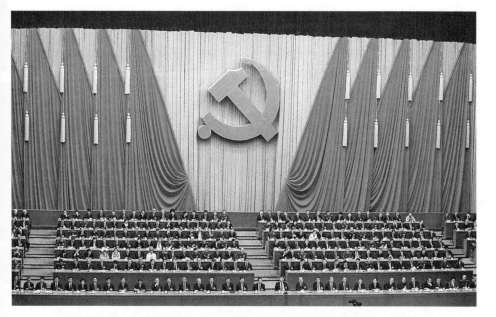

FIGURE 2.2. Closing ceremony of the 19th National Party Congress, 2017
(photo: UPI/Alamy Stock Photo)

First, there is the "Rule of 68": once Politburo members reach the age of sixty-eight, they cannot be reappointed to their current post or appointed to a new one. The rule is therefore abbreviated as "seven up, eight down." Central Committee members cannot be reappointed once they reach sixty-three. This effectively means that State Council ministers and provincial party secretaries and governors also cannot be appointed or reappointed once they reach sixty-three, because they are also Central Committee members.[25] Second, leaders can serve two five-year terms but then must either be appointed to a new position or retire.

These are norms for party leaders, but for government leaders they are constitutional provisions. The state constitution adopted in 1982 set the length of a term of five years for president, vice president, prime minister, vice prime minister, NPC Standing Committee chair and vice chairs, and established a limit of two consecutive terms for holders of those posts. The party's own constitution does not spell out these term limits, but it does say that party leaders at all levels are "not entitled to lifelong tenure" and must abide by state laws. Similarly, the "Rule of 68" is not a formal rule but was widely understood to influence the selection of top leaders. The practical result has been that party leaders normally face the same constraints of age and term limits that are imposed on government leaders.

Term limits in the United States and other countries serve the same purpose: to prevent officials from holding power indefinitely. However, in democratic countries, term limits serve an additional purpose: making elected officials more representative of and responsive to public opinion. Being more representative is not a priority for the CCP in its leadership promotion process, and as later chapters will describe, it is often willing to be responsive to public opinion but refuses to be accountable to the public through elections or other institutions.

Along with the establishment of age limits and terms limits, a related practice was the identification of a successor well before the leadership transition. This was designed to provide more certainty in leadership succession and minimize the competition among rivals that can trigger a political crisis. Hu Jintao was handpicked by Deng Xiaoping to be Jiang Zemin's successor, and he was publicly identified as such in 1992, ten years before the transition took place. In 2007, the 17th Central Committee elevated Xi Jinping and Li Keqiang to the Politburo Standing Committee, indicating that they would become the next general secretary and prime minister five years later. The identification of a successor further solidified the perception of an institutionalized succession process and a unified party leadership able to reach an early consensus on the next leader.

Do institutions actually constrain authoritarian leaders? The case of China suggests that leaders create the institutions necessary to carry out their preferred policies, all the while being careful not to tie their own hands.[26] In order to facilitate the regular rotation of leaders (and to reduce the winner-take-all aspect of factional fighting), China's leaders created regulations on term limits and mandatory retirement ages for party and government officials at all levels of the political system. At the very top, members of the Politiburo, its Standing Committee, and the General Secretary abided by these limits, but they were informal norms and not formal rules that applied to other leaders. As a result, the rules were frequently broken.

Jiang Zemin's reappointment as general secretary in 1997 violated the age limit, which was originally set at seventy and later reduced to sixty-eight. The new age limit forced the retirement of one of Jiang's rivals on the Politburo Committee, Qiao Shi, yet Jiang, already seventy-one, was allowed to remain as general secretary for another term in order to provide continuity in political leadership. This first adoption of an age limit is a good example of the political maneuvering among China's leaders that is not visible to outside observers.

When Jiang's two full terms as general secretary and president were finished in 2002 and 2003, respectively, he should have also resigned as chairman of the Central Military Commission. But he did not. Instead, he repeated the example of Deng Xiaoping, who remained as chair of the CMC for several months before Jiang was given that title.[27] Jiang eventually resigned as CMC chairman in 2004, reportedly at the behest of PLA leaders who preferred their commander-in-chief also be head of state and, more significantly, head of the party. Jiang may have hoped to replicate Deng as China's unofficial though formally retired leader, but Jiang was no Deng. He retired from all his posts, and while he remained an influential figure behind the scenes, he was not as influential as Deng had been.

However, with the exception of Jiang, all other party and government leaders abided by the limits on age and term, creating a nearly wholesale turnover of political leaders every ten years. So, even though these norms have been in place for decades, they have not been practiced in enough leadership transitions to be fully institutionalized. At the same time, the media coverage of them created the perception of a more institutionalized process for appointing and replacing leaders. The transition from Hu to Xi was more clear-cut: Hu resigned as general secretary, CMC chair, and president when his second terms in each of those posts expired. The institutionalized nature of leadership change in China avoided the intense political rivalry of the Maoist and early post-Mao period, and of most other authoritarian regimes.

Xi Jinping further eroded the formal constraints on his power. After only one term as general secretary, Xi began to undo the norms of leadership change in order to consolidate his power. Previous general secretaries Jiang Zemin and Hu Jintao both had their successors identified while they were still in office. Following these precedents, Xi's successor should have been announced at the 19th Party Congress in 2017, when Xi began his second term as general secretary. But this did not happen, suggesting that Xi did not intend to resign after two terms. Party rules did not require it: term limits are binding on government positions, but not on top party leaders. Nevertheless, the party's own propaganda publicized these norms of term limits and age limits since the 1990s. Under Xi, the party's media began denying that the Rule of 68 even existed. At the 19th Party Congress, no successor was identified. However, all members of the Politburo Standing Committee who were over sixty-eight were not reelected at this congress; only Xi and Li Keqiang remained from the Standing Committee elected in 2012. The five new members were all under sixty-eight. This was a mixed message— no successor, but age limits still constrained appointments.

That ambiguity was clarified in spring 2018 when the National People's Congress revised the state constitution to eliminate the two-term limit on the presidency. This would avoid an awkward situation where different people would be leaders of the party and the state. In other words, Xi could remain in both roles indefinitely, even though it violated past norms. In addition, Xi's ally Wang Qishan, who carried out the ambitious anticorruption campaign during Xi's first term, was appointed vice president, even though he was sixty-nine at the time and had retired from the Politburo Standing Committee just a few months before. This was the first time the Rule of 68 was broken since Jiang Zemin. Since Xi's hold on the posts of president and general secretary is no longer term limited, he has the potential to remain as China's top leader indefinitely. The full effects of this action will not be known for years to come, but it certainly means the undoing of the rules that have guided elite politics in China for the past generation. This exception to constitutionally mandated term limits applies only to the president; term limits on the prime minister, vice prime ministers, NPC chairman and vice chairmen remain in place.

Xi's assault on these norms of succession indicated how fragile they were. It was no surprise that he wanted to enhance his hold on power—incumbents usually do. Most observers saw the elimination of term limits as a significant step backward in China's political development. There seemed to be no resistance from fellow leaders, some of whom must have recognized the value of institutionalized norms of succession and a regular rotation of leaders. The elimination of term limits benefited Xi as an individual leader, but at the expense of institutionalized leadership succession.

In short, despite the creation of term limits and age limits, leadership transitions have only followed these rules in 2007 (when Xi was identified as successor) and 2012 (when Xi became general secretary). Hu Jintao was the only Chinese leader to follow these rules in full. It is no coincidence that Hu is also seen as the weakest of China's top leaders. He followed the rules because he was not strong enough to bend or break them. Jiang was able to bend them, although other leaders eventually forced him to resign in favor of Hu. Xi was able to break the rules altogether by revising the constitution to allow him to reign indefinitely.

Getting to the Top

The interplay of competence and connections is best seen in the career paths of the people who made it to the pinnacle of power in China: the general secretaries of the CCP. Their career paths also illustrate another distinctive feature of the CCP's leadership selection process: each of them rotated through a variety of party and government posts at the central and local levels in order to gain broad experience and test their leadership skills before being handed the reins of power.

Deng Xiaoping was China's paramount leader until his death in 1997, yet he never held the top position in the party or government. Deng was in political exile at the start of the post-Mao era: a few months before Mao died, he purged Deng from all his posts after concluding that Deng would not carry on his policies after he died. He was not wrong: after Deng's rehabilitation in 1977, he lost little time in pushing out his rivals, installing his people in top positions, and implementing the ambitious reform and opening policies that launched China's economic modernization. Deng wanted to avoid the succession crisis that would ensue if he died in office. By having protégés in top posts, his successors were already in place.

After maneuvering Mao's chosen successor, Hua Guofeng, out of his posts as head of the party, government, and military, Deng handpicked replacements. He made his longtime lieutenant Hu Yaobang head of the party, but lost confidence in him after the student protests in late 1986. He replaced him with Zhao Ziyang, but soon lost confidence in him too. During the midst of the large-scale student protests in spring 1989 that culminated in the bloody crackdown on June 4, he finally selected Jiang Zemin to be general secretary. He later selected Hu Jintao as Jiang's successor. Only Xi became general secretary without Deng's blessing.

Jiang Zemin (1989–2002)

Jiang had not anticipated becoming general secretary. His career trajectory was more typical of local officials who need to prove themselves and develop ties with higher level patrons in order to gain promotion.[28] Like many other Third Generation leaders, he was a technocrat: a bureaucrat with technical background (an expert, in the Maoist terminology). He graduated from Shanghai Jiaotong University in 1947 with a degree in electrical engineering. In 1946, while still a student, he joined the CCP.

Beginning in the 1950s, Jiang held a series of administrative positions in various government agencies tasked with industrial development, including automobiles, electrical equipment, and thermal power machinery. Throughout the post-Mao period, his career cycled through a series of government and party posts, mostly in Shanghai and Beijing, involving foreign trade and the development of China's electronics industry, often spending just a year or two in a job before being promoted. During the 1980s, he supported Deng's priorities: promoting economic reform while maintaining party control. Whereas Hu Yaobang was criticized for tolerating student protests that broke out in December 1986, and as a result was ousted as general secretary, Jiang negotiated a peaceful end to student protests in Shanghai.

If not for the public demonstrations that broke out in spring 1989 in Beijing and throughout the country, Jiang would probably have retired as Shanghai's party secretary when he reached the mandatory retirement age of sixty-five in 1991. Instead he became general secretary, in large part because he was not directly associated with the martial law decision, was not tainted with the bloodshed that ended the protests, and was acceptable to the different factions in Beijing. As leader in Shanghai, he struck a conciliatory tone with protesters (as he had in 1986), and the protests there ended without relying on the military. He may not have been anyone's favored candidate to become China's top leader, but he proved to be acceptable to them all.

Jiang had extensive international experience before becoming general secretary. In 1954, he went to the Soviet Union to study energy resources, power conservation, and managing power stations and networks. In 1974, he led a delegation to Romania. In 1980, he led a forty-day, UN-sponsored world tour of import-export centers and free trade areas in twelve countries. As mayor and party secretary of Shanghai, he hosted many foreign leaders. He speaks several foreign languages, including English and Russian. During a speech at Harvard in 1997, he shifted smoothly into English halfway through his speech. He is also a somewhat comical figure. When meeting with foreign leaders, he loved to sing Italian opera and quote the Gettysburg Address.

In Shanghai, he was mocked as a "flowerpot," someone who preferred ribbon-cutting ceremonies and greeting visiting dignitaries over the hard work of governing. He was also a bit of a sycophant, escorting leaders from Beijing when they visited Shanghai, willing even to do menial tasks like personally delivering their suitcases to their rooms. This was all part of his strategy for building ties with other powerful leaders which ultimately—and unexpectedly—allowed him to reach the top of the party hierarchy.

Hu Jintao (2002–12)

Hu Jintao was also handpicked by Deng to become eventual party leader, but his path to the top post was notably different.[29] He was designated as Jiang's successor in 1992, then spent the next ten years in a prolonged internship, handling a variety of administrative and diplomatic tasks. Most important was that he did not commit any major mistakes that would cause Deng or other leaders to reconsider his status as heir apparent.

Like Jiang, Hu Jintao was trained as an engineer. He got a degree in hydroelectric engineering from Tsinghua University in 1965, the year he also joined the CCP. After working as a researcher and political instructor at Tsinghua, he was sent to work at a power plant in Gansu, a poor and remote province in western China. While in Gansu, he caught the eye of Song Ping, then party secretary of Gansu, who had close ties with Deng Xiaoping. Song arranged for Hu to study at the Central Party School in Beijing in 1980, where he was classmates with the son of Hu Yaobang, who later became a key benefactor to Hu Jintao's career. In 1981, he returned to Gansu as secretary of the provincial Communist Youth League (CYL), a CCP organization for those under thirty-five whose members often became party members and whose leaders are often transferred to more prominent posts in the party bureaucracy.[30] High-level officials whose careers began in the CYL are often known as the Youth League Faction, or *tuanpai*. Hu Jintao was seen as the leader of this faction, as well as the greatest beneficiary of relationships he developed as head of the CYL.

Hu's rapid rise came during a time when the CCP was looking for young and professionally qualified leaders. His degree from Tsinghua University and early career as an engineer established his credentials, and his performance in those posts earned him promotions. He then relied on his political patrons to appoint him to higher positions. When Hu Yaobang was looking for young officials to promote into the Central Committee in 1982, Hu Jintao was one of those chosen. At thirty-nine, he was the youngest alternate member of the Central Committee.[31]

After serving as secretary of first the Gansu provincial CYL (1982) and then the national CYL (1982–85), Hu was appointed party secretary in Guizhou (1985–88). As provincial party secretary, Hu visited every county, city, and district in the province and became well acquainted with local problems. But he initiated no major reforms, and hewed closely to Beijing's line. Guizhou was dirt-poor when Hu arrived in 1985, and it was dirt-poor when he left in 1988.[32] Hu focused instead on poverty alleviation and reducing inequality, priorities that would later characterize his time as general secretary. Whereas Jiang and the others who were born or had career experience in Shanghai, and therefore known as the Shanghai Gang, were focused on promoting rapid development along the coast, even at the expense of growing inequality between coastal and inland provinces and between urban and rural areas, Hu championed balancing growth with equity, both in Guizhou and later as general secretary.

In December 1988, Hu was appointed the party secretary of Tibet. His main accomplishment was imposing martial law to suppress protests in March of 1989. These protests were unrelated to the protests that swept Beijing and the rest of China in mid-April. As a result, when demonstrations broke out in the rest of the country, Tibet was already locked down. Hu was one of the first provincial leaders to declare his support for Deng's decision to declare martial law in Beijing. Given his emphasis on maintaining political stability and party control, these steps earned Hu great credit in Deng's eyes.

Although Hu was officially party secretary in Tibet until 1992, he spent most of that time living in Beijing in order to avoid the physical discomfort of Tibet's high elevation (Tibet's capital, Lhasa, is twelve thousand feet above sea level). While in Beijing, he ran the Organization Department, formally directed by his longtime patron Song Ping. Deng also put Hu in charge of the planning for the 14th Party Congress in 1992, at which he was promoted from the Central Committee to the Politburo Standing Committee and the heir apparent to Jiang Zemin as general secretary. His promotion to the Politburo Standing Committee was unusual, both because of his age (forty-nine) and, more important, because he catapulted directly from the Central Committee to the Standing Committee without first serving on the full Politburo. This promotion was encouraged by Song Ping and endorsed by Deng, illustrating how the rise to the top is made possible only with the support of powerful patrons.[33]

Between 1992 and 2002, Hu served as Jiang's apprentice, displaying loyalty to Jiang's priorities and competence in his work more generally. During these years he gradually acquired other titles, including president of the Central Party School (1992), vice president (1998), and vice chair of the Central Military Commission (1999). He was in charge of the planning for the 15th Party Congress in 1997 (where his rank in the party hierarchy rose from seventh to fourth), led a group editing Jiang's collected works, and handled the fallout from Jiang's ouster of his rival Chen Xitong as party secretary of Beijing. Jiang also gave him difficult foreign policy tasks, including the public protests against the NATO bombing of China's embassy in Belgrade in 1999 and the crisis in US-China relations during the incident concerning a US Navy EP-3E spy plane in 2001 (these episodes are described in more detail in chapter 7). At the same time, Jiang kept Hu away from other politically influential roles in favor of his own protégés. For example, he put his right-hand man Zeng Qinghong in charge of the daily work of the Central Committee; appointed him as head of the Organization Department during his second term as general secretary, which allowed Jiang to appoint his supporters to key posts in the central and provincial bureaucracies; and assigned Zeng to draft the party reform proposal adopted at the 15th Party Congress in 1997. Hu handled the logistical details, but Zeng prepared the more important policy document coming out of the congress.[34]

Hu successfully cultivated ties on the right and left. Along with Hu Yaobang and Hu Qili, he was one of the "three Hus" known for favoring greater liberalization. At the same time, his patron, Song Ping, was known as a skeptic on reform issues and favored a more conservative approach. In between was Deng Xiaoping, who wanted both economic liberalization and political stability under the control of the CCP. Hu's rise to the top was due to his ability to play the political game so effectively that he gained the support of leaders on the right and the left. By the time he became general secretary in 2002, many expected him to be a committed reformer, due to some of his political ties and the reform-promoting studies he sponsored as president of the Central Party School. However, he did not initiate any significant political reforms during his years as general secretary, especially if political reform is defined in terms of democratization. At the end of his tenure, his ten years as general secretary were often described as a "lost decade." Yet, in light of the repressive turn of the Xi era, the lost decade is now grimly referred to as a "golden era."

Although Hu became general secretary at the 16th Party Congress in 2002, Jiang managed to stack the Politburo and Central Committee with his supporters. The tension between Jiang's Shanghai Gang and Hu's Youth League supporters would be a prominent theme of Hu's ten years as China's leader, hampering his efforts to initiate his own agenda as party leader. Instead of fighting over policy priorities, he sought to balance growth (favored by the Shanghai Gang) with equity (the priority of the Youth League Faction). When his second terms as general sectary and chair of the CMC expired in 2012 and as president in 2013, he dutifully resigned. Unlike Jiang before him, he was unable to pack the incoming leadership with his own supporters.

Xi Jinping (2012–Present)

Xi Jinping's rise to the top is distinctive in several ways.[35] Unlike Jiang Zemin and Hu Jintao before him, Xi was not handpicked by Deng. After Deng died in 1997, a new method was used to choose the next generation of leaders: a straw poll of senior leaders. Also unlike his immediate predecessors, Jiang and Hu, Xi is not a technocrat. His career has been in strictly administrative and political positions. And unlike previous general secretaries, Xi has experience in the military bureaucracy. He was not a soldier or officer but served as a political appointee in the military. Nevertheless, this allowed him to assume the post of general secretary with personal and professional ties to the People's Liberation Army. He did not have to spend years cultivating relationships as a means to consolidate his power, but this does not mean that the PLA has outsize influence in Xi's administration. During his first term as general secretary, he undertook a massive reform of the PLA, which further strengthened his control over the military.[36]

Finally, unlike the general secretaries who came before him, Xi's rise to the top was not the result of notable achievements in his previous posts. He spent twenty-five years in local party and government posts, culminating in a short stint as Shanghai's party secretary, before moving to Beijing as a member of the Politburo Standing Committee in 2007. In those posts, he hewed close to the mainstream. He was a faithful adherent of reform policies as approved by the central leadership, but was not himself an innovator or trendsetter. His career success is based on several factors: he is a "princeling"[37] whose father, Xi Zhongxun, was a veteran of the communist revolution in China and also a key ally of Deng Xiaoping; he had warm ties with multiple leaders but none served as his patron; similarly, he had good relations with key factions but was not a member of any of them; he had a reputation for fighting corruption; and above all, he had no enemies.

Xi was born in 1953 and joined the party in 1974 when he was twenty-one. This was during the Cultural Revolution, and Xi was among the "sent-down youth," young urbanites who were sent to live and work in the countryside, in Xi's case the western province of Shaanxi.[38] He was allowed to return to Beijing in 1975 to attend Tsinghua University. However, this was before the university had returned to normal after the chaos of the Cultural Revolution and before professors had resumed teaching regular classes. He graduated in 1979 with a degree in chemical engineering, but the quality of his education was always suspect and his career was unrelated to his degree. Similarly, his 1982 PhD in law (more accurately, Marxism) from Tsinghua was done as a part-time student, and his dissertation was reportedly ghostwritten.[39] His career was not built on his academic degrees or technical skills, unlike Jiang and Hu, who were well known as technocrats.

Xi benefited from connections with those around Deng, including his father, Xi Zhongxun, a revolutionary veteran whose career was up-ended after being accused of opposing Mao and who spent much of the Cultural Revolution in prison. After being rehabilitated by Deng Xiaoping in 1978, he regained his seat on the Politburo and was appointed party secretary and governor of Guangdong Province and political commissar of the Guangdong Military Region. As leader of Guangdong, Xi Zhongxun promoted and implemented Deng's reform and opening policies. In particular, he built and ran Shenzhen, the first special economic zone. After his father's political rehabilitation, Xi Jinping used his father's connections to become the secretary to Minister of Defense

Geng Biao. This gave Xi an early connection with the PLA that would prove helpful in later years.

Xi was ambitious, however, and advancement within the military hierarchy would not make him eligible for higher political office. Rather, he recognized that the route to the top in China is best accomplished by working in the provinces. In 1982, he transferred to Zhengding County in Hebei, first as deputy party secretary and then party secretary of the county and political commissar of the Zhengding County Military Affairs Department. In 1985, he transferred again to became vice mayor of Xiamen, a city in the coastal province of Fujian. The party secretary of Fujian was a friend of his father's and also a leader of the Youth League Faction, giving Xi a good tie to another key group. He then spent the next seventeen years in Fujian in a series of party, government, and military posts, culminating with deputy party secretary and governor of Fujian. Despite the many years in Fujian and his steady promotions, he did not distinguish himself there with economic results or reform initiatives. However, he had a record for fighting corruption and developing good ties with other officials and the common people.

Despite this slim record, Xi became governor of Zhejiang Province in 2002 and party secretary the following year. These provincial posts allowed him finally to show whether he could run a prosperous coastal province. Xi led the technological upgrading of hundreds of backward enterprises and closed many others. He promoted environmentalism and experimented with grassroots democracy, in both cases without clear achievements. He supported the expansion of the private sector, although this policy was in place before he became Zhejiang's leader. Zhejiang experienced strong economic growth during his years there, although it is hard to determine if that growth was the result of Xi's leadership or the strong base he inherited from his predecessors.

In 2007, Xi was appointed party secretary of Shanghai after the incumbent, Chen Liangyu, was removed from office for his involvement in a pension scandal and more generally for opposing Hu Jintao's efforts to balance growth with equity. Xi held this post for only seven months before being promoted to Beijing as a Politburo Standing Committee member, but it was nevertheless important for Xi. It helped his standing with the Shanghai Gang and created an important link between Jiang's faction and Xi's princelings. Combined with his previous ties to the PLA and the Youth League Faction, this gave Xi important connections with all leading groups in the party. His time in Shanghai also showed his ability to rebuild unity among top party and government officials and restore Shanghai's financial and economic reputation. During his time in Zhejiang and Shanghai, Xi was often described as a member of Jiang's Shanghai Gang, but he never totally fit into that group. He worked mostly in coastal areas, but did not have a close personal connection with Shanghai or Jiang. Once he became general secretary, he showed no favoritism toward Jiang or his protégés.

The Shanghai Gang and the Youth League Faction were known for their policy preferences: the Shanghai Gang favored rapid economic growth based on the comparative advantages of coastal areas, whereas the Youth League Faction was known for fighting poverty and spreading the benefits of economic development to rural areas and inland cities that lagged behind the coast. In contrast, princelings like Xi are known for their backgrounds, not their policy goals. Although there are still echoes of the Shanghai Gang and Youth League Faction in Xi's China, they have much less influence than under Jiang and Hu. This may explain why Xi has been so slow to devise a clear policy agenda: he did not rise to the top in order to advance certain policy goals, he got there due to his ambition, pedigree, and demeanor. However, factional alignments under Xi are even more opaque than they were in the past.

Early in his career, he relied on the women in his life to make connections with top leaders. His sister Qi Qiaoqiao served as a liaison with other princeling families, especially after their father opposed Hu Yaobang's ouster in 1987 and was therefore ostracized. While Xi was serving in local posts, he had little opportunity to socialize with the other princelings in Beijing, so his sister's ties proved beneficial. Xi's second and current wife, Peng Liyuan, is a singer made famous by her many TV appearances.[40] In many ways, she was better known than Xi for most of his career. She is also a civilian member of the PLA and holds the rank of major general, which gave Xi another important connection to the PLA. She was also instrumental in introducing Xi to the

Shanghai Gang through her connections with Zeng Qinghong, Jiang Zemin's right-hand man.[41]

Xi's selection as the designated successor to Hu Jintao as CCP general secretary was unique in the history of the PRC. He was not handpicked by Hu, or even by Jiang or Deng. Since there was no clear consensus on Hu's successor, an informal straw poll of more than four hundred incumbent and retired party leaders was conducted in 2007. Hu reportedly favored Li Keqiang, a leader in his own Youth League Faction, but Li did not enjoy broad support among other top leaders. Xi tallied the most votes, and Li came in second.[42] At the 17th Party Congress in 2007, both Xi and Li were promoted directly into the Politburo Standing Committee, even though they had not previously been Politburo members. Xi was ranked above Li on the standing committee, signifying that he would be the next general secretary at the 18th Party Congress in 2012, and Li would become prime minister when new government leaders were announced in 2013.

For most CCP officials, rising in the party requires both competence and connections, as illustrated by Jiang and Hu. Xi is a partial exception to that rule: although he did not have notable successes in his many party and government posts, he also had not accumulated any major policy mistakes. What he had in abundance was connections—personal relations to many prominent leaders, many the result of family ties. Xi's career indicates that connections are both necessary and sufficient to reach the top in China.

*　*　*

The CCP's routine process for rotating its leaders is a distinctive aspect of China's political system. It is in sharp contrast to the Maoist era and to the practice of most authoritarian regimes, where leaders are normally replaced only through death or coup. In China, lower-level leaders are generally evaluated on the basis of their objectively measured performance. Before reaching the top, potential leaders are assigned a variety of party and government jobs in the provinces and Beijing to gain experience and test their skills. This adds a meritocratic element to the criteria for selecting and promoting officials, while still leaving room for political connections and patronage at higher levels of the system. Despite the institutional arrangements described throughout this chapter, the top of the Chinese political system remains defined by personal ties.

The tenures of central-level party and government leaders are constrained by a combination of formal regulations and informal norms. The formal regulations on age limits and term limits mostly apply to government leaders and have generally been enforced at times of leadership change. On the party side, the constraints are more informal and apply to some but not all leaders. The transition from the third generation of leaders to the fourth mostly upheld these informal norms, although Jiang Zemin remained chairman of the Central Military Commission for several additional years. The transition from the fourth to the fifth generation abided entirely by the norms on age limits and term limits, an indication that they had been fully institutionalized.

Yet these norms have been challenged with Xi Jinping's tenure as CCP general secretary. Not only has he failed to appoint a successor but he has revised the state constitution to eliminate term limits on the presidency, which is normally held concurrently with the post of general secretary. In so doing, he has created the possibility of remaining China's leader indefinitely. This unravels the norms of leadership succession first practiced under Deng Xiaoping and continued since. If Xi does remain in power after he turns sixty-eight and his two terms as general secretary are over in 2022, there will be less turnover at the top, fewer opportunities for upward mobility, and fewer leaders with new ideas rising up the hierarchy—all the problems Deng's reforms were designed to alleviate. The consequences may be good for Xi but bad for the CCP.

3

HOW ARE POLICIES MADE?

In 2003, China was hit by an epidemic of severe acute respiratory syndrome (SARS). The secrecy inherent to China's political system hampered a quick response. Information about the highly contagious disease was not shared with hospitals, doctors, and other health care workers, much less the general public, allowing it to spread from southern China to other parts of the country and eventually abroad. In the end, more than eight thousand reported cases and 774 deaths were attributed to SARS. A report cosponsored by the Chinese government and the World Health Organization labeled the Chinese health care system as "basically unsuccessful," a remarkable admission for a regime that rarely acknowledges failure.[1]

In the years after, the Chinese government revamped its health care system. It established an ad hoc group to coordinate efforts of fourteen government agencies involved in health care. In 2007, this group invited proposals from China's leading universities, the government's National Development and Reform Commission, the World Bank, the World Health Organization, and McKinsey and Company, a prominent international consulting company. Universities, government agencies, and think tanks in China held public events, published articles, and gave media interviews to promote their preferred health care program. In October 2008, the government released a draft of its proposed new health care plan and invited public comments. During subsequent months, more than thirty thousand comments were submitted by stakeholders, health care professionals, and average citizens. In April 2009,

China's new health care system went into effect. It provided basic health care insurance to most urban and rural residents, gave more emphasis to disease prevention and control, and reformed the primary care and hospital systems to reduce costs and improve the quality of care.

If this had occurred in the United States, it would have seemed routine. Consultations with policy specialists, lobbying by stakeholders, public discussion, and revisions to draft proposals are all common occurrences in the American policy process. The extent to which this also happens in China is not as well known. In different ways, the Chinese political system has become more responsive to public opinion, but the CCP still resists being accountable to the people it governs. In the absence of competitive elections and rule of law, the CCP sees improved governance—including greater transparency and more spending on public goods, such as education, health care, and the environment—as a source of legitimacy. This chapter will focus on the areas where policy options are the subject of prolonged negotiations involving different government ministries and local leaders, where local experiments become the basis for national policy, and where the party welcomes societal input into the policy process. Subsequent chapters will detail how it responds to perceived threats from society.

The study of policy making in China tends to focus on the local level, where decision making and implementation are more visible, participants in the policy process are more accessible to scholars, and regional variation is more amenable to theorizing. However, much decision making happens at the central level, especially on issues where the party's legitimacy and hold on power are at stake—and policy making at the center remains a largely black box. Since 1989, central leaders have maintained a united front with few examples of debate. Even though we know China is a largely top-down political system, the focus is on local patterns because the center remains off-limits to academic research.

This chapter is organized from the top down. Topics that are very politically sensitive and threaten the party's hold on power are decided at the very top of the party leadership with little outside input. Topics that are less sensitive and less threatening to the party provide opportunities for other actors to participate. When there is broad agreement on policy goals but differences on how best to achieve them, central ministries, local governments, and other bureaucratic actors bargain and negotiate to find consensus.

During the first decade of the 2000s, a wide range of actors sought to influence policy decisions. Scientists, journalists, and domestic and international NGOs advocated their policy preferences, often in opposition to what party and government leaders decided. Eventually the public at large was invited to comment on pending laws and regulations. Yet, while the party became more responsive to public opinion, it did so only for selective issues and not in ways that made it directly accountable to the people. Only at the very grassroots level were local officials accountable to the people they governed, and even then only in a limited way, as we will see below.

In short, policy making in China ranges from a very closed to a fairly open process, depending on the issue and the overall political context. The general trend line was greater openness over time—but that trend reversed once Xi Jinping became CCP general secretary in 2012. Decision making became more centralized in the party as Xi restored the political system's Leninist character, and more centralized in Xi personally as he consolidated his own authority. When the party is in command, there is less opportunity for the people to be heard.

The Mass Line in Theory and Practice

In describing the party's relationship with the people in the policy-making process, it is best to start with Chairman Mao's concept of the "mass line." During the pre-1949 civil war years in China, the CCP recognized the need to gain popular support by adopting policies that reflected public opinion. This gave rise to the "mass line" concept, one of the CCP's most important traditions. The mass line encouraged party leaders to seek the views of the masses and adjust policies in light of this mass feedback. As Chairman Mao described it,

[T]ake the ideas of the masses (scattered and unsystematic ideas) and concentrate them (through study turn them into concentrated and systematic ideas), then go to the masses and propagate and explain these ideas until the masses embrace them as their own, hold fast to them and translate them into action, and test the correctness of these ideas in such action. Then once again concentrate ideas from the masses and once again go to the masses so that the ideas are persevered in and carried through. And so on, over and over again in an endless spiral, with the ideas becoming more correct, more vital and richer each time.[2]

The mass line is one of the few Maoist traditions that has not been abandoned or discredited by China's post-Mao leaders. In theory, the mass line compels party leaders to listen to the masses and shape policies that respond to their concerns. In practice, the mass line is more about going to the masses to sell the policies the leaders have decided upon and less about soliciting mass opinion. The masses have little opportunity to offer feedback, and little incentive to challenge the leaders' decisions directly.

But to dismiss the mass line as mere lip service would go too far. The CCP does respond to public opinion, and replaces officials and adjusts policy in light of feedback. It does not act responsively in a mechanical fashion, as the rudimentary explanation of the mass line feedback loop would imply. It responds in a selective way, on some types of policies more than others: in short, they are unlikely to respond on political issues that are usually framed in zero-sum terms where the survival of the regime is at stake, and more likely to respond on economic and social issues that are not zero-sum in nature. When it is willing to solicit feedback from society, it uses the mass line concept as the rationale.

Policy Making during Crises

On issues of greatest salience to the CCP, such as suppressing discussion of democracy and maintaining stability, all key decisions are made within the CCP, especially within the Politburo and its Standing Committee, with little or no outside input. We know little about debates within these bodies, but they are the location for the most authoritative policy decisions.

The COVID-19 epidemic of 2020 illustrates several of the best-known aspects of the Chinese political system: its focus on maintaining stability over all other goals, its lack of transparency, and its willingness to use all means necessary to achieve policy goals. When facing this kind of crisis, the CCP is very risk averse. It would rather overreact than risk instability.

In January 2019, Xi Jinping warned top officials of "black swans": unforeseen events that could suddenly pose an existential threat to the CCP. The CCP tends not to be very adept at handling new situations, and the COVID-19 epidemic demonstrated that anew. Rather than take proactive measures to forestall a crisis they see coming, CCP leaders tend to react only once the crisis is upon them. Whatever lessons had been learned from the SARS crisis in 2003 had been forgotten by the time COVID-19 hit in 2020.

Like most countries around the world, the Chinese government was slow to respond to reports of the new virus. Xi Jinping reported news of the virus in a speech to the Politburo in early January 2020, but no action was taken for two weeks.[3] Xi announced a new task force to handle the response, but he named Prime Minister Li Keqiang to lead the task force. Like Trump and Putin, Xi did not put himself in charge of handling the crisis, although he had the most to lose. With so much at stake, these leaders put others in charge, perhaps in order to blame them if the epidemic was not handled well. As the disease began to spread, the Chinese government was slow to share information with foreign governments and international organizations like the World Health Organization, often relying on press releases instead of the details that health care professionals needed. Xi also disappeared from public view for almost two weeks without explanation. This was highly unusual for someone who dominates the news coverage in China—creating speculation that he was either ill or in political trouble.[4]

In Wuhan, where the epidemic began, local leaders tried to suppress information about the new virus. They first learned of it in December 2019 but did not report it to the central government. Local leaders are often reluctant to report bad news to their superiors for fear of being fired, and indeed, the party secretaries of Wuhan and Hubei were replaced in February 2020. When a group of eight doctors in Wuhan sent information about the new virus to other doctors, the local public security department detained them for several days and forced them to issue a public apology for spreading false information.

Except it was not false information, but an early warning of the pandemic that was to come. One of those doctors, Li Wenliang, returned to work at his hospital, caught the virus, and died; he became a hero on social media for trying to help the people and becoming a victim of the repressive arm of the state. Rather than take preemptive steps that might have slowed or even stopped the spread of the virus, Wuhan officials instead chose to suppress the information they feared would cause a panic among the people and jeopardize their own positions. Their ultimate concern was maintaining stability, and they were intent on doing so, even though this decision led to far worse problems.

China's social media revealed the public's understandable outrage at the mishandling and cover-up of the virus, but most of their ire was aimed at local leaders, not the central party and government. This is a common theme in Chinese politics, that people have much higher levels of trust and support for central leaders than for their local officials, and it was prominent during the COVID-19 epidemic in 2020.

Once the CCP decided to act, it showed its continued capacity to respond quickly and effectively. But it was also a very heavy-handed response. It completely shut down Wuhan, a city of more than 11 million, and the surrounding Hubei Province. Other cities imposed two-week quarantines for newly arrived people, even people who were returning home. The economy largely ground to a halt as factories, offices, restaurants, and shops closed. The party deployed a mix of old-fashioned and high-tech measures for monitoring the population. Police set up checkpoints at the entrances of cities and main intersections. In major cities, hundreds of thousands of volunteers were mobilized to check IDs and question people who wanted to enter neighborhoods and residential buildings. This was reminiscent of the Maoist era, when people were mobilized on a massive scale to achieve short-term goals. People were required to use phone apps to track their location and report their temperature and general health every day to their local governments. To further pinpoint people's locations, they had to use QR codes (unique digital "quick response" codes) to enter buses, office buildings, and other public places.

Xi Jinping visited Wuhan for first time on March 10 and declared the epidemic there over; in mid-March, China reported its first day without new cases. The severe lockdown in Wuhan was finally lifted on March 25 and other cities slowly began to reopen. The concern then became the possibility of a second wave of cases, in particular from Chinese returning from overseas, where the novel coronavirus was still spreading. When Wuhan reported six new cases in May, the government announced plans to retest all 11 million residents in just ten days.[5] Later outbreaks in Beijing, Qingdao, and other cities were also met with immediate lockdowns and extensive testing within just a few days. The enormous scale and short time frame of these plans were also reminiscent of campaigns of the Maoist era, as well as examples of the party's tendency to overreact to even small threats.

In their fight against COVID-19, China's leaders used military language: it was not simply an effort to contain an epidemic but an all-out people's war against the virus. Once Xi declared victory in Wuhan, the party's propaganda machine began describing it as a great victory, demonstrating the party's leadership. It compared its strong response to the slow and halting efforts of other countries, especially the United States and Europe. Ironically, it tried to use the epidemic in China as a source of nationalist pride and not the human tragedy it was.

By the time it had declared the epidemic over in March 2020, China had officially reported more than eighty thousand cases and over four thousand deaths. Most outside observers believed the actual numbers were much higher, for several reasons. First of all, it is clear that the CCP was worried about how the public would react if the true extent of the epidemic were revealed. Local governments restricted funerals so mourners could not share stories with other families or see how many people died.[6] As always, threats to stability are the party's greatest concern. Relatedly, the party's propaganda machine needed to support Xi's visit to Wuhan. Although there were reports of additional unreported new cases in Wuhan, testing stopped after Xi announced the epidemic was over, so as not to undercut his declaration of victory.[7] There were also technical problems. For example, China initially did not count asymptomatic cases, even when they tested positive. Hong Kong media reported more than 43,000 asymptomatic cases, suggesting that up to one-third of cases were going unreported.[8] The Chinese government later changed how it counted cases to include asymptomatic ones but did not revise previous numbers. And, finally, the tests themselves may not have been very accurate. The Spanish government reported it stopped using Chinese COVID-19 tests because they were only 30 percent reliable.

Though the novel coronavirus came as a surprise to everyone, for those who watch Chinese politics the CCP's response to it was all too predictable. But most policy issues do not pose this same level of threat to the party and do not produce this type of response. In any complex organization, whether a government, a corporation, or a university, not all decisions are made at the top. The top leadership simply does not have the bandwidth to decide every issue. And so it is in China. Once the top CCP leadership has set policy priorities, the policy-making process becomes more complicated with the inclusion of more actors. The party sets broad policy priorities (in the post-Mao era, that has meant economic modernization and political stability) with more room for bureaucratic bargaining and even public participation about how to achieve those goals.

Fragmented Authoritarianism

The Chinese state is not a unified actor; political authority is fragmented.[9] It is fragmented vertically, in the sense that decisions made at higher levels are not always faithfully implemented at lower levels. Different levels of the political system have different priorities, based on the local context and the interests of local officials. For example, the central leadership has set improving the environment as a key priority. This is a nationwide problem, more intense in some areas than others.

But in order to address this problem, local leaders have to be willing to meet the pollution targets set by Beijing. However, as will be described in more detail below, local leaders have greater incentives to emphasize economic growth than environmental protection. As a result, many localities have been slow to enforce the stricter standards for air and water pollution set by Beijing. In China, as in other countries, protecting the environment is a long-term goal that is too often seen as being at odds with the immediate task of economic development.

Political authority is also fragmented horizontally: at every level of the political system, different ministries and agencies have different policy preferences. These bureaucracies act as interest groups, lobbying decision makers to adopt their preferred policies and rescind the ones that harm their interests. As noted above, environmental protection is often pitted against business interests. Ministries in charge of economic development and oil and gas exploration typically have different preferences than those responsible for the environment. Similarly, agricultural interests are not always compatible with industrial interests because industrialization encroaches on farm land. Developing new land for farming also leads to deforestation, which in turn leads to soil erosion, desertification, and the destruction of habitats for animals, all of which concern environmental protection agencies. Because most policies touch on multiple interests, policy change requires extensive bargaining before a decision is reached.

Resolving policy conflicts is further complicated by bureaucratic ranks in the Chinese political system. For example, the heads of central ministries have the same bureaucratic rank as provincial leaders, and none of them has authority to impose a decision on the rest. Often the result is continual bureaucratic bargaining among equally ranked leaders. Moreover, like most complex organizations, the Chinese state is stovepiped, meaning that information flows within a given ministry or level of government but is not necessarily shared with other ministries and levels. As a result, information is often incomplete and compartmentalized.

These common bureaucratic pathologies—competing interests, incomplete information, and unclear authority—complicate the policy-making process, leading to delays in reaching decisions and further delays in their implementation.

In China's fragmented authoritarianism, the CCP plays an essential role by integrating and coordinating these fragmented pieces in two key ways. First, it integrates policy making with its central-level "leading small groups" that bring together the leaders of party and government bureaucracies with interests on the same issue. There are more than two dozen of these leading small groups on policy areas, including economics and finance, the environment, state security, and foreign policy.[10] They are not well publicized and their membership is not always known, but they play a key role in coordinating policy across multiple bureaucracies.

The CCP also integrates policy making through the personnel system, which is based on the Soviet *nomenklatura* system, where the party is in charge of appointing all top positions in the party, government, SOEs, universities, banks, and other important institutions. Leaders are expected to represent the interests of their units in which they work, but those who are too recalcitrant or too publicly oppose the top leaders' policy priorities can be removed from office. Through the leading small groups and the nomenklatura system, the CCP integrates China's fragmented authoritarianism and prevents conflicting interests from creating complete policy gridlock.

A good example of this fragmented authoritarianism in action is the Three Gorges Dam project along the Yangtze River.[11] China's rapid economic development has led to growing energy demands. Its domestic sources of oil and gas are limited and China's leaders have been reluctant to be overly dependent on imported sources of energy. One solution has been to build an extensive network of dams on China's many rivers to produce hydropower, thereby helping alleviate China's demand for energy. These dams also help control flooding, a perennial problem in China's heartland. But they have also been controversial. Dams create vast reservoirs that displace the people who live there, disrupt navigation along the rivers, threaten wildlife, and harm cultural landmarks. In building the Three Gorges Dam, these competing interests clashed.

Negotiations on the Three Gorges Dam began in the early 1980s and dragged on for years as different interest groups lobbied, bargained, and

FIGURE 3.1. Three Gorges Dam (photo: Le Grand Portage/Wikimedia,
Creative Commons BY 2.0, https://creativecommons.org/licenses/by/2.0/)

competed. One of the main points of contention was how high the dam
should be. The Ministry of Water Resources favored a high dam that
would control flooding. Local governments behind the dam, such as the
municipality of Chongqing, also supported a high dam because it would
extend the reservoir farther behind the dam, making the cities upstream
more accessible for shipping. Provinces downstream from the dam were
in favor because it would reduce flooding and improve shipping along
the Yangtze River. In contrast, the provincial government in Sichuan
favored a lower dam that would create a smaller reservoir and displace
fewer people, because it would be responsible for resettlement costs.
The Ministry of Energy thought there were better options for hydropower than the Three Gorges Dam and opposed it altogether.[12] With
the costs and benefits so stark and some ministries and provinces

getting the benefits and others bearing the costs, negotiations dragged on for years. The ministries and provincial governments involved in the case had the same bureaucratic rank and none had the authority to make a definitive decision. Top CCP and government leaders were reluctant to impose a solution that would harm the interests of any of the actors involved, preferring to let them reach a consensus.

Ultimately, a compromise was struck. One of the key elements was separating Chongqing from Sichuan and turning it into a centrally administered municipality (as are Beijing, Shanghai, and Tianjin). Chongqing would be responsible for the resettlement of the more than 1.2 million farmers away from the dam's reservoir, which largely resolved Sichuan's opposition. But the Three Gorges Dam remained controversial because of its tremendous costs, corruption in granting construction contracts, the displacement of people who were relocated to make way for the dam and its reservoir, and damage to cultural landmarks. When the plan was put before the National People's Congress for approval, one-third of the deputies registered their disapproval by either voting against the plan or abstaining, an unprecedented show of opposition in what had been a largely rubber-stamp legislature.[13] The Three Gorges Dam was completed in 2006 but remains controversial for its environmental impact, its displacement of almost 1.5 million people, landslides and excessive silting in the reservoir behind the dam, and a variety of technical problems.

As China's reform era progressed into the twenty-first century, the policy-making process expanded to include new groups of "policy entrepreneurs," nonstate individuals and groups who tried to influence the policy process and public opinion. The state-owned media became more commercialized and somewhat more liberalized, creating space for journalists and editors to pursue stories with popular appeal.[14] Academic experts began to offer their views in public forums and through the media. Nongovernmental organizations began to form in growing numbers. Many of them were involved in social welfare services, but others pursued policy goals, including defending workers' rights or protecting the environment. Foreign NGOs like Greenpeace and The Nature Conservancy also became active in China, often in partnership with domestic NGOs. These new policy entrepreneurs modified the policy making process: whereas the original fragmented authoritarian model was focused on bureaucratic actors, "fragmented authoritarianism 2.0" recognized that nonstate actors—and in some cases foreign actors—now influenced domestic policy in China.[15]

The opposition to plans for a series of dams along the Nu River in southwestern Yunnan in the first decade of the 2000s illustrates the new dynamics of fragmented authoritarianism 2.0.[16] This area of Yunnan is very picturesque, revered in China and recognized by UNESCO as a World Heritage Area. But it is also deeply impoverished and indebted. Local officials who promoted building the dams argued that it would boost economic development by generating energy that could be used locally and be sold to other areas of China. They were also in favor of the project because it would fund local development projects that would in turn would boost their career prospects.

A diverse set of policy entrepreneurs—including scientists, environmental activists, journalists, and grassroots and international NGOs—mobilized to oppose the project, highlighting both the cost of resettlement and, more important, the damage to one of China's most cherished cultural heritage sites. They hosted conferences in Yunnan, Beijing, and Thailand to air their concerns. Local and international NGOs organized tours of the region for provincial and national leaders to showcase the pristine beauty of the area that would be irreversibly damaged by the proposed dams.[17] They worked with the media to further publicize their concerns, hoping to get the attention of both the general public and higher-level leaders who were not familiar with the plans. These efforts worked: in 2004, then-Prime Minister Wen Jiabao ordered a halt to the dam project until it could be "cautiously studied and scientifically studied," effectively killing the project.[18] The concerted efforts of China's policy entrepreneurs resulted in a rare victory of cultural heritage and environmental protection over economic modernization.

However, this initial victory did not end the determination of local officials to build the dams or find other ways to boost economic development in the area. Some suggested they might move forward with the dams even if Beijing opposed them and even if they had to find alternate sources of funding.[19] So far, no dam construction has begun, but the desire for development remains strong.[20]

When Xi Jinping became the CCP's leader in 2012, China's policy-making process changed again, becoming less fragmented and more authoritarian. The CCP's role as integrator and coordinator was reemphasized. Xi chairs eight leading small groups, five of which were created after he became general secretary.[21] These groups covered the full range of domestic and foreign policies, reflecting Xi's control over the policy process. The CCP reasserted its control over the media and the internet, limiting what information was available and what voices could be heard. NGOs faced new constraints, especially those with international ties. Xi launched an anticorruption campaign that targeted both "tigers and flies," in other words, central-level party, government, and military leaders, as well as local officials. The message was clear: get in line behind Xi or risk being fired or even imprisoned. In addition to targeting corruption, the campaign also eliminated potential rivals to Xi as China's leader (more details on this in chapter 2). The dynamics of fragmented authoritarianism 2.0 declined, and political authority was once again recentralized under the CCP's control, with Xi unequivocally in charge.

These changes under Xi have not ended the fragmented nature of political authority in China, however. Despite offering an ambitious set of economic reform proposals in fall 2013, including greater reliance on markets, SOE reform, tax reform, and exchange rate liberalization, the CCP has not been able to deliver on most of them. The delays are allegedly due to the vested interests of both bureaucratic actors and local leaders who resist abandoning the economic model based on infrastructure investment and foreign trade for one based more on innovation and domestic consumption.[22] The policy-making process may be less fragmented than in the past, but the conflicting interests among bureaucracies and leaders at different levels of the state continue to exist.

Local Policy Experiments

As an alternative to the bargaining characteristic of the fragmented authoritarian model, another distinctive aspect of the policy process in China is the use of local experiments to try out policy alternatives before adopting on a nationwide scale.[23] This is a continuation of procedures used pre-1949, before the CCP became China's ruling party and was experimenting with how best to achieve its policy goals under different local conditions. The practice has continued up to the present. Local experimentation comes after the CCP's decision on policy priorities. It is designed to determine *how* best to achieve policy goals, not to resolve *what* the goals should be. Once the central leadership decides on a policy, it selects several locations to experiment on policy implementation techniques. The lessons learned from local experiments then inform national policy.

A key example of how local experiments become national policies are China's special economic zones (SEZs). First created in 1979, they allowed the CCP to experiment with market-oriented reforms, private ownership, foreign investment, and foreign trade at a time when the Chinese economy was still managed by the central plan and isolated from the global economy. The CCP leadership had decided to make economic modernization its central task in 1978, but they disagreed on how best to achieve this task. Conservative leaders preferred to maintain the traditional central planning system, a hallmark of a communist system, and saw Deng Xiaoping's reform and opening policies as too much like capitalism and incompatible with communism. Rather than engage in a direct debate over whether the plan or the market was the best way to achieve economic modernization, reformers chose to experiment with the SEZs. Because the SEZs were originally few in number, small in scale, and located in peripheral coastal areas, conservative leaders did not object to the experiment.

The SEZs were literally fenced off from the rest of China, as though they were quarantined to prevent their influence from spreading uncontrolled. If the experiment failed, the SEZs could simply be shut down and not "infect" the rest of the country. But just the opposite happened: the SEZs were so successful in attracting new investment, creating new jobs, and fostering rapid growth that leaders in other localities demanded similar reforms. Fourteen coastal cities were then given permission to adopt these still experimental reforms. These reform and opening policies were gradually expanded to more and more cities and eventually nationwide. Local experimentation not only demonstrated the utility of the reform and opening policies but also created demands for their diffusion through the rest of China.

The CCP also experimented with the registration process for NGOs. Early in the reform era, the CCP was wary of the potential of certain NGOs to be a source of opposition, and therefore made it difficult for them to register and operate legally. Over time, party and government officials began to recognize NGOs' utility in providing social welfare services, and so the party decided to encourage the NGO sector. In the late 2000s, Beijing, Chengdu, Guangdong, Shanghai, and Shenzhen were chosen as experimental points for streamlining the NGO registration process. Their experiences were then adopted as a nationwide policy rolled out in later years.[24]

Responding to the Public

In the post-Mao period, the CCP has introduced different ways to incorporate public opinion into policy making.[25] These reforms are not to be confused with democracy, but in various ways they improve the quality of governance in China through greater transparency and responsiveness to public opinion. In this way they reflect both the logic of the traditional mass line and its inherent limitations.

The War on Pollution

China's rapid economic development has not only raised incomes and improved living standards but has also taken a tremendous toll on the environment. Since 2006, it has been the world's leading contributor of greenhouse gases. Almost 300 million people in China do not have access to safe drinking water. Close to 40 percent of its rivers are heavily polluted, with some not even safe for human contact. Commercial agricultural practices and deforestation for agricultural and industrial development are leading to the desertification of approximately one-quarter of China's land, and more than 15 percent of the land is contaminated with heavy metals from coal plants and industrial discharge.[26]

FIGURE 3.2. Same view of the Beijing skyline on a clear day and during the 2013 "airpocalypse" (photo: Bill Bishop, used with permission)

China's pollution has had dramatic health and economic costs. A study of northern China found that it had 5.5 million excessive deaths per year due to air pollution.[27] The 2008 Olympics in Beijing brought unwanted international attention to Beijing's air pollution. Many athletes arrived wearing face masks, and some even brought their own food due to fears of unsafe meats and vegetables. In 2013, Beijing and other cities experienced an "airpocalypse," causing planes to be grounded for days (see figure 3.2). Severe air pollution in Beijing, Shanghai, and other major cities also caused declines in international tourism.

Growth-oriented policies alone are not to blame. Rising living standards that have accompanied economic growth have played a role as well. Higher incomes led to more demand for personal cars; China is now the world's largest market for cars. Urbanization has produced increased demand for energy in homes and workplaces. There is now greater reliance on packaged foods instead of fresh, creating more garbage. All of these changes are typical of modern urban lifestyles, but also have negative impacts on the environment.

Although the Chinese political system is not known for its transparency, pollution provides its own commentary on transparency: people can see for themselves the smog that obscures the sky and burns the throat and lungs, the water that is opaque, oddly colored, and foul smelling, the expanding deforestation and desertification, the piles of trash. Some forms of pollution are not so easily detected—greenhouse gases and lead in drinking water—but are eventually revealed through lab tests by government scientists and by the work of NGOs and investigative journalists.

The Chinese government's lack of transparency on environmental conditions led others to gather their own information. The US embassy in Beijing used Twitter to report the air quality in its part of the city. During the "airpocalypse," it reported an air quality index of over 700, where 100 is the threshold for a "red alert." Moreover, it used the international standard of PM2.5 (particulate matter of 2.5 microns in diameter), instead of the more lax PM10 standard of air quality used by the Chinese government. This was a quiet but effective way of pressuring the Chinese government to acknowledge the air pollution problem and to do something about it. In 2012, China finally adopted the PM2.5 standard the US embassy and most other countries used. Chinese citizens followed suit, using handheld air quality sensors or smart phone apps to get precise and continually updated information about the extent of air pollution. Party propaganda alone cannot counteract the pollution people can see and feel.

Environmental issues became what the CCP fears the most: a source of political unrest. Plans to build new power plants, chemical factories, and similar projects often triggered NIMBY ("not in my backyard") protests by local residents (more on this in chapter 5). Pollution had the potential to undermine popular support for the party. An innovative study found that daily variations in the air quality in different areas of Beijing were correlated with the rise and fall of people's support for the CCP-led regime: when air pollution went up, support went down.[28] It is remarkable that the level of regime support fluctuated so often across different sections of a single city, but it reinforces a crucial point for China's decision makers: the environment has become one of the most important issues in public opinion and is a prominent source of public protest.

In response to these trends, the CCP took a number of steps to improve the environment. It banned leaded gas for cars and trucks. Car owners in Beijing, Shanghai, and other large cities are restricted to driving on alternate odd-even days based on their license plate numbers. The government closed or moved factories away from population centers, although this did not reduce pollution so much as move it to new and less populous spots. To reduce China's heavy reliance on coal, it has mandated reductions in coal use and the operation and building of coal-fired energy plants. In 2008, it elevated the State Environmental Protection Administration to a State Council-level Ministry of Environmental Protection (MEP), giving it more status and resources. The MEP was then restructured in 2018 as the Ministry of Ecology and Environment and given wider oversight authority. In 2014, Prime Minister Li Keqiang declared a "war on pollution" to undo the damage the CCP's approach to development had on the environment. The need to protect the environment also figured prominently in Xi Jinping's speech to the 19th Party Congress in 2017. A new Environmental Protection Law went into effect in 2015 that, among other things, imposed substantial fines on polluters and those who interfere with environmental impact assessments before construction projects are approved. The Chinese government has put major investments in renewable energies and is now a global leader in this sector. In these different ways, the party signaled that it was responsive to public opinion on the environment.

These various measures had notable impacts on China's environment. As just one example, its air quality improved. In 2006, sixteen of the twenty most polluted cities in the world were in China, according to the World Bank. By 2019, only two of the top twenty were in China, and the country as a whole ranked eleventh in the world.[29] This was in part because China's air quality had improved, but also in part because other countries were getting worse.

Today, China has generally good national policies to protect the environment. The problem is that they are not always implemented locally.[30] In China as in other countries there is a widely perceived tradeoff between economic growth and environmental protection. Local officials are reluctant to take steps to improve the environment that would slow economic growth and thereby harm their chances for promotion. The MEP does not have the same staff, budget, or clout of other State Council ministries. This makes it hard to for it to monitor local compliance with central policies. At the local level, environmental bureaus are under the jurisdiction of the local governments and do not have the autonomy to act as effective watchdogs. Some are more willing to tax pollution in order to raise revenue than to enforce policies to reduce pollution.

Open Government Information

The central government's difficulty in monitoring local implementation of its policies was a main motivation behind the reform initiative known as Open Government Information (OGI). In 2007, China's central government launched the OGI policy to give citizens more access to important information about how well their local governments were doing their work. OGI was adopted for two reasons. First, as a condition for joining the World Trade Organization, China agreed to make certain types of information more accessible and more transparent, such as government budgetary expenditures and tax regulations. This was important for foreign investors and companies interested in doing business with China. Second, and more important, OGI was devised to give the center greater oversight over local officials.[31] Because of China's fragmented authoritarianism, central officials could not depend on local officials to fully and faithfully implement policy and could not effectively monitor whether they were engaging in corruption. By allowing local citizens to ask for information on local government spending, environmental standards, tax codes, and other basic information, the center compelled local officials to be more transparent. This made it easier to determine whether they were properly implementing central policies and whether they were misusing government funds, one element of corruption. In other words, the center and local citizens were tacit allies in monitoring local officials, and OGI was the tool that let them work together. In a political system without direct accountability to the public, this type of proxy accountability can occasionally be a useful strategy.[32]

Even under OGI, local officials often refused to divulge information. As for most policies, there was regional variation in compliance with OGI. For example, one of the types of information subject to OGI was levels of pollution. Local governments were required to publicly reveal how clean the air and water were in their jurisdictions, but not all of them did so. A key explanation for why some complied and others did not was the economic context: in cities dominated by a single industry, and especially when the local economy was dominated by large firms, local officials were less likely to reveal information about the environment in order to protect local industry.[33] For example, in two cities with similar levels of industrial pollution, the one that had several small firms creating that pollution was more likely to reveal information about the quality of its environment than a city dominated by a single large firm. Failure to comply with national environmental standards should lead to heavy fines and other sanctions, but when the local economy was dependent on a heavily polluting industry or firm, local officials often chose to look the other way. In China—as in the United States and other countries—the fear is that enforcing environmental standards can be bad for business, at least in the short run, and since local officials are expected to produce strong economic growth as a condition for promotion, meeting environmental standards and complying with OGI are seen as secondary in importance. Vigorous compliance with OGI will not by itself lead to promotion, but failing to meet economic growth targets will almost surely prevent promotion. Most local officials choose the option that is in their better interests.

Failure to comply with OGI can be seen as a policy failure, but it also has a potential upside. OGI encourages political participation in two ways. First, it provides a legitimate frame for asking for information, even when the government does not want to reveal it. Second, when local officials refuse to comply with requests for information, it provides a legitimate channel for political activists to challenge local officials through the courts.[34] In both of these ways, activists can use OGI to pursue policy goals by utilizing existing official institutions and rhetoric. By working within existing institutions and framing demands in terms of existing laws and regulations, activists can portray themselves as politically unthreatening. They are not demanding new rights or reforms, they are simply availing themselves of rights granted by the CCP.[35] Activists often request information fully expecting their requests to be denied so that they can then publicize the government's failure to comply with OGI provisions.[36]

Studies of compliance with OGI reveal that local governments respond to requests for information between a third and a half of the time. This response rate is on par with studies done in the United States and other developing countries.[37] When requests for information contain an implied threat of collective action and the potential for protests leading to political instability, officials are more likely to respond and more likely to post their responses online so that other citizens can see evidence of the government's responsiveness to local problems. Officials in cities with recent incidents of protest are also more likely to respond. Maintaining stability is an essential goal for local officials, and protests can threaten their chances for promotion. Threats to report officials' refusal to provide information to higher-level officials are also more likely to generate a response. Both top-down oversight and bottom-up societal pressure were shown to be important sources of responsiveness from local officials.

Requests for information can also provide information to local officials about local conditions. Many local governments have a "Mayor's Mailbox" or other similar institution that allows local citizens to air their complaints, seek help for a problem, and request information on an issue. In order for citizens to provide this information, local officials have to be seen as willing to respond.[38] Moreover, these requests can provide information about citizens' displeasure with certain policies or specific leaders, the need for public services, or increasing social conflicts. The willingness to receive this kind of information is not driven just by a fear of protest but also by the need to get reliable information about emerging problems before they get out of control.

All this shows that new opportunities for political participation like OGI do not necessarily undermine the regime. If OGI moves official policy and especially the local implementation of policy closer to the public's preferences, it may paradoxically strengthen the regime by improving public approval of its performance.[39] Local officials may see OGI as undermining their autonomy, but that was one of the goals of OGI. Its purpose was to help the center ensure local implementation of its policies and bring local practice more in line with central promises and public interests.

In short, OGI was primarily an effort to gain greater oversight over local officials, not a commitment to the principle of transparency. But OGI has an important limitation: it only applies to local governments, not the central government. Although OGI has compelled at least some local governments to be more responsive, the center still refuses to be accountable, even in this limited way.

Public Comments

In 2001, the NPC began posting some draft laws online for public comment, and in 2008 announced it would do so for all drafts.[40] Most local people's congresses followed suit. The State Council also posts proposed regulations on its website for public comment. In 2014, the CCP announced that public consultation was one of its "primary pillars of governance."[41] This is an updating of the mass line concept: solicit information from the people in order to devise acceptable policy. Xi himself supported this type of consultation because it used party-controlled institutions like the people's congress system.

The popular response to this public comment initiative has been varied. The labor contract law, eventually passed in 2006, drew more than 190,000 online comments, plus another 150,000 in focus group meetings with workers.[42] The health care law adopted in 2009 attracted over 30,000 comments.[43] In contrast, draft laws on less-hot-button issues, such as tort law and agricultural innovation, received only a few thousand comments.[44] More significant is that those who submitted comments on draft laws did not have much expectation that their opinions would make a difference. In a context where the mass line is more top down than bottom up, citizens had low expectations about their influence. Nevertheless, they took advantage of a new opportunity to make their views known.[45]

A key finding from studies of China's public comment initiative is that higher rates of consultation with the public lead to fewer incidents of protests when the final versions of laws and regulations are announced.[46] By publicizing draft laws and regulations, the public and key stakeholders have the opportunity to express their views before they are adopted. The opportunity for public comment does not necessarily generate support for what gets adopted, but the process of consultation provides a measure of transparency that reduces public protests.

What difference do public comments make? Even though individuals and interest groups have the opportunity to comment on pending laws and regulations, it is not clear if legislators and policy makers take these views into consideration. There are limits to how transparent the CCP is willing to be: unlike in the United States, the comments submitted during the time allotted for public comments are not always publicly revealed, making it difficult for outside observers to assess the views expressed. More often, a select number are made available, and it is likely that they are the ones most in line with the CCP's preferences. However, it is possible to compare the draft laws and regulations with their final versions to see what revisions were made. For example, in response to public comments, the NPC revised the draft labor contract law to make it more labor friendly.[47] However, after continued lobbying by private business organizations, revisions to the law were subsequently proposed to make it more favorable to business, at the expense of labor.[48] Similarly, the central government relaxed some of the provisions in the draft criminal procedure law in 2012, especially regarding the detention of criminal suspects in what are known as "black jails," secretive facilities where suspects could be held without charge and without the ability to communicate with family or lawyers.[49] It did not solicit comments on what kinds of behavior and speech would be illegal, which is the sole prerogative of the party, but only on the procedures for enforcing laws.

As such, the public comment initiative indicates evolution in China's policy-making process but not transformation.[50] The CCP solicits public input on issues only where its authority is not at stake. It is willing to accept outside input in order to break policy stalemates that arise from the fragmented authority in China's political system, but it does not tolerate challenges to the system itself. The opportunity for public comments makes the policy-making process more consultative, but it does not make it more democratic (at least in the Western sense of democracy) and was not intended to. It was designed to solicit suggestions on issues, like health care, where greater political participation does not threaten the CCP's hold on power. By allowing consultation on issues where the political stakes are low but the popular interest is high, it might even have the effect of bolstering popular support for the status quo.

Representation in People's Congresses

China's people's congresses are often derided as rubber-stamping, simply approving whatever party and government leaders put before them. They meet in full session only once per year, and then only for a few days or at most a few weeks at a time. The National People's Congress at the apex of the legislative branch has roughly three thousand members, too large to deliberate or debate legislation. It meets once per year in March for ten to fourteen days, too short a time even to read the many bills presented for approval. Once bills are put to a vote, they always pass with overwhelming majorities. NPC deputies are not accountable to the public: how they vote is not publicly revealed and, more important, they are not directly elected by the public.

At the grassroots level, popular elections for people's congresses occur in townships, counties, and urban districts. Citizens as well as party and government officials are able to nominate candidates. Citizens tend to nominate people they believe can represent them, especially community leaders who have lived in their districts for many years and are familiar with local issues and public sentiments. In contrast, party and government officials tend to nominate people they believe will be loyal to the party's priorities and not oppose them.[51] Above the grassroots level, people's congresses indirectly elect people's congresses at the next-higher level: grassroots congresses elect municipal people's congresses, which elect provincial people's congresses, which in turn elect the National People's Congress.

At all levels, electoral committees dominated by CCP leaders determine the final slate of nominees. This allows the CCP to screen out nominees it deems unsuitable for any reason, such as their favoring democratic reforms that challenge the CCP's legitimacy. These electoral committees also make sure that CCP members predominate in all levels of people's congresses: roughly 70 to 75 percent of people's congress deputies are CCP members. People's congress deputies are disparaged by reform-oriented activists and outside observers as not representing the public and instead being beholden to the CCP.[52]

For all these reasons—CCP control over nominated candidates and elected deputies, the lack of public accountability above the grassroots level, the infrequency and brevity of meetings—people's congresses are no match for the more powerful party and government bureaucracies. As in other parliamentary and quasi-parliamentary systems, policy-making authority is centered in the executive branch. In China, this means the party and government.

However, new research calls this conventional wisdom into question. People's congresses play an important role in China's political system by providing information to party and government officials about what matters most to the Chinese public. Despite the theory of the mass line concept, practically speaking there are few avenues for political elites to learn about the public's true sentiments. The party and government are believed to conduct public opinion surveys, but they are not made public and their quality cannot be determined. The state-controlled media write internal reports for party and government leaders in addition to their published articles, but how widely those internal reports circulate and how they are utilized are not well known. The public comment system allows individuals and groups to comment on pending laws and regulations and propose revisions to them, but does not give them the opportunity to suggest laws and regulations without the CCP's initial blessing. Political leaders are therefore constrained in knowing what policies would be popular and what issues most concern their citizens. Into this void, people's congress delegates can help provide valuable information by reflecting public opinion toward higher-level officials.

At the same time, there are limits on how representative China's people's congress deputies are. First, representing the public's interests is most likely to happen at the grassroots level, where deputies are directly elected.[53] At higher levels, where the deputies are indirectly elected by the people's congress at the level below them, the link with the public is broken. Deputies at higher levels do not have to belong to the congress that elects them and do not even have to live in the districts, cities, or provinces they nominally represent. Second, deputies who are nominated by their fellow citizens are more likely to represent public opinion. In contrast, those nominated by the party and government have less incentive to represent public opinion because their nominations do not depend on public support. Third, given the brevity of the annual people's congress meetings, information on public opinion is not provided during the formal meetings but during informal meetings with party and government officials throughout the year. In fact, private entrepreneurs who become people's congress deputies find the value of being a deputy comes not from being able to vote on bills, budgets, and nominations during once-a-year meetings, but in giving them access to policy makers throughout the year. This offers advantages to their business interests and protection from local officials who may demand bribes and levy random taxes and fees.[54] It is what happens between the formal people's congress meetings that matters most.

Finally, people's congress deputies do not necessarily represent the people who elected them. Candidates in people's congress deputy elections do not campaign on the basis of their policy preferences; most candidates who have policy views that are not aligned with the CCP are screened out by the party-dominated election committees. Instead, candidates emphasize their biographical credentials: their education, profession, and above all their ties to their communities. Most Chinese do not vote in these grassroots people's congress elections and most do not know who their deputies are. Nevertheless, deputies are able to provide information that can be useful to party and government officials: where road work is needed, where garbage is piling up, where crime is increasing, and other local issues that may not otherwise rise to officials' attention.

The results of this informal sharing of information has direct policy impact by providing increased spending on certain public goods issues—building and repair of roads, education, health care, environmental protection—but does not influence the policies themselves. In other words, information on public opinion influences the implementation of policy but not the adoption of policy in the first place. Citizen-nominated and popularly elected deputies deliver "pork" to local communities but they do not challenge the CCP's policy priorities.[55]

Why do local officials respond to this kind of information if they are not accountable to the public? China's cadre evaluation system gives them the incentive to do so. In addition to growing the economy and generating more tax revenue, officials are also required to maintain political stability. In fact, political stability is a "veto" target: the outbreak of protests can nullify all other achievements, prevent the promotion of local officials, and even result in their removal from office. Therefore, getting information about public grievances allows them to remedy problems before they lead to public protests. Moreover, higher public goods spending at the local level helps boost support for local officials.[56] Information from people's congress deputies can tell local officials where additional spending is most needed.

At higher levels of the political system, a different logic of representation prevails. Party and government leaders are even further separated from the public and lack reliable information on a wide variety of issues. They are reluctant to solicit public opinion on sensitive issues but allow and even encourage people's congress deputies to offer motions and opinions on nonpolitical issues. NPC deputies receive training on how to exercise their roles, including how best to use the mass line to reflect public opinion to higher levels.

NPC deputies do not so much represent their "constituents" as offer motions and proposals that serve the public's interests, broadly defined. Because they are not popularly elected and do not necessarily live in the districts or provinces they represent, they are not seen by the public as their representatives. Thousands of motions and proposals are submitted every year, but few of them become law or adopted as policy. Not all motions and proposals are publicly announced, and even fewer are reported in detail. The lack of transparency prevents a fully detailed analysis, but research based on the ones that are revealed shows that the issues highlighted by NPC deputies generally conform to public opinion in the provinces the deputies "represent."[57]

China's political system more often reacts to crises than prevents them. As a result, NPC deputies offer more opinions and motions when major events are in the news—the "airpocalypse" in 2013, the earthquakes in Sichuan in 2008 and 2013, food safety scares, and transportation disasters—as long as they involve issues that do not challenge the CCP's legitimacy. When the events are about politically sensitive issues—corruption and malfeasance of officials, abuse of authority by officials and their families, unrest in Tibet and Xinjiang—NPC deputies make fewer motions and proposals. Not surprisingly, the deputies who are more reform-minded report that their proposals are either dismissed or ignored.[58]

If NPC deputies are not accountable to voters, why would they channel information on public opinion? For some, public spirit may motivate them. But there are also material interests involved. The more proposals they make during their term, the more likely they are to be reappointed. This is consistent with the meritocratic approach to appointments and promotions described in chapter 2: deputies are rewarded for good behavior. Those promoted to the NPC standing committee (which convenes every two months) and special committees that meet throughout the year also submitted higher-than-average numbers of proposals.[59]

In short, people's congress deputies from the grassroots to the national level can influence the implementation of policies even though they are not directly involved in the decision-making process. Their motions and proposals during formal meetings and information shared during informal meetings do not call for democratizing reforms, yet they can lead to increased funding for roads and schools, environmental protection, and regulatory changes. Those changes do not make the country more democratic, but they address everyday issues that help bolster popular support for the regime.

Deliberative Democracy

In the absence of general elections, officials at the central and local levels cannot be certain whether the public is satisfied with the work of the government. Moreover, they cannot be sure if their policy priorities are consistent with the public's preferences. This is where the mass line is supposed to come in. One solution to this problem has been "deliberative democracy," in which leaders call together members of the community to discuss policy priorities and budgetary priorities. It is touted as a possible alternative to competitive elections for discerning the public's policy preferences.[60]

During the first decade of the 2000s, experiments with deliberative democracy were conducted in a few areas, most notably in the coastal city of Wenling in Zhejiang Province. These were sponsored by local party leaders, often in collaboration with scholars who promoted the benefits of greater political participation. In one of Wenling's townships, party and government leaders convened a meeting with a randomly selected group of local citizens. Over a period of days, they discussed and debated different priorities: should they increase the amount of green space in the township or upgrade the sewer system? Roads and schools both needed repairs, but which needed them most? In the end, they ranked a list of twelve priority projects from an initial list of thirty. These twelve projects were then forwarded to the local people's congress, which approved them. In a neighboring township, deliberations went a step further: the groups discussed how much would be spent on each of their priority projects. The government then submitted a revised budget based on input from the deliberative groups and people's congress deputies.

Despite these apparent successes, Wenling's experiments with deliberative democracy did not spread to other areas. Unlike the example of special economic zones described above, where local officials all over China sought permission to adopt similar economic policies, political reform experiments rarely spread to other areas.[61] Local officials are normally too preoccupied with economic growth and maintaining stability to consider political reforms.

Even where deliberative democracy has occurred, local officials have sought to control the deliberations. In Wenling, residents were randomly selected to participate, but officials in other areas were skeptical that randomly selected individuals would be representative. They instead adopted hybrid methods, such as having half be randomly selected and half be chosen from among local officials and elected people's congress delegates.[62] Many communities dispensed with random selection altogether and invited local elites to participate in the deliberative meetings. Those local elites were often well connected with local party and government officials and many were CCP members, but they hardly represented society in general. In communities where only local elites and party and government officials were involved, many citizens were unaware that deliberative democracy was taking place.[63]

From the perspective of local officials, deliberative democracy offered several advantages. First, it allowed them to gain information about true public sentiments. In the meetings in Wenling, local officials were often surprised they had the wrong assumptions about the public's wishes. For example, whereas officials planned to beautify public areas with trees and flowers, local citizens gave higher priority to sewage treatment. Second, they controlled the agenda. In most cases, they decided whom to invite to participate in the meetings and also set the agenda of issues to discuss. The focus was on relatively nonsensitive issues concerning development and spending, and not on issues where the regime's legitimacy was at stake, such as political rights, property rights, fiscal policy, industrial pollution, official corruption, and so on. Third, when done right and local officials did indeed appear to be responsive and the policies they implemented accorded with the public's preferences, it enhanced their legitimacy and limited social grievances. In short, deliberative democracy allowed local officials to appear to be responsive without requiring them to be accountable.

On the other hand, deliberative democracy has not spread, because of the costs involved. It requires extensive briefing materials so that participants can make informed choices. It requires people to miss several days of work in order to participate. It can be embarrassing for local officials when their signature projects are rejected by the community.

More generally, it requires them to cede to society at least some control in policy implementation. Many Chinese officials are unaccustomed to having their decisions publicly questioned.

The Xi Jinping era has seen a retreat from a variety of political reforms. "Intra-party democracy," in which CCP members discuss (and, in some cases, vote on) candidates for key positions in the party bureaucracy, was promoted during the previous Hu Jintao era, but has largely disappeared from the party's lexicon under Xi. The election of township-level officials was also experimented with under Hu but abandoned in 2012, the year Xi became general secretary. However, the CCP increased support for deliberative democracy, or what it prefers to call "socialist consultative democracy," because it provided a veneer of consultation but kept it under party control. The Central Committee formally endorsed the practice in 2013 and the CCP released a document called "Opinions on Strengthening Socialist Consultative Democracy" in 2015. Despite this show of support, local officials did not jump on the bandwagon.[64] The number of localities practicing deliberative democracy grew between 2005 and 2010, but then plateaued and has remained relatively flat since then.[65] Even the CCP's endorsement did not persuade local officials to adopt it. Deliberative democracy may have some advantages, but it seems unlikely to become commonplace throughout China.

Grassroots Accountability

There is one notable way in which local officials are directly accountable to the people they govern. Research on rural China found that villages made up of a single clan or with a temple association to which all villagers belong tended to be better governed than other villages. They were more likely to have paved roads and paths, schools in good repair, homes with running water, and other types of public goods, for two reasons.[66] First of all, the clans and temple associations were able to mobilize fellow villagers to contribute money and labor for projects that benefited the village as a whole. Villages without these groups lacked the means to organize collective action and therefore did not produce these types of collective goods. Second, these groups provided an important source of accountability over village officials. Because they, too, belonged to these groups, shirking their official duties or engaging in corruption would bring a loss of face to them and their families. They were therefore compelled to provide better services. In villages without these groups, officials were less likely to be held accountable by their fellow villagers because they were not cohesive enough to hold officials accountable.

While this type of accountability had important effects in at least some villages, it does not make China's political system, as a whole, more accountable. It only applies to specific types of villages—those dominated by a single clan or a temple association; it does not scale up to larger towns and cities, where no single group encompasses the entire community. Even in those villages where this type of accountability did work, it may not apply as well in the twenty-first century as it did in the twentieth century because villages have been hollowed out in two ways, as noted in chapter 2: by the migration of hundreds of millions from villages to the cities, leaving only the very young and the very old behind; and by township and county governments taking financial responsibilities away from villages, leaving village leaders with less discretion over how they spend public money.[67] The accountability of local officials, most of whom are party members, to their social networks does not mean the party as a whole is therefore accountable to society. Indeed, the party is wary of local leaders who are more accountable to their localities than they are to higher level officials and the CCP.

* * *

There is little question that policy making is under the control of the CCP, but the CCP is not a unified monolith. There is a tremendous amount of negotiating, politicking, and lobbying that is part of the policy-making process in China. The fragmented nature of political authority in China means that there are many competing interests and policy preferences that complicate a simple top-down model of decision making. When the CCP's legitimacy and survival is not at stake, it sets the broad policy priorities but leaves the details of laws, regulations, and implementation to other state actors—including government ministries, local governments, and people's congresses at both the local and national levels.

Another consequence of China's fragmented authoritarianism is incomplete information available to policy makers and officials. The mass line concept was designed to create a steady flow of information between the party and the masses and thereby allow the party to adjust its policies to align more closely with the public's preferences and better suit local conditions. Too often, the mass line runs only one way—from the party to the masses—with no opportunity for meaningful feedback. But the mass line is the rationale for the CCP's efforts to consult with the masses in various ways, including the Open Government Information initiative, public comments on draft laws and regulations, people's congress deputies who offer motions on behalf of the public's interest, and deliberative democracy. These political reforms are not substitutes for democracy, and they were never meant to be. They were intended to improve the quality of governance and in that way increase popular support for the CCP.

Under Xi Jinping, the CCP is attempting to integrate the fragmented qualities of China's political system. More authority is concentrated at the top of the CCP, and what's most important, in Xi's hands. The party's central role in the state and throughout society is being reasserted in ways both dramatic and subtle. This may preempt any potential threats to the CCP and to Xi's personal leadership, but it also comes with a high price: it has made local officials reluctant to engage in the kinds of policy innovations that have characterized much of the post-Mao reform era. Without stronger incentives for innovation, the short-term benefits of political stability and loyalty may be outweighed by the long-term stagnation that centralized power leads to.

Policy making in China in the twenty-first century is dominated but not monopolized by the CCP. Societal actors—activists, experts, and NGOs—also influence policy decisions and their implementation. Their role, and the limits the CCP puts on them, will be explored in more detail in the next chapter.

4

DOES CHINA HAVE
A CIVIL SOCIETY?

The CCP takes a dim view of civil society. Mindful of how civil society groups helped bring down authoritarian governments—in particular, how Poland's Solidarity and Czechoslovakia's Charter 77 challenged the former communist regimes in Eastern Europe—the CCP is determined to suppress or preempt potential threats from civil society in China. Take, for example, the fate of a group known as the New Citizens Movement, started by a group of prominent civil rights activists and rights defense lawyers. Its goal was to create public support for greater transparency in the political system and ultimately a transition to constitutional government in China. Soon after calling for the public disclosure of officials' salaries in 2013, the CCP began arresting its members. One of its founders, Xu Zhiyong, was placed under house arrest in July 2013 and later formally arrested, convicted of "gathering a crowd to disrupt public order" (a common charge against political activists) and sentenced to four years in prison.[1] Other members of the group were also arrested and imprisoned around the same time.[2] Although the New Citizens Movement was committed to peaceful methods, the CCP saw it differently: an effort to overthrow the CCP-led regime and replace it with a constitutional democracy. It therefore crushed the New Citizens Movement.

This is not an isolated example. After Xi Jinping became party leader in 2012, the CCP took measures to better control, if not stifle, China's civil society. In 2013, it issued a secret internal document (subsequently known as Document 9) that identified seven "malicious" Western values, including constitutional democracy and civil society, that should not be taught in school or discussed in the media.[3] In 2015, it passed a law requiring foreign NGOs operating in China to find an official sponsoring agency and register with the Public Security Bureau, the coercive arm of the regime, signifying that the CCP saw them as threats to China's security and not just advocates of human welfare, clean environment, and charitable causes. To dissuade China's domestic NGOs from receiving foreign funding, the CCP required them to disclose their sources of support in annual reports to the government. It also ordered that party cells be created in all NGOs to serve as the eyes and ears of the party throughout China's civil society. Later that year, it arrested more than three hundred lawyers and their staffs who were engaged in human rights cases, including workers' rights and religious freedom. All of these steps created a sense of uncertainty: were these the initial moves in an all-out assault on China's civil society, or were they simply the party's attempt to gain some control over the rapidly growing numbers of domestic and foreign NGOs operating in China?

To answer this question, we need to recognize that the CCP does not uniformly suppress civil society. Rather, its response to civil society, in both formal institutions and informal practices, depends on the type of group involved, the region of the country, and whether the political climate is relatively open (as under Jiang Zemin to some extent and more so under Hu Jintao) or closed (as it is under Xi Jinping at present). There is tremendous regional and topical variation in whether the CCP suppresses, tolerates, or supports civil society groups. The evolution of civil society in China is a good example of how the CCP is responsive without being accountable. As individuals and groups call attention to issues (such as pollution, inequality, the cost and fairness of health care, education, and other social welfare issues) and individuals form groups to advance these causes, the CCP often is willing to work with them. But it does so selectively, on some issues and not others, with some groups and not others. It is willing to be responsive to public opinion but refuses to be formally accountable to the public.

The remainder of this chapter will explore the variation in civil society groups in China and how the CCP's response to civil society has varied over time and in different areas of the country.

Does China Have a Civil Society?

To answer the question of whether China has a civil society, it is first necessary to define what civil society is. Definitions vary, but most emphasize that it consists of social organizations that are created by individuals and groups in society (not by the state); that are largely autonomous from the state (even though they often interact extensively with the state); and in which membership is voluntary (you are not born into it and not required to join at the direction of the government or other supervising body).[4] In other words, civil society is a network of associations that are voluntary, self-governing, and autonomous from the state. By itself, this definition does not say what these associations do or what impact they have; its focus is on how they are founded and how they operate. Civil society organizations may be politically active, but they also include professional associations; philanthropic groups; groups dedicated to education, health care, and various social services; even sports leagues and other forms of recreation. For simplicity, "NGO" will be used to represent this full range of civil society groups.

Why do we care if China has a civil society? Because it is more than just an academic debate over definitions; it is about the potential for political change. Civil society is thought to be a leading cause of democratization in authoritarian regimes. It challenges the state and encourages democratization. For example, in Eastern Europe, civil society groups helped bring down communist governments. In the post-communist countries in Eastern Europe and the former Soviet Union, civil society organizations continued to mobilize the public to join in protests against authoritarian rule. These protests were known as "color revolutions," named for the colors that symbolized the protests: rose in Georgia, orange in Ukraine, and so on. Other protest movements, such as the Tunisia's Jasmine Revolution and Egypt's Lotus Revolution that launched the Arab Spring in 2011, are also included as color revolutions.[5]

They were generally peaceful protests that avoided the turmoil and violence that ensue when regime change is the result of civil war between armed groups. For advocates of civil society, therefore, the presence of a robust civil society offers the promise of a peaceful transition to democracy.

But civil society is also thought to stabilize democracies by promoting better governance, political trust, and, ultimately, political stability. How does the same thing—the existence of civil society—undermine one type of regime while strengthening the other? The key is distinguishing different dimensions of civil society. Just as the state is not a unified, unitary actor, civil societies can also be made up of different types of organizations, some of which challenge the state and advocate political change, others that seek to cooperate with it, and still others that simply want to be left alone.

This need to distinguish different realms of civil society is not new. In the China field, scholars have differentiated groups that are critical of the regime and pursue a political agenda from groups that are largely noncritical of the status quo, preferring to work on economic, social, and cultural issues.[6] In the more general political science literature, this is the distinction between Civil Society I (or CSI), which consists of apolitical NGOs that improve the quality of governance and enhance political stability, and Civil Society II (CSII), which is made up of political organizations that oppose the regime and seek political change, typically toward democracy.[7] These are different labels—economic and social vs. political; noncritical vs. critical; CSI vs. CSII—to describe essentially the same distinction. The debate over whether China has a civil society is largely due to focusing on only one type of civil society to the exclusion of the other.

Civil Society I—made up of economic, social, cultural, and noncritical individuals and organizations—is large and growing in China. China has almost 800,000 registered NGOs, with an estimated 1.5 million more unregistered but still active.[8] This would seem to suggest a robust civil society. But many observers say civil society does not exist in China because these organizations are not fully autonomous from the state and do not engage in political opposition and protest. It is true that most of China's NGOs are not set up to advocate for democratization or regime change. Rather, they are engaged in meeting practical societal needs, such as poverty alleviation and job training; protecting common interests, like homeowners' rights and environmental issues; and pursuing shared interests in sports and hobbies. Rather than challenge and oppose the state, many of them seek to cooperate with it in order to get the political and material support they need to operate.

Cooperation between civil society and the state is not a unique feature of China's civil society: many American NGOs similarly apply for and receive grants and contracts from the federal, state, and local governments. In the democratic countries of Europe and North and South America, governments provided roughly 40 percent of financing for civil society organizations.[9]

Civil Society II is made up of political activists and organizations critical of the regime. These actors are usually repressed by the state when they are detected, as was the New Citizens Movement mentioned above. In China, this realm of civil society is very small, almost invisible. The CCP is wary of the potential for these types of civil society organizations to spawn "color revolutions," and consequently to threaten its hold on power. No less an authority than Russian president Vladimir Putin reportedly warned China's then-president Hu Jintao that without control over NGOs, the CCP could be victim to its own color revolution.[10] That message was not lost on CCP leaders, who have been determined to prevent a color revolution and the foreign support they generate. But, as the next sections will show, how the CCP managed China's civil society varied over time and in different regions of the country.

Rather than speak of civil society in China as an undifferentiated whole, we should think of China as having multiple civil societies, in different relationships with the CCP. We need to make these kinds of distinctions for the simple reason that the CCP does. It cooperates with some groups while cracking down on others, depending on whether it sees them as beneficial or threatening. At the same time, we must also keep in mind that CSI and CSII are ideal types, not hard-and-fast categories. The dividing line between CSI and CSII is neither well defined

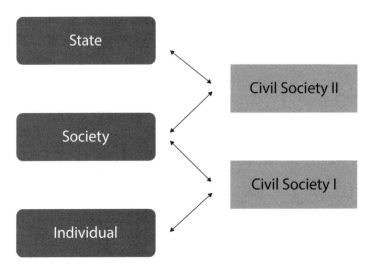

FIGURE 4.1. Civil society I and II

nor stable over time. CSI groups that were allowed to operate in the past have been shut down under Xi. But distinguishing CSI from CSII helps illuminate the CCP's strategy toward China's civil society and how that strategy has changed over time.

The CCP's Changing Approach to Civil Society

The CCP's policy toward civil society has changed over the years, from trying to restrict it during Jiang Zemin's tenure in the 1990s, to encouraging it under Hu Jintao in the 2000s, to current efforts to control it under Xi Jinping.

The CCP is wary of any group that seeks autonomy, which is in conflict with the CCP's monopoly on political organization. In the 1989 demonstrations in Tiananmen Square, one of the key goals of protesters was the recognition of autonomous student and worker organizations. CCP hard-liners saw this as a threat to their power and refused to compromise, eventually imposing martial law and bringing the peaceful protests to a violent end. The demise of communist governments in Eastern Europe beginning in 1989 provided the CCP with further evidence of the danger of civil society to communist rule. The CCP is determined to avoid a similar fate.

The CCP's early attempts to restrict civil society can be seen in its NGO registration requirements, which made no distinction between CSI and CSII groups. In the wake of the 1989 Tiananmen demonstrations, the Ministry of Civil Affairs issued the "Regulations on the Management and Administration of Social Organizations" in October 1989 (revised in 1998). These regulations were intentionally difficult to fulfill in order to prevent the formation of autonomous organizations that had participated in the Tiananmen protests earlier in the year. These regulations followed a largely corporatist logic, in which the CCP wanted to approve a very limited number of groups that would be under its supervision.[11] To limit competition between similar groups, there could be only one group in each community in a given issue area. For example, if there were two fan clubs for the local soccer team, one would be forced to disband or the two would be forced to merge. NGOs could not create regional branches, affiliate horizontally with similar groups in other parts of the country, or organize themselves vertically into a national organization. These measures prevented NGOs from scaling up their operations and coordinating with other groups to be more effective.

In addition, NGOs had to find a public agency to act as their sponsor. This could be a university, a mass organization, or a government agency. If they could not find a sponsor—more specifically, if they could not convince any agency that they posed no threat to the CCP and that their actions would not get the potential sponsor into political trouble—they were unable to register. Finally, the NGOs had to register with the Ministry of Civil Affairs or its local agencies and submit annual reports. All of these features were intended to keep the number of NGOs small and weaken their capacity to advocate policy change, much less challenge party and government officials.

The CCP's corporatist strategy quickly proved unworkable. There were soon too many organizations in one city on the same issues (many of them unregistered), such as business associations, environmental groups, and organizations serving migrant workers. The Ministry of Civil Affairs and its local agencies did not have sufficient manpower to oversee the growing number of NGOs. At the local level, officials learned that NGOs could be useful collaborators on policy issues. Beginning in the 1990s, the CCP began adopting an ambitious social policy agenda with a greater commitment to higher education, health care, poverty alleviation, and other public goods. However, these were unfunded mandates: Beijing announced the commitments but it was up to local governments to deliver on them. Short on staff and budgets, many local leaders turned to relying on grassroots NGOs. Their founders were often experts in their fields, including scholars, scientists, and former officials. Their knowledge, political experience, and personal connections were invaluable resources in making their NGOs effective. Their staff supplemented the limited capacity of local officials; for instance, NGO staff trained in social work were better able to monitor and evaluate programs, identify and assess needs, and measure results than bureaucrats who lacked the necessary training and resources.[12] Over time, local leaders learned that these CSI NGOs were not simply a threat; in some cases, they could actually be an asset.[13]

As a consequence of these changes, the CCP sought to cooperate selectively with civil society groups in the 2000s, when Hu Jintao was CCP general secretary.[14] The CCP also simplified the rules for registering NGOs. Most important, it eliminated the requirement that NGOs had to find a sponsoring agency; under the new rules, they could simply register with the local civil affairs office.[15] The result was an explosion of growth in the number of NGOs: by the end of Hu Jintao's tenure, China had more than 500,000 officially registered NGOs and an estimated 1–1.5 million unregistered but active NGOs.

During this time, the CCP adopted a new approach to civil society in which NGOs supplemented the work of the government. Local governments began signing contracts with NGOs to deliver public goods and services, reducing the government's burdens in these areas. Although the CCP now encouraged NGOs involved in service delivery, it still repressed many of those involved in policy advocacy, defense of rights, and other sensitive issues. In other words, it was more welcoming to NGOs that belonged to Civil Society I, but still opposed to those from Civil Society II.

This new approach was clearly seen in Guangdong Province. Guangdong is on China's southeast coast adjacent to Hong Kong. It is home to Shenzhen and other special economic zones where economic reforms were first experimented with in the early post-Mao period before being rolled out to the rest of China. As a major manufacturing hub for China's export sector, it was a destination for many migrant workers who left rural villages inland to find jobs. With this influx of new workers came NGOs created to protect the rights of workers. In 2012, the Guangdong provincial government and the Provincial Trade Union began reaching out to labor NGOs, many of them unregistered, to provide services to workers and their families, including job and life skills training, medical check-ups, cultural activities, and legal education. It simultaneously began cracking down on other labor NGOs that were more involved in rights protection and labor militancy, showing that it clearly distinguished between CSI and CSII groups. This new initiative had definite benefits: it provided invaluable funding to NGOs, offered necessary services to migrant workers, and created more harmonious ties between the state and labor NGOs. At the same time, the initiative may have been undertaken to limit the NGOs' work. It shifted their focus away from labor rights and collective bargaining toward practical issues such as unpaid wages and compensation for injuries on the job.[16] The financial support given by the government was in short-term contracts, so the NGOs could not afford to engage in sensitive issues or risk the nonrenewal of their contracts. Some NGOs were suspicious that this seemingly benign policy change was in fact designed to neuter their influence.[17]

The party's approach to civil society changed dramatically after Xi Jinping became CCP general secretary in 2012. It did not return to the corporatist strategy of the Jiang Zemin era but adopted a more repressive approach to civil society than had been the case during the Hu Jintao years. Instead of encouraging and cooperating with NGOs, it took steps to control them more directly with new restrictions on which groups could register and how they could raise money. Most notably, the CCP now requires international NGOs (INGOs) to find a sponsoring agency, which domestic NGOs no longer have to do, and to register with the Public Security Bureau, not the Ministry of Civil Affairs as

China's domestic NGOs do. This is an important shift: in the past, INGOs were not required to register in order to operate in China. And because the Public Security Bureau's mandate is to prevent threats to political stability, the new law suggests that INGOs will be handled as a matter of law and order and maintaining political stability, a key CCP priority. This is in line with a more general framing of international influences as incompatible with Chinese values and hostile to the CCP, reflected in 2013's Document 9 noted above. Moreover, even registered INGOs must get permission for each project they undertake. Domestic NGOs that receive foreign funding must now formally disclose that information to the government, which could provide a veto over cooperation between domestic and international NGOs, threatening the survival of NGOs that rely on foreign sources of support for their operations.[18]

The new rules created great uncertainty about whether INGOs would be able to continue operating in China. However, so far they have not had the dire consequences that many feared at first. By the end of 2019, when the rules had been in effect for two years, more than four hundred INGOs had successfully registered. This is much smaller than the number of Chinese NGOs but, as will be described below, INGOs have advantages in resources and expertise that Chinese NGOs lack and can have an outsized influence that numbers alone do not capture. In addition, almost 2,400 filings by unregistered INGOs to conduct temporary activities had been approved.[19] The process for filing temporary activities was simpler than for registering NGOs and the amount of time required for approval was also shorter. For example, Greenpeace decided to register as a company, not an NGO. If it wants to engage in a project, it can partner with a domestic NGO and then file a temporary activity permit. If these trends continue, it suggests that filings may become an acceptable alternative to the more burdensome registration process. In this and other ways, INGOs are learning how to adapt to the new regulations.[20]

However, a closer look at the numbers reveals that INGOs are not equally likely to be approved by the Public Security Bureau. Those that renovate rural schools or provide scholarships to college students (i.e., CSI INGOs) are more likely to be approved. In contrast, those that work on politically sensitive issues such as labor rights, Tibet, or LGBTQ issues (i.e., CSII INGOs), are much less likely to be approved.[21] The INGO law allows the Public Security Bureau to decide which INGOs will be allowed to operate in China and the kinds of issues they will be allowed to promote—in short, those that are consistent with the party's priorities.

In addition to the new rules on INGOs, the CCP began a new crackdown on other CSII NGOs. It put new pressure on unregistered, underground labor organizations, forcing them to shift their activities away from organized protests and collective action to smaller and even individual actions.[22] For example, an unregistered labor organization, "Solidarity in Action," helped organize "flash demonstrations" outside courthouses that lasted only long enough for demonstrators to hold up a sign and take a photo. Another, "Pay It Forward," coached individual workers by texts and phone calls how to seek back pay and workers' compensation.[23] The CCP also took aim at "rights defense" lawyers, so named because they defend the rights of disadvantaged and discriminated against individuals and groups, including workers, churches, and ethnic minorities. On July 9, 2015, it took into custody more than three hundred lawyers and legal staff, as mentioned in the introduction to this chapter. Most were later released without formally being charged, but several were convicted of subversion of state power, "picking quarrels and provoking trouble," and other similar charges and sent to prison.

As part of the CCP's renewed efforts to control civil society, the CCP also revived a classic Leninist technique for monitoring society: it ordered all NGOs to have a party organization within them to manage party members who work there and, more important, to monitor what the NGOs do. In 2012, when Xi became CCP general secretary, only 35.2 percent of NGOs had party organizations; by 2017 that figure rose to 58.9 percent,[24] a two-thirds increase in just five years.[25] Although the CCP has been trying to build party cells within NGOs, it has not emphasized recruiting NGO leaders.[26] In contrast, the CCP's approach to the growing private sector of the economy has been quite different: it has built both party cells in private enterprises (68 percent as of 2017) and also recruited private entrepreneurs into the party.[27] The CCP wants to control and partner with NGOs, but does not see NGO leaders as potential allies as they do China's private entrepreneurs.

As with all changes, the CCP's new approach to civil society has both losers and winners. The main loser will be the small, unregistered, grass-roots NGOs that have little material support except for foreign sources and do not have strong personal ties with local leaders. The individuals and groups that benefit from the work of NGOs—the impoverished, the victims of natural disasters, rural migrants working in cities, and others—will lose out, and may end up resenting the CCP for not provid-ing the support they have come to rely on. These efforts to control civil society may benefit the CCP in the short term by reducing the chance that CSII groups could pose a threat to it, but they may also be detrimen-tal to the CCP's long-term interests by eliminating CSI groups that do not pose a threat to it and provide valued public goods to society.

Then again, the CCP's new approach may create beneficiaries. Larger, more established, and officially registered NGOs should find it easier to seek greater financial support, including from government agencies and domestic foundations in China and even from foreign sources. INGOs that successfully register may also benefit because they will be out of the ambiguous gray area in which they previously existed. Under the new INGO law, INGOs can fund only registered NGOs, in partic-ular those registered as NGOs and not-for-profit enterprises, and this will further incentivize Chinese NGOs to seek official registration.

NGOs that develop a reputation for expertise are more likely to be invited to consult with local governments. Consultation is usually at the invitation of local officials, not on the initiative of NGOs. Despite the recent experiments with open government information and online pub-lic comments on pending laws and regulations (described in chapter 3), what really matters is face-to-face consultation. Having good personal relations is one means of gaining access to policy making and imple-mentation, but being recognized as an expert with policy-relevant knowledge is an increasingly important avenue for interacting with party and government officials. Invitations to consult on policies are typically given only to officially registered NGOs, another way of limit-ing access, advocacy, and influence.

In a more general sense, the CCP's new approach to civil society fits its desire to funnel all interactions between state and society through authorized channels instead of unregistered and unsanctioned organizations that can threaten stability. While this will harm many of the unregistered NGOs, it may compel others to become better institutionalized and rely less on personal connections with leaders to be influential.[28] This could lead them to develop the kind of policy-relevant knowledge and expertise that will improve their operations, and make it more likely they will be invited to participate in the policy-making process. This would be good for both their service delivery and policy advocacy. But, as the example of Guangdong shows, working with the government could also shift the NGOs' agendas toward politically safer areas that will not draw the ire of the CCP.

One example of CSI-type NGOs that have weathered the changes over the years in the CCP's approach to civil society are environmental NGOs (eNGOs). China's alarming environmental degradation, the result of its rapid economic development, industrialization, and urbanization, has also spawned a vast network of environmental eNGOs. Many of them are supported by the government to help educate the public about ecological awareness and monitor the local compliance with environmental regulations. In 1994, Friends of Nature became the first nationwide eNGO in China and now has a national membership of more than thirty thousand. It offers programs on "environmental education, low-carbon household, ecological community, litigation, policy advocacy, and others."[29] Rather than engage in protests, it works through existing institutions to enforce existing laws and regulations. In the 1990s, it filmed a group of local officials planning to cut down virgin forest trees. The film was broadcast on CCTV, the official national television station, and prompted the central government in 1999 to order a ban logging in all virgin forests.[30] More recently, in July 2017 it filed a lawsuit to stop construction on a hydropower plant on the Red River to protect the last habitat of the endangered green peafowl. The project was halted the next month to allow time for an environmental impact study.[31] Its recycling and "Zero Waste" programs in Beijing and Shanghai have been positively covered in *Xinhua*, *Global Times*, and other official media outlets in China. These efforts are not only in line with Xi Jinping's emphasis on stronger environmental protection, they work through existing institutions and do not pose a threat to political stability. This has allowed Friends of Nature to gain extensive domestic and international recognition.

Local Patterns in the Management of Civil Society

In addition to the central policy toward civil society set by the CCP, there is also tremendous regional variation in how open the environment is for NGOs. Some localities, like Beijing, Guangdong, and Yunnan, are known to be more supportive of NGOs.[32] As the nation's capital, Beijing has attracted lots of INGOs willing to invest in China's development, which supports the CCP's agenda. Beijing is also home to many of China's top universities and research institutes, and many NGO founders come from academic backgrounds. Guangdong was a pioneer in both economic and social reforms. NGOs that had not been able to register elsewhere in China were welcomed in Guangdong, but, under Xi, Guangdong has become one of the most conservative in its approach to civil society—in sharp contrast to its liberal reputation. Yunnan's openness to civil society is born more of necessity: it is a relatively poor province with few resources to meet the unfunded mandates on education, health care, and other social welfare policies. Grassroots NGOs and INGOs have moved in to supplement the government's work in these areas.

In contrast, Shanghai is more conservative in its approach to both the economy and civil society. Rather than rely on the private sector to produce growth, as has Guangdong, Shanghai depends more on state-owned enterprises and state-led development. It has likewise been less willing to partner with NGOs in the local distribution of welfare services. Instead the CCP in Shanghai created its own organizations— party-organized, nongovernmental organizations (PONGOs, if you will)—for charitable and social welfare activities, as well as events that publicized the party's mission, promoted patriotic education, and mobilized displays of public support for the party.[33]

The southwestern province of Yunnan is an interesting location for the development of civil society. It is one of China's poorer provinces, home to the Dai minority, and reliant on tourism for economic development instead of agriculture or industry. As a result, its government does not have as many resources to draw upon as the more prosperous coastal provinces do. Because of its proximity to the "golden triangle" region of southeast Asia, it is a conduit for illicit drugs, and because of its reliance on tourism, it is also a draw for the sex industry.[34] These two factors combine to make HIV/AIDS a prominent problem. The provincial government was not equipped to deal with these problems, so NGOs emerged to address drug addiction, prostitution, HIV/AIDS, and other social and medical issues. INGOs like the Gates Foundation and the United Kingdom's Global Fund also focused their attention on Yunnan for the same reasons. By 2009, there were 140 INGOs operating in Yunnan.[35]

Yunnan did not always have cooperative relations with NGOs and INGOs. When local leaders planned to build thirteen dams along the Nu River that would produce much-needed hydropower, a prominent part of the local economy and a major source of government revenue, several domestic and foreign environmental NGOs pushed back (this episode was one of the examples of "fragmented authoritarianism 2.0" mentioned in chapter 3). They argued that the dams would damage the environment and displace the ethnic minorities who lived along the river. In the end, the central government sided with the NGOs and the project was canceled.[36] Even though the NGOs were of the CSI variety and did not challenge party rule, they forced local leaders to abandon a major policy priority.[37]

This setback led to a change in Yunnan's management of civil society. Government officials grew frustrated from their often contentious relations with NGOs and their lack of information about many of the NGOs and INGOs operating in Yunnan. In 2010, it implemented new regulations requiring INGOs to register with the government and to have an official sponsoring agency, and their individual projects had to register with both civil affairs and foreign affairs bureaus. Prior to this, INGOs did not have to register their organizations or their projects. The goal was not to prevent INGOs from operating in Yunnan or discourage more from entering, but to monitor and manage their activities. Most domestic and overseas NGOs were able to register with the government and continued operating. Some smaller NGOs were unable to register, such as those dealing with sensitive issues like minority rights, drug addiction, and prostitution.[38]

The Spectrum of NGOs in China

Just as the CCP distinguishes between CSI and CSII groups, its relationship with them also varies. Some have formal recognition, some are able to operate informally, and others the CCP seeks to suppress altogether. Put differently, there are "red" NGOs that are formally registered (in a communist system like China's, red is the party's color); "black" NGOs that are prevented from operating, like the New Citizens Movement, or operate surreptitiously, like "Solidarity in Action" and "Pay It Forward"; and those in a "gray" area, not formally registered but able to collaborate with local officials on local problems.[39] The red and gray NGOs make up CSI, whereas the black NGOs are CSII. Understanding China's civil society requires distinguishing these different groups.

Mass Organizations and Other GONGOs

Soon after taking power in 1949, the CCP created organizations to be conduits to important social groups. These "mass organizations" included the All-China Federation of Trade Unions (ACFTU), the All-China Women's Federation, and the All-China Federation of Industry and Commerce. Rather than representing the interests of those groups, these mass organizations are often described as simply "transmission belts," conveying the party's perspective to these groups. During the Cultural Revolution (1966–76) they were disbanded but were revived in the post-Mao period as the party tried to restore its relationship with society. They are prominent today not simply because of their public status and the resources the CCP provides to them, but also because they occupy space that would otherwise be filled by civil society groups and thus provide a pretense for not allowing such groups to form. In particular, the CCP has been adamantly opposed to the formation of independent trade unions, insisting that all such groups must affiliate with the ACFTU. The CCP wants to keep tight reins on labor NGOs, not just to maintain political stability but also to provide a more stable business environment in China. During the 1990s and early 2000s, the ACFTU experimented with reforms that would allow it to act in the true interests of workers, but those efforts failed to get CCP support and were eventually abandoned.[40] The message was clear: mass organizations were intended to serve the party's interests, not those of the groups they nominally represented.

Mass organizations are not part of civil society: their leaders are chosen by the CCP, they get their budgets from the CCP, and the CCP sets limits on the range of their activities. For all these reasons, they lack the autonomy expected of civil society groups. They are more accurately referred to as GONGOs: government-organized, nongovernmental organizations.[41] Beyond the mass organizations, there are other prominent GONGOs in China. For example, the Red Cross Society of China is the official charity and enjoys a privileged status as the preferred conduit for charitable donations, although its reputation has suffered from several scandals.[42] Newly created GONGOs are part of China's massive Belt and Road Initiative that links China to countries in Asia, Africa, the Middle East, and Europe.[43] The GONGOs reduce the visibility of the Chinese government in these projects and provide a buffer against popular resistance to Chinese influence in these countries.

Mass organizations and GONGOs do not in and of themselves constitute a civil society. However, they are part of the environment in which civil society operates in China.[44] Other NGOs interact with them. For example, the All-China Women's Federation is the official sponsor of some NGOs that work on women's issues, in particular the special concerns of women in the large migrant worker populations in China's cities. The All-China Federation of Industry and Commerce similarly sponsors business associations.

Registered Red NGOs

Although a key aspect of civil society organizations is that they are organized and operated by members of society, and the vast majority of social organizations in China are of this type, at the same time, some of them seek and receive formal recognition from the state, such as the Friends of Nature mentioned earlier. These can be thought of as "red" NGOs (although not as politically red as the mass organizations and GONGOs). As registered NGOs, they are better able to operate openly and in particular to collaborate with the government on a wide range of projects, mostly related to economic and social issues. Registration, however, may limit their autonomy from the state, which imposes certain conditions on which groups it will approve and on what they can do. Although autonomy is often seen as the sine qua non of civil society organizations, in China autonomy can be both a blessing and a curse. Without close connections with the state, many NGOs in China would lack the political and material support they need to survive, much less operate. On the other hand, if they are too closely tied to the state, they can lose their sense of mission and be diverted to the state's priorities.

Rural Women Knowing All is another example of a registered NGO. It was one of the original NGOs formed to serve the personal and legal needs of migrant workers in China's cities. It is based in Beijing and publishes a magazine, provides job training to female migrants, and offers financial and legal assistance. Its work has benefited from the backgrounds of its leaders. For example, its founder, Xie Lihua, formerly worked for the All-China Women's Federation.[45] Despite its good political connections, it had a difficult time getting officially registered in Beijing, so in 2013 it moved its headquarters to Guangdong, which at the time was known as being more welcoming to NGOs. Rural Women Knowing All is recognized as one of the most effective advocates for China's migrant workers.

Unregistered Gray NGOs

In addition to the nearly 800,000 registered NGOs in China, there are many more unregistered NGOs. The exact number is not known, because, being unregistered, they are impossible to count accurately, but estimates range between 1 and 1.5 million. Being unregistered does not necessarily make them illegal. Unregistered NGOs can be divided into gray and black groups.[46] The gray groups are unregistered but active in their communities, often partnering with local governments to provide valued public goods and services. But their situation is precarious. When their local patron changes jobs, the rules about the work of NGOs change, or as their work ventures into sensitive areas, their survival and continued operation can be jeopardized.

In some cases, local officials actually discourage NGOs from registering. Although central leaders are primarily worried about the threat posed by civil society and therefore see registration as a way of controlling them, the incentives of local leaders are more mixed. If they partner with local NGOs on service delivery, they may not want higher levels to be alarmed by how many NGOs are operating at the local level. They may also want to benefit from foreign funding to local NGOs. Foreign funding to registered NGOs filters through the central government, making it difficult for local officials to take a cut. But foreign funding to unregistered NGOs goes through local governments, allowing them to keep some for themselves and also to determine which unregistered groups will get the rest.[47]

In other cases, NGO leaders find the registration process too difficult and the benefits too small; either they operate unregistered, or they register as another type of organization, such as a private enterprise or, more recently, a social enterprise.[48] Registering as an enterprise is much easier than as an NGO and allows the organizations to open a bank account and have a legal status. But being registered as something other than an NGO also has downsides. For one thing, they cannot accept donations and they must pay taxes. Registration as an enterprise also provides the authorities a pretense for shutting the group down for engaging in activities not permitted for its type of registration.

The Unirule think tank shows the risks of operating in the gray area of China's civil society. It was founded in 1993 by prominent liberal economists including Mao Yushi and Sheng Hong and registered as a private enterprise with a district branch of the Administration for Industry and Commerce in Beijing. According to its website, Unirule does not receive any government support; it relies on donations and grants

from domestic and international foundations.[49] Unirule's advocacy of
market-oriented policies had long been out of step with the CCP's priorities, first under Hu Jintao, who favored equitable development to
narrow the gap between rich and poor, and later in the conservative,
state-led economic program under Xi. For example, it published a study
in 2011 which concluded that all state-owned enterprises would be unprofitable were it not for subsidized loans and cheap land provided by
the government.[50] It also criticized Xi himself. In July 2018, it posted a
critique of Xi on its website after he orchestrated the elimination of term
limits on the presidency in the state constitution, a step that could allow
Xi to remain indefinitely as China's leader. The report was written by
one of Unirule's directors, law professor Xu Zhangrun of Tsinghua University.[51] For publicly criticizing Xi's usurpation of power, Xu was
banned from teaching and put under investigation.[52] In July 2020, he
was taken into police custody for several days and was fired by Tsinghua
upon his release. For posting the critique, Unirule was shut down. The
pretense for this action was a technicality about its registration: it had
begun offering training classes that its registration as a private enterprise
did not allow. This illustrates the CCP's use of legal mechanisms to punish political actions as well as the precariousness of being registered as
a private enterprise but not operating as one.

Unregistered Black NGOs

Finally, there are "black" NGOs that pose a more direct challenge to the
CCP and its policies and are therefore suppressed. While the aboveground, unregistered NGOs exist in a legal gray area, there is less ambiguity about the black NGOs. When the CCP discovers them, it is quick
to crack down. A few risk harassment and even arrest by operating
openly (like the New Citizens Movement); most try to be surreptitious.
They want to avoid the CCP's attention and scrutiny because they are
engaged in issues that are more critical of party policy, such as labor,
religion, ethnic minorities, or democracy promotion. When observers
say there is no civil society in China, it is these underground CSII
groups they have in mind. If civil society is defined this narrowly, then

it is true there is little of it in China. But this is only one aspect of civil society, whether in China or in any other country. If we consider the full range of NGOs—CSI and CSII, red, gray, and black—we can see that civil society is large and diverse, yet also constrained by the CCP.

Further Constraints on Civil Society in China

Civil society in China faces other constraints besides the CCP and its officials in terms of its development and vitality, which include societal, international, and internal constraints.

Societal Constraints

Most NGOs in China are trying to help their fellow citizens, but society does not always see it the same way. Many Chinese are skeptical of NGOs and suspicious of their true motives. Like the CCP, many Chinese do not trust NGOs. When asked how much they trust different types of peoples and groups, they rank NGOs near the bottom of the list, below local officials and staff people and above only complete strangers.[53] Moreover, most Chinese believe it is the government's responsibility to provide social welfare and they do not consider NGOs to be an appropriate substitute.[54] This is a particular problem when they are not personally familiar with NGO leaders and staff and feel no need to trust them. There is also a semantic aspect that breeds suspicion: *non*governmental has the connotation of *anti*government, even though they are different words. In China, where everything remotely political can be sensitive, even using the term "NGO" can raise suspicions.

International Constraints

Many NGOs in China rely upon foreign support to fund their operations and could not survive without it. At the same time, some in the NGO community complain that INGOs hamper their work by shifting their attention away from the issues that motivate them toward measurable outcomes that do not advance their cause.[55] INGOs are knowledgeable about "best practices," which they convey to their counterparts in China through workshops and other training activities. However, they are less familiar with the Chinese context. The goals of Chinese NGOs may be distorted to conform with advice from INGOs and the expectations of foreign donors, especially that they provide evidence of progress and create a robust organizational culture. For example, INGOs often push Chinese NGOs to create a board of directors. This might be a good idea in general, but in the Chinese context, NGOs and local officials are often concerned about getting into trouble because of each other's actions. Convincing prominent people to risk their reputations on an unfamiliar and untested NGO can be a big challenge. To meet this demand from INGOs, Chinese NGOs often create a formal board on paper that does not act like a board in practice. While both Chinese NGOs and INGOs may agree that the goals of accountability, participation, and good governance are valuable, they often struggle to find Chinese words that accurately capture those concepts.[56] This is a familiar trend in many countries: more and more expense and effort are spent on sustaining the organization, at the expense of the mission it was created for.

INGOs can also constrain the development of Chinese NGOs for a very different reason: their lengthy experience, deep expertise, and strong capabilities can crowd out Chinese NGOs who lack each of those things. Local governments are often willing to work with INGOs because they offer expertise and funding that local leaders desperately need. For example, Yunnan officials trying to address the spread of HIV/AIDS in their province were eager to work with the United Kingdom's Global Fund and the Gates Foundation because those organizations had great financial resources and experience in the issue. China's NGOs working on this issue were just as dependent on these international sources of financial support because they received little support from the Chinese national or local governments.[57] In that sense, the new INGO law may protect Chinese NGOs from foreign competition, although the primary objective was to limit their potential political impact.

Internal Constraints

One of the constant challenges for NGOs, in China as in most countries, is finding the financial resources necessary to survive. Without proper funding, NGOs cannot continue to operate, no matter how urgent the need and how committed its members. Financial support is a particular challenge in China because the practice of charitable giving is underdeveloped. People and companies are not accustomed to donating money to NGOs, and tax laws do not provide an incentive. Moreover, many Chinese citizens are skeptical of NGOs, as noted above, and are unwilling to support groups and individuals they do not trust. Getting funding from foreign governments, foundations, and INGOs is problematic, especially when the Chinese NGO is not registered. Those that rely on government funding have to shift their programmatic priorities to fit the government's preferences. As a result, many Chinese NGOs work on shoestring budgets that prevent them from being as effective as they hope to be. However, one hopeful development was the passage of the Charity Law in 2016, which allowed the creation of foundations to fund nonprofit organizations, especially those whose work supports the party's priorities, such as environmental protection and poverty alleviation. This has provided large amounts of new financing to at least some NGOs.[58]

Another constraint on the development of civil society in China stems from the nature of NGOs themselves: they are generally young, small, and poorly institutionalized.[59] The opportunity to form NGOs has emerged only in the last few decades and their numbers have grown steadily. As a result, most Chinese NGOs are relatively new, less than ten years old. Most are also small, with few full-time staff. They rely heavily on part-time staff and volunteers, most of whom are in their twenties and thirties and inexperienced. Idealism is a common characteristic of youth, and that is why so many NGO staff and volunteers are relatively young. With the growing prevalence of college education, more and more young people are becoming aware of problems in China and are meeting classmates with shared interests with whom they can cooperate. The CCP also encourages voluntarism for its priorities—for example, improving the environment by recycling and picking up trash. A new norm of voluntarism may be taking shape in China, especially among the youth, which provides a steady supply of people to staff NGOs.

Natural disasters are a common trigger for groups to form, donations to be made, and volunteers to step up to help. Following the devastating earthquake in rural Sichuan in 2008, there was an outpouring of donations to charities and a flood of volunteers into the region to help with relief and rebuilding efforts.[60] Many of these spontaneous organizations are short-lived, however, and dissolve once the emergency is past.

For these many reasons, Chinese NGOs have limited capacity to expand services to their clients or to train their staff, and the CCP restricts their ability to collaborate with other NGOs, which prevents them from scaling up their operations. Due to low pay, there is high turnover among NGO staff, which prevents them from accumulating institutional knowledge. As a result, the success of NGOs often rests with the personal capabilities of its founders, not the organizational strength of the NGOs themselves.

Most Chinese NGOs have been slow to develop reputations for policy-relevant knowledge, expertise, and competence, and therefore slow to be accepted by local officials into the policy process (environmental NGOs are an exception).[61] Because most NGOs are small and inexperienced, they are more focused on treating the symptoms of social ills than advocating policies to alleviate the problems themselves. As a result, they do not develop policy-relevant expertise, which in turn constrains their ability to engage in policy making.[62] Contracting with local governments on social welfare services like education, elderly care, and child welfare may be a mixed blessing: on one hand, the NGOs get funding and recognition; on the other hand, the local government connection keeps them focused on social services and away from policy advocacy.

China's civil society may be entering a consolidation phase. Just as new markets often attract more firms than they can support, many of China's numerous small grassroots NGOs may not be able to survive unless they increase capacity by means of greater expertise, reliable sources of funding, and institutional ties with the party and government, not just personal relationships. The first generation of NGOs was overwhelmingly made up of small grassroots NGOs with committed staff and volunteers, but their capacity to be effective was limited. Their reliance on personal connections with local officials in order to survive and operate effectively may no longer be sufficient. The regular rotation of local officials means that reliance on personal connections can be ephemeral and unreliable. Once the official is transferred or promoted, the NGO may lose its connection with the local government. The anti-corruption campaign under Xi exacerbated this risk by removing many local officials from office, discouraging others from taking risks or showing favoritism that might appear as corrupt. Moreover, the recentralization of political authority under Xi gives local officials less leeway in how they implement policies. One of the ironies of Xi's efforts to control civil society may be that NGOs will be forced to become more institutionalized and develop greater expertise rather than rely personal connections between their founders and local officials to get things done. Such an outcome would undoubtedly be fine with the CCP.

* * *

The CCP's approach to civil society may seem paradoxical—alternately suppressing and supporting civil society—unless we distinguish the different types of NGOs. It is willing to partner with the registered and unregistered NGOs that offer resources and expertise that support the CCP's social welfare agenda (the red and gray NGOs), but at the same time wants to root out and eliminate the unregistered (black) groups that threaten the CCP's legitimacy, including those that promote labor rights, human rights, religious freedom, and party rule itself. In other words, it has come to accept and even encourage CSI groups, but remains determined to suppress all CSII groups.

The CCP has been alert to any imminent or potential threat to its hold on power. Civil society is a particular focus of its concern. CCP leaders have repeatedly warned of the potential for a color revolution in China that would upend the regime. They have coupled this warning with a related one: civil society organizations offer a front for foreign influences in China that seek to stymie China's further economic development. These two fears—political instability and foreign interference in China's domestic affairs—are constant themes in party propaganda. They also resonate with much of the Chinese population, which is afraid of chaos and highly nationalistic. Many agree with the party's contention that diverse groups with differing perspectives—a hallmark of a vibrant civil society—threaten political stability.[63]

To counter this possibility, the CCP heavily suppresses the political realm of civil society, or CSII. It actively watches for groups with a political agenda that criticize the current party line and incumbent leaders, harassing and often imprisoning those who are critical and shutting down their organizations. The result of this suppression is that China has no any real political opposition, few active dissidents, and even fewer who receive much public support.

But the political realm is only one aspect of civil society. Another dimension of civil society—CSI—does not engage in political activities, but instead is oriented toward economic, social, and cultural activities. It brings awareness to social issues like poverty and economic inequality, provides valued services like job training and legal assistance, and brings people together through shared interests and leisure activities, like soccer and tai chi. It highlights the dangers of pollution, encourages the government to enforce existing laws on air and water pollution, and educates people on the benefits of recycling. In short, it does what many civil society groups do in the United States and other countries: supplement the role of the government in ways that serve the interests of their members and, in many cases, society at large. This too is civil society, and poses no threat to the CCP.

These CSI NGOs, both red and gray, can help improve governance in both democratic and authoritarian regimes, and in that way provide benefits for both the regime and the people. They provide needed goods and services to those who need it most. They benefit local officials by providing trained expertise, committed staff and volunteers, and material resources, all of which enhances their ability to govern more effectively. To the extent that these CSI groups are effective, they can increase regime stability by alleviating burdens, addressing needs, and providing goods and services. Those who receive these benefits do not always recognize who provides them, they just recognize the improvement in their lives.[64] Greater overall life satisfaction is highly correlated with regime stability, so much so that life satisfaction is a good proxy for regime support.[65]

Just as it is wrong to oversimplify the concept of civil society as being only a source of political change, it would be naïve to assume that China's CSI economic and social NGOs offer only benefits to the regime. Local officials who work with these NGOs may develop a measure of trust in them and be willing to engage in further cooperation, but they remain wary that even these groups may develop a more political orientation without proper monitoring. Groups that form for one purpose can be used for another, just as African-American churches in the American South became focal points for organization and information for the 1960s civil rights movement. Groups that serve China's migrant worker population may seek greater representation for them. Groups may spotlight sensitive issues, as those that work on the environment have criticized the CCP for not enforcing its own laws and for pursuing an economic model with such devastating impacts on the environment. And, while officials may trust NGOs with which they have personal experience, they remain suspicious of NGOs they are not familiar with. In short, while the distinction between CSI and CSII is helpful in understanding the CCP's evolving strategy toward civil society, the boundary between them is not fixed.

As the CCP's approach to civil society under Xi becomes the new normal, a second generation of NGOs may emerge. The small grassroots and unregistered NGOs may not survive, perhaps replaced with somewhat larger and more institutionalized ones. This would conform to the emphasis on formal institutions under Xi and the elimination of informal processes and relationships. The registered NGOs will be able to receive funding openly through grants and contracts from domestic and foreign sources, including governments, foundations, and individuals. Domestic and foreign NGOs that register will move out of the gray area that they have operated in, an ambiguous status that made them vulnerable when political winds shifted. Interactions between domestic and foreign NGOs may become more routine, less surreptitious, and therefore less a cause of concern for the CCP. But the party is determined to keep a close eye on them just the same.

5

DO POLITICAL PROTESTS THREATEN POLITICAL STABILITY?

In the spring of 1989, Beijing witnessed a spectacle unlike any other in the history of the PRC. Peaceful protesters—estimated at their peak to number as many as 1 million—marched in the streets calling for political reform. Thousands of protesters, mostly college students, occupied Tiananmen Square, the symbolic center of the country. The protests spread to dozens of Chinese cities. Some top party and government leaders were publicly sympathetic. It seemed as though political change was imminent.

The protesters were careful to frame their demands as patriotic, and thus not a threat to the CCP. These demands included increased funding for education, greater anticorruption efforts, freedom of the press, and a reassessment of deposed CCP leader Hu Yaobang, whose death on April 15, 1989, was the catalyst for the protests. Hu had previously been general secretary of the CCP but was removed from that post for not taking a stronger stand against prodemocracy protests in late 1986.

Hard-liners in the top leadership of the CCP did not accept this patriotic view. They published an editorial in the *People's Daily*, the CCP's official newspaper, declaring that the protests were a "planned conspiracy and a disturbance" and must end. This outraged the students, who added a new demand to their agenda: retract the editorial and declare the movement to be legitimate and patriotic. CCP hard-liners remained intransigent, refusing to compromise and continuing to call for an end to the occupation of Tiananmen Square and the ongoing street marches. Protesters later added a more extreme demand: remove Deng Xiaoping, China's preeminent leader, and Li Peng, the prime minister.

The CCP did not accede to these demands. Instead, on May 19, Li Peng declared martial law in Beijing, although the command was not immediately carried out. That same night, CCP General Secretary Zhao Ziyang, whose plea to negotiate and compromise with the students was rejected by Deng Xiaoping and other leaders, went to the square to talk to the students. "I have come too late," he told them. What had begun as a peaceful, patriotic movement had hardened into a tense stalemate. Party hard-liners were in now in command; reformers like Zhao who were sympathetic to the protesters were sidelined and would eventually be deposed. Zhao himself would soon be under house arrest, where he would remain until his death in January 2005, more than fifteen years after the Tiananmen protests.

On June 4, 1989, the CCP ordered the execution of the martial law decree after seven weeks of peaceful protest. Tanks and armored personnel carriers flooded into Tiananmen Square and surrounding streets. Soldiers fired randomly into the crowds, filling hospitals with the dead and wounded. Protesters fought back with Molotov cocktails, sticks, and metal rods, but they were no match for the weapons of the People's Liberation Army. Estimates on the number of people who died that night range from several hundred to more than one thousand. The protests that seemed to promise so much came to a sudden and bloody end.

The 1989 protests were not a harbinger of mass protests to come. In the more than three decades since, there has been no further sustained, nationwide mass movement on behalf of political change. Most Chinese, even those who participated in the protests, turned their attention to economic opportunities as China's economy began its rapid takeoff in the early 1990s. In the years to come, few were willing to talk about the events of spring 1989: not parents, not teachers, and certainly not the CCP, who actively suppressed all public discussion of the peaceful protests and the violent crackdown, censored online information about it, and even pressured foreign companies, like Google and Zoom, not to provide what it deemed to be sensitive images or commentary to Chinese users of their programs.

Several lessons came out of the 1989 protests. The CCP learned that it needed a domestic security apparatus to respond quickly to protests and social instability without relying on the PLA alone. This lesson was reinforced by the "velvet revolutions" that brought down communist regimes throughout Eastern Europe beginning in the fall of 1989. Beginning in the 1990s, the CCP developed new policies and practices to cope with protest. It increased the budgets, bureaucratic stature, and influence of the public security apparatus, and required local leaders to maintain stability as a condition for their evaluation and promotion.[1] In all these ways, it gave local leaders the means and the incentive to limit social and political unrest.

In contrast, the people learned that the CCP was willing to use lethal force to defend its monopoly on political power. Protests did not end, but they changed in size and purpose. As protest activity changed, the party's response did as well, combining a willingness to compromise with a determination to maintain stability.

Whereas the 1989 protests in Tiananmen Square and throughout the country were a large-scale mass movement involving people of all ages and walks of life; focusing on broad social, political, and economic issues; and targeting national party and government leaders, subsequent protests have been much smaller in size and focused on local issues and local leaders. As in the Wukan protests that opened this book, protesters typically do not demand complete regime change, and rarely even new rights or political reforms. Instead they seek to have national laws, regulations, and policies properly implemented locally. Most do not see democracy as part of the solution (the prodemocracy protests in Hong Kong will be discussed in chapter 7). Protesters often praise the benevolence and wisdom of central leaders even as they criticize the conduct of local officials, making protesters and central leaders tacit allies against local leaders, who bear the wrath of protesters and the punishments imposed by higher-level leaders.[2]

Because most protests since 1989 have not posed an existential threat to the CCP, it has often been responsive to them, conceding or at least compromising on material demands. New industrial plants have been moved to other locales, more compensation has been given to the victims of land grabs, and unpaid wages and pensions have been paid—at least partially. But the CCP is not always responsive, and does not respond in ways that would hold it accountable to the people. Local officials in particular are more likely to repress protests in order to maintain political stability, because their careers may be threatened if protests happen on their watch. Even when concessions and compromises are offered, protest leaders are often arrested and sentenced to lengthy prison terms in order to discourage others with similar complaints from using similar tactics. Protests can be successful in achieving specific goals, but they often come at a very high price. And since Xi became the party's leader in 2012, the balance between repression and responsiveness has tilted decidedly toward the former. The CCP has become less willing to be responsive to public opinion and further distanced from accountability to it.

The remainder of this chapter will flesh out these themes, looking at protest strategies, what triggers protests, and how the party responds.[3] Along the way, we will look at what protests threaten stability and which do not, and how the protesters' strategies and the party's responses vary accordingly.

Popular Protests in Post-Tiananmen China

Protests in China have risen dramatically in number in recent years. In 1993, the central government reported that there were 8,700 protests; in 2005, the number rose to 87,000, a tenfold increase in just over ten years. After this, the Chinese government stopped reporting the number of protests, perhaps alarmed by the public revelation of rising discontent in the country. Sociologist Sun Liping of Tsinghua University in Beijing estimated that there were 180,000 protests in 2010. Even without knowing the precise number of protests, there is general agreement that it has gotten larger over time, although not on the scale of the 1989 protests.

More important is how Chinese citizens have engaged in protest and how the CCP has responded has evolved over time.

Protest Framing

The way protesters frame their demands has evolved over time, from moral claims for justice and fairness, to defense of rights promised but not fulfilled, and eventually to a focus on interests.[4] In the early post-Mao period, protests were commonly couched in the language of socialist ideology and Maoist rhetoric. Workers sought the dignity they had been promised. Farmers wanted enough grain to survive. Pensioners and demobilized soldiers asked for the subsistence-level payments they were due. Slogans such as "We don't want fish or meat, just some porridge" and "Not a yuan in six months, we want rice to eat" reflect this appeal for subsistence.[5] These types of demands reflect a moral economy perspective: protesters were not acting out of self-interest and were not demanding new rights and freedoms, but only just and fair treatment based on what was right and proper and, more significantly, on what the CCP had promised in the past.[6]

Protesters later framed their protests in terms of defending rights already promised by the CCP. Perhaps the most influential concept in the study of political protest in China is that of "rightful resistance."[7] It recognizes that many protests are based not on demanding new rights, freedoms, or liberties, but in getting the state to uphold its promises at the local level. Protesters cite existing laws, regulations, leaders' speeches, and articles in the official media to point out the inconsistencies between what has been promised and what is being delivered. In many cases, these promises have been made by central or provincial leaders but have not been implemented by local officials. Hence, protesters rightfully resist the local officials who refuse to implement the laws and regulations that already exist. Rightful resistance is also generally nonviolent in order to solicit wider support and to avoid giving officials an excuse to repress their efforts.

One of the most common targets of rightful resisters was village elections, which provides a good illustration of the concept. As described in chapter 2, the CCP allowed experiments with village elections in the early 1980s and then mandated these elections beginning in 1987. This was done to help solve the problem of local leadership when the rural communes were being dismantled and replaced with family farms. Villagers began electing their own village chiefs and village councils to govern local affairs.

However, township and county leaders often interfered in these elections, rejecting candidates they did not like or nullifying the results when their preferred candidates did not win. Villagers then protested this outside interference in village affairs and cited violations of the village election law to challenge the meddling of township and county officials. The villagers did not demand a new right that did not exist, such as the right to form new political parties to run against the CCP, nor did they seek changes to the electoral law. They simply demanded that higher-level officials order these township and county meddlers to abide by the existing election law that had already been passed by the National People's Congress.

Rightful resistance is commonly seen in protests in today's China, but it is not necessarily new to contemporary times. Throughout Chinese history, peasants have used official rhetoric to protest the state of affairs.[8] They did not seek the overthrow of the emperor; instead they noted that the responsibility to govern on behalf of the people was not being properly upheld. From this historical perspective, rightful resisters in contemporary China may understand the rules of the game and play by them in order to survive and improve their chances of success. Although they know how to use the rhetoric of the regime to their advantage, pointing out its unfulfilled promises and commitments in their own communities, they may have no real sense of inherent rights and do not seek to challenge the regime. Whether or not rightful resistance is a new tactic, it has been an important concept for understanding how protesters pursue their causes.

The debate between rights and rules consciousness is not just an academic debate over semantics; it has implications for whether rightful resistance poses a threat to regime stability. If protesters are only playing by the rules of the game as set forth by the regime, then their claims do not pose much of a threat to the regime. But if they are developing a concept of inalienable rights that are not simply given by the regime but inherent to individuals, they may push for new rights and freedoms that pose more of a threat to the CCP, if not now, in the not too distant future. Scholars agree that protesters routinely cite existing laws and regulations as a way of legitimizing their demands, but there is debate over the ultimate significance of the practice.

A third and more recent frame for protests is the interests and quality of life of protesters and society at large. This theme is particularly common in environmental protests. Whether the trigger for protests is the building of a chemical plant, incinerator, or high-speed rail near residential areas, protesters cite the threats to their health, quality of life, and property values. The notorious environmental degradation caused by rapid economic growth and urbanization in China has triggered public demonstrations and online criticism, prompting the government to take some remedial measures to improve air quality, such as banning leaded gas, reducing urban traffic, and moving factories and coal burning plants away from population centers. Plans to build hydroelectric dams to produce much-needed energy have occasionally been stymied by the actions of scientists, journalists, and local activists who point out the threats to endangered species and cultural landmarks (as illustrated by the Nu River dams discussed in chapter 3). In these protests, opponents do not simply utilize the regime's rhetoric or the rights it has promised to citizens, but make claims about personal, societal, and even national interests. This type of protest may signify the emergence of inherent individual rights that need protection from state actions, not simply rights as gifts from the state.

These different ways of framing protests are not mutually exclusive. Rightful resisters may claim they seek only enough to survive, in order to deny that they pose a threat to the status quo. Environmental protests may emphasize that local officials did not follow existing laws and regulations, such as conducting a thorough environmental impact review.

This evolution of protest framing—from morality to rightful resistance to material interests—reflects ongoing social changes and may hint at a "revolution of rising expectations" as protests shift from those based on the regime's promises to the interests of individuals and society at large.[9] As of now, however, there is scant evidence that the gap between people's expectations and their reality is large enough to pose an imminent threat to the CCP.

Forms of Protests

There is a wide range of actions people in China can take to protest. Ranging from low to high levels of confrontation, they include writing and signing petitions, filing lawsuits, strikes and sit-ins, and street protests. Protesters often begin with the less confrontational options and escalate when those actions are unsuccessful.

The Chinese state has created several formal channels through which Chinese citizens can raise complaints. One is the petition system. Party, government, legislative, judicial, media, and other official units at all levels of the political system have "letters and visits offices" where citizens can file petitions, individually or collectively, about issues of wrongdoing, typically the malfeasance or corrupt behavior of local officials. These petitions are rarely successful, but they are the first step in an often lengthy process of getting problems solved.[10] If petitions at one level are not successful, petitioners can appeal at higher levels. Some people even become "professional petitioners," devoting their entire lives for years on end to seeking justice for themselves and occasionally offering advice to less experienced petitioners. At the same time, the center has directed local officials not to allow petitioners to travel to provincial capitals or Beijing to file their petitions. Some local governments send police and even hired thugs to force petitioners to return home. Submitting unapproved petitions was also among the list of activities that were subject to "reeducation through labor" (essentially prison camps) before that system was abolished in 2013.[11] This is a familiar contradiction in Chinese politics: officially, people have the right to do this and the state encourages them to do so; but in practice, the state directs local officials to prevent them from doing so in order to maintain stability.

But even when these individual petitions are not successful, a surge in petitions on a specific issue or from a specific region can signal to higher levels that there is a problem that warrants their attention. For example, in the early 2000s, there was a sudden explosion in the number of petitions about rural land seizures and urban home demolitions. National and provincial officials reacted with conferences, statistical studies of the contents of petitions, and debate over whether policy implementation or the policies themselves were to blame. They concluded it was the policies that were at fault and responded with reforms.[12] These reforms did not end the practice of land grabs for redevelopment nor the protests against them, but they did try to alleviate the coercive practices of local officials and the anger those generated. In short, the state was not necessarily responsive to individual petitions, but it was responsive to the issue—illegal land grabs—that had suddenly prompted so many petitions.

The Chinese state also encourages people to use the court system to resolve their problems. In 1989, it passed the Administrative Litigation Law, which allows citizens to sue the government. In 1995, it passed the Labor Law, which allows workers to sue employers for unpaid wages, workers' compensation, and wrongful termination. The state heavily publicized these laws and how to "use the law as a weapon," even though most cases were unsuccessful. The result was "informed disenchantment": aggrieved citizens were better informed about their legal rights and options but became disenchanted when their efforts were for naught.[13]

Why encourage people to use the law and then allow so few cases to succeed? The promotion of the labor law in particular was part of the CCP's strategy for reforming its bloated state-owned enterprises, beginning in the 1990s. It wanted to wean workers off the "iron rice bowl"— the promise of high-paying jobs with generous benefits and lifetime job security. In its place, it wanted to turn labor issues into individual complaints, not a moral commitment that was neither part of a broader social contract nor the basis for a true labor movement in China.[14] SOE workers quickly went from being the labor aristocracy to being among the biggest losers of the reform era.

When using formal channels is not successful, Chinese citizens can adopt more confrontational tactics. Strikes, sit-ins, and street protests

are public events that put pressure on party leaders, government officials, and enterprise owners and managers. Protests can be quite
large, involving thousands of people, although nothing on the scale of
the 1989 protests. The size of the disturbance refers not only to the
number of protesters but also the audience that watches. For example,
during a protest against pollution and its attendant health effects in
the coastal province of Zhejiang, protesters from one of the affected
villages erected a tent that blocked the entrance to an industrial park.
Other villages joined the protest and erected their own tents. People
from surrounding areas came to view the spectacle. Vendors arrived
to sell food and souvenirs to the protesters and spectators, creating a
festival-like atmosphere. Local officials dismantled the tents several
times, only to have the protesters rebuild them. More than a thousand
cadres and security personnel entered the tent city late one night to
dismantle it and force the protesters out, but the effort backfired as
protesters fought back, resulting in hundreds of injuries and multiple
government vehicles being burned. This excessive use of force by the
local government created public sympathy for the protesters and put
pressure on the officials to reach a compromise. After media reports
caught the attention of high-level officials, the local leaders decided
against another use of force against the protesters. Instead they agreed
to close all the factories in the industrial park responsible for the
pollution.[15]

This episode illustrates several common themes in protests in China.
The protesters were seeking a solution to a very specific and local problem: their health and livelihoods were being damaged by pollution from
a nearby industrial park. They had previously tried using the petition
system, even traveling to Beijing to file a petition, to no avail. Only then
did they engage in public protests. The local officials first tried to intimidate the protesters into ending their protest, but once the media picked
up the story and higher-level officials were alerted, local officials con-
ceded to the protesters' demands.

Many protests involve labor issues, especially the problems of migrant workers from rural areas who work in the manufacturing and

construction sectors. Because the official trade union, the All-China Federation of Trade Unions (ACFTU), protects the CCP's interests more than the workers it nominally represents, a variety of NGOs have been formed to serve the needs of workers, and migrant workers in particular. Initial efforts to form independent labor unions were unsuccessful because the CCP sees autonomous organizations as an existential threat and forcefully suppresses efforts to form them. When large-scale strikes also became too risky, labor NGOs began to focus on small-scale and even individual actions.[16] NGO activists secretly trained workers to achieve specific and immediate results by steering clear of politically sensitive issues and demands. Small-scale collective action, such as a flash mob outside a courthouse, proved to be more successful in creating a sense of community through shared suffering and denied rights than in achieving actual goals, but the NGOs hoped that in the long run a true labor movement would emerge. Some NGOs even coached individuals via cell phone calls and texts about whom to talk to and what to say. These were not just individual actions, but organized, orchestrated, and coached actions.

The key to this style of small-scale and individual action—including public suicide—is to threaten social stability. Suicide is a dramatic and alarming form of protest, especially when enacted in a very public display to shame the target of the protest.[17] In 2010, at least fourteen workers committed suicide at Foxconn, a major supplier for Apple and other electronics companies, most by jumping off the roof of the workers' dormitory. Following the rash of suicides, central leaders who had criticized labor practices at Foxconn and Apple executives made their own investigation. Foxconn's immediate response was to build nets on its tall buildings so that jumpers would not fall to their deaths. While conditions improved somewhat at that particular Foxconn plant, labor abuses remain common in private enterprises in China. Individual workers have been able to gain concessions from employers by threatening to commit suicide, which would bring unwanted attention to the employers.[18]

Other forms of individual protest involve people resisting the changes going on around them. In one famous episode involving a so-called nail

FIGURE 5.1. Nets to prevent suicide jumpers at Foxconn Factory in China (photo: Bobby Yip/Reuters, used with permission)

house—so named because the people involved were "hard as nails" and would not listen to reason—a married couple in the southwestern city of Chongqing refused offers to sell their house to developers who were planning on redeveloping the site. Their neighbors had all sold their houses, and the construction work left the "nail house" perched on a narrow pillar of land while a large pit was dug around it to build the foundation for the new facility. After a standoff that lasted more than two years, the owners finally agreed to an undisclosed settlement.

A popular saying during the Hu Jintao years (2002–12) was that a big disturbance brings big results, a small disturbance brings small results, and no disturbance brings no results. In the next section, I will demonstrate that large protests, so long as they did not threaten regime legitimacy or social stability, almost always succeeded in achieving some

FIGURE 5.2. A "nail house" in Chongqing (photo: EyePress image)

compromise, although usually not in meeting all the protesters' demands. Unless there were casualties or substantial media attention, central officials were willing to allow local officials to handle protests. This allows the central leadership to avoid blame when local officials misstep, either by using excessive repression or by offering overly generous concessions: the former can generate a backlash; the latter may encourage others to protest.[19]

The CCP's Strategy for Managing Protests

Maintaining stability has been a top priority in China since the early 1990s. The 1989 protests in Tiananmen Square and elsewhere in China told the CCP it needed a better way to handle mass protests without relying solely on the PLA. The army is designed primarily for national defense and lacks training in nonlethal forms of crowd control.

Moreover, its reputation was tarnished by acts of violence against un-armed protesters. For these reasons, many PLA leaders reportedly op-posed using troops to end the 1989 protests, although their opposition ultimately proved unsuccessful. Afterward, the CCP elevated the status of the public security apparatus responsible for domestic security within the bureaucracy and integrated its top personnel with party leadership at the central and local levels.[20] It expanded the People's Armed Police, a paramilitary police force, to handle large-scale protests and distur-bances. And it created special "stability maintenance" funds to both pay for the expansion of the security apparatus and provide for negotiated settlements to end protests.

The overall budget for public security greatly increased during the 1990s. In 2011, the public security budget for the first time exceeded the military's budget. This indicates the CCP's priority in maintaining do-mestic security, but the simple comparison of the public security and military budgets is slightly misleading. The public security budget in-cludes items that are not used for repression, such as law enforcement and criminal justice.[21] In fact, China's government spending across the board has increased steadily since the early 1990s. Government spend-ing on health care and education rose in tandem with public security spending. In different ways, all were intended to maintain political and social stability.[22] The increased spending on domestic security reflects not only the CCP's priority on maintaining stability but also higher spending overall.[23]

The CCP uses a variety of tactics for managing protests, including both repression and responsiveness. In fact, it can use both options si-multaneously. Local leaders often resolve protests by negotiating a com-promise and also arresting several protesters as a warning against future protests. The complementarity of repression and responsiveness is also evident in aggregate trends. During the years Hu Jintao was CCP gen-eral secretary (2003–12), provinces with increased labor unrest increased their spending on public security and handed down an increased num-ber of prolabor verdicts in mediation, arbitration, and court cases.[24] However, once Xi Jinping became China's leader in 2012, the party shifted decisively toward repression to deal with protests. In the sections below, while the different options are discussed separately, it is important to keep in mind that they are often used together.

Hard Repression

Hard repression is the most visible tactic the CCP uses to manage protests. It includes the use of force against protesters, imprisonment with frequent allegations of torture, house arrests of those who are released from prison—and sometimes the relatives of those still in prison—and occasionally the disappearance of protesters and dissidents for long periods of time. These acts of hard repression are designed to both punish the protesters and deter others. China has the most political prisoners of any country in the world, and is second only to Turkey in the number of journalists in jail.[25]

Local officials not only use security forces and police officers to repress protesters and critics, they frequently hire "thugs," often members of local criminal gangs, to do the dirty work.[26] Hired thugs break up protests, damage homes, and intimidate NGOs and activists in their offices. Similar to how American companies used outside muscle to try to break up unions in the early 1900s, this practice allows the officials to be one step removed from the repressive acts. And, by hiring thugs on an as-needed basis, local officials are able to use force while also saving money by not permanently hiring additional security and police.

Hard repression can often backfire, infuriating protesters instead of intimidating them and also gaining them public sympathy and support. When efforts to crack down lead to an escalation of violence, the media is more likely to pick up the story, and the internet and social media are more likely to spread the word. The increased attention brings scrutiny from higher-level officials, who may send investigation teams to find out why stability is not being maintained. Because the promotions and salaries of local officials are tied to the goal of maintaining stability, party and government officials want to avoid violent and prolonged clashes that will draw the attention of higher-ups. To do this, they must also engage in more indirect, "soft" repression.

Soft Repression

One of the best-known forms of soft repression is interviewing activists (and sometimes scholars) about their activities and organizations, a practice known as being "invited for tea." This is not a full-scale detention and interrogation, just an unofficial talk often held in a government office or even a public place, but it can still be quite unnerving. The purpose is to gather information about potential protests and other activities, about the organization the individual belongs to, and even about other organizations working on the same issues. These meetings also let the activists know they are on the public security's radar and may deter some of their plans. Activists may be invited to tea on a regular basis. While the state may have repressive intentions for these meetings, activists can use them to build some measure of trust with the officials they meet, in the hopes of reassuring them that they do not have a political agenda and do not pose a threat to political stability, much less the CCP. But this relationship is strongly tilted in the state's direction: officials invite activists to tea, determine how often they will meet, and set the agenda for the meetings. The activists do not have the option to decline the invitation.

Party and government officials also use fragmentation to preempt protests. For instance, they take advantage of natural divisions among workers: skilled and unskilled, migrants from the countryside and permanent residents, different dialects, and so on.[27] These differences make it harder to build the mutual trust necessary for successful collective action. In a similar fashion, local officials can pit NGOs and activists against each other by using one to gain information about the others. NGOs and activists are often willing to cooperate in order to ensure their own survival, but the result is mutual suspicion and mistrust, preventing them from working together.[28]

An increasingly common form of soft repression is "relational repression," in which local leaders identify the family and friends of protesters and get them to persuade the protesters to end their protests.[29] Local leaders first determine who the protesters are and investigate their backgrounds to find the people most likely to be influential with them. These people are then tasked with getting the protesters to stop. If they fail, they can be suspended from their jobs or transferred to less attractive posts. For example, young adults may plead with their elderly grandparents to stop protesting the demolition of their homes: if they do not agree to vacate their homes, the job prospects of the grandchildren will be damaged. In a culture where family ties are paramount, this very often works. In some cases prominent local private entrepreneurs are enlisted for this purpose; if they refuse, they can find their business prospects suffer, for instance by having their loan applications rejected. In other words, it is not only the protesters who are punished; their friends, relatives, and the local elites also bear the cost. Relational repression may be effective in the immediate resolution of a protest, but its long-term costs may be huge: by threatening and punishing people who are dependent on the CCP for success in their careers, it risks alienating the very people who are among its core supporters.[30] However, relational repression does not always work: if the protesters are particularly determined, or if the people sent to persuade them do not have close personal or professional bonds with them, their efforts are likely to fail.[31]

Relational repression is not a centrally sanctioned policy, but it is in common use by local officials, whose performance is evaluated according to how well they maintain stability. It is one element in a larger repertoire of soft repression, and is now commonly used to silence vocal critics of the CCP's policies in Xinjiang, including those living outside China. Family members still in Xinjiang call their relatives who have left to persuade them to stop their criticisms and protests lest they be forced into the detention camps the CCP has built in Xinjiang to stymie ethnic mobilization among the Uighurs.[32] (The CCP's policies in Xinjiang will be discussed in more detail in the discussion on nationalism in chapter 7.)

The most important new tool in the party's arsenal of repression is technology. Although the initial post-Mao reforms reduced the party's ability to monitor the people, new technology is allowing a level of monitoring capability previously unheard of. Facial recognition and cell phone tracking software allow the party to track the comings and goings of anyone throughout the country. Attempts are under way not only to recognize an individual's face but to pick out a member of an ethnic group in crowd of people, which would take racial profiling to a new level. Chinese scientists are also trying to develop the technology to use DNA samples to reconstruct a person's face.[33] Phone apps released during the COVID-19 epidemic of 2020 allow the state to track the whereabouts of people under quarantine and those exposed to the virus. The same technology used to fight the spread of disease could easily be converted to monitor dissidents and others the party defines as a threat.

Collecting and analyzing "big data" also allows the party to connect the interactions of multiple people. The party monitors social media not just to block objectionable content but to learn who is communicating with whom. New technology also makes it possible to collect and aggregate information at the micro level. Public security officials in Xinjiang use an Integrated Joint Operations Program (IJOP) for high-tech, integrated surveillance of virtually the entire population. The IJOP app allows officials to collect personal information, including height, the color of one's car, and recent purchases; monitor activities or circumstances the party sees as potentially suspicious, including using a VPN (virtual private network), getting a new phone number, or even not using the front door; and then launch investigations of people flagged by the app, often resulting in detentions in Xinjiang's concentration camps and prisons.[34] All of this information is tied to the person's national identification number. It is the most intrusive surveillance system in China, but it is similar to programs used elsewhere and will likely be adopted on a national scale.

The newly created social credit system may be the ultimate example of the use of big data in soft repression. It is somewhat similar to the financial credit scores that Americans get based on their records of paying off previous loans and credit card debt. However, the Chinese social credit system includes a much wider range of information and behaviors, including business regulatory violations and court judgments. Early reports on the social credit system suggested it would also include such things as work history, relations with neighbors, and online activities, but those fears have not yet materialized. Moreover, it is not a single score but a report. For example, businesses receive a social credit code that consumers can look up to see if a restaurant has been cited for health code violations or a firm has unpaid fines and penalties. The punitive aspects of the social credit system are widespread: those with poor social credit can be denied access to credit, new jobs and promotions, or travel inside and outside China; even the college prospects of their children can be affected. It has primarily been applied to regulatory and legal issues, not wider types of social behavior. Once the social credit system is in place, it will be easy enough to aggregate other types of data into it, but that has not happened yet.[35] Remarkably enough, many Chinese seem receptive to the social credit system, perhaps hopeful that only scofflaws will be victims of it.[36] When I have talked to Chinese students about it, they have been unaware of the potential downsides to this new initiative.

Negotiating Outcomes

The Chinese state does not simply repress all types of protests; it often makes concessions in order to bring protests to a close. This is particularly common when the protests are over monetary issues, such as unpaid wages and pensions; wrongful termination due to injury, pregnancy, or downsizing; compensation for land acquisitions; and resettlement expenses. Local officials have a good deal of discretion in negotiating these types of monetary settlements, even using the "stability maintenance funds" to pay for them, a practice known as "buying stability." These monetary demands are a type of rightful resistance: the protesters are not demanding new rights and freedoms but simply asking for their existing rights to be enforced. These negotiated outcomes, however, turn rights into commodities to be bargained over, rather than seeing them as being inalienable and irrevocable.[37] They treat rights as gifts from the state that need not be made available in their entirety but are subject to negotiation over how much of the right will be granted to what groups in different places at different points in time. The use of stability maintenance funds to buy stability has declined under Xi Jinping in favor of more repressive tactics, as will be discussed below.[38]

The state is also willing to concede or compromise when the dispute is over material interests that do not challenge the legitimacy of the regime. These include NIMBY protests about new construction projects: for instance, a high-speed magnetic levitation (maglev) train that connects Shanghai to the Pudong International Airport about thirty miles away. When local officials began planning an extension of the maglev line, which would pass through residential areas, residents protested the disruption to their community from the construction and the potential for electromagnetic radiation from the trains' operation. In the end, the planned extension of the line was shelved due to the intense opposition.

Protests against environmentally damaging projects are also regularly resisted. Protesters were able to block the construction of paraxylene (PX) plants in a number of cities, including Xiamen in 2007, Dalian in 2011, and Shanghai in 2015. Paraxylene is a highly flammable chemical used in making plastic containers and polyester fabrics. It can be damaging to health when inhaled or absorbed through the skin. Local residents were quick to protest the presence of PX plants in their communities once plans were revealed. In each case, local officials agreed to cancel or move the planned PX plant in response to the public outcry.

The successful anti-PX protests in Maoming in 2014 illustrate this trend.[39] Maoming is a city on the southern coast of Guangdong Province, often referred to as the "oil city of the south" because of its oil refineries and petrochemical industries. When Maoming officials began devising plans to build a PX plant, they tried to preempt protests through a variety of measures, but in the end these efforts failed and even backfired. First of all, they mounted a propaganda campaign extolling the benefits of the PX plant. They distributed informational brochures and ran articles in the local media describing PX as safe and highlighting the economic benefits it would bring. Local citizens were suspicious of this sudden and intense campaign, especially since other anti-PX protests in other cities had highlighted the health and environmental costs. Second, they tried to force students and people working in the petrochemical industry to sign a letter of support. To induce people to sign, they threatened to withhold important benefits, such as entry into college and future promotions. This is a form of soft repression—not violence or imprisonment but denial of benefits. This also backfired, as people began discussing these heavy-handed tactics online, spreading information and opposition. Third, officials hosted a conference promoting PX and invited online activists and opinion leaders. Rather than dispel skepticism, this conference became an opportunity for anti-PX activists to get to know each other.

Successful anti-PX protests in other cities also allowed Maoming protesters to learn what worked and to apply that learning in their city. Previous anti-PX protests had received extensive coverage in the national media and caused local governments to cancel or suspend PX projects. Protesters also learned that keeping protests peaceful was crucial. After the first day of protests ended in violence, with police beating protesters and protesters torching police cars and government buildings, anti-PX activists sent out messages via social media that anti-PX protests in other cities had been peaceful. The key was to remain committed to protesting while also avoiding violence. After a week of protests, the deputy mayor held a press conference at which he condemned the violence and defended the use of force by the police. However, he also announced that there was no timetable for constructing the PX plant and that it would not be built without the public's support. With that, both the plans for the plant and the protests against it came to an end.

Whether local officials choose to compromise or crack down is based in part on local state capacity: the higher the per capita GDP, tax revenue, and ratio of police officers to general population, the more likely authorities are to seek a negotiated outcome with protesters. Strong state capacity allows local officials to monitor local conditions before protests occur; collect information on protesters; deploy the police to prevent escalation of protests; channel protesters into officially sanctioned channels, such as the petition system and the courts; and ultimately negotiate a solution without resorting to mass repression. In contrast, local officials with less state capacity are less able to do those things and have little choice but to rely on repression to end protests.[40]

Even when local officials are willing to concede or compromise, they also take punitive steps to discourage similar protests in the future. They identify several protesters as leaders of the protest, arrest them, and sentence them to often lengthy prison sentences. In 2002, SOE workers in the northeastern rust-belt city of Liaoyang protested the closing of their factories. The workers were further angered by the chair of the local people's congress, who stated in a nationally televised interview that there were no unemployed workers in Liaoyang, even though thousands had been laid off. Tens of thousands of laid-off workers marched to demand back pay and an investigation into the corrupt means by which their factories had been liquidated after being declared bankrupt. Local officials eventually negotiated a compromise with the workers, giving them most of the back pay they were owed. The manager of the bankrupted factory was convicted of corruption and imprisoned. The provincial governor who approved the bankruptcy was charged in a separate bribery case and sent to prison.[41] The provincial government also responded to these massive protests by revising the bankruptcy procedures, including ensuring that workers receive severance pay.[42] At the same time, they arrested several of the protest leaders, and two were sentenced to prison sentences of four to seven years. Their arrests also led to the fragmentation of the movement when one of the arrested leaders reportedly informed on the others in order to get a reduced sentence. This generated hostility and mistrust among the protest leaders, which inhibited further cooperation among them.

To avoid having leaders arrested and imprisoned, protesters have learned to conceal the identity of protest leaders and claim they are engaging in spontaneous, unorganized action. In order to negotiate a compromise, however, local officials will let the protesters select several people as their representatives in order to bring the protest to a close without it escalating into violent clashes. The protesters selected to negotiate with officials are typically not arrested afterward. To do so would be counterproductive: it would undermine the negotiated compromise and likely trigger a resumption of the protest.

Not all protest leaders are arrested as punishment for creating instability. In some cases, as in the Wukan village protests, these leaders are co-opted into leadership positions in order to gain their cooperation and reduce the risk of their leading future protests. In labor protests, private enterprise owners and managers of state-owned enterprises will co-opt workers into management, hoping that once the activists have been bought off, the other workers will be less able to organize and mobilize.[43]

Preemptive Repression

The CCP does not simply wait for protests to occur before reacting; it also tries to preempt them at predictable times, such as significant anniversaries, high-level political meetings, and the hosting of international events in China.[44] Before and during these times, the CCP rounds up the "usual suspects," such as known dissidents and NGO activists, puts them under house arrest or into detention or temporarily relocates them to another city. Leaders of underground churches and labor NGOs are warned to keep a low profile and avoid speaking to the media. Traffic in and around Beijing is restricted. Police and security forces are more visible at prominent public places. In these many ways, the CCP demonstrates its unwillingness to tolerate any threat to political stability.

In anticipation of the June 4 anniversary of the Tiananmen Square protests, every year surveillance by uniformed and plainclothes police increases on college campuses and public spaces where protests are likely to occur, internet traffic slows to a crawl, groups are monitored even more closely, and restaurants are warned not to host parties. The international Labor Day (May 1) and the National Day anniversary of the founding of the PRC (October 1) are also times of tightened security. The year 2019 was marked by such anniversaries: the hundredth anniversary of the May Fourth movement, in which nationalist protests turned into antigovernment protests; the seventieth anniversary of the founding of the PRC in 1949; the thirtieth anniversary of June 4. This string of anniversaries made for a particularly heightened sense of insecurity for the CCP, which was taken occasionally to a farcical extent, such as warning businesses and hotels not to hold meetings of more than fifty people. This might have curtailed the risk of protests, but it also impinged on the usual conduct of business, including sales and marketing meetings. That the CCP would go this far indicates how risk averse it has become to even the remotest possibility of dissent, protest, or instability.

In addition to anniversaries, the CCP treats major political, diplomatic, and international events as times for tightened security. For example, the National Party Congress, which meets every five years; the Central Committee, which meets once or twice per year; and the annual meetings of the National People's Congress are times of tight security in Beijing, as are visits by foreign leaders and events like the Beijing Olympics in 2008 and the Shanghai Expo in 2010. These sensitive days are important for protesters as well: some groups and activists avoid them so as to not embarrass the regime and trigger a crackdown, but others leverage these days as rare opportunities to press their cause, especially with the international media.[45]

Protests as Feedback

Given how obsessed the CCP is with maintaining stability, why does it allow protests at all? One reason concerns resources: the CCP simply lacks the capacity to preempt or repress all protests. Even if it did have sufficient manpower and equipment to stymie all protests, it would be costly to do so. It would be economically costly, and it would be politically costly: when protesters have legitimate grounds for protesting, the CCP risks stoking resentment by rejecting their demands. Local protests also serve as a pressure release valve, allowing citizens to air grievances instead of letting tensions fester and build and finally explode into public protest.

More importantly, protests provide information to high-level party and government leaders about conditions at the grass roots. [46] They indicate what problems may be emerging and if they are isolated events or indicative of more widespread problems that require their attention, as in the example about rural land grabs and urban housing demolitions noted above. They also provide information about incompetent, malfeasant, or corrupt leaders who need to be replaced. The CCP has historically lacked reliable institutions for monitoring its local leaders, except in episodic anticorruption campaigns that are costly and disruptive. Although local officials do their best to suppress protests in order to maintain stability, and to prevent negative news from rising to higher levels, protests, paradoxically, also provide a rare form of feedback about public opinion at the local level.

Allowing some protests to occur also provides information to potential future protesters about what kinds of demands and rhetoric will be tolerated, thereby limiting the scope of the protests. But this willingness to allow protests to gather information is conditional: the grievances have to be serious, not raise political issues that would challenge the CCP, and not provide a precedent that encourages other groups to mobilize. Protests may be a costly way to gather feedback, but to the CCP they are preferable to other alternatives, such as free and fair elections that would require the CCP to be more accountable and might even threaten its hold on power.

Changes under Xi

Under Xi Jinping, the CCP's management of protests has changed in three significant ways, all of which involve more repression and less responsiveness.[47] First, the CCP has criminalized protests and claims against the state that occur outside official state-sanctioned institutions. NGOs and activists are no longer simply subject to sporadic harassment, such as being invited to tea and being confronted by hired thugs. In the past, NGOs and activists could cope with these kinds of intimidation by simply lying low or moving their offices to a new location. Under Xi, they are more likely to be arrested by police and public security agents and charged with specific crimes, such as disrupting stability or "picking quarrels and causing trouble." Their offices are then permanently and forcibly closed. After their arrests, they are often forced to make televised confessions, both to shame them and to warn others.

The second key change has been to rely more on preemptive repression rather than simply to react to events as they occur. For example, an attempt at launching a #MeToo movement in China was immediately repressed before it could get under way. A few accusations were made against prominent TV personalities and scholars, but the state intervened before the movement could pick up steam, in part by censoring online discussion.[48] A group known as the "feminist five" who wanted to publicize sexual harassment were arrested in 2018 and charged with "illegal assembly" before they were able to hold protests. Although their mission—against harassment and for women's equality—was in line with the CCP's ideology, they represented a bottom-up movement and coordinated their actions in several major cities, both red lines for the CCP, especially under Xi.[49] The state has also moved against existing groups to prevent their making new claims. Feminist groups that had been sponsored by universities and other organizations have been forced to close when those affiliations were severed and they could not find new places to open their offices.[50] A prominent women's group, Feminine Voices, had its online Weibo account shut down on March 9, 2018—the day after International Women's Day. The group's founder speculated it was being punished for publicizing the #MeToo allegations.[51]

The third key change concerns the state's framing of protests and activism. In the past, they were characterized as threats to stability; under Xi, they are described as threats to national security. In April 2013, soon after Xi became CCP general secretary, the CCP issued a secret, internal document known as Document 9 that described a variety of political and social topics as Western influences that were a threat not only to the CCP but to the Chinese nation. Viewed this way, civil society groups are not just an everyday nuisance and a threat to social stability but also ideological, existential threats with foreign influences. NGOs that receive foreign funding now have to disclose that information. This has had the effect of shutting off China's NGOs from foreign sources of financial and logistical support. In many ways, this is a greater threat to their continued operations than the more repressive tactics they also face: without funding, they cannot survive.[52] Activists used to be able to find sympathetic allies in China's fragmented party and government bureaucracies, but officials are less willing to help activists when they are characterized by the CCP as threats to national security.

In all three ways, the CCP is making it clear that it is less tolerant of bottom-up social mobilization. It is not willing to tolerate even some groups that espouse the CCP's traditional ideology. Students at several universities in Beijing, Guangzhou, and Nanjing formed Marxist groups to promote the interests of workers. Some took leaves of absence from school in order to work in China's factories. Others held rallies outside enterprises calling for better working conditions and the right to unionize. All this would seem to be in keeping with the CCP's line, and indeed similar to the CCP's actions in the pre-1949 period. However, these actions were taken without the CCP's leadership, and the Marxist groups did not support the party's new priorities of fostering growth and maintaining stability. Under Hu Jintao, these groups probably would have been tolerated and perhaps even encouraged because Hu was trying to balance growth with equity, offering more protection to China's poor and disadvantaged. In contrast, under Xi they have been suppressed and their leaders arrested or simply disappeared, presumably into state custody but not yet formally charged. After their arrests, four leaders of the Marxist student groups made televised confessions that included apologies to students and workers for their actions and beliefs. They also claimed to have received foreign funding for their groups, an admission that turned their prolabor positions into national security threats.[53] This represents the turn toward a national security framing under Xi. The crackdown on these Marxist student groups may seem perplexing, since the CCP still pays lip service to Marxism, but it is also not too surprising. Xi does not tolerate criticisms of the party's line by anyone—even Marxists.

The CCP under Xi has relied almost exclusively on repression to manage protests, but the turn to repressive tactics began before Xi took over. The shift can be traced back to the months leading up to the 2008 Olympics in Beijing, when the CCP began cracking down on dissidents, activists, NGOs, underground churches, and others it deemed to be potential threats. This was a rare moment when the foreign media and international audiences would be focused on Beijing, and the CCP wanted to preempt any hint of protest. Although it had agreed to let individuals and groups apply for licenses to hold demonstrations, in the end none was approved. The message coming out of the Olympics was that China was strong and united, not driven by disputes. Who was in charge of managing the Olympics? None other than Xi Jinping, at that time newly promoted into the Politburo Standing Committee and heir apparent to become CCP general secretary and president. His handling of the games and the repressive tactics used to stifle protests was a foreshadowing of what he would do once he became CCP leader in 2012.

Although the CCP has taken further repressive and legalistic action under Xi, it has also continued to encourage participation through sanctioned channels, such as petitions, the courts, and the official mass organizations such as the All-China Federation of Trade Unions and the All-China Women's Federation. These channels have become more important under Xi, precisely because the CCP is now less tolerant of unsanctioned public protests outside authorized channels.[54] However, these channels are not very effective for making claims against the state or employers and therefore are less likely to satisfy the demands of protesters. By channeling participation in this way, the CCP under Xi is increasing the likelihood that protesters will find their appeals rejected or unenforced. This may successfully maintain stability in the short run, but the accumulation of unresolved and even unexpressed grievances may result in greater instability in the long run.

The Impact of the Internet

The internet is often seen as a tool with which a disenchanted society can challenge an oppressive state. In China, online activism has been described as part of the long revolution that is unfolding as social, political, and cultural values undergo change.[55] Even though citizens cannot mobilize on behalf of regime change, netizens may be able to use the relative safety of the internet to do so. But just as netizens learn how to express their opinions and meet kindred spirits online, authoritarian states have learned how to manage the internet to protect their regimes and isolate their critics.[56] It is a cat-and-mouse game without a clear winner.

Rather than see the internet in China pitting a monolithic and repressive state against a liberal society, it is important to recognize that both state and society are fragmented. As explained in chapter 3, the state is fragmented vertically, in the sense that central and local governments have different priorities and therefore different strategies—in this case, for managing the internet—and fragmented horizontally, with different parts of the government (such as propaganda, public security, and economic development) viewing the internet in quite different ways. Similarly, Chinese netizens hold diverse views and interests. They are as quick to challenge each other as they are the state. Conservatives and liberals challenge the integrity and patriotism of each other. Conservatives and nationalists dismiss liberals as unpatriotic and dupes of the West. Liberals see conservatives as apologists for the regime. There are few heroes on the Chinese internet, no one who enjoys broad public support, and certainly no one who represents a political opposition with a wide following.[57] For those who are waiting for regime change in China, this conclusion will come as a big disappointment.

The number of internet users in China has grown dramatically, from 22.5 million in 2000 to 854 million in 2020. This constitutes 59.3 percent of the total population, lower than the United States (almost 90 percent) but in line with the global average of 59.6 percent.[58] With that many people online, the CCP simply cannot monitor each and every one of them. At any given time, there are numerous critical comments online about the CCP and its policies, some direct and some oblique. These criticisms are occasionally censored but are often allowed to remain. What the CCP cares most about are online attempts to organize street protests or public demonstrations. CCP sees these types of collective action as particularly threatening and is much more likely to censor them and punish the people involved.[59]

The CCP's internet censorship practices are referred to as the Great Firewall. Like the Great Wall itself, it is able to block most efforts to climb over it but cannot stop those who are most determined to jump over. Entire websites are unavailable in China, including Google, YouTube, Facebook, the *New York Times*, and other social and news media the CCP wants to block. The only way to access them while behind the Great Firewall is by using a VPN, but even that option is now heavily restricted in China. This approach has drawbacks: it has the potential to annoy people who are not engaged in antiregime activities but are paying the costs of censorship anyway. An American student told me a story from when she was studying at a university in northeast China. Her Chinese roommate asked if she could borrow her laptop when she went out because the Chinese student was not allowed to use a VPN. However, with access to the global web, the Chinese roommate did not read the *New York Times* or CNN, look for information about Tiananmen, communicate with prodemocracy activists, or do anything the CCP would be worried about. Instead she watched makeup videos on YouTube because she wanted to start her own website about doing makeup and was looking for other examples. This shows how the CCP's censorship policies have the potential to backfire by infringing on people who pose no danger to it.

Besides blocking websites, the CCP's Propaganda Department regularly issues directives about names, events, and topics that cannot be discussed in the media or online. These can include such things as June 4, the names of dissidents, or breaking news about natural disasters or political scandals.[60] Censors can use algorithms to scan the web for key terms, but netizens have ways of avoiding these scans, using euphemisms and homonyms. For example, netizens used "Winnie the Pooh" as a code name for Xi Jinping because of their physical resemblance—at least, until censors picked up on the practice and banned it.

Given the CCP's desire to control the flow of information, it is no surprise that China's internet service providers are state-owned telecoms. However, China's content providers are typically privately owned companies, including Sina, which owns Weibo; Tencent, which owns WeChat, the most popular social media in China; and Alibaba, the world's largest e-commerce company. Although privately owned, they abide by the CCP's censorship policies in order to avoid its censure, including fines, public criticism of their business practices, investigation of their finances, and (at the extreme) being shut down altogether.[61] In this sense, the CCP has outsourced censorship to these private companies, relieving itself of the burden and expense of monitoring and censoring the ever-growing number of internet users.

The CCP also ensures the cooperation of China's internet companies by co-opting their leaders. Like many of China's large private firms, the heads of China's internet companies are closely tied to the CCP. For

FIGURE 5.3. Winnie the Pooh and his real-life counterpart Xi Jinping
(left: *Art of Drawing* / Alamy Stock Photo; right: Peter Probst / Alamy Stock Photo)

instance, Jack Ma, the founder of Alibaba and at one time China's richest individual, is a "red capitalist," a capitalist who also is a member of the CCP.[62] Ma Huateng (often referred to as Pony Ma), the founder and CEO of Tencent, belongs to the local People's Congress in Shenzhen and is a delegate to the National People's Congress. Robin Li, cofounder and CEO of Baidu, China's most popular search engine, is a member of the Chinese People's Political Consultative Conference, a largely honorific body made up of economic and social elites supportive of the CCP.

In addition to direct censorship, the CCP uses friction and flooding to deter Chinese citizens from accessing what the CCP sees as sensitive information.[63] Friction refers to the practice of slowing down the speed at which they load or intermittently blocking access to it. Flooding works differently: instead of directly censoring controversial or critical stories, the CCP floods the internet with lots of irrelevant news and proregime cheerleading. This makes it harder for people to find out about stories or events the CCP does not want them to know about. If you ever ignored reviews on Yelp or Amazon because you could not distinguish the genuine from the artificial, you have experienced how effective flooding can be.

Most internet users in China are not aware of the Great Firewall because they go online for innocuous reasons, as do Americans: they shop, watch videos, browse the news, and chat with friends. For these users, friction and flooding are largely effective. If the CCP throttles a website so it takes longer to load, the typical netizen in China will switch to a different website, not try to jump the firewall. If they want to get news about a current event, they will be inundated with lots of progovernment posts, making it hard to find the needle in the haystack of information.

Roughly 10 to 15 percent of Chinese internet users report encountering censorship online.[64] This is likely an underestimate. Given the CCP's strategy of friction and flooding, many internet users experience censorship without realizing it. Censorship rarely intimidates those who encounter it. Few react with fear or worry that they will be punished. More commonly they say it does not matter, either because they have ways of evading it or can switch to other websites for the information they seek. Some are angered by it, and criticize the censors rather than be scared into silence. When the designer of China's Great Firewall opened a Sina Weibo account, the criticism against him was so intense that he immediately closed the account.[65] Others respond with mockery and puns. The best-known example is the response to Hu Jintao's goal of creating a "harmonious society," which in part motivated the CCP's censorship efforts. Netizens responded with a "grass-mud horse" (which sounds similar to "f**k your mother") fighting a "river crab" (a homonym for "harmonious").[66] Videos and stories circulated online, T-shirts and other items were sold offline. Once the censors figured this out, they censored even this parody of censorship.

The "Fifty Cent Party" plays a key role in the flooding strategy, which involves a large but unknown number of people who are paid nominal amounts (fifty Chinese cents are equivalent to seven US cents) to post messages to counter online criticism.[67] Rather than debate critics of CCP leaders, policies, and programs, or persuade other readers with an alternative argument, the Fifty Cent Party simply floods the Chinese internet with positive propaganda, patriotic slogans, and irrelevant information. There are other, unpaid netizens who challenge regime critics, not because they are paid to do so but because they adamantly disagree with the critics' views.

Divisions within China's online communities allow the CCP to manage the internet in ways that prevent it from being solely a source of criticism and opposition. Through its direct and indirect forms of censorship, it has also found ways to make the internet a potential source of regime stability.

The Significance of Political Protest in Twenty-First-Century China

Do protests in China threaten political stability, or even regime survival? That certainly seems to be the fear of the CCP, especially under Xi Jinping. But this fear seems overwrought for several reasons. First of all, in the years since 1989, when peaceful protests were brought to a violent and tragic end, there has been no broad-based, nationwide movement promoting political change. Instead, the growing number of protests since then have been about local and material issues, which are easier to resolve and contain. They are ad hoc protests about specific events and grievances, and not indicative of broader political ambitions. At least so far, there is greater interest in responsiveness than accountability.

A second reason is related to the first: there seems little popular support for political change, much less democracy in China. Indeed, most Chinese believe that democratization has already been under way throughout the post-Mao era. However, they define "democracy" not in terms of elections, rule of law, and other institutional arrangements, but in terms of the state governing in the public's interests. (The meaning of democracy in China is explored further in chapter 8.)[68] The protests in China have little or nothing to do with democracy or political change, and need not lead to wider instability if handled properly.

The way in which protests are framed is a third reason in which protests need not threaten stability. Protesters often cite existing laws and regulations to justify their claims. Does rising rights consciousness indicate budding support for democracy? Will awareness of rights given by the regime lead people eventually to demand new rights and freedoms that restrict the regime's powers, leading ultimately to democratization? Or is rightful resistance more a tactical response, adopting the regime's rhetoric to make demands seem less threatening? In other words, does it indicate that protesters are aware of their rights, or simply aware of the rules of the game they need to play by? Both sides in the "rightful resistance" debate agree that protests utilizing the state's rhetoric to enforce rights promised but not delivered are not intended to overthrow the regime and may not even be indicative of protodemocratic attitudes in the making.[69] In fact, compromising with rightful resisters may legitimate the regime by making small concessions seem like big victories.[70]

The growing numbers of local protests and their increasing assertiveness may be part of the reason for the CCP's more repressive tactics. Although these kinds of local protests have not coalesced into a broader social movement, they have the potential to do so. Indeed, efforts to link efforts across multiple cities have occurred but are quickly suppressed as soon as they are discovered. Scholars have been watching for a fundamental value shift, the point where the gap between what people come to expect and what the CCP is willing to provide becomes so extreme that political change becomes more likely. Scholars have found scant evidence of this so far, but the CCP is undoubtedly looking for such a shift as well.

The Arab Spring of 2011 also holds an important lesson for the CCP: an isolated and seemingly insignificant protest can suddenly and rapidly snowball into a social revolution that can destabilize authoritarian regimes and even depose their leaders. The Arab Spring was triggered by a female police officer in Tunisia who slapped a street vendor, confiscated his scale, and overturned his cart; he, in turn, angered at having his livelihood threatened and humiliated by being slapped by a woman in public, set himself on fire and died several days later of his injuries, becoming a symbol of helpless citizens against an unaccountable regime. His death triggered protests that soon spread throughout the Middle East and North Africa, toppling leaders like Mubarak in Egypt and Qaddafi in Libya, overthrowing the regime in Tunisia, and producing civil war in Syria and Libya. For risk-averse leaders, the preferred response to protest is to clamp down rather than address the underlying tensions and sentiments that give rise to revolutionary movements. Chairman Mao famously wrote that a single spark can start a prairie fire, alluding to the potential for unexpected events to spark a revolution. The CCP rose to power following this strategy. It does not want to be the victim of the same strategy in the hands of others. Whereas the CCP used to follow the "fire alarm" model, responding to discontent once it exploded into view, it now aims to reduce the political "oxygen" that activists and NGOs need to survive, thereby preventing a spark from becoming a firestorm.

By shutting off the potential for protest, the CCP under Xi is also closing down an important source of information about public discontent.[71] In the past, the CCP used bottom-up mobilization to reveal problems in policy implementation and law enforcement and about corrupt and malfeasant local officials. It responded to this information in various ways: by adopting new laws and policies or revising existing ones; by replacing local officials who were rightly targeted by these protests; by conceding to NIMBY disputes; and by making compromises on demands for unpaid wages and pensions, unsafe working conditions, inadequate compensation for confiscated land and housing, and similar material demands. In each of these ways, the goal was to reduce tensions between the party and the people. Xi seems not to trust information that percolates up from below, preferring instead to rely on the CCP's own institutions to monitor local trends and local officials from above, to preempt protests rather than have to respond to them, and to label protesters and activists as criminals and threats to national security.

In the past, the CCP struck a rough balance between repression and responsiveness: it repressed direct threats to its legitimacy, while responding to other types of protests with concessions and compromises. Under Xi, however, it treats all protests as existential threats and overreacts to public signs of discontent by cracking down fast and hard. At the local level, excessive repression can lead to a backlash. Will a similar backlash arise when the center is no longer seen as a potential ally against local officials and now is orchestrating the repression? This is the risk of relying exclusively on repression to manage protest.

Without well-functioning feedback mechanisms, organizations decline.[72] This is particularly true for monopolies, which do not have to be better than competitors to survive, and it applies to organizations of all kinds: firms, parties, even states that ignore—or are unaware of—signs of trouble until it is too late. The CCP has a monopoly on political organization in China. Under Xi, it is resistant to feedback of all sorts, but does so at its peril. In the short run, it may suppress real and perceived threats, but in the long run those threats will fester and grow until they can no longer be contained. As the sudden collapse of communist regimes in the Soviet Union and Eastern Europe demonstrated, communist parties appear to be invincible until they are not, and their demise can be surprisingly quick. If the CCP hopes to avoid that fate, it—and most of all Xi—will need to return to responding and adapting to the public's discontent.

6

WHY DOES THE PARTY
FEAR RELIGION?

Beijing's Shouwang church is one of China's largest and best-known "house churches," unregistered churches that often meet in people's homes.[1] Because it is not officially registered with the government, it has faced continual challenges in holding worship services. In May 2008, the local Beijing government announced a new ban on "illegal" worship services, meaning those that took place outside official sanctioned churches. Government officials and police broke up a Shouwang worship service and recorded names and ID numbers. Church members soon began receiving threatening phone calls at home and work. Local officials began pressuring the church's landlord to revoke its lease. He refused because the rent was prepaid, but he did not renew the lease when it expired in October 2009.

Unable to renew their lease or find other appropriate indoor space for worship gatherings, church leaders announced they would worship outdoors. An estimated four hundred worshippers attended the first outdoor service in November 2009.[2] The second week, the crowd was even larger, even though the church's pastor was prevented from leaving his house and police used loudspeakers and megaphones to disrupt the service.

The issue got enough press coverage to attract the attention of the CCP's general secretary at the time, Hu Jintao. He stepped in to achieve what the local government had failed to do: end the public dispute with the Shouwang church. Hu offered to let Shouwang worship indoors in a facility owned by CCTV, the official state television station; if they persisted in worshipping outdoors, he would send in thousands of riot police to forcibly stop them. The Shouwang leaders agreed to this arrangement. For the next several months, the Shouwang church held its weekly worship services in the government building Hu Jintao had provided.

Local officials were stung by Hu's intervention and the implication that they had been unable to fulfill their duties. They waited until central leaders were no longer monitoring the case, and then moved in. In spring 2011, they forced Shouwang out of their government-supplied space and warned nearby landlords not to rent to the church. Shouwang thereupon resumed its outdoor services. This time, local officials were better prepared. Again they prevented the church's pastor from leaving his house, and now also arrested church members as they left their houses, as well as the few who were able to get past police barricades to the place of worship.

For years after, church leaders remained under house arrest each weekend. Shouwang continued to communicate with its members via the church's website (which was moved to overseas servers to escape government censors). Some members grew tired of the constant pressure and split off to form a new church, but others continued in smaller Bible study groups. During a new wave of repression against unregistered churches, Beijing government officials broke up a Shouwang Bible study meeting in March 2019, announced the church would be closed, and took worshippers to a nearby school for questioning.

The example of Shouwang illustrates several prominent themes about religion in contemporary China. First, the CCP does not have a uniform policy toward religion. It recognizes some, tolerates others, and suppresses still others. Moreover, the boundaries between recognition, tolerance, and suppression have varied over time and in different parts of the country at any given time. Second, religious policy in China includes both formal institutions and informal practices. In the post-Mao era, there was a general relaxation in religious policy, but there has been a tightening under Xi Jinping. The CCP under Xi is trying to funnel all types of political and social activities into state-sanctioned institutions, and that is also the case for religion. But many worshippers resist worshipping where, when, and how the CCP mandates. Third, just as local officials variably recognize, tolerate, and suppress different religious groups, those groups in turn resist, avoid, and cooperate with the CCP's policies. Finally, "house" church can be a misnomer. While some house churches are quite small, others like Shouwang have more than one thousand members and worship not in private homes but in their own buildings or rented office space—sometimes rented from the local government.

The CCP requires its leaders and members to be atheists, but it recognizes that many Chinese are religious. To allow them to practice their faiths and, just as important, to monitor how religious individuals and organizations operate, the CCP provides an official framework in which religion is practiced. It recognizes only five religions—Buddhism, Taoism, Protestantism, Catholicism (Protestantism and Catholicism are treated as separate religions, not two varieties of Christianity), and Islam. (The specific cases of Tibetan Buddhists and the Muslim Uighurs in Xinjiang will be covered in more detail in the next chapter.) It has established official churches, temples, and mosques and supervisory bodies for each of these faiths. However, there are also unofficial and even underground groups that also are a part of the religious landscape in China, and some of them have informal ties to the official bodies.

Just as China's civil society organizations can be distinguished into different types (see chapter 4), we can say that China has three distinct types of religious organizations: one that is officially recognized (red), one for banned religious groups (black), and one for those that operate in between, neither officially recognized nor banned but mostly tolerated (gray).[3] Indeed, in the post-Mao period, much of the growth in religion, especially Christianity, is happening in this informal, loosely defined gray area.

This chapter will emphasize the varied experience of religion, religious policy, and religious believers in China. While the party has employed unnecessarily harsh treatment of some groups and believers, it does not repress all groups and does not persecute all believers. Instead, religious policy and practice exists along a continuum, with official rec-ognition on one end, outright prohibition on the other, and various degrees of tolerance and even cooperation in between. To understand the complexity and contradictions of the party's policy toward religion, it is necessary to examine trends over time, in different parts of the country, different religions, and even different groups within the same religion.

The Administration of Religion in China

The combination of faith and politics makes the CCP wary of religion, for both historical and contemporary reasons. The Chinese state has historically had a tempestuous relationship with religion. Christian in-fluences were part of large-scale rebellions in modern Chinese history.[4] The Taiping Rebellion, which lasted from 1850 to 1864, was led by Hong Xiuquan, who claimed to be the younger brother of Jesus. At its peak, the Taipings governed 30 million people and controlled much of south-ern China. By the time the rebellion ended, tens of millions of Chinese had died and millions more were displaced from their homes.

The Boxer Rebellion of 1899–1901 targeted Christian missionaries and other foreign influences in China. In response, an eight-nation alliance of Western countries, Russia, and Japan sent troops to fight the Chinese Imperial Army, which supported the Boxers, and defended their citizens living in China. Once the rebellion and the Imperial Army were defeated, the Chinese government agreed to extensive reparations to the foreign countries to pay for the damages to their properties in China.

In more contemporary times, the CCP is aware that religion has con-tributed to regime change in other countries. Catholic and Protestant churches helped trigger democratization in the Philippines, South Korea, Taiwan, Brazil, and elsewhere. In particular, the church played an important role in the demise of communism in Eastern Europe, es-pecially in Poland.[5] The CCP wants to avoid the interplay of domestic and international forces—in this case religion—that can challenge, un-dermine, and potentially overthrow authoritarian regimes like China's.

After the CCP took power in 1949, it established quasi-governmental associations to manage the five recognized (or "red") religions: the China Protestant Three-Self Patriotic Movement (TSPM),[6] the Chinese Catholic Patriotic Association (CPA), the China Buddhist Association, the China Islamic Association, and the China Taoist Association. These associations were disbanded during the Cultural Revolution when the CCP outlawed all religious organizations and activities, but were revived in the post-Mao period. They are tasked with ensuring conformity on doctrinal and theological matters and reining in diversity by, among other things, training priests and pastors, organizing worship services, and restricting the contents of sermons.

The CCP recognizes only these five religions. The TSPM also eliminated denominations in 1957. Whereas separate Presbyterian, Methodist, Lutheran, and other Protestant denominations had churches in China before 1949, they all became simply Protestant after 1957. Today, many unregistered and house churches are affiliated with the traditional denominations, but the official TSPM is still nondenominational. The CCP does not recognize other prominent religions, including Orthodox Christianity, Judaism, Mormonism, and Baha'i.

The CCP does not include Confucianism as a religion, even though it is the most prominent philosophical and cultural tradition in China and the rest of East Asia. Strictly speaking, it does not have the common features of a religion: it does not recognize a deity, lacks a creation story, and does not offer the promise of an afterlife. However, it does provide extensive rules for governing the country and for managing social and familial relationships, and these rules are based on firm moral principles. Confucianism was also the basis for ancestor worship (an extension of filial piety), which provided some idea of an afterlife: people burn paper money so their dead ancestors will have money to spend, offer food and drink so they have nourishment, and seek their help in dealing with life's challenges. These rules are of human origin and not divinely inspired. Confucius was a historical figure, as were Mencius and others who made important contributions to the Confucian tradition. Their philosophy was derived not from study of religious doctrine but from practical lessons of public life. During the post-Mao period, the CCP has gradually begun again to embrace Confucianism as it tries to tie its legitimacy to Chinese traditions and not simply Marxism-Leninism, but it does not treat it as a religion.

As noted throughout this book, China's political system is not monolithic. The variety of party and government organs involved in most policy areas have overlapping jurisdictions. This feature of China's political system gave rise to the fragmented authoritarian model of policy making described in chapter 3. This is also the case with religious policy. There are different formal institutions by which the CCP manages religion.[7] First of all, its United Front Work Department is in charge of the CCP's interactions with nonparty groups, including religious organizations and religious leaders.[8] It is involved in publicizing religious policy and limits on religious activities; relations with religious organizations; management of property used by churches, temples, and other religious groups; and also the training and management of religious personnel.

In addition to the CCP's United Front Work Department, the government has its own organs for managing religion. At the central level, the State Administration for Religious Affairs (SARA) is part of the State Council, China's cabinet.[9] SARA includes departments and centers that produce research on religious affairs and provide training. Throughout the post-Mao period, the government has promoted the "scientific" study of religion in order to improve knowledge about religious affairs.[10] At the local level, from the provincial to the grassroots level, there are religious affairs bureaus (RABs) that monitor religious activities. Although the SARA and local RABs have important responsibilities, they are not powerful actors in China's political system. SARA's leader has historically had lower standing than other government ministers and is even outranked by provincial and municipal party secretaries. It has the smallest staff and department size of all ministerial-level organizations. SARA also has very limited supervisory and oversight capacity over the local implementation of religious policy, which remains under the control of local officials.[11]

Finally, the CCP's management of religion is focused on security. China's public security apparatus is responsible for the monitoring and surveillance of house churches and informal religious groups. It is also part of the CCP's coercive approach to Xinjiang's Uighur Muslims and Tibetan Buddhists. For instance, in recent years the party secretaries in Xinjiang have come out of the public security system. Unlike SARA and the five religious associations, the public security bureaus at the central and local levels are among the most powerful bodies in the Chinese political system. Their main responsibility is the maintenance of political stability, and religion is one of the potential threats to stability that most concern party leaders.

The Resurgence of Religion in Post-Mao China

During the years of the Cultural Revolution (1966–76), religious believers were persecuted for engaging in religion, which was denounced as superstition. Temples, churches, and mosques were destroyed or converted into buildings for other purposes, such as storing grain in the countryside or schools and hospitals in the cities. Religion did not so much disappear as it went into hiding. The faithful still worshipped, but in secret. Some families and small groups of believers continued to worship in their homes. Others would retreat to remote areas, like woods and hills, where they were less likely to be detected.

Just as economies may grow rapidly after the ravages of war come to an end, religion grew in post-Mao China because the CCP was no longer trying so hard to eradicate it. What had been hidden during the upheavals of the Cultural Revolution was able to emerge from hiding as the CCP's policy toward religion softened.

How fast has religion grown? That simple question is hard to answer, for several reasons. First, the numbers vary widely, depending on the source. The PRC's official statistics on religiosity in China, based on membership in the officially recognized churches, are at the low end of estimates. By its count, in 2018 there were 38 million Protestants, 6 million Catholics, and 20 million Muslims. It does not report the numbers of Buddhists or Taoists because "it is difficult to accurately estimate their numbers as there are no set registration procedures which ordinary believers must follow as part of their religion."[12] At the other extreme are estimates from the World Religion Database, which in 2015 counted 125 million Christians (not separating out Protestants and Catholics), 23 million Muslims, and more than 222 million Buddhists.[13] In between are estimates from Freedom House: 185–250 million Buddhists, 58 million Protestants, 12 million Catholics, and 21 million Muslims in 2014.[14] These unofficial estimates try to count all religious believers, not just the ones in official temples, churches, and mosques.

The second reason the numbers vary so much is that reported numbers are not reliable. Local officials have the incentive to underreport the number of believers in order to improve their chances of promotion: the rapid growth of religious believers is seen as a potential threat to political stability. Even unofficial Protestant and Catholic churches do not keep accurate records of their members (including baptisms) in order to protect their safety.

A third reason the numbers on religious believers vary so widely is related to another difficult question: What does it mean to be religious? Repeated studies in China have found that many people admit to doing religious practices, but few admit to belonging to a religion. This is particularly the case when counting Buddhists and Taoists: people are more likely to practice these religions informally and privately, without belonging to formal institutions. According to data from the World Values Survey, China has the lowest levels of religiosity among the countries in the survey.[15] The survey measured religiosity as belonging to a religious organization; attending religious services other than weddings, funerals, and christenings; and whether a person is an atheist, nonreligious person, or religious person. But many people engaged in religious practices even though they did not identify with an organized religion. These religious practices include consulting fortune-tellers, geomancy (feng shui), burning incense, burning paper money for ancestors, and other forms of ancestor worship. Given this discrepancy between religious identity and religious practice, it may well be that "China is a godless country with a temple on every corner."[16]

Other studies found similar levels of religious practices without religious identities. A study by Horizon, a well-known survey firm in China, found that 85 percent of respondents engaged in religious practices or had religious beliefs, but did not necessarily claim to be religious or belong to a religion.[17] They consult fortune-tellers to find an auspicious date for weddings and other significant events. They consult with feng shui masters to determine where to build a house or furnish a room or office. Students light candles or burn incense for "good luck" before a test. A study by China's State Administration College found that the majority of party and government officials engaged in similar practices.[18] But are these really religious practices, or more akin to superstitious behavior, like carrying a lucky coin or rabbit's foot? Without knowing where to draw the line, it is difficult to get an accurate count of religious believers in China.

While an accurate count may be difficult to obtain, there is, however, general agreement that the number of religious believers in China is growing. This is in sharp contrast to the United States and other Western countries, where religious membership has been declining steadily for decades. But even though the number of religious believers in China may be growing rapidly, it is starting from a very low base following the persecution of the Maoist years. And even though the numbers are growing, as a share of China's population they are still quite small. In a variety of public opinion polls, roughly 15 percent of respondents claim to have any sort of religious faith. This is a very small percentage, but given China's enormous population (1.4 billion), even a relatively small percentage means a lot of people: 15 percent of China's current population translates to 210 million people. By way of comparison, the CCP has roughly 90 million members and is growing (by design) much more slowly.

Why is religion growing in China? Some reasons have to do with state initiatives, others with societal and individual factors. Put differently, there has been an increase in both the supply of and demand for religion, as explained in the following sections.

The Evolution of the Party's Policy toward Religion

As the CCP launched its economic reforms, the opportunity to practice religion increased because the political environment itself became more open. When the CCP grew concerned over potential threats to its hold on power, it narrowed the space for religion. However, local practice often deviated from central policy, as will be explained below.

The PRC constitution adopted in 1982 states that "Citizens of the People's Republic of China enjoy freedom of religious belief" (Article 36). But that article went on to reveal the limits of religious freedom in China: "No one may make use of religion to engage in activities that disrupt public order, impair the health of citizens or interfere with the educational system of the State." This established the constraints in which religion operates in China.

Also, in 1982, the CCP announced a new policy toward religion, spelled out in what became known as Document 19. This new policy acknowledged that even though the CCP remained committed to atheism and its basic task was still to build a modern socialist country, it would provide more space for religious belief and practices. At the same time, the coexistence of religion with the CCP was predicated on the principle of "love country, love religion" (with religion notably in second place). All religions should be self-managing but also comply with the CCP: "All patriotic religious organizations should accept the leadership of the party and government."[19]

The CCP's policy toward religion evolved in later years, and not always in a consistent fashion.[20] In the early 1990s, after the 1989 demonstrations in Tiananmen Square and elsewhere around China, and after Catholic and Protestant churches contributed to the collapse of communist regimes in Eastern Europe, the CCP grew more concerned about the security implications of religious groups. But in 1993, then-general secretary Jiang Zemin asserted that religion was compatible with socialism. However, the next year the CCP issued a new set of restrictions on the religious activities of foreigners and the registration of religious venues, reflecting its intent to continue its somewhat contradictory policy of both encouraging and controlling religion.

During the years when Hu Jintao was general secretary (2002–12), the CCP tried to institutionalize religious policy and practice. The "Regulations on Religious Affairs" released in 2005 state that religious activities could occur only at fixed places of worship, implicitly targeting the growing number of unregistered house churches.[21] They granted religious communities increasing autonomy and authority over the management of their internal affairs, as part of a broader systemic effort of the Chinese government to redefine state-society relations.[22] They also hinted at the possibility that unregistered house churches could officially register without joining the official Three-Self Patriotic Movement (TSPM). However, local officials did not implement the regulations this way. When Beijing's Shouwang church sought to register without joining the TSPM in 2006, its application was rejected.[23] The ultimate goal of the new regulations was to standardize religious policy, not to allow religious freedom.

The CCP took a somewhat softer approach toward religion in "Decisions on Major Issues of Building a Socialist Harmonious Society," issued in 2006. Among other things, this document called on religious believers to play a positive role in promoting social harmony. It signaled that the CCP was becoming being more open-minded and practical about religious groups and was seeking a better relationship with the growing numbers of Chinese religious believers. Religious leaders quickly adopted the language of "harmonious society" to show that religion was compatible with CCP priorities.[24] Protestant pastors—both in TSPM and house churches—drew on Bible passages about harmony in their sermons, especially when they knew RAB officials were present. Adopting official rhetoric and linking it to religious traditions sends the message that religion is compatible with regime goals. This is especially important for "foreign" religions like Christianity and Islam, but even the favored Buddhists are willing to cooperate in this way. The phrase was featured prominently at the First World Buddhist Forum, held in Beijing in 2006.

Chinese Pentecostal and charismatic churches (a large portion of unregistered churches) often promote a strongly patriotic message.[25] Pastors offer blessings and prayers for the country and its leaders, as well as broader themes of national development and economic modernization; they use social media to express the patriotism of church and religious leaders in order to convey the message that they do not pose a threat to the state, society, or other Protestant churches; and they engage in community-based charity work (including social welfare, poverty alleviation, and disaster relief), downplaying their religiosity while emphasizing their civic-mindedness. These types of patriotic messages and actions are designed to show that Christians are productive and patriotic citizens, which in turn allows leaders to strengthen their churches' work and improve the negative image they have among party and government officials and mainstream society. Within the churches, these patriotic messages may also help the churches grow by appealing to the patriotic sentiments that are prominent in society at large.

The emphasis on economic growth during the post-Mao period also gave local officials an incentive to cooperate with religious organizations. Some local officials have supported the repair and renovation of religious sites in order to boost tourism and solicit foreign investment. Especially on holidays, Buddhist temples and other religious sites can be packed with both the religious faithful and domestic and international tourists (some believers, others just curious), and these crowds provide revenue for local government coffers.[26] Local governments benefit from religious tourism by taking a share of entrance fees and taxes on vendors at religious sites. They also benefit from the ripple effects of tourism: extra business for hotels, restaurants, tour guides, and taxis, all of which create jobs and produce tax revenue.

The Buddhist Nanputuo temple is located in the southeast coastal city of Xiamen, directly across from Taiwan.[27] Like other religious sites, it was shut down during the Cultural Revolution and its property was used for a factory and school. In the post-Mao period, the temple was restored and reopened for both religious activities and tourists. By 2001, the temple was the home of more than six hundred clerics. It trained a new generation of young, well-educated monks to replace the elderly and often illiterate monks who had been with the temple before the Cultural Revolution. It attracts thousands of domestic and international visitors, especially at the times of Buddhist holidays and festivals. Officials in both Beijing and Xiamen saw Nanputuo's potential to attract financial investments and political support from overseas Chinese in Taiwan and Southeast Asia. In fact, Nanputuo was so successful at earning money from religious rites and running small businesses, including a vegetarian restaurant and souvenir shop, that conflicts inevitably

FIGURE 6.1. Holiday crowds at Nanputuo Temple
(photo: Imaginechina Limited/Alamy Stock Photo)

emerged between the temple, the local Buddhist Association, and the local RAB. These conflicts were resolved only with the intervention of higher-level Buddhist Association officials and the death of the head abbot at Nanputuo, which allowed the local RAB to appoint a new abbot and to separate the leadership of the temple and the local Buddhist Association. Nanputuo shows both the acceptance of religion by central and local officials as well as the inherent tensions between material interests and spiritual beliefs.

Religious groups that provide financial revenue to the local government are treated more leniently than those that do not. Temples and other sites associated with folk religion are not able to register as religious sites, because folk religion is not one of the five officially recognized religions, but they can register as cultural heritage sites.[28] For example, a local government near Shanghai supports a folk religion that has links to forty-nine stone bridges which have become sites for tourism and pilgrimage. At the same time, the same local government has periodically cracked down on Protestant churches, temples, and qigong groups that are part of the same community.[29]

A district government south of Shanghai rebuilt a temple in order to attract tourists and investments. They succeeded: a wealthy Taiwanese businessman helped pay for the temple's restoration. However, the temple was not registered with the local RAB as a place of worship, only as a museum. The same government agreed to build and restore a mosque but registered it as a museum to attract more tourists. The mosque's imam and the local Islamic Association agreed to this arrangement because they had no other way to pay to renovate the temple, which was then used for both worship and tourism.[30]

At the local level, cooperation between government and religious organizations—both formal and informal—can be mutually beneficial. Religious groups can establish businesses (typically small in scale) that generate taxable income for the government. As noted in chapter 2, local officials are expected to produce economic growth and especially tax revenue in order to be promoted. Local governments are therefore more likely to tolerate churches when their affiliated businesses and factories feed the local economy and in turn advance their career prospects.[31] Some factories double as unregistered churches with worship services on evenings and weekends. In China it is common for large enterprises to provide dorms, dining halls, clinics, and shops for their workers, and it is easy to add a church to this mix of buildings without drawing the attention of local officials. Some local officials even offer new churches to lure new investments. For example, when local officials in Shanghai, Beijing, Chengdu, and Tianjin were seeking new factories from the Semiconductor Manufacturing International Corporation (SMIC), a large firm based in Taiwan, they agreed to provide a TSPM church to the new SMIC factories where workers and managers could worship without leaving factory grounds.[32]

Local officials also benefit from the philanthropic work of religious organizations. By providing aid to the poor and needy, these organizations lighten some of the burden on local governments to provide social welfare services and allow them to devote scarce resources to

other projects. For example, religious organizations often open and operate orphanages, hospitals, and institutions for the severely disabled. They
provide relief following natural disasters, such as earthquakes and floods.
Some even get involved in infrastructure projects, such as building roads
to isolated villages. Religious groups can also improve their relations
with local officials by contributing to state-sponsored charities and welfare organizations. Because these donations are often made public, both
the donors and the local officials have political incentives to make and
receive large donations.[33] While many contribute to community philan-
thropy and relief efforts, some house church pastors are unwilling to
donate and volunteer in the name of their church in order to keep it away
from official scrutiny. They may contribute to look like good citizens, but
do not want to draw attention by publicly identifying as Christian.

Under Xi Jinping, however, the political atmosphere in general has
become more repressive and the CCP has pursued a more coercive and
politicized approach to religion.[34] There has been renewed pressure on
unregistered churches, as the example of Shouwang, above, shows. Xi
called for the "sinicization of religion" suggesting that Tibetan Buddhism, Islam, and especially Christianity are not indigenous to China
and should adopt "Chinese characteristics." This is part of Xi's general
crackdown on Western influences in China, as reflected in 2013's Document 9, which highlighted the dangers of Western ideas and influences.
It also reflects the CCP's goal of constraining ethnic identities among
its minority groups, after concluding that ethnic separatism contributed
to the demise of the Soviet Union.

The CCP has also reasserted and strengthened the regulatory framework for managing religion. "China's Policies and Practices on Protecting Freedom of Religious Belief," first enacted in 2005, was revised by
the State Council and put into effect in 2018. The revisions layered new
bureaucratic procedures on new construction and hiring of religious
leaders, commercial activities, and "religious extremism."[35] At the local
level, however, officials were slow to implement the new regulations and
Xi's goal of sinicizing religion. They dutifully used the slogans but did
not carry out the extremist actions that the revised regulations allowed.
They were also unsure how to put into practice Xi's strategy of

sinicization, which was long on rhetoric but short on concrete directions.[36] As noted in chapter 3, central policy is not always implemented immediately or fully at the local level in China.

One concrete manifestation of the new repression of religion was a wave of attacks on churches, temples, and mosques. In some cases, the suppression was complete: buildings were razed and religious leaders arrested. More commonly, only the visible symbols of religion were removed: crosses were taken down from atop churches and Buddhist statues were moved inside temples. Even the patriotic churches were not exempt from the crackdown: among the many churches whose crosses were removed were TSPM and CPA churches. The removal of crosses may be a local compromise between complying with central directives and allowing religious activities. As will be shown below, local officials are often willing to cooperate with local religious organizations, even unregistered ones, so long as they keep a low profile.

The Appeal of Religion in Contemporary China

The resurgence of religion in China was not just due to the CCP's policies and practices. New people are also being drawn to religion for other reasons. One has to do with the search for meaning in a rapidly changing world. With the decline of ideology, some people are seeking an alternative system of values to believe in. Rapid urbanization and industrialization have uprooted people from their traditional social networks (especially the millions of migrant workers). Religion is appealing to many Chinese because it provides comfort for the rapid and sometimes wrenching economic, political, and social changes in post-Mao China.[37] The unrelenting emphasis on material development—measured by growth in GDP, personal incomes, sales revenue, and so on—leads some Chinese to seek spiritual development by turning to religion, whether out of curiosity or conviction.

In the countryside, Protestant Pentecostalism has spread rapidly in provinces such as Henan and Anhui. Some rural Chinese found Pentecostalism, with its emphasis on miraculous healing, exorcism of demons, and prayers for good health and prosperity, an easy substitute for the folk religion they were used to.[38] For others, Christianity—especially mainstream Protestantism—is a symbol of modernity, a gateway to urban life for migrant workers from the countryside.

The equality that is at the heart of most religions can be appealing in China's otherwise very hierarchical political and social systems. Even language conveys countercultural mores, especially in Christian churches. Instead of being referred to as elder brother (*gege*) and younger brother (*didi*), or elder sister (*jiejie*) and younger sister (*mei-mei*), new visitors to churches in the coastal city of Wenzhou are greeted as simply brother (*xiongdi*) or sister (*zimei*), regardless of their age.[39] This can be refreshing for people who are new to the faith and/or seeking escape from the unrelenting political, economic, and social pressures in contemporary China.

Christianity's appeal as a modern and cosmopolitan set of beliefs and practices attracted political activists. Many of China's dissidents (including those in exile) and human rights lawyers have Christian backgrounds, either from their parents or themselves.[40] After the imposition of martial law in Tiananmen Square on June 4, 1989, many of the participants who escaped into exile explored Christianity. For some, it was a momentary phase in their search for modernity; for others, it was a source of spiritual solace following the violent and deadly end to a peaceful movement and led to a full religious conversion. Chai Ling, for example, was one of the more radical of the student leaders who fled China to escape the crackdown. After settling in the United States, receiving her MBA, and getting married, she converted to Christianity.[41]

Many of China's "rights defense" (*weiquan*) lawyers (so named because they defend clients whose rights have been violated) are Christian. This gives their political and legal goals an additional dimension: it is not just their political ideals that lead them to press for change; their religious faith provides an important impetus as well. These lawyers defend religious believers against state prosecution, even including groups banned as "evil cults," such as Falun Gong. Their faith also provides a rationale for the suffering they endure for their political activities. Gao Zhisheng was once identified by the Chinese government as one of China's top lawyers but was later imprisoned for his defense of religious freedom, including banned groups like Falun Gong. He converted to Christianity while defending a pastor charged with illegally possessing Bibles.

The evangelical zeal of Protestant preachers and congregants is another reason the numbers of Protestants have grown so rapidly in the post-Mao era. Whether in the countryside, in urban factories, or university campuses, Protestants have sought to share their faith with friends, family, and even strangers.[42] That is one reason why Protestantism has grown faster than Catholicism and Islam in China.

Informal Local Policies and Practices

Although formal organizations of the CCP and the government are used as tools to manage and control religion, the more common practice is informally to tolerate and work with religious groups. For much of the post-Mao reform era, the CCP relied more on persuasion than coercion to manage its religious affairs, but there has been a noticeable return of coercive practices under Xi Jinping. The CCP's goal is to minimize differences between nonbelievers and religious believers, so long as they accept the CCP's leadership.[43]

Most of the newly emerging Protestant and Catholic churches exist in a gray area, neither officially recognized nor outright prohibited. Local party and government officials allow them to operate as long as they follow certain understood but not explicitly stated rules.[44] First, they cannot take part in political activities. They cannot advocate democracy, either in public or from the pulpit, or other types of political reform, including the freedom of religion. Second, they must keep a low profile. Their congregations should be relatively small so they do not draw attention or complaints from their neighbors. As a consequence, many of them are based in office buildings that are otherwise vacant in the evenings and on weekends so that there is no one to complain about the music, singing, and numbers of people coming and going. Third, they should not have ties with other churches inside China or religious organizations outside China. The CCP is very suspicious of any group that is part of a broader network, especially those with foreign ties, because it fears they could be involved in political protests and other forms of collective action against the party. It is more willing to tolerate unregistered churches as long as they do not pose a direct threat to the party or to political stability.

This containment strategy allows local officials to avoid the extra costs associated with coercion, such as resources needed for surveillance and imprisonment. At a time when maintaining political stability is the top priority for the CCP, they also avoid the potential for public protests against more heavy-handed tactics. Because the CCP remains committed to atheism, local officials may not wish their superiors to realize that the numbers of local churches and their members continues to grow. The containment strategy keeps them off the radar.

The strategy is also cheaper than co-optation, the approach the CCP uses toward private entrepreneurs, intellectuals, and other elites. Co-optation entails bringing new groups into the party and the political system, including at least honorary appointments to local people's congresses and advisory bodies (such as the political consultative conferences that meet annually in tandem with the people's congresses) and creating formal organizations that give them easy access to party and government officials.[45]

Containment provides a cheaper alternative to coercion and co-optation, allowing local churches to exist and grow but always under the very watchful eye of the security apparatus. If church leaders violate any of the conditions that containment is based on—if they become political, if they become publicly visible, if they join together with other churches to pursue shared goals—local party and government leaders are prepared to adopt more coercive measures at any time.

The local containment strategy itself has a "divide and conquer" quality to it. Among house church leaders, there is a sharp divide between those who are willing to work with local leaders and those who feel that such behavior is a betrayal of religious principles. This creates mistrust and makes cooperation on collective goals much less likely—which, in the end, is a key goal of this strategy.[46] For leaders of "contained" churches, it also raises a dilemma: when they consent to containment, they indirectly reinforce the CCP regime.[47]

The Varying Experiences of Different Religions

The CCP uses a variety of formal institutions and informal practices to manage and control religion in general. There are also some that are specific to different religions.[48]

Protestantism

The CCP tries to control the spread of Protestantism by training pastors. It provides limited funding for national, regional, and provincial TSPM seminaries (and Bible schools).[49] The TSPM seminaries prefer younger students, who are believed to be more impressionable. Age barriers and the realities of job placement (and the prospect of a low salary or living in poverty as a pastor) have not decreased the number of applications. The TSPM and RABs use academic and political tests, as well as background checks, to narrow the pool of applications. After graduation, the RAB is closely involved in the appointment and promotion of TSPM personnel. With so few pastors, ordained church workers often lead smaller TSPM churches as assistant pastors/teachers and elders. The party restricts the number of seminaries to train new pastors, although many house churches run their own unofficial seminaries. (These unofficial seminaries often have ties to the official TSPM seminaries, and TSPM teachers will often teach in the unofficial seminaries.) It restricts education and training for new members and religious leaders, and officially bans Sunday school for children (although many house churches provide it). It restricts the publication, sale, and circulation of religious books and materials.

Just as the CCP has a varied strategy for dealing with religious groups, including recognizing, tolerating, and suppressing them, religious groups also have varied strategies for responding to the CCP, including resisting, cooperating, and avoiding.

The Shouwang church that opened this chapter is an example of a church resisting the CCP's formal institutions and informal practices. Shanghai's All Nations Missionary Church (known by its Chinese name, Wanbang) faced similar pressure. It enjoyed explosive growth in membership from a single Bible study group in 1999 to a congregation of three hundred in 2006 and to fifteen hundred by 2009. In addition to its size, Wanbang also violated another element of the containment strategy: the church's pastor organized a group of unregistered church leaders from around China and hosted a series of meetings of the group that grew from less than ten at its first meeting in 2007 to more than seventy in 2009. In order to avoid scrutiny from the international media that would accompany Obama to Shanghai in late 2009, local officials closed the church just before his visit.[50] They posted a sign on the locked doors saying services had been moved to another location, which turned out to be a TSPM church. Shanghai officials pressured congregants to quit the church: they made threatening phone calls and spread rumors that Wanbang was an illegal cult. These pressure tactics worked: within a few months, two-thirds of the members and half of the staff had left the church. The rest returned to small Bible study groups and did not worship as a full church.[51]

But not all large, unregistered churches choose to resist the CCP's efforts to control them; others choose to cooperate. Another unregistered "megachurch" in Beijing, the Zion Church, remained open and active when Shouwang and Wanbang faced pressure, even though it had signed a letter supporting Shouwang. In part, the different treatment given to the Zion Church relates to the containment strategy: unlike Shouwang and Wanbang, Zion did not engage in open resistance. In addition, there was a personal dimension: the founder of the Zion Church had gone through a TSPM seminary and worked for a decade as a pastor in a TSPM church before starting his own church. This experience gave him informal ties in the local RAB and other government offices that allowed him to expand his church at a time when Shouwang and Wanbang were under pressure. However, Beijing officials moved to close the Zion Church during a new wave of repression in 2018.[52]

Still other churches simply try to avoid the scrutiny of party and government officials altogether. They worship in small groups in private homes or out of the way places so as not to draw attention to themselves. Some unregistered churches even borrow from the CCP's own playbook in order not just to survive but to expand. The China Gospel

Fellowship (CGF) is a network of house churches with more than 1 million members.[53] Just as the CCP borrowed religious imagery and rituals to gain support during the civil war years,[54] the CGF adopted some of CCP's techniques for building clandestinely. The CGF network is built on a "fractal" organizational structure: if any one house church is discovered, it will not imperil other CGF churches. It sent members to proselytize in the countryside, where they offered to work in the fields and perform odd jobs in exchange for room and board, as did CCP cadres in the pre-1949 period. Its members gained status as "model workers" in factories, giving them special status and allowing them to share their faith with coworkers. Unlike the CCP, however, the CGF's organizational structure and deployment of its members did not have a revolutionary intent. They were used to ensure the church's survival and growth but not to overthrow the regime. The CGF has not escaped the recent crackdown on underground churches. The local United Front Work Department and police raided a meeting of pastors in the CGF network and arrested all 150 in attendance.[55]

A distinctive style of Protestantism has emerged in Wenzhou, a coastal city well known for its private entrepreneurs (and initially for its shady products). It also became known as "China's Jerusalem" because many of its successful entrepreneurs were benefactors of local churches, building large and extravagant buildings and paying the salaries of pastors and church staff. They are often referred to as "boss Christians," reflecting their leading roles in both the business and religious communities. Their combined business and religious activities have made Wenzhou famous for both its entrepreneurship and the prevalence of Christianity, especially among the city's economic elites. They exhibit a Chinese variant of the so-called prosperity gospel, in which their business success is seen as a sign of God's favor. Wenzhou's entrepreneurs frequently cite Max Weber's classic *The Protestant Ethic and the Spirit of Capitalism* to explain the intersection of their religious and business activities.[56] Because of their close ties with local party and government officials and their extensive business contacts around the country, Wenzhou's Boss Christians have enjoyed a degree of autonomy not found elsewhere in China.

But even Wenzhou has been the site of periodic crackdowns on Christianity, as in 2013–15 when local authorities demolished some church properties. Of the fifty-one cases reported in the media, most involved removing crosses in front of or on top of churches, which in Wenzhou can be enormous as the churches compete for attention.[57] Others involved the removal of church signs, the destruction of part of the church, or the conversion of the church into a cultural center. Only twelve involved the destruction of entire churches. Somewhat surprisingly, most of these actions targeted TSPM churches, not house churches. This crackdown did not prohibit religious practice but reflected the CCP's determination to restrict the visibility of it.[58]

Catholicism

Like the TSPM, the CPA runs seminaries for those wishing to become Catholic priests. Also, like the TSPM seminaries, teachers in the official CPA seminaries unofficially visit house churches to provide theological training to priests with limited understanding of the Bible. In some areas, underground Catholic priests and those in the official CPA lead services in the same churches, and parishioners worship in both the official and house churches, further blurring the distinction between them.

Catholicism has not spread as rapidly as Protestantism in China, in part because it is seen as less progressive and modern than Protestantism. Nevertheless, the CCP has been wary of Catholicism for political reasons. As noted above, the Catholic church was actively involved in democratization in Latin America, the Philippines, and Poland. The CCP therefore sees the Catholic church as a potential threat to its hold on power.

The CCP is also highly sensitive about any infringement on China's national sovereignty by the Vatican. It worries that Catholics owe ultimate allegiance to the pope in Rome and not the CCP.[59] And it sees the Vatican's appointment of Chinese priests, bishops, and cardinals as meddling in Chinese domestic affairs. It has frequently imprisoned bishops appointed by the pope without Beijing's approval. In one particularly prominent case, Father Thaddeus Ma Daqin was approved by both Beijing and the Vatican to become auxiliary bishop of Shanghai. At his ordination ceremony, he stunned those in attendance—including CCP officials—by announcing his resignation from the CPA. He was immediately placed under house arrest in a local seminary where he remained under investigation for four years. He later rejoined the CPA but was not installed as bishop and instead was identified only as Father Ma Daqin.[60]

In 2018, the Vatican announced an agreement with Beijing on the future appointments of cardinals and bishops.[61] This removed a major irritant in relations between China and the Vatican and could lead to formal diplomatic ties between the two. However, the announcement conveyed no details about the specific content of the agreement. Will Rome or Beijing have final authority on the appointment of cardinals and bishops, and how will disagreements between them be resolved? Will it provide amnesty for cardinals and bishops the Vatican appointed in the past without Beijing's approval, many of whom were then imprisoned? It remains to be seen what the scope of the agreement is and how well it will be implemented. As one indication of compromise, a priest approved by the Vatican in 2010 to become a bishop but rejected by the CCP was finally installed as bishop in Inner Mongolia's Jining city in August 2019. As a further concession, China allowed a bishop in the underground church to attend the ceremony, which was seen as a tacit endorsement of his status.[62] A second bishop was installed a few days later in Shaanxi province.[63] Beijing and the Vatican were satisfied enough with the agreement that they agreed to a two-year renewal in 2020.

Islam

Like Christianity, the CCP sees Islam as a foreign religion and treats it with suspicion. Islam is often associated—in China as in other countries—with terrorism, and the CCP has been involved in an extended but unsuccessful effort to suppress Islamic practices in dress, eating and drinking, and even the naming of children. As will be described in the next chapter, the CCP is relentlessly trying to eradicate Islam from the western province of Xinjiang, the traditional home of the predominantly Muslim Uighur ethnic group. After years of repression, propaganda, and education did not achieve this goal, the CCP built prison camps where Uighurs and other Muslim groups have been detained for months at a time.

The Hui minority is another Islamic minority, but has generally been spared from the CCP's repression. Many Hui live in Ningxia in western China, but others live throughout China. The Hui are fully assimilated into China: they do not seek autonomy, much less independence, speak Mandarin, and are often visibly indistinguishable from the Han majority except for men's prayer caps and women's headscarves. For much of the post-Mao era, they have not been subject to the same restrictions as the Uighurs: they have been able to fast during Ramadan and allowed to join the annual hajj to Mecca.

However, the increased "sinicization" of religion under Xi has affected even the Hui. Arabic language schools in Ningxia have been forced to close. Minarets and domes on mosques have been torn down and replaced by traditional Chinese-style roofs. Arabic lettering has been removed from public spaces. Hui contractors are instructed to remove their prayer caps when meeting with local officials.[64] A top party official in Ningxia even suggested, "We should draw experiences from the good practices and measures of Xinjiang."[65]

Buddhism

Buddhism is seen by the CCP as an indigenous religion, unlike Christianity and Islam, and therefore as less threatening.[66] Although Buddhism originated in India, it arrived in China roughly two thousand years ago via the Silk Road trading route. Today it is the largest religion in China. With the very important exception of Tibetan Buddhists, international human rights organizations have not criticized the Chinese government for its treatment of Buddhists, and Buddhists have not been at the forefront of political protests in China (at least outside Tibet). Even in South Korea and Taiwan, which are predominantly Buddhist, they were not involved in those cases of democratization.[67] However, Buddhists occasionally venture into political territory. In July 1989, soon after the crushing of the Tiananmen protests, the Nanputuo temple held a midnight service "to console the spirits of students and other citizens killed in Beijing."[68]

The Buddhist Association has a more constructive role with Buddhist monks and laypeople than do the Protestant and Catholic associations. Its personnel are familiar with the language used by the CCP and Buddhists. It can convey the CCP's regulations in a manner acceptable to Buddhist monks and also translate the wishes of monks into Marxist-Leninist terminology.[69] In contrast, the unregistered Christian churches have a more disparaging view of the TSPM and the CPA, which they see as emphasizing political authority at the expense of biblical teachings.

Buddhist institutions provide useful services to both local society and local governments. Foreign investors and philanthropic organizations provide funds to renovate and operate Buddhist sites and foreign tourists provide customers for local businesses. These foreign sources of investment, donations, and tax revenue help local governments address poverty and the potential for local unrest, two of their key policy goals. The Buddhist temples also provide social welfare services to local citizens. In these different ways, Buddhist institutions help reduce social tensions that can threaten political stability.[70]

Not all Buddhist leaders are willing to cooperate in the commercialization of religious landmarks, which betrays their religious values and can also alienate religious believers.[71] For example, the Shaolin temple in central Henan is as famous for its kung fu training as for its Buddhist heritage. Despite its fame, its extreme commercialism has made it the target of public criticism online. The head abbot, Shi Yongxin, is often referred to as the CEO monk. He received a VW SUV from the local government for his "extraordinary contribution to developing local tourism." These same contributions also led to accusations of corruption and misuse of money. He was tried in 2017 but cleared of all charges.[72] When the #MeToo movement began in China, he was accused of sexual misconduct, including fathering several children despite the vow of celibacy that all Buddhist monks take. He denied all charges, and China's state-run media soon dropped the stories. But the controversies surrounding Shi's business activities and personal life damaged

Shaolin's reputation. As part of Xi's tighter regulation of religious affairs, these kinds of commercial activities are now facing greater scrutiny.

Tibetan Buddhism is quite different from the form of Buddhism practiced elsewhere in China. One of the key differences between Tibetan Buddhists and other Buddhists in China concerns the Dalai Lama, who is Tibet's spiritual leader but not recognized by most Buddhists outside Tibet. He fled Tibet in 1959 and since then has resided in Dharamshala in India.[73] He has traveled extensively around the world, meeting with political leaders and the public to promote the cause of Tibetan autonomy. He won the Nobel Peace Prize in 1989, not coincidentally the same year as the suppression of the Tiananmen protests.

According to Tibetan tradition, when the current Dalai Lama dies, he will be reincarnated in another living person. The Dalai Lama has suggested that he may reincarnate outside Tibet, and may not even reincarnate at all because after fourteen reincarnations the Dalai Lama may have fulfilled its purpose. The CCP has rejected any such deviations from the traditional way of determining the new Dalai Lama and insists it will have the final say. This is no idle threat: in 1995, the Panchen Lama, the second-highest lama in Tibetan Buddhism, died. The Dalai Lama selected a young Tibetan boy as the new Panchen Lama but his choice was rejected by the CCP. It selected another boy for the post and sent him to Beijing for education and training. The boy selected by the Dalai Lama was taken into custody and not seen again. If a similar controversy occurs in identifying the next Dalai Lama, a new conflict between Tibetans and Beijing is all but certain.

"Evil Cults"

The "black" market of religions includes groups not recognized by the CCP and what it deems to be "evil cults."[74] This label was originally used against the Falun Gong spiritual group, which emerged out of the "qigong fever" in the 1990s.[75] Its mix of traditional Buddhist and Taoist meditation, slow-movement exercises, and modern mysticism attracted millions of members throughout the country, even including party, government, and military officials. Its charismatic founder, Li Hongzhi, taught his followers to abandon material well-being at a time when the party was basing its legitimacy in large part on improving living standards.[76] Instead, it encouraged Falun Gong members to develop supernatural powers through its practices. It promised miracle cures for ailments at a time when China's SOEs were being reorganized and millions of people lost their jobs and access to health care. It also created social bonds among the large numbers of people who would gather to exercise in public parks. At its peak, it may have been larger than the Chinese Communist Party, which at the time had around 60 million members. It was originally a member of the official state-run China Qigong Scientific Research Association, but later was expelled from that group as its claims and millennial language became more extreme.

The state-run media frequently criticized Falun Gong and its members in turn protested this treatment and demanded a retraction of the media criticism. When its demands were rejected, in April 1999 it organized a silent protest around Zhongnanhai, the compound in central Beijing where most of the top party and government officials live and work. More than ten thousand of its members, some having chartered buses to bring them to Beijing, stood in silent protest for a full day. This shocked the CCP leadership, which was generally unaware of its size and organizational prowess. The party saw Falun Gong's size, mobilization capacity, and teachings to be a threat to its power and its priority on economic modernization. It launched a full-scale crackdown on Falun Gong, branding it an illegal and "evil" cult, imprisoning and reportedly torturing its members. The Chinese Buddhist Association supported the CCP's efforts to suppress Falun Gong and other newly formed Buddhist organizations in order to maintain its monopoly over the practice of Buddhism in China. This intense and long-term crackdown largely eliminated Falun Gong from public view. While there are undoubtedly members who continue to meet in private, the group as a whole was thoroughly and vigorously suppressed.[77]

The CCP also applies the "evil cult" label to groups like Eastern Lightning (also known as the Church of the Almighty God), whose founder claimed that a woman from rural China was the second coming of Christ. The two fled together to the United States in 2000, playing into the CCP's contention that foreign influences are behind religious extremism in China. The group employed aggressive tactics to gain adherents. It once kidnapped dozens of CGF pastors in order to get them to join the group, but eventually released them. It gained domestic and international notoriety in 2014 when several of its members confronted a woman at a McDonald's and beat her to death when she refused to join. The assailants were quickly arrested, two were sentenced to death, and the rest received lengthy prison sentences, while the CCP launched a broader campaign to identify and suppress its members.[78]

* * *

Religion is resurgent in China. The CCP has tried to manage and control the resurgence of religion but has had limited success. It recognizes five religions, each with an official regulatory body, and pressures the faithful to worship in officially approved churches, temples, and mosques. This pressure has increased under Xi Jinping, who wants all types of activities to occur within officially approved institutions.

The relationship between religion and the state in China is not just about formal institutions, however; informal practices also figure prominently. Local governments in China have great leeway in their approach to religion and how they enforce national laws and regulations. State policy toward religion ranges—from time to time and from place to place—from suppression to tolerance to cooperation. Similarly, the religious faithful respond in varied ways: some resist, others try to avoid the attention of local officials, and still others seek ways to cooperate on shared goals of renovating and restoring religious properties (which often entails attracting foreign investments), providing social welfare services and charity, and generating revenue from religious tourism.

To avoid suppression, religious leaders in both the official and unregistered churches—the red and the gray churches—work with local officials to build goodwill and create safe spaces for their churches' worship and mission work. Unregistered church leaders who are willing to cooperate with local officials still refuse to register with the official churches. They avoid political messages in their sermons; do not criticize the regime in public; limit the size of their congregations; share information with local officials about their own churches' activities, as well as those of blacklisted Christian sects that try to infiltrate house churches; and do not link up with other house churches to pursue collective goals, whether political or religious. Leaders of unregistered churches who do not consent to the conditions of the containment strategy face a more repressive response from local officials. Their worship services may be interrupted, their members investigated, and they themselves may be imprisoned. As was the case for civil society groups (see chapter 4) and private entrepreneurs—groups often assumed to be antagonistic to autocrats—the informal practices on the ground do not fit a simple state domination versus popular resistance framework.

The CCP is wary of religion. It sees matters of faith, and especially the desire of the faithful to be free to worship as they see fit, as a potential challenge to its status as China's ruling party. Religion offers an alternative belief system in a political system that is officially atheistic. Christianity is a particular cause of concern because it was a source of instability in China's modern history and has been involved in several cases of democratization in other countries in recent decades. The CCP seeks to manage religion to avoid facing a similar fate. Though the party has not stopped the spread of religion, it has prevented religion from posing a political threat.

7

HOW NATIONALISTIC
IS CHINA?

During 2012, a wave of anti-Japanese protests broke out in more than two hundred Chinese cities. The focus of the protests was the disputed Diaoyu Islands (known as the Senkakus in Japan) in the East China Sea. These islands have been the cause of frequent diplomatic tensions between China and Japan as well as anti-Japanese protests in China. The protesters denounced the Japanese government's purchase of the islands from their owner, a Japanese citizen. Among the many signs opposing Japan's claims to the islands, one read, "Diaoyu belongs to China, and Bo [Xilai] belongs to the people."[1] This was an unusual sign to see at a nationalist protest; Bo, the popular party secretary of the megacity Chongqing in southwestern China, was a political rival of Xi Jinping. At the time of the protest, he was embroiled in a criminal investigation about his wife's involvement in the murder of a British businessman, which was seen by many as politically motivated.[2]

This episode illustrates the double-edged nature of Chinese nationalism. On one hand, antiforeign sentiments have been visible in recurring antiforeign protests against Japan, the United States, France, and foreign countries more generally. These protests include not only street demonstrations but also attacks on foreign businesses and calls to boycott foreign-made goods. On the other hand, these antiforeign protests can easily become antigovernment protests, aiming not just at foreign countries but at China's own government—as with the sign in support of one of Xi's rivals. Nationalist protests can also become an occasion for other types of complaints, such as corruption, unemployment, and other shared grievances. For these reasons, nationalism in China is a cause of concern, not just for foreign observers but for the CCP, too.

This chapter will examine some common assumptions about Chinese nationalism: that it is rising, especially among the youngest generation; that it is the result of Chinese education and propaganda policies; that the CCP mobilizes and orchestrates nationalist protests; and that nationalism drives China's foreign policy. In each case, the available evidence runs counter to these assumptions. Surveys of public opinion and studies of nationalist protests indicate that the link between party propaganda and popular attitudes is not as tight and the CCP's control over nationalist protests not as strong as is often assumed.

Is China Increasingly Nationalistic?

There is no doubt that nationalist sentiments are very prominent in China. Indeed, global surveys of public opinion suggest that China is the most nationalistic country in the world. The International Social Survey Program's (ISSP) national identity survey asked respondents in thirty-six countries about their degree of nationalism: if they would rather be a citizen of their own country than any other; if the world would be a better place if people in other countries were more like their country; if their country was better than most countries; and if they felt proud when their country did well in international sports competitions. These same questions were asked in a 2008 survey in China to provide a comparison. The results showed that China ranked highest on these questions (the United States ranked second).[3]

Young Chinese are seen as especially nationalistic. In China, they are known as "angry youth" because of their strident animus against foreign countries, especially Japan and the United States.[4] Many studies of Chinese nationalism focus only on young people, either college students or urban internet users, who are younger and better educated than the population as a whole. This gives a biased look at nationalism in China because it does not consider whether young Chinese are any different from their elders. However, a closer look at the evidence finds just the opposite: every public opinion survey that includes the full age range of the Chinese population finds that young people are less nationalistic than older generations—the opposite of what the conventional wisdom suggests.

The most conclusive study of trends in Chinese nationalism is based on the Beijing Area Survey (BAS), which is conducted every two to three years.[5] Starting in 1998, the BAS has included questions on nationalism, including two questions from the ISSP survey noted above (whether respondents would prefer to be a citizen of China than any other country, whether they thought China is a better country than most), plus one more (whether they should support the country or government even when it was wrong). Comparing fifteen years of survey data from 1998 to 2013, two trends are readily apparent. First of all, nationalist sentiments have not risen during these years. Instead, nationalism peaked around the time of the Beijing Olympics in 2008 and declined thereafter. Second, young respondents are less nationalistic than older respondents. On each of the three questions noted above (prefer to be a citizen of China, believe China is better than most countries, and have blind trust in the country or government) and in each year of the BAS, older respondents were more nationalistic than younger respondents. Neither of these findings fits the conventional wisdom of steadily rising nationalism in China.

The findings of the BAS may not be generalizable to the population as a whole: it is limited to Beijing, whose population is wealthier and better educated than in most Chinese cities, and because the early years of the BAS did not include the growing number of migrant workers, it may not have even been representative of the Beijing population. However, the BAS has some advantages that other surveys lack: it provides a baseline to measure change over time, and Beijing, being the nation's capital, is more likely to have a higher concentration of nationalist sentiments among its residents. But the two key findings question the conventional wisdom about Chinese nationalism: the level of nationalism has not continued to rise ever higher, and China's youth are not more nationalistic than their elders.

Other surveys find similar results. In the 2008 China Survey and the East Asian Survey, also conducted in 2008, older Chinese are more nationalistic than younger Chinese.[6] In my nationwide survey of urban China in 2014, older cohorts were also more likely to have nationalist attitudes.[7] Figure 7.1 compares different generations in China: those who "came of age" (that is, turned fifteen) around the time of the founding of the PRC in 1949, during the Cultural Revolution, during the early reform years (late 1970s through the 1980s), and in the 1990s and later. This last group underwent "patriotic education" while in school (which will be explored in the next section) and is generally thought to be the most nationalistic. The survey asked the two questions also used in both the ISSP and BAS surveys and added a third, to find out whether, "When other people criticize China, it is as though they are criticizing me." On all three questions, the survey responses indicate that nationalist sentiments are highest among the oldest generation and steadily decline in each subsequent generation. Most notable is the decline in the percentage of those who strongly agree with each statement.

Each of these surveys challenges the conventional wisdom that young Chinese are most nationalistic. This finding is strengthened by the range of questions used to measure nationalism: regardless of how the question is asked, the finding is the same: we should have more confidence in these findings when different measures and survey designs yield the same results.

What we cannot tell from these surveys, however, is whether the relationship between age and nationalism is due to generational or life cycle effects. If it is due to generational effects, then we would expect each cohort to have relatively stable views: as one generation passes from the scene and is replaced by another, the level of nationalism across the whole population would decrease. Alternatively, if it is due to life cycle effects, then we would expect to find that people become more nationalistic as they get older. Whether the observed trend is due to generational or life cycle effects is apparent only when we have panel data, where the same questions are asked of the same respondents over a long period of time. Short of that, we can examine trends in survey data spread over several decades. However, survey research in China is

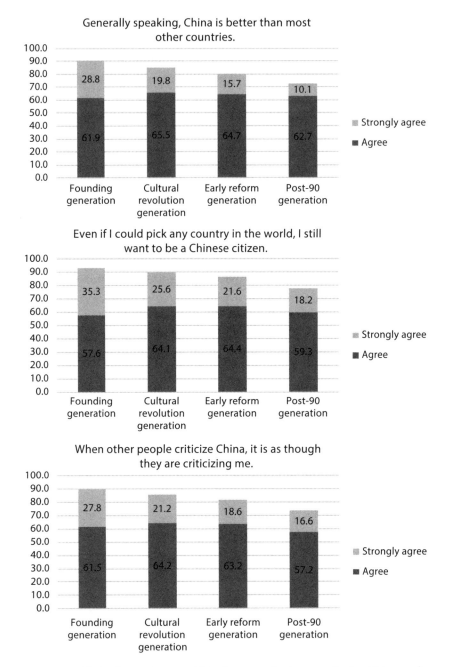

FIGURE 7.1. Nationalist sentiments in China (source: author's survey of urban China, 2014)

still relatively new and we do not have either those kinds of panel data or long-term time series data. With the information currently available, all we can say is that the conventional wisdom appears to be wrong: young Chinese are not the most nationalistic; moreover, each generation is successively less nationalistic than older ones.

Why is this important? If Chinese youth are the most nationalistic, we would expect that nationalism in China would continue to rise in the years ahead and potentially push the CCP to adopt a more assertive foreign policy.[8] But the surveys to date all show that Chinese youth are not more nationalistic than their elders, and the BAS showed that nationalist sentiments peaked in 2008 and declined afterward. That should not make us complacent—China is without question highly nationalistic, but not increasingly so.

Yet, during the years of these surveys, nationalist rhetoric and protests became more common. How does that square with the finding that Chinese are becoming less nationalistic? Nationalist protests have been increasing even though nationalist sentiments have not, in large part because nationalism is the only form of dissent that the CCP allows.[9] Whereas other forms of protest are often suppressed (see chapter 5), activists now recognize that nationalist protests are handled differently. The state-run media is more likely to support the goals of nationalist protests, while also warning of threats to stability, one of the CCP's top concerns. The CCP puts an end to nationalist protests by issuing warnings in the media and even sending out text messages to uphold political stability, clearly signaling to those paying attention that it will no longer tolerate protests. Unlike most other forms of protest, the CCP does not send thugs to attack nationalist protesters, nor are the leaders of nationalist protests routinely arrested as a warning to others.

It is also true that young people, especially college students, are more likely to participate in nationalist protests than other groups, adding to the perception that young Chinese are particularly nationalistic. But that is not distinctive to China: young people are more likely to protest in most countries. College students are especially prone to protest. They are more idealistic and more interested in current affairs. They live in close proximity to one another, which allows them to communicate and organize more effectively. They are more technologically savvy, making it easier for them to share information. All of these skills and traits incline young college students to protest when they are animated by an issue or event.

Because nationalist protests are handled differently than other protests, they also provide opportunities for other types of political critiques. The vignette that opened this chapter is one example of how nationalist protests also provide cover for other complaints. It is not unusual to see marchers in nationalist protests carrying signs of Chairman Mao or denouncing corruption. Mao's portrait is often used as an implicit critique of current leaders, many of whom are seen as corrupt. Despite the widespread suffering during the Maoist years, there is notable nostalgia for a past in which local leaders may have abused their power in political campaigns like the Cultural Revolution, but they did not enrich themselves in the process.[10] Citizens cannot call out current leaders by name for their corrupt ways, but they can hold high Mao's portrait during nationalist protests as a not so subtle critique of corruption. Nationalist protests therefore provide an opportunity to protest other types of grievances.

Nationalist sentiments may not be rising, but nationalist protests are more common, because the CCP is willing to tolerate them, at least to a point; because protesters know they will be tolerated, at least for a time; and because they provide a venue for other types of issues, at least at the margins. At the same time, the CCP is not willing to be the target of those attacks nor let them pose a threat to political stability. As will be shown below, it wants to promote nationalism as a source of legitimacy, but at the same time does not want nationalism to trigger unrest or turn against the CCP. That tension—between promoting and constraining nationalism— is a key challenge for the CCP's survival as China's ruling party.

Is the CCP the Source of Chinese Nationalism?

After the CCP imposed martial law in 1989 to end the peaceful demonstrations in Tiananmen Square and elsewhere around China, it embarked on a new propaganda campaign to rebuild popular support.

Known as the Patriotic Education Campaign, it changed how modern Chinese history was taught in schools and conveyed in popular culture. Through textbooks, movies, songs, and books, the CCP sought to convince the people, and young Chinese in particular, that foreign countries had oppressed China in the past and continue to have hostile intentions toward China. As part of this campaign, the CCP also promoted "red tourism" by designating battlefields, museums, monuments, and other historical sites as "patriotic education bases" for students, families, and tourist groups to visit. The message of this campaign was plain: being patriotic means supporting the party.

Whereas the CCP used to portray China as a victor that defeated the Japanese in World War II and expelled foreign influences from China, after 1989 party propaganda framed China's involvement with the outside world in a victimization narrative. According to this narrative, beginning with the Opium Wars of the 1840s until the CCP took power in 1949, China was the victim of more powerful foreign forces that took advantage of China's relative backwardness, forced it to sign unequal treaties, and violated China's national sovereignty and national interests more generally. This view of the pre-1949 period portrays China as the victim of foreign manipulation, including the Opium Wars; unequal treaties with England, France, Russia, the United States, Japan, and other Western countries; and colony-like areas known as "concessions" that were carved out of Chinese territory and under the control of foreign countries. This foreign aggression against China reached its peak with Japan's invasion and occupation of large areas of China from 1937 to 1945, and the atrocities committed during that occupation. This ended in 1949, once the CCP unified the country and drove out foreigners and foreign ideas, but—according to this victim narrative—foreign countries continue to impinge on China's interests and reputation.

When foreigners behave badly in China, when foreign governments and companies do not recognize China's territorial claims, and when foreign leaders and international institutions criticize China's domestic and foreign policies, these are denounced by the Chinese media and many Chinese citizens as current manifestations of the perceived longstanding effort to keep China weak. For many scholars, this Patriotic

Education Campaign is emblematic of the CCP's efforts to stoke nationalism for its own ends.[11] However, the CCP's portrayal of foreign aggression against China, especially by Japan, resonated with the personal experiences and popular memories of many Chinese. In addition, it is important to note that the CCP did not invent this victim narrative during the post-1989 era. It merely echoed a similar narrative about the century of humiliation used by the Nationalist government in the pre–1949 years.[12] The CCP first replaced the Nationalist's victim narrative with its own victor narrative after it took power in 1949, and then revived the victim narrative after 1989 as it tried to repair its image at home and abroad.

How well has the Patriotic Education Campaign succeeded in producing a form of nationalism that looks at international affairs through this lens of victimization? Not so well, if we compare older and younger generations. In my nationwide survey in 2014, respondents were asked whether they agreed with statements about China being the victim of international forces.[13] Those who came of age after the beginning of the Patriotic Education Campaign were much less likely to agree with those victimization statements (see figure 7.2). The differences are not as large as for the nationalist sentiments shown in figure 7.1: there the differences between the oldest and youngest generations were 15 to 20 percent, here they are around 10 to 12 percent, depending on the question. This is true even when controlling for personal characteristics such as level of education, gender, ethnicity, and party membership. This finding is in line with the findings of every other study comparing the nationalist sentiments of younger and older Chinese as noted above. In this particular case, young Chinese are less likely to agree with the CCP's victim narrative. Nevertheless, we should also note that the belief in the victim narrative is quite high across all age groups. Even among the youngest generation, between 70 to 80 percent of respondents agree with each of the questions about China being the victim of past and present humiliations.

It is possible that in the absence of patriotic education, young Chinese would be even less nationalistic than they are today. This is the implication of one study that surveyed high school students in several

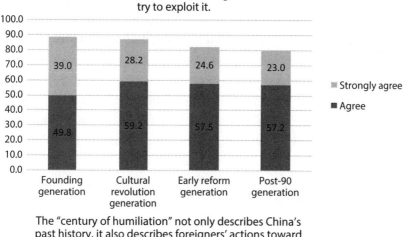

Unless China becomes modern, foreign countries will try to exploit it.

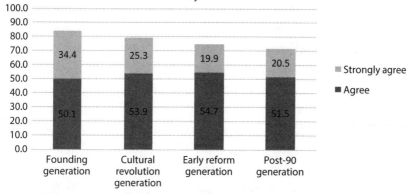

The "century of humiliation" not only describes China's past history, it also describes foreigners' actions toward China today.

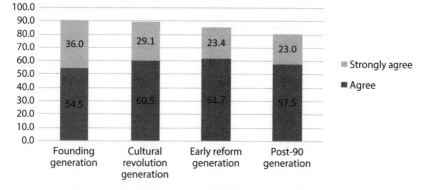

China's early modern encounter with Western imperial powers was a history of humiliation in which the motherland was subjected to the insult of being beaten because we were backward.

FIGURE 7.2. Public opinion on the "century of humiliation" (source: author's survey of urban China, 2014)

Chinese cities, conducted in-depth interviews with students and teachers, and analyzed the textbooks used in these high schools. It found that years of education in general reduced nationalist sentiments, but that specifically attending patriotic education events increased students' nationalist attitudes.[14] It is not clear from the study if there is selection bias at work: are patriotic students more likely to attend patriotic events, or does attendance at patriotic events produce more patriotism? That is the bane of these kinds of studies: we can identify the correlation between patriotic sentiments and attendance at patriotic events, but we cannot determine which is the cause and which is the effect without knowing people's attitudes before attending the events. Even so, this study offers an important insight: we should not assume all the party's propaganda has its desired effect. Patriotic messages embedded in high school textbooks do not necessarily produce patriotic feelings in the students who read them.[15]

The CCP's strategy in launching the Patriotic Education Campaign was to rebuild its legitimacy by distracting Chinese public opinion away from its own failures in the present and toward foreign aggression in the past. It was successful to a large degree, but it also let loose waves of public activism on foreign policy issues that it has struggled to contain. In particular, it made more people aware of Japanese atrocities, but it could not control what people did with that knowledge. The anti-Japanese sentiments that were a key part of the Patriotic Education Campaign had the biggest impact on older cohorts with personal memories of the Japanese occupation. As these memories were revived by the Patriotic Education Campaign, their anti-Japanese animus grew. However, it failed to increase anti-Japanese sentiments among China's youth.[16]

Patriotic education is also intended to shape popular views of the problems besetting China today. If patriotic education is having its intended effect, we should expect that the people who have been exposed to this curriculum would be more likely to blame foreign influences as the source of China's problems. But the opposite is true. In response to the question "Today, China faces many difficulties in different aspects of its development. Do you see these problems as being due to foreign influence or to problems within China?" younger generations that received

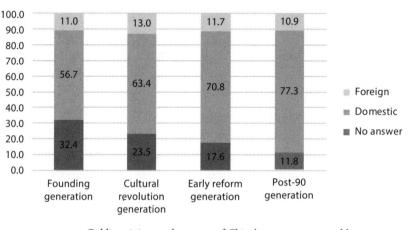

FIGURE 7.3. Public opinion on the source of China's contemporary problems
(source: author's survey of urban China, 2014)

patriotic education in school are more likely to see domestic sources for
China's problems (see figure 7.3).[17] The difference between the oldest and
youngest generations was more than twenty percentage points. Combined with the statements about the century of humiliation in figure 7.2,
the results reported in figure 7.3 indicate that we should not automatically assume the CCP's propaganda is absorbed by China's youth.

Patriotic Education in Tibet and Xinjiang

Patriotic education campaigns have a more coercive component when
they are aimed at ethnic minority populations that seek greater autonomy from Beijing's control, if not outright independence. Of China's
more than 1.4 billion people, almost 92 percent are Han. The remaining
8 percent belong to fifty-five officially recognized ethnic minorities. The
CCP targets patriotic education at the Tibetans and Xinjiang's Uighurs (a
largely Muslim group) because they have continuously resisted Beijing's
efforts to incorporate them into the larger Chinese nation, whereas other
ethnic minorities, such as the Mongolians and Koreans, have been less

resistant to assimilation and Han domination.[18] The CCP has forced
many Tibetan Buddhists and Xinjiang's Uighurs to undergo patriotic education as a means of imposing its depiction of a multinational China of
which Tibet and Xinjiang are inseparable parts. In Tibet, this includes
requiring Buddhists to renounce their allegiance to the exiled Dalai Lama;
those who refuse face prolonged imprisonment and other forms of pressure, including torture. In fact, part of the patriotic education campaign
in Tibet asserts that Buddhism was not originally part of Tibetan culture.[19] This is an ironic claim, because elsewhere in China among the majority Han ethnic group, the CCP treats Buddhism as an "indigenous"
religion, in contrast to "foreign" religions such as Christianity and Islam.

One of the key ways the CCP instills its values in Tibetan children is
to send them to boarding schools outside Tibet. More than one-third
of young Tibetans are sent to central China for secondary education
and are rarely allowed to return home until they graduate.[20] Classes are
taught in Mandarin and contain little to no information about Tibetan
culture and traditions. Isolating school-aged children from their homes
and communities helps achieve the CCP's goals of indoctrinating Tibetans with its version of history and politics, but it comes with a tremendous social cost. When they graduate and return to Tibet, they are
unfamiliar with the values and language of their fellow Tibetans.

The CCP pushed a new wave of repression in Tibet after violent protests in 2008. The protests began on the anniversary of the March 10,
1959, uprising that ended with the Dalai Lama's flight into exile in India,
where he and many of his supporters have remained. Anniversaries are
often the occasion for protests in China, and it is remarkable that Tibetan leaders were not prepared for this one. In fact, the top leaders left
for Beijing to attend the annual meeting of the National People's Congress in early March 2008, even though it coincided with this important
anniversary. Tibet had been relatively stable following the imposition
of martial law in March 1989 (unconnected with the martial law in Beijing in June 1989), and leaders may have been overconfident that no
protests would occur while they were away. When protests did break
out, the remaining leaders in Tibet were slow to react and the protests
spread rapidly. By the time the protests ended, at least eighty Tibetans

and eighteen Han Chinese had been killed, and numerous businesses— mostly owned by Han Chinese—had been damaged or destroyed. The PRC shut off media access to Tibet and ordered all foreigners to depart. Constraints on visiting Tibet have continued in the years since.

As part of the crackdown in Tibet, Tibetans were subjected to another patriotic education campaign. Interviews with Tibetans afterward indicated that the campaign had been totally ineffective. For one thing, the campaign's emphasis on the benefits of economic modernization did not resonate with Buddhism's antimaterialist beliefs, especially among monks and nuns. The campaign may even have been counterproductive: monks who were apolitical before the classes ended up with a more developed understanding of politics and religion. Instead of becoming patriotic, they became more nationalistic Tibetans.[21] Denouncing the Dalai Lama was the central component of this and previous patriotic education campaigns, and also the most divisive. Tibetans who refused to comply—even children—were typically sent to prison.

Although the CCP's propaganda had little effect on Tibetans, it had a significant impact on the Han Chinese. After years of denigrating the Dalai Lama, most Chinese had little difficulty accepting the CCP's depiction of him as being intent on dividing China. Given the low levels of religiosity among the Han (see chapter 6), there was little sympathy for Tibetans' desire for greater religious freedom. Many Han Chinese saw Tibetans as ungrateful for the economic opportunities offered by the CCP's development policies.[22] CCP propaganda emphasized the new economic modernization efforts in Tibet, but did not mention that the main beneficiaries were recently arrived Han Chinese. The Han Chinese also believed the Tibetan protests presented China in an unflattering light to foreign audiences on the eve of the 2008 Olympics in Beijing.

Outright defiance by the Tibetans against the CCP's rule is not common, but other forms of resistance are. Many Tibetans engage in acts of everyday resistance, such as carrying photos of the Dalai Lama or not attending patriotic education classes because they are "ill." Other types of protests are more public, like raising the Tibetan flag or shouting slogans. The individuals who do these things recognize they will likely be imprisoned and tortured but act out of their personal convictions.

Estimates on the number of Tibetan political prisoners range from five hundred to two thousand.

A more gruesome form of resistance is self-immolation. According to the International Campaign for Tibet, the organization for Tibetans in exile, more than 150 self-immolations have occurred since February 2009, of which 131 resulted in death. These events peaked in 2012 (85 self-immolations) and declined sharply afterward.[23] Most of these have occurred outside the formal boundaries of the Tibetan Autonomous Region (the official name of Tibet in today's China) in the neighboring provinces of Sichuan, Gansu, and Qinghai that are part of the traditional Tibetan homeland. These self-immolations—not reported in the Chinese media—indicate the determined resistance of Tibetans to the CCP's policies of forced assimilation into the Chinese nation.

The repressive aspect of patriotic education is also evident in Xinjiang, where the CCP is engaged in a prolonged effort to eradicate Islamic influences, including bans on long beards for men, wearing hijabs for women, and even giving Muslim names to newborns. The CCP requires Uighur-run restaurants to remain open on religious holidays and to sell alcohol, both of which are proscribed by their religion. Beginning in 2018, the CCP began building internment camps for upward of 1 million Uighurs, Kazakhs, and other Muslim groups in Xinjiang. The Chinese government claims these camps are for reeducation and job training, but the repressive aspect of the camps reveals their true purpose. In these camps, inmates are required to sit through long patriotic education classes and are expected to denounce what Beijing considers extremist views associated with Islam. Those who refuse can remain in the camps indefinitely and can have their family members threatened with similar detention. To deter Uighurs and Kazakhs living outside China from criticizing the camps and other CCP policies in Xinjiang, the CCP uses "relational repression,"[24] meaning that relatives living in China are punished for the words and actions of those outside China. These relatives are even pressured to call those outside China to implore them to keep quiet.

The CCP intends to indoctrinate even the Uighurs who do not live in Xinjiang. It created a special "Xinjiang Class" in 2000, and in subsequent years tens of thousands of young Uighurs were forced to attend.

FIGURE 7.4. Internment camp in Xinjiang (photo: Thomas Peters/Reuters)

The CCP used this program to "instill Chinese patriotism, feelings of ethnic unity and the values of the CCP in young Uighurs."[25] But the program was almost entirely ineffective. Not only did young Uighurs not alter their ethnic identities, the program deepened their commitment to Islam, including attending Friday prayers at the Sudanese embassy in Beijing and taking Arabic classes for reading the Qur'an. Like patriotic education in Tibet, the CCP's heavy-handed efforts to indoctrinate young Uighurs backfired.

Beijing has built an intensive surveillance state in Xinjiang, with numerous police stations and substations, police armed with assault weapons on the streets, multiple cameras in public locations, facial recognition software to monitor the comings and goings of all people, and other tactics.[26] Chinese companies are developing facial recognition software to not only identify specific individuals but to distinguish Uighurs from other ethnic groups. These high-tech surveillance techniques were used on a trial basis in Xinjiang but were gradually rolled out elsewhere in

China. In fact, the companies developing these programs are advertising them to foreign governments. More than a dozen countries have purchased surveillance technology from China, including authoritarian regimes like Zimbabwe and Pakistan but also democracies like Germany.[27] The export of China's surveillance state provides a new dimension to the "China model": not only state-led economic development but also state-sponsored, high-tech repression.

Beijing's propaganda against Uighurs has caused many Han to fear Uighurs as potential terrorists. Terrorist attacks by Uighurs outside Xinjiang amplified this fear. In 2013, a car with three Uighurs inside crashed into a crowd of tourists in Tiananmen Square in Beijing and burst into flames. All three Uighurs and two tourists died, and more than thirty were injured. Another such attack occurred at the train station in Kunming, Yunnan, in 2014. Eight Uighurs with long knives attacked travelers in the train station, killing thirty-one people and injuring nearly one hundred fifty; four of the attackers were also killed. Extensive coverage of these events in the official media and shared by social media conveyed the implicit message that all Uighurs were potential terrorists. Uighurs who travel outside Xinjiang can face discrimination in employment and be denied access to hotels and other locations. The resentment against Uighurs even extends overseas. Chinese students at McMaster University in Canada launched a harsh online criticism against a Uighur activist who had been invited to speak on campus about the detention camps in Xinjiang, even criticizing the Chinese embassy in Ontario for not opposing the talk.[28]

The PRC took advantage of the global war on terror to justify its repressive tactics in Xinjiang. Protests and acts of random violence, previously labeled as the work of separatists, became incidents of terrorism. This message was widely received within China.[29] With the start of the global war on terror, China was able to persuade other governments to support its position. Multiple foreign governments, including the United States, United Kingdom, the European Union, and Russia labeled the East Turkestan Islamist Movement a terrorist organization. However, more recently international public opinion has turned against Chinese antiterrorism policies. Most governments have been unwilling to condone China's widespread repression in Xinjiang, and in particular have criticized its use of internment camps, which came to international attention in 2018. Ironically, majority Muslim countries like Saudi Arabia have generally remained silent on the camps and the general mistreatment of Xinjiang's Muslims.

Although the CCP has tried to promote its brand of nationalism with its Patriotic Education Campaigns, it has had limited success. The youth who have been most exposed to this campaign are less nationalistic than older cohorts who did not go through school with the patriotic education curriculum. In Tibet and Xinjiang, patriotic education has largely backfired by reinforcing ethnic identities over Chinese national identity. As a result, the CCP has resorted to coercion to achieve what it could not with persuasion.

Chinese Nationalism vs. Hong Kong Identity

For much of 2019, large-scale and often violent protests roiled Hong Kong. These protests against Beijing's influence in Hong Kong were quite different from those in Tibet and Xinjiang. Whereas those protests were about ethnic identity, in Hong Kong, where most people are Han, they were not. Instead, the Hong Kong protests have been about civic identity: What values do the Hong Kong people identify with and how do they contrast with the values and priorities emphasized by the CCP? The underlying question is the same—who belongs to the Chinese nation—but the reasons behind the answers given in Tibet, Xinjiang, and Hong Kong differ in important ways.

Some background on Hong Kong's status is helpful to understand the protests there.[30] Until 1997, Hong Kong was a British colony. In 1842 the island of Hong Kong was granted to Great Britain in perpetuity after China's surrender in the first Opium War. The adjacent peninsula of Kowloon was granted in perpetuity in 1860 after the second Opium War.

The much larger area of the New Territories was leased to Great Britain for ninety-nine years in 1898. These three parcels of territory, collectively known as Hong Kong, were then ruled as a British colony until

1997. For the CCP, Hong Kong's status as a British colony exemplified the "century of humiliation."

In 1982, negotiations began over the future of Hong Kong. With the ninety-nine-year lease on the New Territories about to expire, the British government recognized that keeping Hong Kong island and Kowloon was not feasible. The Thatcher government first hoped to renew the lease, but China refused. In 1990, China adopted the "Basic Law" for Hong Kong, based on the "one country, two systems" framework in which Hong Kong would be under Chinese sovereignty but would have a high degree of autonomy as a Special Administrative Region for at least fifty years. In 1997, Hong Kong reverted back to Chinese control.

With the Basic Law, China tried to shape Hong Kong political institutions to minimize opposition and maintain control. It allowed some democratic procedures but controlled the outcomes to ensure compliance with its priorities. The chief executive is formally elected by an electoral committee but effectively is appointed by Beijing. Half of the members of the Legislative Council (LegCo) are elected from local districts and half elected from functional groups to allow Beijing to control candidates and elected legislators. There are also district councils whose members are mostly directly elected. They are not important in governing Hong Kong, but they played an important role in the 2019 protests, as will be explained below.

Although Beijing tried to control Hong Kong politics in these ways, changing conditions in Hong Kong changed people's willingness to comply. First of all, there has been emerging Hong Kong identity based not on ethnicity but on local issues; distrust of the government (which is seen as pro-China); and civic values such as democracy, civil liberties, and the rule of law.[31] Relatedly, there was growing resentment toward Chinese influence in Hong Kong, not just in terms of Beijing's efforts to micromanage Hong Kong affairs but also the visible presence of Chinese tourists and businessmen. These changing sentiments were especially strong among those born after Hong Kong's return to Chinese sovereignty in 1997. This younger generation had a strong commitment to democracy that ran contrary to the CCP's intention to control Hong

Kong. The result has been repeated public protests against some of Beijing's initiatives, most significantly in 2014 and 2019.

The "umbrella movement" of 2014 (so named because the protesters used umbrellas to protect themselves from the tear gas fired at them by the police) was a prodemocracy protest seeking direct election of the chief executive and the LegCo.[32] The protest was triggered by Beijing's announcement that the rules for electing the chief executive and LegCo members would remain as laid down in the Basic Law. This angered prodemocracy groups in Hong Kong that had hoped to reduce Beijing's influence in Hong Kong by letting the voters elect Hong Kong's leaders. Protesters occupied major intersections throughout Hong Kong, disrupting traffic and economic activity for over two months. The business community and much of the public initially supported the protesters, but over time they grew weary of the disruptions and sought a return to normalcy. With this loss of public support, the protests came to an end. Afterward, several key leaders were arrested, tried, and sentenced. China also asserted greater influence over Hong Kong's universities, whose students and professors had been the leaders of the umbrella movement.

More violent and long-lasting protests broke out in 2019 after Chief Executive Carrie Lam introduced a draft extradition bill to the LegCo. If adopted as law, the bill would have allowed the Hong Kong government to extradite its citizens when other governments—including China's—charged them with crimes. Many in Hong Kong opposed the bill because they worried it would provide yet another way for China to undermine rights and freedoms in Hong Kong by charging its critics there with crimes.

The 2019 protests were different from the umbrella movement in several key ways. First, the 2019 protests involved more violence. Most of the protesters remained peaceful during a brief occupation of LegCo, repeated attempts to shut down the airport, calls for general strikes, and regular street marches that drew up to an estimated 1 million people (out of a total population of 7.4 million). However, some threw bricks and Molotov cocktails at police, defaced government symbols at the Chinese government's Central Liaison Office in Hong Kong, and vandalized businesses of people suspected to be pro-China. These protesters saw violence as the only option against a stubborn government that had lost the public's trust and refused to negotiate. Second, there were no identifiable leaders in the 2019 protests. Protests were loosely organized through social media; protesters wore masks to prevent identification by facial recognition software and spray-painted surveillance cameras.[33] As a result, there was no one for the government to either arrest or negotiate with to bring the protests to a close. Instead, police used mass arrests to try to foil the protests but without success. Third, public support remained strong even after several months of ongoing protests that brought much of the transportation system and the economy to a stop.

Beijing's response to the protests was stronger in words than action. Official state media used nationalistic rhetoric to denounce the protesters. It blamed the high school curriculum for creating critical thinkers instead of loyal patriots.[34] It criticized the United States, Great Britain, and other countries for fomenting the protests, seen as another example of alleged foreign interference in China's domestic affairs right in line with the CCP's victimization narrative. Zhang Xiaoming, director of the Chinese government's Hong Kong and Macao Affairs Office, likened the protests to the kind of "color revolutions" that brought down governments in Eastern Europe and the former Soviet Union,[35] insinuating that the protests were a threat to regime survival and national security. Pro-Beijing organizations, politicians, and businesspeople in Hong Kong mobilized to denounce the protesters. Hong Kong's diplomats and students abroad also criticized the protests and even encouraged violence against them and their supporters overseas.[36] When a student at Emerson College in Massachusetts wrote an article for the student newspaper entitled "I Am from Hong Kong, Not China," the article went viral and attracted harsh criticism from many Chinese who accused the author of denying her Chinese identity, but it also drew supportive comments from other students from Hong Kong, Taiwan, and Singapore who had received similar criticism.[37] By contrast, when the general manager of the NBA's Houston Rockets tweeted support for Hong Kong, China's official media and social media erupted in outrage.[38]

FIGURE 7.5. Hong Kong protests, 2019 (photo: Joseph Chan/Unsplash)

Beyond this rhetoric, China had few good options for resolving the protests. It hinted it would send in PLA troops or People's Armed Police to put down the protests and restore order, and even staged antiprotest drills across the border in Shenzhen to intimidate the protesters, but in the end left the Hong Kong authorities to deal with the protests. It pressured Chief Executive Carrie Lam, but she had already lost the trust of much of the Hong Kong public. In September she withdrew the extradition bill that had provoked the protests but refused to negotiate on four other demands: investigation of police brutality against protesters, release of arrested protesters, retraction of official description of protests as "riots," and Lam's own resignation followed by elections for a new chief executive and LegCo based on universal suffrage. The Hong Kong police used tear gas, rubber bullets, batons, and water cannons against the protesters, to no avail. In at least one incident, thugs allegedly from criminal triads attacked and beat protesters. This is a common CCP tactic for handling protests, as mentioned in chapter 5. Hiring thugs allows the government and police to deny responsibility while also sending a clear message. Despite these efforts, protests continued unabated throughout the summer and fall.

November elections for district councils were widely seen as a referendum on the protests, and the results were definitive: prodemocracy parties won control of seventeen of eighteen district councils and increased their share of seats by 27.4 percent, to 85.8 percent.[39] With these results indicating strong public support for the prodemocracy movement, neither Beijing nor the Hong Kong government could pretend the public did not support the protests. Sporadic protests continued for a time after the district council elections, but the outbreak of COVID-19 in December 2019 quickly shifted the attention of both the public and the government toward this looming threat. The new crisis brought the months-long protest to an end, but not the underlying tension between China's influence in Hong Kong and the growing Hong Kong identity. As one indication of this, the Hong Kong government in April 2020 began arresting prodemocracy activists, signaling that it—and its overseers in Beijing—had no intention of being responsive to the people of Hong Kong, even in the midst of a pandemic.[40] The head of Beijing's liaison office in Hong Kong said it had the right to supervise events in Hong Kong, in opposition to the Basic Law's promise of a high degree of autonomy.

Then, in order to remove any doubt about China's intentions, in June 2020 the NPC in Beijing passed a new National Security Law (NSL) for Hong Kong that bans foreign interference, secession, terrorism, and subversion of state power against the governments of Hong Kong and China and makes these actions punishable by potentially life imprisonment.[41] These vaguely worded provisions were designed to end protests in Hong Kong after 2019's tumult, and came at a time when much of the world's attention was focused on the COVID-19 pandemic. The wording of the NSL seemingly applies not just to people in Hong Kong but to anyone anywhere.[42] Any statement or action to which Beijing takes offense could potentially violate the NSL, even if it occurs outside China and Hong Kong. In the weeks after the law was passed, the Hong Kong police arrested prominent democracy activists and the publisher of the prodemocracy newspaper the *Apple Daily*. The NSL effectively ends the autonomy promised in the Basic Law and imposes a "one country, one system" model on Hong Kong.

Does the CCP Orchestrate Nationalist Protests for Its Own Purposes?

In addition to the Patriotic Education Campaign, the CCP also uses nationalistic rhetoric in its media reports, official speeches, and propaganda. In his speech on the seventieth anniversary of the founding of the PRC in 2019, Xi Jinping said, "There is no force that can shake the status of this great nation. No force can stop the Chinese people and the Chinese nation forging ahead."[43] Many observers, especially in the media and the policy community, see this rhetoric as a means to mobilize Chinese society in support of the government's foreign policy. For example, this was the main interpretation for anti-US protests in 1999, when Chinese students protested the US bombing of the Chinese embassy in Belgrade. The missile hit a room on the second story of the building, killing three Chinese journalists and injuring twenty others. The room reportedly held intelligence equipment used to monitor NATO activities in Belgrade and report back to Beijing.[44] Because countries have sovereignty over their embassies, an attack on an embassy is equivalent to an attack on the country's territory. As soon as the bombing of the Chinese embassy in Belgrade became known, Chinese students were so outraged that their request to protest in front of the US embassy in Beijing was readily approved by their universities and the government. The spontaneous protests in Beijing quickly evolved into orchestrated protests under the CCP's control. Groups of students were bused to the US embassy in Beijing, where they yelled and threw rocks at the embassy for a set period of time, then were bused back to their campuses and replaced by students bused in from another campus. After several days, the protests came to an end.

This looks like a simple case of the CCP orchestrating nationalist protests. However, an alternative interpretation is that such protests were the result of popular nationalism that emerged in the 1990s. This coincided with the CCP's shift to the victim narrative, but popular nationalism had its origins in the intellectual ferment within society regardless of the CCP's actions and intentions.[45] Popular nationalism has an emotional component that makes it so volatile and potentially threatening to the CCP. China's nationalists do not always wait for a signal or permission from the regime before springing to action. Anti-US protests began in Beijing, other Chinese cities, and on foreign campuses as soon as reports of the bombing of China's embassy in Belgrade appeared. Rather than orchestrating the protests at the American embassy, the CCP may have been trying to bring order out of chaos. Before it began busing students between the embassy and their campuses, students were protesting spontaneously at the embassy's gates. Ambassador James Sasser said at the time that he was worried that the protesters would break down or climb over the gates and that the safety of embassy staff was in danger. By arranging buses for the students, the government could limit how many students were outside the embassy and for how long. Once their time was up, they were whisked away on the buses. This allowed the protests to occur, while preventing them from escalating out of control.[46]

Many of China's most vocal nationalists were not fans of the CCP and its leaders. They wanted the CCP to take a stronger line against foreign countries, especially the United States. As the title of one best seller from the 1990s aptly put it, *China Can Say No*. Books like this capitalized on popular nationalism by encouraging China's leaders to be equally nationalistic.[47] Such books could not be published today. Xi Jinping wants adulation, not advice, from intellectuals.

Chinese nationalists are not only critical of the regime, they are also critical of fellow Chinese who they feel are not sufficiently patriotic, including those who favor democracy in China. In 2017, a Chinese student gave a graduation ceremony address at the University of Maryland in which she praised the "fresh air of free speech" in the United States.[48] This was taken as an oblique criticism of the political atmosphere in China. In retaliation for her comments, she was immediately attacked online and by the Chinese media and even received death threats, as did her family members back in China. Li Na, China's best-known tennis player, was frequently criticized for saying she played for herself more than her country. When she suffered an upset loss in the French Open in 2013, she rejected the need to explain her loss to her fans back home: "Do I need to get on my knees and kowtow to them? Apologize to them?"[49] She was roundly criticized by both the Chinese media and netizens.

The CCP may try to stoke nationalism, but Chinese nationalism has a popular base that is independent of the CCP's control. China's nationalists are not necessarily party supporters, although the party tries to link love of country and support for the party as one and the same. Popular nationalism presents a potential threat to the CCP: it may eclipse the CCP's own propaganda, criticize the CCP for not being sufficiently vigilant in protecting China's national interests, and even compel it to adjust its foreign policy to accommodate nationalistic public opinion. This last possibility is explored in the next section.

Does Popular Nationalism Drive Chinese Foreign Policy?

What if the CCP is not the cause of Chinese nationalism but is captive to it? The popular nationalism perspective argues that nationalism is rooted in Chinese society regardless of the CCP's actions. Rather than creating nationalist sentiments and mobilizing them in support of its policies, the CCP may be forced to take a harder line than it prefers in order to prevent itself from being the target of nationalist protests. Although Chinese youth may not be more nationalistic than older generations, they may be more hawkish in their foreign policy views, which may further constrain foreign policy makers who do not want to face a popular backlash.[50]

This would not be the first time that a Chinese government was challenged and weakened by nationalists. After World War I, Chinese students and other intellectuals were angered when the Chinese territories formerly controlled by Germany, such as the port city of Qingdao, were given to Japan instead of being returned to full Chinese sovereignty.[51]

But their anger turned to outrage when they discovered that China's representatives at the Versailles Peace Conference in 1919 had agreed to this outcome. They criticized the Chinese government for being too weak to stand up for Chinese national interests against foreign powers. Bowing to student protests and public opinion, the Chinese representatives in the end refused to sign the Treaty of Versailles, but by then the damage to the government's reputation had already been done. These protests and critiques became known as the May Fourth movement, a period marked by intellectual ferment and popular protest that questioned many orthodoxies in China, including subservience to political powers. The CCP itself was founded a few years later in 1921, and many of its founding members were active in the May Fourth movement. It therefore has a keen appreciation for how popular nationalism can challenge an incumbent regime.

Another occasion of nationalists challenging the government also involved Japan, which invaded Manchuria in northeast China in 1931 and gradually expanded its control over more and more Chinese territory. On December 9, 1935, Chinese students protested the Nationalist government's weak response to Japan's aggression. The December 9 protests did little to change the Nationalist government's policy toward Japan, much less slow Japan's advance, but remained a vivid reminder of nationalist protests against unpopular government policies. In recent years, Chinese students have tried to mark the anniversary of this event and Japan's invasion of China on September 18, 1931, with new protests to voice their opposition to Japan's contemporary policies and actions, although these efforts have generally been suppressed by the CCP.[52]

Does public opinion push the CCP to take more assertive policy toward foreign countries? An answer in the affirmative suggests that Chinese leaders prefer a more accommodating foreign policy but are pushed to adopt more belligerent policies by public opinion. The alternative—that China's leaders stoke nationalism to support its more assertive and even aggressive actions—is clearer and more straightforward, but most studies of Chinese nationalism reject it in favor of arguments involving interaction between popular nationalism and CCP leaders in the shaping of Chinese foreign policy.

During the 2000s, anti-Japanese sentiment was strong in China. Not only was the national government criticizing Japan in its media and education curriculum but also private actors at the local level were promoting strong anti-Japanese messages. These local efforts were without central approval, and seemingly without central support. Anti-Japanese history activists used the Patriotic Education Campaign to publicize Japanese atrocities during World War II. They conducted new research, published books and articles, and even opened new museums to document and publicize these historical events.[53] When controversies involving Japan—including historical issues and contemporary diplomatic and territorial disputes—broke out in this context, the public quickly mobilized around demands to take a harder line toward Japan than the CCP's rhetoric initially suggested. By 2005, China's Japan policy was under challenge from public opinion.

Beijing's rhetoric, negotiating strategies, and policy changes toward Japan during these years all seemed to be the result of the public's influence and not simply a response to Japanese policies. Public mobilization regarding Japan arose outside CCP control and without CCP mobilization and it influenced both decisions and rhetoric toward Japan. Nevertheless, CCP efforts to tamp down public mobilization, reshape public opinion, and demobilize activists were largely successful. China's leaders could bring these protests to a close with a combination of persuasion, repression, and pointed warnings in the media and text messages whenever the protests began to challenge international interests and domestic stability.

The media may also influence how popular nationalism puts pressure on China's foreign policy. When popular nationalism is aroused by reports in the official media, it can pressure Beijing to take a more hardline stance toward Japan.[54] The impact of the official media is amplified by the internet, as social media users repost media reports to reach an ever larger audience. The CCP clamps down on online discussions on hot-button topics once they are seen as potentially destabilizing, but by then the discussion has often reached a crescendo. In that sense, the official media both transmits and appeals to popular nationalism. Tracing the timeline of media reports and government statements regarding

Japan during the 2000s and early 2010s shows that the government's rhetoric began to take a stronger position only after the official media and social media spread more nationalistic and anti-Japanese language. Beijing's statements were initially mild and showed no willingness to confront Japan on a variety of issues, including Japan's bid to gain a permanent seat on the United Nations Security Council, territorial disputes, or Japanese textbooks that obscured its atrocities in China. But then nationalist rhetoric began to pour out from below, both on the internet and local media. Over a short period of time, Beijing's rhetoric began to match what was rising up from below.

Did popular nationalism influence Chinese foreign policy toward Japan? Without access to Chinese decision makers, we cannot see what was happening behind the scenes. It is possible, for example, that official statements were mild to avoid stirring up the public, but that stronger statements were being made through private channels to the Japanese government. If so, the strategy failed: the mildness of Beijing's official rhetoric galvanized the Chinese public to demand a stronger line, and that was the eventual result. It is also possible that China's leaders had a range of opinions on this issue, as is true for most policy issues (see chapter 3), and that the more hard-line rhetoric was the result of internal debates. Without access to foreign policy decision makers, it is impossible to determine if the increasingly harsh rhetoric was in response to public opinion, infighting among political leaders, or other factors.

A more intriguing possibility is that the CCP's response to nationalist protests is designed to send signals to foreign governments about the constraints it faces in international negotiations. Because nationalism is part of the CCP's claim to legitimacy, it would pay a high price if it made concessions to foreign countries that angry patriots did not approve of. Their outrage could potentially trigger an uprising that would overthrow the CCP. The new regime could be even more nationalistic because new regimes—even new democratic regimes—often adopt strong nationalist policies to rally public support.[55] Seeing popular nationalism in action, foreign governments may feel compelled to forgo certain demands, recognizing that the CCP cannot comply without threatening its hold on power. Conversely, when the CCP suppresses nationalist protests, it signals that it is willing to risk the wrath of its citizens in order to achieve a certain foreign policy goal, making its commitment to that goal more credible. This is a diplomatic version of the "good cop, bad cop" routine: the Chinese government signals that the foreign government is better off making an accommodation with it or risks having a more nationalistic alternative come to power. This negotiating strategy can be credible when nationalist protests arise spontaneously but is undermined when the CCP is thought to be orchestrating those protests.

Two episodes in US-China relations illustrate this argument.[56] The first was the 1999 anti-American protests after the bombing of the Chinese embassy in Belgrade, described earlier. These protests were generally seen as being orchestrated by the CCP, although the initiative seems to have come from university students. In contrast, the CCP responded quite differently during another episode in 2001 involving an American EP-3 intelligence-gathering aircraft. The United States routinely flies surveillance planes like the EP-3 in international airspace along China's coast. The Chinese government protests that these flights are a violation of its sovereignty and occasionally sends fighter jets after the American spy planes. In one such incident on April 1, 2001, a Chinese fighter pilot flew too close to the American plane and clipped its wing. The Chinese jet crashed into the ocean, and its pilot died in the crash. The damaged American plane was forced to make an unauthorized landing on the island of Hainan off China's southern coast. The American crew was held in custody at a military barracks while the two governments negotiated a resolution. Although many Chinese citizens were again outraged by the collision and the death of the Chinese pilot, the CCP did not allow protests to occur. US officials interpreted this as symbolizing the CCP's determination to maintain the US-China relationship at the start of George W. Bush's first term in office.[57] That it was willing to do so even in the face of popular anger indicated that the CCP was prepared to pay a domestic price for its commitment to the US-China relationship. After ten days, on April 11, 2001, the US crew was allowed to leave China.[58]

An alternative explanation of the CCP's different responses in these two events may be what triggered them: the CCP allowed protests when it was the victim, but suppressed them when it was the instigator. US jets undeniably bombed the Chinese embassy in 1999, and the Chinese pilot undeniably collided with the EP-3 in 2001.

This simpler explanation fits the two cases of anti-American protests, but it does not explain the more numerous episodes of anti-Japanese protests. When China and Japan have been committed to improving diplomatic relations and broadening their economic ties, the CCP has been willing to suppress nationalist protests; but when China's leaders believe that Japan is deviating from their agreement to shelve territorial disputes and set aside historical grievances, the CCP allows protests to occur as a way of signaling its opposition to Japan's moves. In 1985, Japanese Prime Minister Yasuhiro Nakasone paid an official visit to the Yasukuni Shrine in Tokyo, which includes a memorial to those who died in World War II (including Tojo and other war criminals). His visit was seen as an insult to the memory of the estimated 6 to 10 million Chinese who died and the countless others who suffered atrocities at the hands of Japanese soldiers during World War II.[59] Chinese students immediately began anti-Japanese protests, which spread across college campuses for several weeks. Concerned that his visit was threatening China's reform agenda of domestic reform and international opening, Nakasone canceled plans for a second visit.[60] Other Japanese prime ministers, including Junichiro Koizumi and Shinzo Abe, also visited the Yasukuni Shrine. Some of those visits led to reprisals, as when China canceled a planned visit by the Japanese foreign minister after Koizumi visited the shrine in 2013, but not the large anti-Japanese protests that followed Nakasone's visit. These varied responses suggest that the CCP selectively uses popular nationalism to achieve its policy goals.

During the 1990s, when the CCP was trying to repair its international reputation and maintain domestic stability after the tragic end to the 1989 demonstrations in Tiananmen Square and throughout China, it was more willing to suppress anti-Japanese protests. In addition, the CCP did not want nationalist protests to become a springboard for other types of citizen grievances, such as corruption, the economy, or democracy, and therefore suppressed protests of all kinds in its effort to maintain domestic stability. But when Japan campaigned to become a permanent member of the United Nations Security Council in 2005, the CCP allowed protests and petitions to occur in order to achieve its diplomatic goal of defeating Japan's bid. The CCP then suppressed anti-Japanese protests for several years as China and Japan sought to repair their relations. When Japan took steps to reassert its claims of sovereignty over the disputed Diaoyu/Senkaku islands in the East China Sea in 2012, angry and occasionally violent protests broke out in more than two hundred Chinese cities, as described in the vignette that opened this chapter.[61] China's leaders saw Japan's actions as upsetting the status quo over the islands and therefore allowed the protests to snowball, but only for a short while. After a few days, the CCP sent out text messages warning students to abide by the law and maintain stability. The protests came to an abrupt end. The CCP's preoccupation with maintaining stability inevitably takes priority over even nationalist protests. They may be the only form of dissent the CCP allows, but they are not always allowed and they are not allowed indefinitely.

Whether popular nationalism influences Chinese foreign policy may depend largely on the context: in other words, what triggered the diplomatic crisis and the state of bilateral relations with the country involved. The evidence is somewhat ambiguous and fits both the conventional wisdom that the CCP mobilizes nationalism and the alternative argument that it responds to popular nationalism. Without access to decision makers, we cannot make a definitive call. Given that ambiguity, neither perspective should be dismissed out of hand. Policy makers in other countries should be mindful of the potential constraints the CCP faces—it also has a domestic audience it cannot ignore. The CCP may be promoting nationalism with its victim narrative, but it is also determined not to be the victim of the nationalism it has unleashed.

* * *

There is no question that nationalism runs high in China, perhaps the highest of anywhere in the world. But the causes and consequences of Chinese nationalism are less well understood. This chapter has examined four of the main assumptions about Chinese nationalism, and has found each of them wanting. Nationalism is not continuing to rise, and young Chinese are less nationalistic than their elders; the CCP's Patriotic Education Campaign has had very mixed results, and in Tibet and Xinjiang it appears to have backfired; popular nationalism has its own dynamic that is not simply a response to CCP mobilization, and it may push the CCP to take a hard line on foreign policy issues.

The CCP does not control Chinese nationalism, nor is it entirely beholden to it. Nationalist protests are a common form of protest that the CCP is at pains to control. Since the early 1990s, it has been promoting the notion that China was a victim of foreign countries during a "century of humiliation" from the Opium Wars of the 1840s until the establishment of the People's Republic in 1949. This Patriotic Education Campaign is not just a history lesson, it is also intended to show that international forces are once again working to slow China's development and impinge on its national interests. Nationalist protests that make these same allegations cannot simply be suppressed, because the protesters are responding to the CCP's message. After basing its legitimacy for almost seventy years at least in part on nationalism, it cannot suppress nationalist protests without also threatening its own legitimacy.[62]

But the CCP also worries that these protests can backfire on it. If it does not respond to perceived foreign insults as forcefully as protesters call for, the protesters may turn on the CCP for not defending the nation's pride, reputation, and interests. If the protests snowball out of control, there is the potential for instability. In the CCP's political priorities, maintaining stability is more important than promoting nationalism. Large-scale protests—even nationalist protests—do not happen without the CCP's tolerance, approval, or even encouragement; but protesters are not mere puppets doing the party's bidding.[63] When the two are at odds, stability wins.

The CCP's response to nationalist protests—encourage, tolerate, or suppress—therefore depends on the interplay of its diplomatic and domestic goals. It is willing to encourage or at least tolerate nationalist protests when it reacts to the actions of other countries, when it wants to show support for nationalist sentiments to its domestic audience, and when it wants to signal its constraints to foreign governments. However, when its own actions trigger a diplomatic crisis, when it wants to signal goodwill to foreign governments, and, most important, when its concerns for maintaining stability outweigh its support for popular nationalism, it is able to bring the protests quickly to an end or preempt them all together.

As shown throughout this book, the CCP is often responsive to public opinion. If Chinese foreign policy evolves in a hard-line direction in response to popular nationalism, and even if Beijing seeks concessions from foreign governments in its efforts to remain in power, it would be yet another example of the CCP's responsiveness. In actuality, connecting the dots between popular nationalism and changes in foreign policy is challenging. China's foreign-policy decision makers are normally not available for interviews to confirm whether or not they were indeed responding to popular nationalism, or if changes in foreign policy or even official rhetoric were for other reasons. Whether public sentiments actually *caused* those changes, or were mostly background noise, is difficult to determine. It may well be that divisions among Chinese leaders are a better explanation for foreign policy decisions than public opinion.[64] If China's leaders are as nationalistic as the people they govern, they may not need prodding from society to take assertive foreign policy actions.

8

WILL CHINA BECOME DEMOCRATIC?

Throughout the post-Mao era of reform in China, scholars have debated the potential for China's democratization. Because an increasingly marketized economy is thought to be incompatible with an authoritarian regime, and because economic modernization triggers social changes requiring a more open political system, many observers inside and outside China expected that political reform would eventually have to catch up to economic reform. But this was not the intention of China's leaders. Going back to Deng Xiaoping and continuing under Xi Jinping, the CCP expected that economic modernization, if handled properly, would produce popular support for the party and solidify its hold on power. China's leaders saw economic modernization as a means of prolonging party rule, and were determined to avoid political liberalization that would weaken the party's hold on power, even if liberalization yielded better economic results.

Is democracy the inevitable consequence of economic modernization? Will future economic growth be stymied if not accompanied by political reform? Is Chinese society developing a preference for democracy, or does public opinion favor the continuation of authoritarian rule? China watchers have offered a range of answers—but many scholars would argue these are the wrong questions. What is more important is whether the CCP will survive as China's ruling party. This is the necessary prerequisite for democratization in China. In order to

understand the prospects for democratization, we also have to understand what keeps the party in power and what are the potential threats
to its survival.

This chapter will assess the ongoing debate about party rule in China
and offer a comparative perspective on the likelihood of democratization. While all countries are unique, a comparative perspective
draws attention to broad trends that are relevant for China's future. Just
as China's leaders study foreign countries for insights and ideas, so
should we as outside observers. At the same time, we should also pay
close attention to the unique features of the CCP and the specific
changes brought about by Xi Jinping. There are reasons to expect
democratization in China, other factors that caution against such expectations, and uncertainty about what type of regime will govern
China if and when the CCP loses its hold on power.

Why We Should Expect
Democratization in China

The changes under way in China throughout the post-Mao period have
given rise to speculation that economic growth in one way or another
will lead to political change. The rationale for this speculation is based
on several well-established findings in political science. When applied
to China, this conventional wisdom has made many optimistic about
the prospects for democratization.

Modernization Theory

Proponents of democratization in China often point to modernization
theory to make their case. Modernization theory is based on one of the
best established and least controversial findings in political science:
the close relationship between prosperity and democracy. In short, the
most prosperous countries tend to be democracies. The only exceptions to this are the OPEC countries of the Middle East, whose wealth
is derived from the export of oil and not the economic modernization

that accompanied democratization in other countries; and Singapore, a city-state with great economic prosperity and still under an authoritarian regime, and therefore a model for many in China who want to preserve the current political system while also pursuing economic modernization.

Why is this so? The essence of modernization theory is not that prosperity itself produces democratization but that economic modernization brings social and cultural changes that favor democratization: an increasingly urban population, higher levels of education and income, moderate and mostly secular values, all of which result in a middle class with a desire to protect its interests and policy preferences.[1] China's rapid economic modernization has triggered these changes that modernization theory says lead to democracy. People are moving from the countryside to the cities in search of better-paying jobs. Levels of education are increasing. New forms of communication allow wider flows of information. Higher standards of living allow people to focus less on basic survival and economic security and more on equality, freedom, and self-expression.

All these developments give hope to some observers that democracy is in China's not too distant future. For example, Stanford's Henry Rowan predicted that China would be "partly free" (in the terminology of Freedom House) by 2015 and "fully free" by 2025. The first prediction was wrong—Freedom House continues to categorize China as "not free"—and the second prediction will likely also go unfulfilled.[2] Ronald Inglehart and Christian Welzel also predicted that China would "make a transition to liberal democracy" by around 2025 due to socioeconomic liberalization and experiments with local democracy.[3] These are straight-line predictions based on trends that did not remain straight. Liberalization has largely stalled since the time they wrote. More significant is that the social and attitudinal changes that create support for democratization have not taken hold in China. For example, there is a large and rapidly expanding middle class with an interest in protecting its property and financial resources from the state (as shown in the NIMBY protests in chapter 5), but it is still not seeking the expansion of political rights and freedoms that would favor democracy.[4]

Compatibility of Democracy and Capitalism

The affinity of democracy and capitalism provides a second argument in favor of democratization in China. As China's economy became more market driven (despite continued state control over strategic sectors like energy, telecommunication, aviation, and finance), it would inevitably become more democratic. Otherwise, the supposed incompatibility of a market-oriented economy and an authoritarian political system would stymie continued economic development.[5]

At the end of the Cold War and following the collapse of communism in the Soviet Union and Eastern Europe, Francis Fukuyama famously proclaimed "the end of history": humankind had reached the point where the combination of democracy and capitalism no longer faced any ideological rivals.[6] Fascism had been defeated in World War II, communism had proven to be anything but a paradise, and no appealing alternatives existed. Not all countries had yet adopted democratic political systems and capitalist market economies, but no other alternatives posed a challenge to the growing dominance of democracy and capitalism throughout the world. This was hubris of the finest kind, but it quickly became apparent that democracy and capitalism were not the only options available.[7] The "China model" of development—the combination of authoritarian politics and an economic system that was market oriented but still dominated by the state—had appeal for many governments, especially in Africa and Latin America.[8]

The expected link between democracy and capitalism also inspired US policy toward China for much of the post-Mao era. The US government promoted trade with China and China's integration into the international community. The somewhat romanticized notion that economic modernization inevitably leads to democratization has suggested to some that there was little need to push democratization on China because it would happen on its own. Similarly, there was little pressure on China to reciprocate the opening of its market to US and foreign firms, because many people expected, or at least assumed, this would happen eventually.[9] But China's openness has stalled, and in many ways reversed since the international financial crisis that began in 2007 and especially after Xi Jinping became China's leader in 2012. Under these conditions, the prospects for democratization in China look less rosy. Even former US government officials have acknowledged that their expectation that economic liberalization would lead to political liberalization was misplaced.[10]

International Factors

A third set of arguments for China's democratization is based on international factors. One source of international influence is normative: the supposed desire of China's leaders to be accepted as part of the global community. Since most major powers are democracies, China's leaders will want to democratize in order to gain full membership in the international community, or so the thinking goes. This perspective was more common at the beginning of the reform era in China, and especially the immediate post–Cold War era, but less so now for a variety of reasons. China's role in the international community has increasingly grown without the need of democratizing. There was little pressure on China to become democratic because most countries were content to trade with China. The Trump administration took a more confrontational approach toward China but still focused on trade and economic policy and not regime change. As citizens in many democracies have lost trust in their leaders and institutions, and democratic countries like Poland, Hungary, Brazil, and the Philippines have seen backsliding in their commitment to democracy,[11] the value of democracy as an international norm is less pertinent than it was even a few decades ago—and less appealing to nondemocracies like China.

Another international factor is "snowballing": when a country becomes democratic, pressures for democratization in neighboring countries also increase. Snowballing was a feature of democratization in Latin America; it helped bring down communist governments in Eastern Europe and challenged authoritarian leaders in the Middle East and North Africa in the Arab Spring. But China does not directly border on a democratic country, except for Mongolia and a small shared border with India (a source of recent military tensions). Its southeast Asian neighbors—Vietnam, Laos, and Myanmar—are authoritarian. It shares borders with countries that used to be part of the Soviet Union—Russia, Kazakhstan, Kyrgyzstan, Tajikistan—all nondemocracies. Japan, South Korea, and Taiwan are consolidated democracies, but they do not border directly on China. China's economic development model borrowed extensively from its East Asian neighbors, but it has shown less inclination to learn from their democratization. In short, there is little chance of democratization in China due to snowballing.

An alternative source of international influence has to do with one of the hoped-for consequences of democratization. "Democratic peace" theory is based on another well-established finding in political science: democracies don't fight each other.[12] Therefore, if China were to democratize, the potential for war between China and the United States or its Asian neighbors would diminish. The democratic peace is an outcome and not a cause of democratization, and as a result it is not a reason for predicting that democracy is likely in China but instead a potential reason for hoping it will become democratic.

Why We Should Not Expect
Democratization in China

While expectations for China's democratization are mostly based on broad generalizations drawn from the experiences of other countries, the reasons for being skeptical are based on more specific aspects of authoritarian regimes, especially China's case. The real question is not whether China will democratize but whether the CCP will remain in power. The answer to that question has to do with regime characteristics, including the nature of one-party rule, the party's adaptability, the unity of party leaders, the legitimacy of the party, and popular and elite attitudes toward democracy. For each of those factors, the changes brought about by Xi Jinping will also influence the continuation of party rule in China.

Durability of One-Party Regimes

When investigating the potential for political change in authoritarian regimes, we first need to distinguish different types of authoritarian regimes and not simply distinguish democratic and nondemocratic regimes. The most common types of authoritarian regimes are military dictatorships, personalist rule by strongmen and monarchs, and one-party regimes like China's. Research by political scientists has shown that one-party regimes are more durable than other types of authoritarian regimes: one-party regimes last the longest, military dictatorships the shortest, and personalist (or strongman) regimes fall in between.[13]

Why? What is it about one-party regimes that have made them longer lasting? Unlike personalist regimes, a one-party regime is more likely to survive the death of its founder because power is not entirely concentrated in the hands of one individual. The CCP survived the death of Mao with limited turmoil. After Mao, it experienced peaceful transfers of power between several generations of leaders, as described in chapters 1 and 2. Leadership transitions in authoritarian regimes are often times of great uncertainty because the death or overthrow of the leader can trigger a struggle for power among potential successors. The CCP's routine process for appointing and replacing leaders largely reduced that uncertainty. Both the party and the people knew well in advance who the next leader would be: Hu Jintao was identified as Jiang Zemin's successor ten years before he replaced Jiang, and Xi Jinping similarly as Hu's successor five years before becoming party leader. This regular and peaceful style of leadership transition has been an important source of regime stability.

Xi upended that process after becoming the CCP's general secretary in 2012. By removing term limits from the state constitution, he signaled his intention to rule indefinitely. By not naming a successor at the 19th Party Congress in 2017, he created uncertainty over who would replace him and even how his successor would be chosen if he were to die or become incapacitated.[14] The concentration of power in Xi's hands makes him vulnerable to policy failures or other crises. But his tight control over the party, the military, and the public security sector will make it difficult and dangerous for other leaders to challenge him.

One-party regimes are durable also because they are more likely to co-opt new elites with access to higher education and plum jobs. These new elites, rather than being treated as if they pose a threat to the regime, are brought in and made stakeholders in the status quo. The CCP has recruited private entrepreneurs into the party and appointed them to (mostly symbolic) political positions.[15] In the years after 1989, it actively recruited college students, making college campuses the main source of new party members. Party membership is seen by many as advantageous to their careers, not only in the party and government bureaucracies but also in the private sector.[16] Co-opted entrepreneurs and intellectual elites have a stake in protecting the status quo.

Unlike military regimes, which are often divided between those who enjoy governing and those who prefer to focus on national security threats, leaders of one-party regimes are more likely to prefer the status quo than any alternative. One-party regimes like China's are not monolithic; their leaders have a greater incentive to coexist with rivals rather than risk losing power. Some may have strong policy preferences, some may seek power and influence, and some may simply want to enrich themselves through the perks of office, but all have a strong motivation to remain in power. Military leaders can "return to the barracks" and still protect their institutional interests, including their own careers. For example, military leaders in Brazil forced democratic leaders to grant them permanent amnesty before agreeing to end their dictatorship. In contrast, civilian leaders of authoritarian regimes do not fare so well once they lose power. Many end up in prison or in exile. In South Korea and Taiwan, even democratically elected presidents went to prison after they left office. The conclusion is straightforward: in order to remain free, CCP leaders have to remain in power.

One-party regimes that come to power via armed struggle may be especially durable because they had to be better organized to win power in the first place. Once in power, they have more extensive and effective institutions for implementing policies and suppressing the rise of an organized opposition.[17] The CCP came to power after a protracted civil war, and several of Mao's maxims, including "political power grows out of the barrel of a gun" and "the party controls the gun," continue to be true. More to the point, the Leninist features of the CCP, including its integration with the government, the military, SOEs, and the media; its network of party cells throughout workplaces and neighborhoods; and its ability to monitor and sanction what people say and do, continue to be characteristics of its rule. These features waxed and waned throughout the post-Mao era but have returned with a vengeance under Xi. The CCP's monopoly on political organization makes it difficult for other groups to form, and its control of the media and censorship policies make it difficult for opponents to communicate with each other without being detected. These core features of a Leninist party system greatly increase the difficulty of engaging in collective action against the party.

The party has been relying more and more on a big-data approach to surveillance, particularly facial recognition software and national identification cards. During the COVID-19 epidemic in 2020, it took this a step further, requiring people to scan QR codes when they enter buildings or buses and report their daily health status to the local government with a smartphone app. These technologies are ostensibly part of the battle against the virus, but they also allow the party to track people's whereabouts on a micro scale at any given time. Continued use of these technologies will further ratchet up the cost of collective action by making it easy for the party to track people in real time.

Among one-party regimes, communist regimes have been the longest lasting.[18] The Soviet Union lasted for seventy-four years before it broke up in 1991; the People's Republic of China marked its seventieth anniversary on October 1, 2019. This highlights a fact about the PRC that is easily overlooked: it has already lasted much longer than other authoritarian regimes, even one-party regimes, and now has retained power almost as long as the previous record holder for longevity among communist regimes. Moreover, the CCP shows no obvious signs of imminent demise. Predictions of its downfall—either due to democratization or collapse—have been common throughout the post-Mao era,[19] but so far all such predictions have failed to materialize.

The CCP's Adaptability

One-party regimes may be more durable in general than other types of authoritarian regimes, but why has the CCP in particular been so successful in defying the expectations of its demise? The first reason is its adaptability. Although the CCP has been the ruling party since 1949, it has not been a static ruling party. Its policies have changed dramatically over the years, mostly in response to changes in top leaders, as outlined in chapter 1. During the post-Mao period, it abandoned central planning for greater reliance on markets for economic development. It replaced economic autarky with ever greater integration into the global community. It abandoned class struggle as the basis for the party's relations with the people. Instead, it became more willing to co-opt former "class enemies," including capitalists and critical intellectuals, into the CCP. Rather than appoint officials primarily for their political loyalty, it began to require professional qualifications for many positions in the party and government bureaucracies. Personal connections continued to matter, as detailed in chapter 2, but the appointment and promotion of officials became increasingly meritocratic. It modified its policies toward economic development, the environment, education, health care, and other prominent issue areas in light of public opinion, as noted in chapters 3 and 5. Being adaptive and responsive in these ways allowed it be more resilient.

There are long-term trends that may influence its longevity for better or worse. For example, the economy has reached the point where the developmental policies that were so successful in the past are no longer useful.[20] The population is rapidly aging, and because of the one-child policy the labor force is not growing the way it once did. Cities are experiencing tremendous growing pains that challenge the party's ability to meet society's expectations.[21] All of these issues present serious governance challenges for the party. But it has been able to manage these trends so far by adapting its policies, its message, and even its members to fit changing conditions.

Xi's tenure as party leader has been marked less by adaptability than by the return of strongman rule akin to Mao. His key slogans have been the "China Dream" and "Socialism with Chinese Characteristics for a New Era," but both slogans are fronts for poorly articulated policy goals. His signature campaign was the anticorruption campaign during his first term as general secretary, but even this campaign took a lower profile after his second term began in 2017. By then he had removed many of his opponents, replaced them with his followers, and warned others not to challenge him. In this way, as in other examples discussed throughout this book, repression has taken priority over responsiveness in political life during Xi's time as China's leader. If adaptability has been a key source of the party's resilience under previous post-Mao leaders, under Xi it has been less adaptive, less responsive, and potentially less resilient as a result. In short, Xi's style of leadership may be good for Xi, but is not necessarily good for the longevity of the party.

Elite Unity

A second reason for the CCP's survival has been its relatively high degree of elite unity. Although Chinese politics is replete with political rivalry, it has not been as explosive or as publicized as it was during the Maoist and early post-Mao periods. There have not been wide-scale purges of political leaders as in the Cultural Revolution. Policy difference have narrowed: leaders are no longer divided over whether to pursue radical leftist goals or pragmatic economic development, and instead debate how best to achieve economic modernization. The outpouring of protests in 1989 made it clear that perceived divisions among China's top leaders created openings for political challenges to the party's rule. Since 1989, China's leaders have more vigorously maintained public unity. The policy differences between leaders and factions do not play out in competing media articles or public speeches, as they did in the 1980s.[22]

But even episodes of elite conflict have typically not ended with the deaths of the losing side. This is what allowed so many post-Mao reformers to be rehabilitated and restored to influential positions. Some had spent time in prison during the Maoist era, some had been sent into internal exile, but within the top echelon of leaders only Liu Shaoqi died, and that was due to neglect (he died of complications of diabetes while in prison). There are many stories of personal tragedies, and the treatment of many people opposed to the CCP has been inhumane and unjustifiable. But one reason for the longevity of the CCP has been the limited political conflict among top leaders. When losing a political struggle does not risk losing your life, the stakes are lower and the conflict less intense.

There were no successful or even attempted coups in China after the arrest of the Gang of Four in October 1976, a month after Mao died. The 1989 Tiananmen demonstrations ended the careers of very few top officials. Zhao Ziyang was placed under house arrest after being removed as general secretary in 1989. He never faced formal charges, much less prison or execution, although he remained under house arrest until his death in 2005. Others close to Zhao fared much better. Wen Jiabao was one of Zhao's top aides; he was not punished for this affiliation, and later became prime minister. Hu Qili was a leading reformer at the time of the demonstrations and a member of the Politburo Standing Committee, China's inner circle of political power. He was removed from office for supporting the students but later had a limited political rehabilitation. He served first as vice minister and then minister of the Ministry of the Machine-Building and Electronics Industry between 1991–98, and as vice chairman of the Chinese People's Political Consultative Conference, a largely honorary post. But none of the top leaders removed from office in 1989 for sympathizing with the protesters was imprisoned, much less executed. An initial attempt to identify and investigate those within the party, government, and universities who supported the protesters was soon abandoned once it became clear that few people wanted to cooperate.

Since 1989, CCP leaders have been able to portray a remarkably high degree of party unity for public consumption. The 1989 protests, the collapse of communist governments in Eastern Europe later that year, and the breakup of the Soviet Union in 1991 convinced China's leaders they needed to project greater unity, at least in public.[23] Political rivals were occasionally removed from office, but their removals did not lead to more widespread purges. In 1995, CCP general secretary Jiang Zemin was able to orchestrate the removal of his rival, Beijing party secretary and Politburo member Chen Xitong. Chen was charged with corruption and sentenced to sixteen years in prison but released in 2006 after serving only eight years. In a similar fashion, Jiang's successor, Hu Jintao, used a corruption scandal to eliminate Shanghai's party secretary and Politburo member Chen Liangyu (no relation to Chen Xitong) in 2006. Chen was accused of siphoning money from the Shanghai pension fund, but his real crime was belonging to a rival faction and resisting "scientific development," Hu's policy to balance rapid economic growth with a more equitable distribution of wealth. Chen was sentenced to eighteen years in prison in 2008.

However, the case of Bo Xilai may be an exception to this norm of party unity. Bo Xilai was party secretary of the southwestern municipality of Chongqing and member of the Politburo at the time of his downfall in 2012. He was a charismatic and ambitious politician and thought to be a candidate for the Politburo Standing Committee, and according to some rumors wanted to become general secretary, even though the party elite had decided on handing that post to China's current leader, Xi Jinping. But Bo's plans fell apart after Chongqing's police chief, Wang Lijun, took refuge in the American consulate in Chengdu and claimed that Bo's wife, Gu Kailai, was responsible for the murder of a British businessman (Wang's request for asylum was denied, and he was handed over to state security officials sent from Beijing). Wang's story was quickly covered by the Western and Chinese media, and Bo and his wife were taken into custody, put on trial, and convicted. Bo received a life prison sentence, Gu a death sentence later commuted to life in prison, and Wang a fifteen-year sentence. Bo's downfall was more like a soap opera than the usually staid public demeanor of elite politics in China.

What makes Bo's case exceptional was what reportedly happened next: according to widespread rumors, his allies in the security apparatus attempted a coup, including the dispatch of armored personnel carriers into the central party and government compound known as Zhongnanhai, part of the former Forbidden City in Beijing. These were only rumors, but the ferocity of Xi's anticorruption campaign, which targeted some party and military leaders previously thought to be untouchable, may have been a response to Bo's challenge to the party's planned leadership succession and especially the (rumored) attempted coup. The sentences doled out to those convicted of corruption in this campaign were relatively mild. In the past, some corrupt officials received death sentences. There were no executions among the thousands of party, government, and military officials found guilty during Xi's anticorruption campaign, but many received lengthy prison sentences, including life sentences.

Saying that Chinese elites do not try to kill each other may seem like damning with faint praise. If the question is how humane the regime is, or how fairly the party treats the people, then simply noting that Chinese leaders agree to coexist does not tell us much. But if the question is why the regime survives when so many have predicted its downfall, then elite unity is very much part of the explanation.

Performance Legitimacy

Another reason that the CCP has remained in power is its performance legitimacy. Because of China's prolonged period of economic growth, most people in China have experienced higher incomes and better quality of life. Some are doing better than others, of course, and growing inequality has been a prominent political issue. But even though the benefits of growth have not been evenly distributed, most have seen significant improvement. Hundreds of millions have been lifted out of poverty: China's poverty rate was 66.2 percent in 1990 but only 0.5 percent by 2016.[24] For the younger generations in China, they have known only progress. The bad old days of the Maoist era are hard to imagine for people who did not live through them, and many Chinese parents and grandparents do not share their past sufferings with their kids and grandkids. Even for rural migrant workers, the dangerous, dirty, and low-paying jobs they end up in are preferable to the conditions they left behind when they moved from the countryside to the cities.[25]

The key to the CCP's performance legitimacy is not economic growth per se, but whether people's own incomes are rising.[26] Despite growing economic inequality, the vast majority of Chinese believe their incomes and quality of life have been growing, and they remain optimistic about continued growth. This is roughly equivalent to "pocketbook voting" in democracies: those with rising incomes tend to support the incumbents. The same logic applies to China: rising incomes are one of the most reliable predictors of support for the status quo.

As incomes grow, and people begin to take for granted the level of prosperity they have come to know, modernization theorists predict they will develop new expectations of what they expect from the government. In anticipation of that, the CCP has been improving its provision of public goods, especially concerning health care, access to higher education, and more generous social welfare policies for the poor and elderly.[27] Whereas in the 1990s it was an outlier—the Chinese government spent much less than other middle-income countries—it has now caught up. More significantly, the central government has taken on a larger share of the burden, relieving local governments of what had been unfunded mandates.

These two aspects of performance legitimacy—rising incomes and improved governance—go a long way in explaining why so many in China are willing to accept—if not fully support—continued rule by the CCP.[28] China's slowing economy now puts the CCP's performance legitimacy to the test. Will China's leaders be able to achieve a soft landing for the economy, reverse the decline, or cause an economic collapse? Economic crises are the primary threat to any ruling party in any type of regime.[29] The CCP's fate may well depend on how well it can continue to deliver improved living standards despite the economic slowdown. Much will depend on how well the CCP manages the transition from its current economic model that emphasizes exports and infrastructure spending to one that relies more on services and domestic consumption. The trade war with the United States and the impact of the coronavirus could further threaten the CCP's performance legitimacy in the years to come. The CCP has already been stoking nationalist sentiments among the public by blaming foreign countries for China's economic problems, as it previously did with its victimization narrative.[30]

Popular Attitudes toward Democracy

Although China is rapidly modernizing, it has not experienced the type of value change that modernization theory says is the basis for democracy. The Chinese public is more concerned with material issues of wealth and security than normative goals of equality and freedom. This is in part because of China's recent political history. Many recognize, in light of the tragic outcome of the 1989 protests, that pushing for democracy is dangerous and unlikely to succeed. Since 1989, there has been no sustained, nationwide social movement for democracy in China. Moreover, there is little public support for the political activists who continue to call for democracy. Even in online discussions, which afford people a degree of anonymity not possible in public protests, people who support China's democratization are often ridiculed as elites and dupes of Western countries.[31] Many dissidents have been forced into exile, where they become irrelevant and spend time fighting each other instead of fighting for democracy. As a result, there is no Chinese equivalent of Nelson Mandela, someone who has broad social support and credibly speaks on behalf of Chinese society writ large.

Despite the problems in contemporary China, there is a recognition that the range of freedoms today is wider than in the Maoist period (at least for those who experienced that period; others take the current situation for granted). These changes are best described as liberalization without democratization: a less intrusive state, more economic opportunities and more social mobility, but still without competition between parties and rule of law. The party is more responsive to public opinion, even if it is still not accountable. So long as the CCP is tacitly responsive, few are willing to call for the formal mechanisms of accountability (such as elections, generally seen as the essential element of democracy). The absence of a free press and the party's strict monitoring of civil society groups further ensure its lack of accountability.

But the repressive turn under Xi has rolled back much of the liberalization that characterized the post-Mao era. He has revived the traditional practices of Leninism and added high-tech surveillance programs. This retreat from liberalization has not triggered pushback from large segments of society, at least not yet. The willingness to "eat bitterness"—that is, to endure hardship and disappointment—is a well-established norm in China's traditional political culture and may be an asset to the party. But the frequency of protests throughout China (described in chapter 5) reveals that there are limits on the people's willingness to acquiesce to the party's overreach. Those protests are most often about the improper implementation of policy, not about policies themselves. If protests arise over the party's repressive tactics, however, they will be more political in nature and the party will be less likely to be responsiveness to those types of demands. Protests against the core characteristics of the regime are rarely tolerated.

Perhaps most surprising of all is the reason that so few Chinese are willing to advocate for democratization—because they believe it is already happening. Repeated public opinion surveys reveal that the vast majority of Chinese believe that China has become increasingly democratic during the post-Mao period and has already attained a relatively high level of democracy.[32] This may seem counterintuitive, and indeed it is. From the perspective of democratic countries, China has little in common with what we expect to find regarding basic rights and freedoms and institutions like elections, rule of law, and an independent media. Major projects that track political change throughout the world, including Freedom House and Polity, show minimal change over this period of time. And yet most Chinese see it differently. How can this be?

The answer lies in the definition of democracy. For most in China, democracy is not defined in terms of elections, the rule of law, political freedom, and equal rights (as we would emphasize in Western countries), but rather in terms of outcomes. Improved governance, a growing economy, and better quality of life are seen as evidence that democratization is occurring. This is a paternalistic view of democracy that is based more on what the state does and not how its leaders are chosen or whether they can be held accountable. It is a view of democracy rooted in the principle of *minben*, the traditional belief that the state should act in the best interests of the people, in contrast to *minzhu*, the Chinese term for democracy, which was not commonly used before the Western impact on China in the nineteenth century.[33] If you define democracy as governing in the public's interest, then it is less surprising to view China as increasingly "democratic," even though that is not how democracy is understood in democratic countries.

Should people who have not experienced democracy be expected to define it? Not necessarily. But if they define it in terms of government responsiveness alone, they are less likely to support calls for democracy as it is understood in democratic countries. For many Chinese, democracy is not something they do, it is something they receive. As long as the party is responsive to their needs, they are less likely to demand accountability. As long as incomes continue to rise, higher education is more accessible, health care more available and affordable, air more breathable, and so on, they are not likely to demand competitive elections, a multiparty system, rule of law, free speech, and the other institutional features of democracy.

Those "as long as" clauses are key: Chinese society does not simply passively accept the status quo, it also has expectations formed over several decades of extensive economic reform and more limited political liberalization. If those expectations of continued progress are not met, then the party will likely face a more demanding public. This has been the pattern in other countries that faced calls for regime change and democratization. If the CCP is basing its legitimacy on its policy performance, then continued improvement in standards of living and public goods is essential. So far, it has been able to do so. But can the trajectory of change always move upward? That is one of the questions that likely keep party leaders up at night.

CCP Opposition to Western-Style Democracy

Finally, perhaps the most prominent obstacle to democratization in China is the CCP's opposition to it. Deng Xiaoping was the main sponsor of political reform in the early post-Mao era, but he made it clear that political reform was not to include democratization. In particular, he was opposed to democratic checks and balances that would limit the CCP's power. He favored political reforms, if they were limited to those that would allow the party to govern more effectively without making it accountable. For example, he favored a retirement policy for aging cadres, which in turn would allow younger and better-educated people to assume leadership positions at all levels. He was in favor of age limits and term limits for top leaders (described in chapter 2). He wanted to separate the party and government in order to create a division of labor between them and not have too much power in the hands of individual party leaders. All of these things seem like bureaucratic tinkering, not political reform, and certainly not democratization. But that was Deng's intent—to improve the political system, not replace or reinvent it. He claimed that these types of political reforms, along with his reform and opening economic policies, amounted to a "second revolution," as important in their own way as the revolution that brought the CCP to power.[34]

Deng's antipathy toward Western-style democracy imposed strict limits on political participation. During the "Democracy Wall" movement that began in late 1978, people were able to complain about the excesses of the Cultural Revolution, call for the rehabilitation of party and government officials who had been purged during that time, and criticize leaders of the time who publicly declared their support for maintaining Mao's priorities. All this supported Deng's agenda of sidelining the beneficiaries of the Cultural Revolution and he tacitly supported the movement. But once some people began calling for Deng's own ouster, he quickly shut down the movement and imprisoned some of its bolder voices. He announced the "Four Cardinal Principles" of party rule in China that could not be questioned: the socialist path, the dictatorship of the proletariat, the leadership of the CCP, and Marxism-Leninism-Mao Zedong Thought. Similarly, he supported an abrupt and decisive end to prodemocracy demonstrations on some college campuses in late 1986. Most famously, Deng opposed the popular demonstrations in 1989, labeling them as turmoil and favoring the imposition of martial law, which led to the deaths of hundreds and perhaps thousands of protesters and even innocent bystanders. Each of these episodes revealed Deng's and the CCP's determination to preserve its monopoly on political organization. Deng was a political reformer, but he was no democrat.

Other CCP leaders have also made clear that they do not support Western-style democratization. Wu Bangguo was the head of China's National People's Congress, China's legislature, from 2003 to 2012 and concurrently a member of the Politburo Standing Committee. In 2011, he declared that China would never adopt "a system of multiple parties holding office in rotation; . . . [or] separate executive, legislative, and judicial powers."[35] Soon after Xi became general secretary in 2012, the party issued the notorious Document 9, which banned discussion of several so-called Western ideas, first and foremost being constitutional democracy. In a speech in Belgium in 2014, he said China had tried multiparty democracy in the past (alluding to a brief period in the early twentieth century after the collapse of the Qing dynasty) but it failed and need not be tried again.[36]

If Chinese leaders fear democratization, their fears are well founded. Democratization in most other countries has led to the ruling party losing power and in some cases to the imprisonment of its leaders. In Romania, the deposed president Nicolae Ceaușescu and his wife were executed after a brief show trial, and their dead bodies were then displayed on TV. Even in established democracies like Taiwan, South Korea, and Brazil, former presidents often go to jail once their terms are over, most often based on accusations of corruption. These accusations may be on target, but they also send a clear message to incumbent leaders in China and other authoritarian countries: if they want to maintain their perks, they must hold on to power.

Regime Change Does Not Guarantee Democratization

In considering the prospects for democracy in China, a key consideration is what happens after the CCP-led regime is over. Democratization will not happen without regime change, but regime change by itself does not guarantee democratization. In fact, most cases of regime change in authoritarian countries lead to a new authoritarian regime. Therefore, we should not assume that the only alternative to the CCP is a democracy.

During the third wave of democratization that began in the mid-1970s, there was great optimism among practitioners and scholars that more and more countries would soon be democratic.[37] For countries that had not yet democratized, the research question became why not. The assumption was that democracy was on the upswing, and the absence of democratization required explanation.

By the 1990s, that sense of optimism began to wane as the pace of democratizations around the world slowed. The end of communism in the former Soviet Union and Eastern Europe illustrates this well: of the twenty-nine formerly communist countries in Eastern Europe and the former Soviet Union, only ten became democracies. The rest had personalist dictatorships or at best hybrid regimes. The Arab Spring uprising is another reminder that regime change more often than not brings a new authoritarian regime. Of the seventeen countries in the Middle East and North Africa that experienced upheavals in 2011, only one—Tunisia—became democratic. Instead of the hoped-for peace, prosperity, and respect for political rights and freedoms, regime change in these countries more often led to instability, weak states, and economic decline.

In recent years, new cases of democratization have been exceedingly rare. According to Freedom House, the percentage of democratic countries throughout the world peaked in 2007 at 46.1 percent and declined to 42.6 percent in 2019.[38] Moreover, the quality of democracy has declined in many established European democracies and even the United States. For promoters of democracy, these trends are disheartening.[39] Regime change still happens, but the most common result is the replacement of one authoritarian regime with another.

How regime change occurs may influence whether democratization is the result and how stable and long-lasting it is. There are three main modes of democratization: an elite-led transformation in which incumbent leaders initiate and preside over the transition; a bottom-up replacement, in which a social movement challenges and overthrows an authoritarian regime; and a pacted transition, in which the incumbents negotiate with the political opposition over the terms of the new regime.[40] Many cases of democratization have elements of more than one of these modes of transition, but most cases fall into one mode more than the others.

An elite-led transformation is the easiest and most direct mode of democratization. Incumbent leaders initiate the transition to democracy and may continue to participate in and even rule the new regime. Taiwan is a good example of an elite-led transformation ending in democracy. In 1986, the ruling Kuomintang (KMT; the same party that had lost the civil war with the CCP and retreated to Taiwan in 1949) announced it would lift martial law and allow the formation of opposition parties. It won the first fully contested presidential election in 1996 and remains a prominent (now opposition) party. However, other cases did not end the same way. The collapse of the Soviet Union is most relevant for considering the fate of the CCP. It was primarily the consequence of communist leaders battling each other for power. Boris Yeltsin became the main opponent of Mikhail Gorbachev, who initiated policies of glasnost and perestroika ("openness and reform") to revive the Soviet economy and improve relations between state and society. Yeltsin used the language of democracy, but once he became president of Russia after the breakup of the Soviet Union, he did not champion democracy. Although he initiated some political reforms, he also created a strong presidency with weak legislative oversight. And what little progress toward democracy had occurred under Yeltsin was quickly rolled back under Vladimir Putin. An elite-led transformation may be the most peaceful mode of regime change, but it does not always lead to democratization.

A bottom-up revolution is a second mode of regime change. The society-led overthrow of authoritarian rule can be exciting and exhilarating, the culmination of popular desires for more freedom and more accountability over the government. It can be contagious, as a social movement in one country can inspire similar movements in nearby countries. This was the experience in Eastern Europe as the Solidarity-led protests in Poland later spread to East Germany, Hungary, and Czechoslovakia. Similarly, Tunisia's Jasmine Revolution soon spread to other countries in the Arab Spring of 2011.

But the popular overthrow of authoritarian rule can also be violent and messy, especially if the government tries to suppress the movement and if the political opposition is itself not well organized. Such a movement can result in an unstable new democracy, or be hijacked by political elites who do not support democracy but see the movement as an opportunity to gain power.

This was the case in Egypt. After the overthrow of Mubarak, new elections brought the Muslim Brotherhood to power. Widespread protests against the new government's Islamist policies and continued economic hardship eventually led the military, under the leadership of General Abdel Fattah el-Sisi, to arrest President Mohamed Morsi and other top leaders and install a new military dictatorship. Many of the officials in the new Sisi government had also served under Mubarak. Despite the tremendous political upheaval of 2011 and the opposition's aspirations for a genuine democracy, the outcome was a new regime that was quite similar to the old regime. As Pete Townshend once said in a very different context, "Meet the new boss, same as the old boss."

A similar social movement in China would have an uncertain outcome. The lessons of 1989 weigh heavily on anyone who prefers a democratic China. The CCP proved it was willing to do whatever it takes to remain in power, including the use of deadly force against unarmed civilians. The conditions that would trigger such a movement would be different (perhaps an economic crisis, an environmental disaster, or some other type of legitimacy crisis), and China's current leaders might opt for a different response, but the risks for anyone who initiates such a movement are high indeed. The party's traditional Leninist features combined with modern surveillance technology will make a bottom-up revolution difficult to organize and sustain.

A third and more promising path to democracy is a pacted transition, in which the authoritarian leaders negotiate with the political opposition about the transition to democracy, the timing of elections, and whether the incumbents will be imprisoned and tried for corruption and human rights abuses or receive amnesty for their crimes. This was the case in South Africa, where the apartheid government released Nelson Mandela from prison and negotiated with him the terms of the political transition. Though still marked by sporadic violence by both the government and the opposition, the eventual transition to democratic rule was successful. This type of pacted transition requires (1) an opposition leader who has broad social support, (2) an organized political opposition, and (3) a regime leader who, like South Africa's F. W. de Klerk, is willing to abandon repressive tactics and negotiate the terms of regime change leading to democratization.[41] All three conditions are lacking in China's case, making this mode of democratization unlikely, even it is preferable.

Regardless of the mode of transition, one commonality stands out: the end of an authoritarian regime most often does not guarantee a new democracy. Over the past twenty-five years and more, the end of an authoritarian regime most often gives rise to a new authoritarian regime. We should not assume the outcome will be different for China.

What to Watch For

Will China become democratic? This is a crucial question for the future of Chinese politics, for the welfare of Chinese citizens, for the international community, and for theories of democratization and regime change. But when it will happen, how it will happen, and above all if it will happen remain highly uncertain.

If China does become a democracy, it would lead to a government that is both responsive and accountable to the public. As previous chapters showed, the CCP has been responsive in a variety of ways, adjusting its policy agenda in response to changes in public opinion, but it refuses to be accountable. Democratically elected leaders do not have that same luxury. A democratic China could also lead to improvements in China's human rights situation, as long as a strong rule of law accompanied democratization. If the "democratic peace theory" continues in force, then a democratic China would also be less of a military threat to its neighbors and the international community as a whole. This has important implications for the United States, where many officials, pundits, and scholars believe conflict with China is inevitable.[42] A democratic China would presumably pose less of a threat to American interests and to China's neighbors.

For those expecting or hoping for democratization in China, there are several signs to look for.

First, economic crises pose a threat to all regimes. Ruling parties in democracies are more likely to lose elections when the economy is bad, and authoritarian regimes are more likely to collapse when an economic crisis occurs. A gradually slowing economy by itself would not create a crisis for the CCP, but a recession might. That is why party and government leaders at both the central and local levels have resorted so often to stimulus spending to boost the economy, even at the expense of growing debt. It is also why the annual meeting of the National People's Congress in 2020—postponed for two months due to the COVID-19 epidemic—did not announce an economic growth target for the year, the first time since 1994 it had not done so. The Chinese economy shrank 6.8 percent during the first quarter of 2020 as economic activity was sharply curtailed in response to the spread of the coronavirus.[43] This was precisely the type of "black swan" event that Xi warned party leaders of in 2019: an unforeseen event that would threaten the party's grip on power. In the past, the CCP has been able to avoid a severe economic crisis, but black swan events like this put its leadership to the test. In this case, they passed the test: economic growth rebounded once the worst of the coronavirus was past. By the end of 2020, China had modest but positive growth for the year. Other more likely events, such as a financial crisis brought on by China's mounting debt burden or a collapse of its real estate market due to inflated prices, would pose a more direct threat to the party because they would be the result of its own policies. Such crises have long been predicted but have yet to occur.

Second, a split within the leadership—as occurred in 1989—would create an opportunity for democratic activists to mobilize against the CCP. If democrats believe they have friends in high places, they will be more likely to take the risk of engaging in public protest. The CCP has been able to maintain a public façade of unity since 1989. The few episodes of elite conflict, such as the Bo Xilai affair, have been struggles for personal power more than open clashes between reformers and hardliners. A more dramatic development, such as top leaders advocating a reassessment of the party's verdict on the 1989 demonstrations, would be a clearer indication of elite support for political change, but is highly unlikely. China watchers used to wonder who would be China's Gorbachev, a leader who would usher in fundamental political and economic reforms. But once glasnost and perestroika led to the fall of communist regimes in the Soviet Union and Eastern Europe, economic collapse in many of those countries, and the dissolution of the Soviet Union, Yugoslavia, and Czechoslovakia into separate countries due to ethnic conflicts, no Chinese leader wants to follow Gorbachev's example.

Relatedly, a third sign of potential democratization would be an increase in popular support for democratic activists. These protests can have a cascade effect: as more people show more support for change and less for the status quo, increasing numbers of people feel it is safe to join the ranks.[44] This played out in 1989 in China, in 1989–91 in other communist countries, and in 2011 during the Arab Spring. To a lesser degree it has also occurred in Hong Kong, where the public support for prodemocracy protests was larger and more long lasting in 2019 than in the past. But popular support for democracy is not enough to guarantee democratization. The Arab Spring did not result in democratization throughout the Middle East and North Africa. In Hong Kong, Beijing looks intent on tightening its control over the territory, not acceding to protesters' demands. Popular support for democracy may be necessary for successful democratization but is not by itself sufficient to bring it about.

Fourth, a significant international loss could also trigger regime change, as nationalists come to believe that the CCP is not strong enough to defend the nation's interests. Examples of international losses that have triggered regime change in other countries include defeat in war and severe economic sanctions. China has had skirmishes with many of its neighbors—Japan over the Diaoyu/Senkaku islands, Vietnam and the Philippines over disputed territories in the South China Sea, India along their shared border—but none have escalated to full-scale war. China has made threatening moves against Taiwan through increasingly assertive language, sending fighter jets through Taiwanese air space, and holding military exercises to simulate invading an island, but it has not yet used force in its quest to unify Taiwan with the mainland. The United States and China have occasionally exchanged heated rhetoric or engaged in shows of force but have been careful to avoid a direct clash. Even in the crises in 1999 and 2001, described in chapter 7, the two countries negotiated a compromise in order to avoid military escalation and a complete split in the relationship. A significant loss in these types of situations could result in nationalist outrage against the CCP. Crippling economic sanctions are unlikely, given how interdependent most countries are with China, and could even backfire if the CCP framed sanctions as yet another example of its victimization narrative, rallying nationalist sentiments instead of being the target of them.

Whether China becomes democratic is also a test for prevailing theories of democratization and regime change. Adherents of modernization theory expect China to democratize because economic modernization is creating rapid changes in China's social structure and in the future may produce value change leading to support for democracy. In contrast, the CCP's strategy is to pursue economic modernization in order to enhance its legitimacy. As Marxists, CCP leaders believe the most important interests are material ones: rising incomes, job security, and living standards. By improving the material aspects of life, they expect to produce popular support. Modernization theory expects the opposite outcome: as people come to take prosperity and economic security for granted, they begin to develop new interests, such as equality, fairness, and self-expression. For the foreseeable future, the continuation of the status quo in China is the most likely scenario, but modernization theory reminds us that the status quo does not remain static indefinitely.

China's democratization could also have ripple effects in other authoritarian regimes that see China's current one-party system as a role model. If the "China model" comes to include democratization, and if China's support for existing autocracies ends as a result, others may follow suit. Though China's support is not as consequential as Soviet support for communist governments in Eastern Europe, withdrawal of its support could still weaken other autocratic leaders and embolden their citizens to protest against their governments.

Conversely, as long as the CCP remains China's ruling party, other authoritarian regimes will face less pressure to reform. International pressure on authoritarian regimes to democratize, become more transparent, improve their human rights records, and undergo other types of political reform have less chance of success when major countries like China do not go along. With its well-publicized resistance to foreign interference in its internal affairs, China rarely cooperates in international efforts to overtly pressure other countries to change. Moreover, its combination of economic modernization and authoritarian rule provides an appealing model for other autocrats. In contrast to the West, China's foreign aid and lending programs are not conditional on the receiving country's governance and human rights records, which allows them to receive much-needed capital without changing how they govern.

However, democracy is not a panacea. Democracies are definitely better at promoting freedom and equality than authoritarian regimes, but they are not necessarily better at achieving economic growth, effective governance, or political stability.[45] In fact, new democracies often experience economic decline, even to the point of creating nostalgia for the former authoritarian regime.[46] Partisan conflict can prevent consensus on even the most pressing policy issues. Democratization could also make China less stable politically. For example, groups representing various interests could openly protest to get their voices heard. Local leaders could challenge the authority of the national government. Minorities in Tibet and Xinjiang could seek greater autonomy or even independence, which would be a critical test of the new government's ability to maintain national unity. Democratization could also make China pursue a more nationalistic foreign policy, as new leaders often use antiforeign rhetoric to build legitimacy.[47]

And it is important to remember that even the end of CCP rule would not guarantee the beginning of democracy in China. Most cases of regime change in recent years have resulted in new authoritarian regimes, not new democracies. This is a sobering thought for all those who work for or hope for the future of democracy in China.

* * *

Chinese politics in the twenty-first century is a study in contrasts: repressive yet responsive, authoritarian yet adaptable, conflictual yet cooperative. The balance between these paired features has varied over time, in different parts of the country, and on some issues more than others. The first half of each pair largely defines the conventional wisdom on contemporary China; the second half is revealed by in-depth research in the field. Both must be kept in mind to best understand how the Chinese political system has changed over time and what may lie ahead.

The CCP has various frailties, explored throughout this book, that make its survival questionable: Xi's autocratic style; the party's ever greater use of repression and declining responsiveness; the absence of effective accountability; the policy stalemate on economic reforms; the challenges of coping with modernization, urbanization, and so on. But as a Leninist party it also has attributes that have allowed it to remain in power for more than seventy years: control over the government, legislature, military, and media; the appointment of party and government leaders at all levels; party cells to monitor what is happening at the grassroots level, now bolstered with surveillance technology and big-data analytics; and, above all, its monopoly on political organization. These same features are likely to keep it in power for the foreseeable future. The evolving relationship between the party and the people will continue to define the nature of Chinese politics in the years to come.

NOTES

Chapter 1: What Keeps the Party in Power?

1. Tony Smith, *Thinking Like a Communist: State and Legitimacy in the Soviet Union, China, and Cuba* (New York: W. W. Norton, 1987).

2. The goal here is not to detail these decades of CCP rule in China but to summarize in order to compare and contrast them. For a more detailed discussion, see Roderick MacFarquhar, ed., *The Politics of China*, 3rd ed. (New York: Cambridge University Press, 2011).

3. Roderick MacFarquhar and Michael Schoenhals, *Mao's Last Revolution* (Cambridge, MA: Harvard University Press, 2006).

4. Harry Harding, "The Chinese State in Crisis," in MacFarquhar, ed., *Politics of China*, 148–247; MacFarquhar and Schoenhals, *Mao's Last Revolution*.

5. Andrew G. Walder, "The Decline of Communist Power: Elements of a Theory of Institutional Change," *Theory and Society* 23, no. 2 (April 1994), 297–323.

6. Barry Naughton, *Growing Out of the Plan: Chinese Economic Reform, 1978–1993* (New York: Cambridge University Press, 1995).

7. David Shambaugh, *China's Communist Party: Atrophy and Adaptation* (Berkeley and Washington, DC: University of California Press and Woodrow Wilson Center Press, 2009).

8. Many of the most momentous changes of the Jiang Zemin era were not Jiang's initiatives but those of his prime minister, Zhu Rongji. Zhu was responsible for ending the boom and bust cycles in the Chinese economy. He was able to achieve a "soft landing" in the 1990s, slowing China's red-hot economy without throwing it into recession. He negotiated China's entry into the World Trade Organization (and was pilloried online, in the press, and on the streets, with Jiang letting him take the heat for a policy he nonetheless approved). Unlike Jiang, Zhu stayed out of the public spotlight after his retirement in 2003, except for appearances at his alma mater Tsinghua University. For a profile of Zhu, see Orville Schell and John Delury, *Wealth and Power: China's Long March to the 21st Century* (New York: Random House, 2014), 325–52.

9. Samuel P. Huntington, *Political Order in Changing Societies* (New Haven, CT: Yale University Press, 1970), 20.

10. Bruce J. Dickson, *Red Capitalists in China: The Party, Private Entrepreneurs, and Prospects for Political Change* (New York: Cambridge University Press, 2003); and *Wealth into Power: The Communist Party's Embrace of China's Private Sector* (New York and London: Cambridge University Press, 2008).

11. Kellee S. Tsai, *Capitalism without Democracy: The Private Sector in Contemporary China* (Ithaca, NY: Cornell University Press, 2007).

12. Economic inequality is commonly measured by the Gini coefficient, which ranges between 0 and 100, where 0 means perfect equality (everyone has the same amount of wealth) and 100 means perfect inequality (one person has all the wealth). China's Gini coefficient peaked in 2008, when it reached 49.1. In 2016, China's Gini coefficient of 46.5 (according to the CIA Factbook) ranked it as the thirty-first-highest level of inequality in the world. However, estimates for many countries vary widely and are not available for every year.

13. Nicholas Lardy, *The State Strikes Back: The End of Economic Reform in China?* (Washington, DC: Peterson Institute for International Economics, 2019); Arthur R. Kroeber, *China's Economy: What Everyone Needs to Know* (New York: Oxford University Press, 2016).

14. Schell and Delury, *Wealth and Power*.

15. See http://news.xinhuanet.com/mrdx/2017-10/21/c_136695470.htm (accessed November 29, 2017).

16. Jiangnan Zhu and Dong Zhang, "Weapons of the Powerful: Authoritarian Elite Competition and Politicized Anticorruption in China," *Comparative Political Studies* 50, no. 9 (August 2017), 1186–220.

17. At the 17th Party Congress in 2007, scientific development and the goal of achieving a "harmonious society," another slogan identified with Hu, were included in the long preamble of the constitution, but not identified as part of the party's guiding ideology.

18. Chris Buckley, "As China's Woes Mounts, Xi Jinping Faces a Rare Rebuke at Home," *New York Times*, July 31, 2018, https://www.nytimes.com/2018/07/31/world/asia/xi-jinping-internal -dissent.html, accessed August 1, 2018; Peter Martin, "Is Xi Jinping's Power Grab Starting to Backfire?" *Bloomberg Businessweek*, August 7, 2018, https://www.bloomberg.com/news/articles /2018-08-07/is-xi-jinping-s-bold-china-power-grab-starting-to-backfire, accessed August 7, 2018.

19. Suisheng Zhao, "Xi Jinping's Maoist Revival," *Journal of Democracy* 27, no. 3 (July 2016), 83–97.

20. The app is reported to include software that allows it to monitor all other parts of the user's phone, including voice, text, photos, videos, web activity, and user's location. See Anna Fifield, "Chinese App on Xi's Ideology Allows Data Access to Users' Phones, Report Says," *Washington Post*, October 16, 2019, https://www.washingtonpost.com/world/asia_pacific /chinese-app-on-xis-ideology-allows-data-access-to-100-million-users-phones-report-says /2019/10/11/2d53bbae-eb4d-11e9-bafb-da248f8d5734_story.html, accessed October 16, 2019.

21. Anne-Marie Brady, *Marketing Dictatorship: Propaganda and Thought Work in Contemporary China* (Lanham, MD: Rowman & Littlefield, 2009); Daniela Stockmann, *Media Commercialization and Authoritarian Rule in China* (New York: Cambridge University Press, 2012).

22. China's formal political system does not include its villages, which are deemed self-governing and, more significantly, self-financing units.

23. Perhaps the only example where this slim margin of choice mattered came in 1987. Deng Liqun, the leading conservative ideologue of that era and a vocal opponent of Deng Xiaoping's reforms (the two Dengs were not related), had been chosen by party leaders for a seat on the Politburo which requires membership on the Central Committee. However, he was so unpopular among other party members that he was not elected to the Central Committee and therefore could not be on the Politburo.

24. The municipalities of Beijing, Chongqing, Shanghai, and Tianjin and the "minority autonomous regions" of Guangxi, Inner Mongolia, Ningxia, Tibet, and Xinjiang have provincial-level status.

25. One well-known vote by the Politburo Standing Committee may be an apocryphal story. During the Tiananmen Square protests in 1989, the Standing Committee reportedly took a vote on imposing martial law. Li Peng and Yao Yilin were in favor, Zhao Ziyang and Wan Li were opposed, and Qiao Shi abstained. Because of this stalemate, they sought Deng Xiaoping's advice. He was in favor. Martial law was announced May 20, leading ultimately to the violent end to peaceful protests on June 4. See Andrew J. Nathan and Perry Link, eds., *The Tiananmen Papers* (New York: Public Affairs, 2001), 191–93. However, Zhao Ziyang claimed in his memoir that no vote was ever taken. See *Prisoner of the State: The Secret Journal of Zhao Ziyang* (New York: Simon and Schuster, 2009), 29–30.

26. The term in Chinese is *zhuxi*, literally "chairman," but "president" is the international norm for referring to heads of state and that is how the term is translated into English.

27. The NPC's role in the policy process will be examined in chapter 3.

28. In the 1990s, local people's congresses rejected a few of the party's nominees for government positions. As a result, the party tightened its nomination process to avoid these rare but embarrassing cases of rejection. See Melanie Manion, "When Communist Party Candidates Can Lose, Who Wins?" *China Quarterly*, no. 195 (September 2008), 607–30.

29. China has eight so-called democratic parties, holdovers from the pre-1949 era. But they do not compete for votes and do not operate as opposition parties.

30. Also on the Politburo's Standing Committee is the chairman of the Chinese People's Political Consultative Conference, a holdover from the pre-1949 era. It is made up of mostly non-CCP elites and meets simultaneously with the NPC and people's congresses at lower levels. It can make recommendations, but they are nonbinding. It does not have the authority to pass laws or oversee the government. It is therefore seen as a largely symbolic institution filled with people friendly to the CCP.

31. John P. Burns, "Strengthening Central CCP Control of Leadership Selection: The 1990 *Nomenklatura*," *China Quarterly*, no. 138 (1994), 458–91; Melanie Manion, "The Cadre Management System, Post-Mao: The Appointment, Promotion, Transfer and Removal of Party and State Leaders," *China Quarterly*, no. 102 (June 1985), 212–19; Kjeld Erik Brødsgaard, "Management of Party Cadres in China," in Kjeld Erik Brødsgaard and Zheng Yongnian, eds., *Bringing the Party Back In: How China Is Governed* (Singapore: Eastern Universities Press, 2004), 57–91.

32. Carl Minzner, *End of an Era: How China's Authoritarian Revival Is Undermining Its Rise* (New York: Oxford University Press, 2018).

Chapter 2: How Are Leaders Chosen?

1. Kevin J. O'Brien, "Implementing Political Reform in China's Villages," *Australian Journal of Chinese Affairs*, no. 32 (July 1994), 33–59; Daniel Kelliher, "The Chinese Debate over Village Self-government," *China Journal*, no. 37 (January 1997), 63–86; Tianjian Shi, "Village Committee Elections in China: Institutional Tactics for Democracy," *World Politics* 51, no. 3 (April 1999),

385–412; Baogang He, *Rural Democracy in China: The Role of Village Elections* (New York: Palgrave, 2007).

2. Minxin Pei, "'Creeping Democratization' in China," *Journal of Democracy* 6, no. 4 (October 1995), 65–79.

3. Pei, "Creeping Democratization," 76; Thomas Bernstein and Xiaobo Lu, "Taxation without Representation: Peasants, the Central and the Local States in Reform China," *China Quarterly*, no. 163 (September 2000), 742–63; Kevin J. O'Brien and Lianjiang Li, "Accomodating 'Democracy' in a One-Party State: Introducing Village Elections in China," *China Quarterly*, no. 162 (June 2000), 465–89.

4. Melanie Manion, "The Electoral Connection in the Chinese Countryside," *American Political Science Review* 90, no. 4 (December 1996), 736–48.

5. Lianjiang Li, "The Politics of Introducing Direct Township Elections in China," *China Quarterly*, no. 171 (September 2002), 704–23.

6. Jie Lu, *Varieties of Governance in China: Migration and Institutional Change in Chinese Villages* (New York: Cambridge University Press, 2014).

7. Graeme Smith, "The Hollow State: Rural Governance in China," *China Quarterly*, no. 203 (September 2010), 601–18.

8. Kevin J. O'Brien and Rongbin Han, "Path to Democracy? Assessing Village Elections in China," *Journal of Contemporary China* 18, no. 60 (June 2009), 359–78; Melanie Manion, "How to Assess Village Elections in China," *Journal of Contemporary China* 18, no. 60 (June 2009), 379–83.

9. John James Kennedy, "The Price of Democracy: Vote Buying and Village Elections in China," *Asian Politics and Policy* 2, no. 4 (2010), 617–31; Meina Cai and Xin Sun, "Institutional Bindingness, Power Structure, and Land Expropriation in China," *World Development* 109 (September 2018), 172–86; Tan Zhao, "Vote Buying and Land Takings in China's Village Elections," *Journal of Contemporary China* 27, no. 110 (2018), 277–94.

10. The CCP has revised the end date of the Cultural Revolution to fit prevailing policy. It originally ended in 1969 with convening of the Ninth Party Congress, although the political struggles among China's leaders continued until after Mao's death. The Cultural Revolution is now said to have ended in 1976 following Mao's death in September and the arrest of the Gang of Four in October. After a brief interval, the post-Mao reform era officially began in December 1978 at the Third Plenum of the 11th Central Committee, which officially declared the end of class struggle and other types of political campaigns and adopted economic modernization as the main task of the CCP.

11. Kevin J. O'Brien and Lianjiang Li, "Selective Policy Implementation in Rural China," *Comparative Politics* 31, no. 2 (January 1999), 167–186; Maria Edin, "State Capacity and Local Agent Control in China: CCP Cadre Management from a Township Perspective," *China Quarterly*, no. 173 (March 2003), 35–52; Susan Whiting, "The Cadre Evaluation System at the Grass Roots: The Paradox of Party Rule," in Barry Naughton and Dali Yang, eds., *Holding China Together: Diversity and National Integration in the Post-Deng Era* (New York: Cambridge University Press, 2004), 101–9.

12. Martin Dimitrov, "Vertical Accountability in Communist Regimes: The Role of Citizen Complaints in Bulgaria and China," in Dimitrov, ed., *Why Communism Did Not Collapse:*

Understanding Authoritarian Regime Resilience in Asia and Europe (New York: Cambridge University Press, 2013), 276–302.

13. Pierre F. Landry, Xiaobo Lu, and Haiyan Dai, "Does Performance Matter? Evaluating Political Selection along the Chinese Administrative Ladder," *Comparative Political Studies* 51, no. 8 (2018), 1074–1105; Xiaobo Lü and Pierre F. Landry, "Show Me the Money: Interjurisdiction Political Competition And Fiscal Extraction in China," *American Political Science Review* 108, no. 3 (August 2014), 706–22; Genia Kostka and Xiaofan Yu, "Career Backgrounds of Municipal Party Secretaries in China: Why Do So Few Municipal Party Secretaries Rise from the County Level?" *Modern China* 41, no. 5 (September 2015), 467–505; Hongbin Li and Li-An Zhou, "Political Turnover and Economic Performance: The Incentive Role of Personnel Control in China," *Journal of Public Economics* 89, nos. 9/10 (2005), 1743–62; Victor Shih, Christopher Adolph, and Mingxing Liu, "Getting Ahead in the Communist Party: Explaining the Advancement of Central Committee Members in China," *American Political Science Review* 106, no. 1 (February 2012), 166–87.

14. Landry, et al., "Does Performance Matter?"

15. Much of the research focuses on these economic targets, which are easiest for scholars and also higher-level officials to measure and compare. Finding valid and reliable indicators of competence is a well-recognized problem for scholars and officials alike.

16. There is some evidence that the criteria for promotion are different for party and government posts, even though individuals typically alternate between party and government bureaucracies in different parts of their careers.

17. More precisely, there are 2,852 counties, 288 prefectures, and 31 provincial units.

18. Chien-Wen Kou and Wen-Hsuan Tsai, "'Sprinting with Small Steps' Towards Promotion: Solutions for the Age Dilemma in the CCP Cadre Appointment System," *China Journal*, no. 71 (January 2014), 153–71.

19. Landry et al. find that age limits are strictly enforced at the provincial level, less so at the prefecture level, and less still at the county level. But they acknowledge this pattern may be due in part to measurement error.

20. Minxin Pei, *China's Crony Capitalism: The Dynamics of Regime Decay* (Cambridge, MA: Harvard University Press, 2016); Andrew Wedeman, *Double Paradox: Rapid Growth and Rising Corruption in China* (Ithaca, NY: Cornell University Press, 2012).

21. Kou and Tsai, "Sprinting with Small Steps"; Kjeld Erik Brødsgaard, "Politics and Business Group Formation in China: The Party in Control?" *China Quarterly*, no. 211 (September 2012), 624–48.

22. Charlotte P. Lee, *Training the Party: Party Adaptation and Elite Training on Reform-Era China* (New York: Cambridge University Press, 2015).

23. Informally, the National Party Congress also provides an opportunity for friends and factions to meet. To prevent congress delegates from coordinating activities without the leaderships' knowledge, local delegations are housed at separate hotels. Central party leaders then meet with local delegations in their hotels.

24. In years past, some Chinese scholars discussed the notion of institutionalizing these informal factions, which are formally prohibited by the CCP. These formally organized factions would then compete for members and support within the CCP (similar to Japan's Liberal

Democratic Party) and be a precursor to a multiparty system. Such ideas are now a thing of the past as the party has no intention of democratization.

25. Zhengxu Wang and Anastas Vangeli, "The Rules and Norms of Leadership Succession in China: From Deng Xiaoping to Xi Jinping and Beyond," *China Journal*, no. 76 (July 2016), 24–40.

26. In a similar vein, Yuhua Wang argues that the CCP promotes the rule of law only in areas where its authority is unlikely to be challenged, for example in commercial law but not political rights, and more specifically in areas where investment comes from foreign business but not where it comes from domestic Chinese investors. See his *Tying the Autocrat's Hand: The Rise of the Rule of Law in China* (New York: Cambridge University Press, 2015).

27. Deng also remained chairman of the government's central military commission until the next NPC elected government leaders in spring 1990. Jiang similarly kept this title until March 2005.

28. Details on Jiang Zemin's career come from Bruce Gilley, *Tiger on the Brink: Jiang Zemin and China's New Elite* (Berkeley: University of California Press, 1998); Robert Lawrence Kuhn, *The Man Who Changed China: The Life and Legacy of Jiang Zemin* (New York: Crown Publishers, 2004); Cheng Li and Lynn White, "The Fifteenth Central Committee of the Chinese Communist Party: Full-Fledged Technocratic Leadership with Partial Control by Jiang Zemin," *Asian Survey* 38, no. 3 (March 1998), 231–64; David Shambaugh, "The Dynamics of Elite Politics during the Jiang Era," *China Journal*, no. 45 (January), 101–11.

29. Details on Hu Jintao's career come from Kerry Brown, *Hu Jintao: China's Silent Ruler* (Singapore: World Scientific Publishing Company, 2012); Richard Daniel Ewing, "Hu Jintao: The Making of a Chinese General Secretary," *China Quarterly*, no. 173 (March 2003), 17–34; Willy Wo-Lap Lam, *Chinese Politics in the Hu Jintao Era: New Leaders, New Challenges* (Armonk, NY: M. E. Sharpe, 2006); Cheng Li, *China's Leaders: The Next Generation* (New York, NY: Rowman & Littlefield, 2001); Alice Miller, "The Succession of Hu Jintao," *China Leadership Monitor*, no. 2 (Spring 2002), 1–8; Frederick C. Teiwes, "The Politics of Succession: Previous Patterns and a New Process," in John Wong and Yongnian Zheng, eds., *China's Post-Jiang Leadership Succession: Problems and Perspectives* (Singapore: Singapore University Press and World Scientific Publishing, 2002), 21–58.

30. Serving in the CYL is advantageous for ambitious leaders. They are able to transfer to an equivalent post in party and government bureaucracies, but they are at a younger than average age. This reduces the age constraint on them, allowing them to gain experience in a wider variety of areas. The Youth League Faction is in large part the consequence of the large proportion of party and government officials who started their careers in the CYL system. See Kou and Tsai, "'Sprinting with Small Steps.'"

31. In addition to the roughly two hundred people elected to the Central Committee, another group of alternate members are elected. When an opening occurs on the Central Committee (due to death, retirement, or political downfall), a member from the list of alternates fills the vacancy.

32. Although Guizhou has been a laggard in terms of economic growth, it has been a leader in poverty alleviation and narrowing the level of economic inequality. See John A. Donaldson, *Small Works: Poverty and Economic Development in Southwest China* (Ithaca, NY: Cornell

University Press, 2011); Daniel B. Wright, *The Promise of the Revolution: Stories of Fulfillment and Struggle in China's Hinterland* (Lanham, MD: Rowman & Littlefield, 2003).

33. Jiang Zemin reportedly wanted to appoint Hu as a government minister to take advantage of his technocratic background, but was overruled by Deng who saw his potential as a political leader; Willy Wo-Lap Lam, *Chinese Politics in the Hu Jintao Era: New Leaders, New Challenges* (Armonk, NY: M. E. Sharpe, 2006), 10.

34. This ambitious plan for party reform largely stalled after Zeng retired from the Politburo Standing Committee in 2007. See David Shambaugh, *China's Future?* (Cambridge and Malden, MA: Polity, 2016), 110–14.

35. Details on Xi Jinping's career come from: Zhiyue Bo, *China's Elite Politics: Political Transition and Power Balancing* (Singapore: World Scientific Publishing Company, 2007); Jean-Pierre Cabestan, "Is Xi Jinping the Reformist Leader China Needs?" *China Perspectives*, no. 2012/3 (2012), 69–76; Willy Wo-Lap Lam, *Chinese Politics in the Era of Xi Jinping: Renaissance, Reform, or Retrogression?* (New York, NY: Routledge, 2015); Cheng Li, *Chinese Politics in the Xi Jinping Era: Reassessing Collective Leadership* (Washington, DC: Brookings Institution Press, 2016); Alice Miller, "Who Does Xi Jinping Know and How Does He Know Them?" *China Leadership Monitor*, no. 32 (Spring 2010), 1–8; Yongnian Zheng and Gang Chen, "Xi Jinping's Rise and Political Implications," *China: An International Journal* 7, no. 1 (March 2009), 1–30.

36. Phillip C. Saunders et al., eds., *Chairman Xi Remakes the PLA: Assessing Chinese Military Reforms* (Washington, DC: National Defense University Press, 2018).

37. Princelings like Xi are the offspring of party and military veterans, constituting a hereditary elite who believe they are entitled to rule China. Their close family ties and career experiences of their fathers (including the suffering they endured during Maoist campaigns like the Cultural Revolution) create a bond between them that is not shared with other leaders. In that sense, Xi and other princelings believe it is their right to rule, given their backgrounds and upbringing. It is this same attitude that creates such intense resentment against them. In an increasingly meritocratic system, princelings have influence because of their pedigree and political connections, not their performance.

38. Xi reportedly applied to join the party ten times before he was admitted (Xinhua 2017a). This was during a time when his father was in prison for allegedly opposing Mao.

39. Lam, *Chinese Politics in the Era of Xi Jinping*, 277; "Plagiarism and Xi Jinping," *AsiaSentinel* (September 24, 2013), at https://www.asiasentinel.com/politics/plagiarism-and-xi-jinping/, accessed July 17, 2018.

40. Xi married Ke Xiaoming, whose father was China's ambassador to the United Kingdom, in 1980, but they divorced after Xi became deputy party secretary in Hebei in 1982. Ke moved back to England. Her name is among the many censored search terms in China.

41. Zeng's brother Zeng Qinghuai was a patron of Xi's wife, Peng Liyuan, and was beneficial in her career.

42. Ironically, he was troubled by the efforts of some leaders to coordinate bloc voting in the straw poll he won. As general secretary, he has been opposed to using elections, even informal ones, or wider consultation in the appointment and promotion of leaders. He prefers insulating these decisions from political maneuvering, but in the process retreating from any semblance

of democratic practices. As part of the process for deciding the new Politburo membership in 2017, Xi had one-on-one interviews with dozens of top leaders, including those already retired, but avoided the kind of group deliberations that brought him to power.

Chapter 3: How Are Policies Made?

1. *An Evaluation of and Recommendations on the Reforms of the Health System in China: Executive Summary* (Beijing: State Council Development Research Council, 2005).

2. "Some Questions Concerning Methods of Leadership," *Selected Works of Mao Tse-Tung*, vol. 3 (Beijing: Foreign Languages Press, 1967), 119.

3. "Rare Release of Xi's Speech on Virus Puzzles Top China Watchers," *Bloomberg News*, February 17, 2020, https://www.bloomberg.com/news/articles/2020-02-17/rare-release-of-xi-s -speech-on-virus-puzzles-top-china-watchers, accessed February 17, 2020.

4. Anna Fifield, "China's Conspicuously Absent Leader Reemerges—For an Audience with a Friendly Autocrat," *Washington Post*, February 5, 2020, https://www.washingtonpost.com/world /chinas-conspicuously-absent-leader-reemerges--for-an-audience-with-a-friendly-autocrat/2020 /02/05/507e6d02-47de-11ea-91ab-ce439aa5c7c1_story.html, accessed February 6, 2020.

5. Sui-Lee Wee and Vivian Wang, "Here's How Wuhan Plans to Test All 11 Million of Its People for Coronavirus," *New York Times*, May 15, 2020, https://www.nytimes.com/2020/05/14 /world/asia/coronavirus-testing-china-wuhan.html?referringSource=articleShare, accessed May 15, 2020.

6. Amy Qin and Cao Li, "China Pushes for Quiet Burials as Coronavirus Death Toll Is Questioned," *New York Times*, April 3, 2020, https://www.nytimes.com/2020/04/03/world /asia/coronavirus-china-grief-deaths.html, accessed April 4, 2020.

7. Emily Rauhala, "China's Claim of Coronavirus Victory in Wuhan Brings Hope, but Experts Worry It Is Premature," *Washington Post*, March 25, 2020, https://www.washingtonpost .com/world/asia_pacific/china-wuhan-coronavirus-zero-cases/2020/03/25/19bdbbc2-6d15 -11ea-a156-0048b62cdb51_story.html, accessed March 25, 2020.

8. Josephine Ma, Linda Lew, Lee Jeong-ho, "A Third of Coronavirus Cases May Be 'Silent Carriers', Classified Chinese Data Suggests," *South China Morning Post*, March 22, 2020, https:// www.scmp.com/news/china/society/article/3076323/third-coronavirus-cases-may-be-silent -carriers-classified, accessed March 31, 2020.

9. Kenneth Lieberthal and Michel Oksenberg, *Policy Making in China: Leaders, Structures, and Processes* (Princeton, NJ: Princeton University Press, 1988); Kenneth G. Lieberthal and David M. Lampton, eds., *Bureaucracy, Politics, and Decision Making in Post-Mao China* (Berkeley: University of California Press, 1992).

10. Chris K. Johnson, Scott Kennedy, and Mingda Qiu, "Xi's Signature Governance Innovation: The Rise of Leading Small Groups" (Washington, DC: Center for Strategic and International Studies), October 17, 2017, https://www.csis.org/analysis/xis-signature-governance -innovation-rise-leading-small-groups, accessed August 21, 2019. There are almost sixty other leading small groups under the Central Government.

11. Much of this recounting of the Three Gorges Dam project comes from Lieberthal and Oksenberg, *Policy Making in China*, chapter 6.

12. At different times, the ministries for water resources and energy were merged into a single ministry to force them to reach a consensus on the issue, or split into separate ministries because they could not reach a consensus.

13. The role of the NPC and local people's congresses in policy making will be further discussed below.

14. Daniela Stockmann, *Media Commercialization and Authoritarian Rule in China* (New York: Cambridge University Press, 2012); Susan L. Shirk, ed., *Changing Media, Changing China* (New York: Oxford University Press, 2010).

15. Andrew Mertha, "'Fragmented Authoritarianism 2.0': Political Pluralization in the Chinese Policy Process," *China Quarterly*, no. 200 (December 2009), 995–1012; Kjeld Erik Brødsgaard, ed., *Chinese Politics as Fragmented Authoritarianism: Earthquakes, Energy, and Environment* (New York: Routledge, 2017).

16. This description of the Nu River dam project is based on Andrew C. Mertha, *China's Water Warriors: Citizen Action and Policy Change* (Ithaca, NY: Cornell University Press, 2008), chapter 5.

17. Jessica C. Teets, *Civil Society under Authoritarianism: The China Model* (New York: Cambridge University Press, 2014), 114–15.

18. Mertha, *China's Water Warriors*, 122.

19. Ibid., 134.

20. See Tom Phillips, "Joy as China Shelves Plans to Dam 'Angry River,'" *Guardian*, December 2, 2016, https://www.theguardian.com/world/2016/dec/02/joy-as-china-shelves-plans-to-dam-angry-river, accessed August 19, 2019.

21. Johnson, Kennedy, and Qiu, "Xi's Signature Governance Innovation." The older leading small groups cover policy toward Taiwan, economics and finance, and foreign affairs; the new ones cover national security, comprehensively deepening reforms, national defense and troop reform, cybersecurity and informatization, and central military and civilian integration.

22. Elizabeth C. Economy, *The Third Revolution: Xi Jinping and the New Chinese State* (New York: Oxford University Press, 2018).

23. Sebastian Heilmann, "From Local Experiments to National Policy: The Origins of China's Distinctive Policy Process," *China Journal*, no. 59 (January 2008), 1–30; Sebastian Heilmann and Elizabeth J. Perry, eds., *Mao's Invisible Hand: The Political Foundations of Adaptive Governance in China* (Cambridge, MA: Harvard University Asia Center, 2011).

24. Jude Howell, "NGOs and Civil Society: The Politics of Crafting a Civic Welfare Infrastructure in the Hu-Wen Period," *China Quarterly*, no. 237 (March 2019), 58–81.

25. Shaoguang Wang, "Changing Models of China's Policy Agenda Setting," *Modern China* 34, no. 1 (January 2008), 56–87.

26. These examples come from Economy, *The Third Revolution*, chapter 6.

27. Brad Plumer, "Coal Pollution in China Is Cutting Life Expectancy by 5.5 Years," *Washington Post*, July 8, 2013, http://www.washingtonpost.com/blogs/wonkblog/wp/2013/07/08/chinas-coal-pollution-is-much-deadlier-than-anyone-realized/, accessed May 19, 2020.

28. Meir Alkon and Eric H. Wang, "Pollution Lowers Support for China's Regime: Quasi-Experimental Evidence from Beijing," *Journal of Politics* 80, no. 1 (January 2018), 327–31.

29. https://www.iqair.com/us/world-most-polluted-cities, accessed May 20, 2020.

30. Elizabeth C. Economy, *The River Runs Black: The Environmental Challenge to China's Future* (Ithaca, NY: Cornell University Press, 2004).

31. Jonathan R. Stromseth, Edmund J. Malesky, and Dimitar D. Gueorguiev, *China's Governance Puzzle: Enabling Transparency and Participation in a Single-Party State* (New York: Cambridge University Press, 2017); Greg Distelhorst, "The Power of Empty Promises: Quasi-Democratic Institutions and Activism in China," *Comparative Political Studies* 50, no. 4 (2017), 464–94; Jidong Chen, Jennifer Pan, and Yiqing Xu, "Sources of Authoritarian Responsiveness: A Field Experiment in China," *American Journal of Political Science* 60, no. 2 (April 2016), 383–400.

32. Dimitrov, "Vertical Accountability in Communist Regimes," 276–302.

33. Peter Lorentzen, Pierre Landry, and John Yasuda, "Undermining Authoritarian Innovation: The Power of China's Industrial Giants," *Journal of Politics* 76, no. 1 (January 2014), 182–94; Denise van der Kamp, Peter Lorentzen, and Daniel Mattingly, "Racing to the Bottom or to the Top? Decentralization, Revenue Pressures, and Governance Reform in China," *World Development* 95 (July 2017), 164–76.

34. Distelhorst, "Power of Empty Promises."

35. This is a key tactic for political activists and will be explored in chapter 5; see Kevin J. O'Brien, "Rightful Resistance," *World Politics* 49, no. 1 (October 1996), 31–55; and Elizabeth J. Perry, "Chinese Conceptions of 'Rights': From Mencius to Mao—and Now," *Perspectives on Politics* 6, no. 1 (March 2008), 37–50.

36. Distelhorst, "Power of Empty Promises."

37. Chen, Pan, and Xu, "Sources of Authoritarian Responsiveness"; Greg Distelhorst and Yue Hou, "Constituency Service under Nondemocratic Rule: Evidence from China," *Journal of Politics* 79, no. 3 (July 2017), 1024–40.

38. Distelhorst and Hou, "Constituency Service under Nondemocratic Rule."

39. Distelhorst, "Power of Empty Promises."

40. Jamie Horsley, "Public Participation in the People's Republic: Developing a More Participatory Governance Model in China" (2009), available at https://law.yale.edu/system/files/documents/pdf/Intellectual_Life/CL-PP-PP_in_the__PRC_FINAL_91609.pdf, accessed August 21, 2019.

41. Stromseth, Malesky, and Gueorguiev, *China's Governance Puzzle*, 293.

42. Stromseth, Malesky, and Gueorguiev, *China's Governance Puzzle*, 176–77.

43. Steven J. Balla, "Information Technology, Political Participation, and the Evolution of Chinese Policymaking," *Journal of Contemporary China* 21, no. 76, (2012), 655–73; Yoel Kornreich, Ilan Vertinsky, and Pitman B. Potter, "Consultation and Deliberation in China: The Making of China's Health-Care Reform," *China Journal* no. 68 (July 2012), 176–203.

44. Stromseth, Malesky, and Gueorguiev, *China's Governance Puzzle*, 217–18.

45. Balla, "Information Technology, Political Participation, and the Evolution of Chinese Policymaking."

46. Stromseth, Malesky, and Gueorguiev, *China's Governance Puzzle*, 195. To measure the extent of consultation, the authors included not only public comments on draft laws and regulations but also proposals made to the Chinese People's Political Consultative Conference (a largely honorary body that meets in tandem with the people's congresses at all levels, although

its proposals are nonbinding); and the number of registered NGOs which provide opportunities for consultation.

47. Stromseth, Malesky, and Gueorguiev, *China's Governance Puzzle*, 177; Steven J. Balla and Zhou Liao, "Online Consultation and Citizen Feedback in Chinese Policymaking," *Journal of Current Chinese Affairs* 42, no. 3 (2013), 104.

48. Mary E. Gallagher, *Authoritarian Legality in China: Law, Workers, and the State* (New York: Cambridge University Press, 2017), 216–27.

49. Balla and Liao, "Online Consultation and Citizen Feedback in Chinese Policymaking," 102.

50. Steven J. Balla and Zhoudan Xie, "Online Consultation and the Institutionalization of Transparency and Participation in Chinese Policymaking," *China Quarterly*, forthcoming.

51. Melanie Manion, *Information for Autocrats: Representation in Chinese Local Congresses* (New York: Cambridge University Press, 2015).

52. Rory Truex, *Making Autocracy Work: Representation and Responsiveness in Modern China* (New York: Cambridge University Press, 2016).

53. Manion, *Information for Autocrats*.

54. Yue Hou, *The Private Sector in Public Service: Selective Property Rights in China* (New York: Cambridge University Press, 2019); Dickson, *Wealth into Power*.

55. Manion, *Information for Autocrats*.

56. Tony Saich, *Providing Public Goods in Transitional China* (New York: Palgrave Macmillan, 2008); Ethan Michelson, "Public Goods and State-Society Relations: An Impact Study of China's Rural Stimulus," in Dali L. Yang, ed., *The Global Recession and China's Political Economy* (New York: Palgrave Macmillan, 2012), 131–57; Bruce J. Dickson, Pierre Landry, Mingming Shen, and Jie Yan, "Public Goods and Regime Support in Urban China," *China Quarterly*, no. 228 (December 2016), 859–80.

57. Truex, *Making Autocracy Work*, 85–90.

58. Ibid., 68.

59. Ibid., 118–19.

60. James S. Fishkin et al., "Deliberative Democracy in an Unlikely Place: Deliberative Polling in China," *British Journal of Political Science* 40, no. 2 (April 2010), 435–48; Baogang He and Mark Warren, "Authoritarian Deliberation: The Deliberative Turn in Chinese Political Development," *Perspectives on Politics* 9, no. 2 (Summer 2011), 269–89.

61. Joseph Fewsmith, *The Logic and Limits of Political Reform in China* (New York: Cambridge University Press, 2013).

62. Baogang He, "Reconciling Deliberation and Representation: Chinese Challenges to Deliberative Democracy," *Representation* 51, no. 1 (2015), 35–50.

63. Deyong Ma and Szu-chien Hsu, "The Political Consequences of Deliberative Democracy and Electoral Democracy in China: An Empirical Comparative Analysis from Four Counties," *China Review* 18, no. 2 (May 2018), 21.

64. Ma and Hsu, "The Political Consequences of Deliberative Democracy and Electoral Democracy in China," 26.

65. Baogang He and Mark Warren, "Authoritarian Deliberation in China," *Daedalus* 146, no. 3 (Summer 2017), 159.

66. These temples were not necessarily affiliated with the official Buddhist or Taoist associations, but more commonly were examples of local folk religion, which is not recognized by the CCP as an official religion. Lily Lee Tsai, *Accountability without Democracy: Solidary Groups and Public Goods Provision in Rural China* (New York: Cambridge University Press, 2007). See also Kenneth Dean, "Local Communal Religion in Contemporary South-East China," *China Quarterly*, no. 174 (June 2003), 338–58.

67. On migration, see Jie Lu, *Varieties of Governance in China: Migration and Institutional Change in Chinese Villages* (New York: Oxford University Press, 2014); on financial responsibilities, see Smith, "The Hollow State," 601–18.

Chapter 4: Does China Have a Civil Society?

1. After his release, he was again arrested in early 2020 after calling for the resignation of Xi Jinping for mishandling the COVID-19 crisis.

2. Andrew Jacobs and Chris Buckley, "Chinese Activists Test New Leader and Are Crushed," *New York Times*, January 14, 2014, https://www.nytimes.com/2014/01/16/world/asia/chinese-activists-test-new-leader-and-are-crushed.html, accessed September 19, 2019.

3. Official party documents are often identified by the order in which they are issued in a given year; hence this was the ninth document issued in 2013. An English translation of Document 9 is available at http://www.chinafile.com/document-9-chinafile-translation, accessed September 18, 2019.

4. Larry Diamond, "Rethinking Civil Society: Toward Democratic Consolidation," *Journal of Democracy* 5, no. 3, July 1994, 4–17; Robert D. Putnam, *Making Democracy Work: Civic Traditions in Italy* (Princeton, NJ: Princeton University Press, 1993).

5. The CCP was so worried the Jasmine Revolution would spread from the Middle East to China that it temporarily censored the word *jasmine* from internet searches, email, and social media in spring 2011.

6. Yanqi Tong, "State, Society, and Political Change in China and Hungary," *Comparative Politics* 26, no. 3 (April 1994), 333–53; Gordon White, Jude Howell, and Shang Xiaoyuan, *In Search of Civil Society: Market Reform and Social Change in Contemporary China* (Oxford: Oxford University Press, 1996); Jonathan Schwartz and Shawn Shieh, eds., *State and Society Responses to Social Welfare Needs in China: Serving the People* (New York and London: Routledge, 2009).

7. Michael W. Foley and Bob Edwards, "The Paradox of Civil Society," *Journal of Democracy* 7, no. 3 (July 1996), 38–52.

8. As of April 2018, the Ministry of Civil Affairs reported a total of a total of 783,764 NGOs, including 360,399 social organizations, 416,733 private noncommercial enterprises, and 6,632 foundations. See http://www.mca.gov.cn/article/sj/tjjb/sjsj/2018/20180608021510.html, accessed June 16, 2019.

9. Shaoguang Wang, "Money and Autonomy: Patterns of Civil Society Finance and Their Implications," *Studies in Comparative International Development* 40, no. 4 (Winter 2006), 3–29.

10. David Shambaugh, *China's Communist Party: Atrophy and Adaptation* (Berkeley: University of California Press, 2008), 91.

11. Tony Saich, "Negotiating the State: The Development of Social Organizations in China," *China Quarterly*, no. 161 (March 2000), 124–41; Jonathan Unger and Anita Chan, "China, Corporatism, and the East Asian Model," *Australian Journal of Chinese Affairs*, no. 33 (January 1995), 29–53; Howell, "NGOs and Civil Society."

12. Diana Fu, *Mobilizing without the Masses: Control and Contention in China* (Cambridge: Cambridge University Press, 2017), 74ff. Her case study of the "Social Engineering" NGO (a pseudonym to protect its identity) shows how some NGOs provide trained social workers to assist local officials in providing basic public goods and services.

13. Jessica C. Teets, *Civil Society under Authoritarianism: The China Model* (New York: Cambridge University Press, 2014).

14. Howell, "NGOs and Civil Society," 58–81.

15. Karla Simon, *Civil Society in China: The Legal Framework from Ancient Times to the "New Reform Era"* (New York: Oxford University Press, 2013).

16. Fu, *Mobilizing without the Masses*.

17. Jude Howell, "Shall We Dance? Welfarist Incorporation and the Politics of State-Labour NGO Relations," *China Quarterly*, no. 223 (September 2015), 702–723.

18. Ivan Franceschini and Elisa Nesossi, "State Repression of Chinese Labor NGOs: A Chilling Effect?" *China Journal*, no. 80 (July 2018), 111–29.

19. Jessica Batke, "'The New Normal' for Foreign NGOs in 2020," *ChinaFile*, January 3, 2020, https://www.chinafile.com/ngo/analysis/new-normal-foreign-ngos-2020, accessed January 7, 2020.

20. "Professor Jia Xijin: Two Years of the Overseas NGO Law," China Development Brief: *NGOnews*, December 12, 2018, https://mp.weixin.qq.com/s/jQggzCN-5TpG9NeTWImbBw, accessed July 15, 2019.

21. Batke, "'The New Normal' for Foreign NGOs in 2020."

22. Fu, *Mobilizing without the Masses*.

23. The names of these organizations are pseudonyms used to protect the identity of their members. See Fu, *Mobilizing without the Masses*, chapters 5–6.

24. The CCP stopped reporting this after 2017.

25. This number may be inflated. According to other reports, NGOs were slow to implement the party's directive to create party cells, and local party officials did not make this a priority; see Jessica Teets and Oscar Almen, "Advocacy under Xi: NPO Strategies to Influence Policy Change," *Nonprofit Policy Forum*, 2018. One reason for the delayed implementation is the nature of NGOs themselves: most are small, with less than ten employees, and there have to be at least three party members to create a party cell. The CCP's report is probably based on registered NGOs that meet the requirements for having their own party cell; the total population of NGOs is much larger.

26. Patricia M. Thornton, "The New Life of the Party: Party-Building and Social Engineering in Greater Shanghai," *China Journal*, no. 68 (July 2012), 58–78.

27. Dickson, *Red Capitalists in China*; Dickson, *Wealth into Power*.

28. Teets and Almen, "Advocacy under Xi: NPO Strategies to Influence Policy Change"; Carolyn Hsu and Jessica Teets, "Is China's New Overseas NGO Management Law Sounding the Death Knell for Civil Society? Maybe Not," *Asia-Pacific Journal* 14, issue 4, no. 3 (February 15, 2016).

29. http://www.fon.org.cn/index.php?option=com_k2&view=item&layout=item&id =12930&Itemid=260, accessed July 17, 2019.

30. Michael Wines, "Liang Congjie, Chinese Environmental Pioneer, Dies at 78," *New York Times*, October 10, 2010, https://www.nytimes.com/2010/10/30/world/asia/30liang.html, accessed July 17, 2019.

31. Feng Hao, "Green Peafowl Lawsuit Exposes Dam Damage," *China Dialogue*, November 19, 2018, https://www.chinadialogue.net/article/show/single/en/10939-Green-peafowl -lawsuit-exposes-dam-damage, accessed July 17, 2019.

32. Jennifer Y. J. Hsu, Carolyn L. Hsu, and Reza Hasmath, "NGO Stratiegies in an Authoritarian Context, and Their Implications for Citizenship: The Case of the People's Republic of China," *Voluntas* 28, no. 3 (June 2017), 1157–79.

33. Thornton, "The New Life of the Party."

34. Elanah Uretsky, *Occupational Hazards: Sex, Business, and HIV in Post-Mao China* (Stanford: Stanford University Press, 2016).

35. Hildebrandt, *Social Organizations and the Authoritarian State in China*; Teets, *Civil Society under Authoritarianism*.

36. Mertha, *China's Water Warriors*.

37. Teets, *Civil Society under Authoritarianism*.

38. Jessica C. Teets, "The Evolution of Civil Society in Yunnan Province: Contending Models of Civil Society Management in China." *Journal of Contemporary China* 24, no. 91 (2015), 158–75; Hsu and Teets, "China's New Overseas NGO Management Law."

39. This typology of red, gray, and black groups is adapted from a similar model used to described religious organizations in China, and will be used in that way in chapter 7 on religion. See Fenggang Yang, *Religion in China: Survival and Renewal under Communist Rule* (New York: Oxford University Press, 2012); and Karrie J. Koesel, "The Political Economy of Religious Revival," *Politics and Religion* 8, no. 2 (June 2015), 211–35.

40. Anita Chan, "Revolution or Corporatism? Workers in Search of a Solution," in David S. G. Goodman and Beverly Hooper, eds., *China's Quiet Revolution: New Interactions between State and Society* (New York: St. Martin's Press, 1994), 162–93; Jude Howell, "All-China Federation of Trade Unions beyond Reform? The Slow March of Direct Elections," *China Quarterly*, no. 196 (December 2008), 845–63.

41. GONGOs are not unique to China. In fact, the United States has them too. The National Endowment for Democracy and Freedom House are both prominent GONGOs tasked with promoting the cause of democratization around the world. The March of Dimes and the Points of Light Foundation began as GONGOs with presidential sponsors (Franklin Roosevelt and George H. W. Bush, respectively) and then later became independent. See Reza Hasmath, Timothy Hildebrandt, and Jennifer Y. J. Hsu, "Conceptualizing Government-Organized Non-Governmental Organizations," *Journal of Civil Society* 15, no. 3 (2019), 267–84.

42. Bruce J. Dickson, *The Dictator's Dilemma: The Chinese Communist Party's Strategy for Survival* (New York: Oxford University Press, 2016), 132.

43. Jennifer Y. J. Hsu, Timothy Hildebrandt, and Reza Hasmath, "'Going Out' or Staying In? The Expansion of Chinese NGOs in Africa," *Development Policy Review* 34, no. 3 (May 2016), 423–39.

44. Hasmath, Hildebrandt, and Hsu, "Conceptualizing Government-Organized Non-Governmental Organizations."

45. Dickson, *The Dictator's Dilemma*, 143–46.

46. The distinction between gray and black NGOs corresponds to what Diana Fu in *Mobilizing without the Masses* calls above ground and underground groups, respectively.

47. Timothy Hildebrandt, *Social Organizations and the Authoritarian State in China* (New York: Cambridge University Press, 2013), 71–72.

48. Social enterprises are "businesses with a social mission that are sustainable because they do not rely on donations or grants." They are a relatively new addition to China's civil society environment. See Jessica C. Teets and Shawn Shieh, "CSOs as Social Entrepreneurs in China: Strategic Rebranding or Evolution?," forthcoming.

49. http://english.unirule.cloud/about/, accessed June 18, 2019.

50. Matthew Campbell and Peter Martin, "China's Latest Crackdown Target Is Liberal Economists," *Bloomberg Businessweek*, May 11, 2019, https://www.bloomberg.com/news/features/2019-05-11/china-s-latest-crackdown-target-is-liberal-economists, accessed May 5, 2019.

51. An English translation of this report is available at http://chinaheritage.net/journal/imminent-fears-immediate-hopes-a-beijing-jeremiad/, accessed July 5, 2019.

52. Chris Buckley, "A Chinese Law Professor Criticized Xi. Now He's Been Suspended," *New York Times*, March 26, 2019, https://www.nytimes.com/2019/03/26/world/asia/chinese-law-professor-xi.html, accessed July 5, 2019.

53. The survey was done in 2014; see Dickson, *Dictator's Dilemma*, 142. Other specialists on China's civil society have told me that their interviews reveal the same type of distrust.

54. Reza Hasmath and Jennifer Y. J. Hsu, "Isomorphic Pressures, Epistemic Communities and State-NGO Collaboration in China," *China Quarterly*, 220 (December 2014), 936–54; Carolyn L. Hsu and Yuzhou Jiang, "An Institutional Approach to Chinese NGOs: State Alliance versus State Avoidance Strategies," *China Quarterly*, no. 221 (March 2015), 100–22.

55. Anthony J. Spires, "Lessons from Abroad: Foreign Influences on China's Emerging Civil Society," *China Journal*, no. 68 (July 2012), 125–46; Hsu and Teets, "China's New Overseas NGO Management Law."

56. Spires, "Lessons from Abroad."

57. Hildebrandt, *Social Organizations and the Authoritarian State in China*.

58. Shawn Shieh, "Remaking China's Civil Society in the Xi Jinping Era," *ChinaFile*, August 2, 2018, https://www.chinafile.com/reporting-opinion/viewpoint/remaking-chinas-civil-society-xi-jinping-era, accessed June 22, 2020.

59. Anthony J. Spires, Lin Tao, and Kin-man Chan, "Societal Support for China's Grass-Roots NGOs: Evidence from Yunnan, Guangdong and Beijing," *China Journal*, no. 71 (January 2014), 65–90; Reza Hasmath and Jennifer Y. J. Hsu, "Communities of Practice and the NGO Sector in China," working paper.

60. Shawn Shieh and Guosheng Deng, "An Emerging Civil Society: The Impact of the 2008 Sichuan Earthquake on Grass-roots Associations in China," *China Journal*, no. 65 (January 2011), 181–94; Jessica C. Teets, "Post-Earthquake Relief and Reconstruction Efforts: The Emergence of Civil Society in China?" *China Quarterly*, no. 198 (June 2009), 330–47.

61. Hasmath and Hsu, "Isomorphic Pressures."

62. Hsu, Hsu, and Hasmath, "NGO Strategies in an Authoritarian Context."

63. This is a consistent finding in public opinion surveys in China. See Tianjian Shi, *The Cultural Logic of Politics in Mainland China and Taiwan* (New York: Cambridge University Press, 2015); Dickson, *Dictator's Dilemma*; Jie Chen, *A Middle Class without Democracy: Economic Growth and the Prospects for Democratization in China* (New York: Oxford University Press, 2013).

64. Hsu and Jiang, "An Institutional Approach to Chinese NGOs," 107.

65. Ronald Inglehart, *Modernization and Postmodernization: Cultural, Economic, and Political Change in 43 Societies* (Princeton, NJ: Princeton University Press, 1997).

Chapter 5: Do Political Protests Threaten Political Stability?

1. Yuhua Wang and Carl Minzner, "The Rise of the Chinese Security State," *China Quarterly*, no. 222 (June 2015), 339–59.

2. Martin Dimitrov refers to this tacit alliance between higher level officials and local citizens as "proxy accountability"; see "Vertical Accountability in Communist Regimes." This is complementary to my use of the term *accountability* in this book, where local officials are ultimately accountable to their superiors, not to the people they govern. But in some cases, protesters can get the attention of higher-level officials and cause them to remove the local officials who are the targets of their protests.

3. For a book-length treatment of these questions, see Teresa Wright, *Popular Protest in China* (Medford, MA: Polity Press, 2018).

4. Feng Chen and Mengxiao Tang, "Labor Conflicts in China: Typologies and Their Implications," *Asian Survey*, 53, no. 3 (May/June 2013), 559–83.

5. Ibid., 568.

6. Marc Blecher, "Hegemony and Workers' Politics in China," *China Quarterly*, no. 170 (June 2002), 283–303; Lee, *Against the Law*; Perry, "Chinese Conceptions of 'Rights,'" 37–50; Neil J. Diamant, *Embattled Glory: Veterans, Military Families, and the Politics of Patriotism in China, 1949–2007* (Lanham, MD: Rowman & Littlefield, 2009).

7. O'Brien, "Rightful Resistance," 31–55; Kevin J. O'Brien and Lianjiang Li, *Rightful Resistance in Rural China* (New York: Cambridge University Press, 2006).

8. Perry, "Chinese Conceptions of 'Rights.'"

9. James C. Davies, "Towards a Theory of Revolution," *American Sociological Review*, 27, no. 1 (February 1962), 5–19.

10. Lianjiang Li, "Political Trust and Petitioning in the Chinese Countryside," *Comparative Politics* 40, no. 2 (January 2008), 209–26; Xi Chen, *Social Protest and Contentious Politics in China* (New York: Cambridge University Press, 2012).

11. Sebastian Heilmann, ed., *China's Political System* (Lanham, MD: Rowman & Littlefield, 2017), 321.

12. Christopher Heurlin, *Responsive Authoritarianism in China: Land, Protests, and Policy-Making* (New York: Cambridge University Press, 2016).

13. Gallagher, *Authoritarian Legality in China.*

14. Ching Kwan Lee, *Against the Law: Labor Protests in China's Rustbelt and Sunbelt* (Berkeley: University of California Press, 2007); Gallagher, *Authoritarian Legality in China.*

15. Kevin J. O'Brien and Yanhua Deng, "Repression Backfires: Tactical Radicalization and Protest Spectacle in Rural China," *Journal of Contemporary China* 24, no. 93 (2015), 457–70; Yanhua Deng and Kevin J. O'Brien, "Relational Repression in China: Using Social Ties to Demobilize Protesters," *China Quarterly*, no. 215 (September 2013), 533–52.

16. Diana Fu, *Mobilizing without the Masses: Control and Contention in China* (Cambridge: Cambridge University Press, 2017).

17. Sing Lee and Arthur Kleinman, "Suicide as Resistance in Chinese Society," in Elizabeth J. Perry and Mark Selden, eds., *Chinese Society: Change, Conflict, and Resistance* (London and New York: Routledge, 2000), 221–40.

18. Fu, *Mobilizing without the Masses.*

19. Yongshun Cai, "Power Structure and Regime Resilience: Contentious Politics in China," *British Journal of Political Science* 38, no. 3 (July 2008), 411–32.

20. Wang and Minzner, "The Rise of the Chinese Security State."

21. Sheena Greitens, "Rethinking China's Coercive Capacity: An Examination of PRC Domestic Security Spending, 1992–2012," *China Quarterly*, no. 232 (December 2017), 1002–25.

22. Dickson et al. "Public Goods and Regime Support in Urban China," 859–80.

23. Diana Fu and Greg Distelhorst suggest that a recent change in reporting public security spending shows a sharp decline, but that it is probably due to recategorizing the components of this spending, not necessarily to a decline in actual spending. See their "Grassroots Participation and Repression under Hu Jintao and Xi Jinping," *China Journal*, no. 79 (January 2018), 100–22.

24. Manfred Elfstrom, "Two Steps Forward, One Step Back? Chinese State Reactions to Labour Unrest," *China Quarterly*, no. 240 (December 2019), 255–79.

25. Arch Puddington, "China: The Global Leader in Political Prisoners," Freedom House blog post, July 26, 2018, https://freedomhouse.org/blog/china-global-leader-political-prisoners, accessed August 28, 2019; Elana Beiser, "Hundreds of Journalists Jailed Globally Becomes the New Normal," Committee to Protect Journalists, December 13, 2018, https://cpj.org/reports/2018/12/journalists-jailed-imprisoned-turkey-china-egypt-saudi-arabia.php, accessed August 28, 2019.

26. Xi Chen, "Origins of Informal Coercion in China," *Politics and Society* 45, no. 1 (March 2017), 67–89; Lynette Ong, "'Thugs-for-Hire': Subcontracting of State Coercion and State Capacity in China," *Perspectives on Politics* 16, no. 3 (September 2018), 680–95; Ong, "Thugs and Outsourcing of State Repression in China," *China Journal* 80 (July 2018), 94–110.

27. Elizabeth J. Perry, "Labor Divided: Sources of State Formation in Modern China," in Joel Migdal, Atul Kohli, and Vivienne Shue, eds., *State Power and Social Forces: Domination and Transformation in the Third World* (New York: Cambridge University Press, 1994); Lee, *Against the Law*; Fu, *Mobilizing without the Masses*; Diana Fu, "Fragmented Control: Governing Contentious Labor Organizations in China." *Governance* 30, no. 3 (July 2017), 445–62; Xi Chen, "The Logic of Fragmented Activism among Chinese State-Owned Enterprise Workers," *China Journal* 81 (January 2019), 58–80.

28. Fu, *Mobilizing without the Masses*; Fu, "Fragmented Control."

29. Deng and O'Brien, "Relational Repression."

30. Kevin J. O'Brien and Yanhua Deng, "The Reach of the State: Work Units, Family Ties and 'Harmonious Demolition,'" *China Journal* 74 (July 2015), 1–17.

31. Deng and O'Brien, "Relational Repression."

32. Tara Francis Chan, "China Released a Uyghur Mother to Silence Her U. S. Son—Then Sent Her Back to Detention the Next Day," *Newsweek*, May 25, 2019, https://www.newsweek .com/xinjiang-uyghur-release-threaten-us-citizen-1435984, accessed May 25, 2019.

33. Sui-Lee Wee and Paul Mozur, "China Uses DNA to Map Faces, with Help from the West," *New York Times*, December 10, 2019, https://www.nytimes.com/2019/12/03/business/china -dna-uighurs-xinjiang.html?smid=nytcore-ios-share, accessed December 20, 2019.

34. Human Rights Watch, "China's Algorithms of Repression: Reverse Engineering a Xinjiang Police Mass Surveillance App," May 1, 2019, https://www.hrw.org/report/2019/05/01 /chinas-algorithms-repression/reverse-engineering-xinjiang-police-mass-surveillance, accessed May 9, 2019.

35. Jamie Horsley, "China's Orwellian Social Credit Score Isn't Real," *Foreign Policy*, November 16, 2018; https://foreignpolicy.com/2018/11/16/chinas-orwellian-social-credit-score-isnt -real/, accessed September 2, 2020.

36. Genia Kostka, "What Do People in China Think about 'Social Credit' Monitoring?" *Washington Post*, March 21, 2019, https://www.washingtonpost.com/politics/2019/03/21/what -do-people-china-think-about-social-credit-monitoring/?utm_term=.b90e91139d44, accessed March 21, 2019.

37. Ching Kwan Lee and Yonghong Zhang, "The Power of Instability: Unraveling the Microfoundations of Bargained Authoritarianism in China," *American Journal of Sociology* 118, no. 6 (May 2013), 1475–508.

38. Yuqing Feng and Xin He, "From Law to Politics: Petitioners' Framing of Disputes in Chinese Courts," *China Journal* 80 (July 2018), 130–49.

39. Zi Zhu, "Backfired Government Action and the Spillover Effect of Contention: A Case Study of the Anti-PX Protests in Maoming, China," *Journal of Contemporary China* 26, no. 106 (2017), 521–35.

40. Xiaojun Yan and Kai Zhou, "Fighting the Prairie Fire: Why Do Local Party-States in China Respond to Contentious Challengers Differently?" *China: An International Journal* 15, no. 4 (November 2017), 43–68.

41. Philip P. Pan, *Out of Mao's Shadow: The Struggle for the Soul of a New China* (New York: Simon and Schuster, 2008), 144.

42. Ching Kwan Lee, *Against the Law: Labor Protests in China's Rustbelt and Sunbelt* (Berkeley: University of California Press, 2007), 111.

43. Xi Chen, "Elitism and Exclusion in Mass Protest: Privatization, Resistance, and State Domination in China," *Comparative Political Studies* 50, no. 7 (June 2017), 908–34.

44. Rory Truex, "Focal Points, Dissident Calendars, and Preemptive Repression," *Journal of Conflict Resolution* 63, no. 4 (April 2019), 1032–52.

45. Fu, *Mobilizing without the Masses*; Feng and He, "From Law to Politics."

46. Peter L. Lorentzen, "Regularizing Rioting: Permitting Public Protest in an Authoritarian Regime," *Quarterly Journal of Political Science* 8, no. 2 (2013), 127–58; Lorentzen, "Designing

Contentious Politics in Post-1989 China," *Modern China* 43, no. 5 (September 2017), 459–93; Jidong Chen and Yiqing Xu, "Why Do Authoritarian Regimes Allow Citizens to Voice Opinions Publicly?" *Journal of Politics* 79 no. 3 (July 2017), 792–803; Wenfang Tang, *Populist Authoritarianism: Chinese Political Culture and Regime Sustainability* (New York: Oxford University Press, 2016).

47. Fu and Distelhorst, "Grassroots Participation and Repression."

48. Javier Hernandez, "She's on a #MeToo Mission in China, Battling Censors and Lawsuits," *New York Times*, January 4, 2019, https://www.nytimes.com/2019/01/04/world/asia/china-zhou-xiaoxuan-metoo.html?_ga=2.50293414.1022361453.1549433306-1393789027.1549433306, accessed March 18, 2019.

49. Leta Hong Fincher, *Betraying Big Brother: The Feminist Awakening in China?* (London: Verso, 2018).

50. Fu and Distelhorst, "Grassroots Participation and Repression," 112–13.

51. https://theinitium.com/project/20181021-metoo-in-china/, accessed March 18, 2019.

52. Franceschini and Nesossi, "State Repression of Chinese Labor NGOs: A Chilling Effect?" 111–29.

53. Yuan Yang, "Inside China's Crackdown on Young Marxists," *Financial Times*, February 13, 2019, https://www.ft.com/content/fd087484-2f23-11e9-8744-e7016697f225, accessed March 28, 2019; Gerry Shih, "'If I Disappear': Chinese Students Make Farewell Messages amid Crackdowns over Labor Activism," *Washington Post*, May 25, 2019, https://www.washingtonpost.com/world/asia_pacific/if-i-disappear-chinese-students-make-farewell-messages-amid-crackdowns-over-labor-activism-/2019/05/25/6fc949c0-727d-11e9-9331-30bc5836f48e_story.html?utm_term=.e5cce0288eeb, accessed May 25, 2019.

54. Fu and Distelhorst, "Grassroots Participation and Repression."

55. Guobin Yang, *The Power of the Internet in China: Citizen Activism Online* (New York, NY: Columbia University Press, 2009).

56. Marc Lynch, "After Egypt: The Promise and Limitations of the Online Challenge to the Authoritarian Arab State," *Perspectives on Politics* 9, no. 2 (June 2011), 301–18.

57. Han, *Contesting Cyberspace in China*.

58. Internet World Stats, https://www.internetworldstats.com/top20.htm, accessed October 6, 2020.

59. Gary King, Jennifer Pan, and Margaret E. Roberts, "How Censorship In China Allows Government Criticism But Silences Collective Expression," *American Political Science Review* 107, no. 2 (2013), 326–43. King, Pan, and Roberts further argue that critical comments are not censored. Dimitar Gueorguiev and Edmund Malesky challenge this contention, noting that King, Pan, and Roberts include public comments solicited by the CCP on draft laws and regulations (described in chapter 3). When these types of online comments are excluded, Gueorguiev and Malesky find that unsolicited critical comments do indeed get censored. See "Consultation and Selective Censorship in China," *Journal of Politics* 81, no. 4 (October 2019).

60. The China Digital Times website keeps an inventory the directives from the Propaganda Department (https://chinadigitaltimes.net/china/censorship/) and a list of banned search terms: https://chinadigitaltimes.net/2013/06/grass-mud-horse-list/.

61. Raymond Zhong and Paul Mazur, "Tech Giants Feel the Squeeze as Xi Jinping Tightens His Grip," *New York Times*, May 2, 2018, https://www.nytimes.com/2018/05/02/technology/china-xi-jinping-technology-innovation.html, accessed August 17, 2018.

62. In late 2020, Jack Ma fell into political trouble for challenging the state's control over the financial sector and for having too large a public profile. He disappeared from public view, and his companies were investigated for violating various laws and regulations.

63. Margaret E. Roberts, *Censored: Distraction and Diversion inside China's Great Firewall* (Princeton, NJ: Princeton University Press, 2018).

64. Roberts, *Censored*, 136–37; Dickson, *The Dictator's Dilemma*, 258.

65. Roberts, *Censored*, 113.

66. Han, *Contesting Cyberspace in China*, 88–89.

67. Han, *Contesting Cyberspace in China*.

68. Tianjian Shi, *The Cultural Logic of Politics in Mainland China and Taiwan* (New York: Cambridge University Press, 2015); Dickson, *The Dictator's Dilemma*.

69. O'Brien, "Rightful Resistance"; Perry, "Chinese Conceptions of 'Rights.'"

70. Kevin J. O'Brien, "Rightful Resistance Revisited," *Journal of Peasant Studies* 40, no. 6 (2013), 1051–62.

71. Wright, *Popular Protest in China*.

72. Alfred Hirschman, *Exit, Voice and Loyalty: Responses to Decline in Firms, Organizations, and States* (Cambridge, MA: Harvard University Press, 1970).

Chapter 6: Why Does the Party Fear Religion?

1. The name Shouwang means "lookout" and is taken from Isaiah 21:6: "For thus the Lord said to me: 'Go, post a lookout, let him announce what he sees.'" Carsten Vala, *The Politics of Protestant Churches and the Party-State in China: God above Party?* (London and New York: Routledge, 2017), 175. This vignette on Shouwang is based on Vala.

2. The timing of these events is significant: this first crackdown came during the run-up to the 2008 Olympics in Beijing, the second prior to President Barack Obama's first visit to China in 2009. As noted in chapter 5, major international events like these are times of preemptive repression.

3. Yang, *Religion in China*; Koesel, "The Political Economy of Religious Revival," 211–35. Yang's original typology of red, black, and gray markets depicted the gray market as a quasi-religious category. For example, the cult of Mao included singing songs of praise and performing a loyalty dance in front of Mao's portrait, confessing shortcomings and promising personal improvement, and studying Mao's quotations in the "Little Red Book," a type of secular scripture. In the post-Mao period, it is more useful to think of the gray market as an intermediate realm between the approved activities of the five officially recognized religions and the black zone of illegal and suppressed activities, including what the CCP deems "evil cults."

4. André Laliberté, "Managing Religious Diversity in China: Contradictions of Imperial and Foreign Legacies," *Studies in Religion* 45, no. 4 (December 2016), 495–519; Carsten T. Vala, "Protestant Christianity and Civil Society in Authoritarian China: The Impact of Official Churches and Unregistered 'Urban Churches' on Civil Society Development in the 2000s," *China Perspectives*, no. 3 (July 2012), 43–52.

5. Samuel P. Huntington, *The Third Wave: Democratization in the Late 20th Century* (Norman: University of Oklahoma Press, 1991).

6. "Three-Self" refers to self-governing, self-supporting, and self-propagating. Along with "Patriotic," the name denotes the CCP's intention that China's Protestants be free of foreign influence.

7. Laliberté, "Managing Religious Diversity in China," 495–519.

8. The United Front department is also the liaison for private entrepreneurs, overseas Chinese, and other groups. Gerry Groot, *Managing Transitions: The Chinese Communist Party, United Front Work, Corporatism, and Hegemony* (New York and London: Routledge, 2004).

9. As part of the strengthening of CCP's authority under Xi, the SARA was reportedly moved from under the State Council (a government body) to the CCP's United Front Work Department. See Chang, "New Wine in Old Bottles," 38 n. 10.

10. Yang, *Religion in China.*

11. James Tong, "The Devil is in the Local: Provincial Religious Legislation in China, 2005–2012," *Religion, State and Society* 42, no. 1 (March 2014), 66–88.

12. Official PRC: http://www.scio.gov.cn/zfbps/32832/Document/1626734/1626734.htm. This report also says there are around 222,000 Buddhist clerical personnel and more than 40,000 Taoist clerical personnel.

13. https://www.worldreligiondatabase.org/.

14. Freedom House: https://freedomhouse.org/report/china-religious-freedom.

15. Wenfang Tang, "The Worshipping Atheist: Institutional and Diffused Religiosities in China," *China: An International Journal,* 12, no. 3 (December 2014), 1–26.

16. Ibid., 14.

17. Yang, *Religion in China,* 119.

18. Ibid., 140.

19. "The Basic Viewpoint on the Religious Question during Our Country's Socialist Period," (Document 19), quoted in Yoshiko Ashiwa and David L. Wank, "The Politics of Reviving a Buddhist Temple: State, Association, and Religion in Southeast China," *Journal of Asian Studies* 65, no. 2 (May 2006), 340.

20. André Laliberté, "The Politicization of Religion by the CCP: A Selective Retrieval," *Asiatische Studien—Études Asiatiques* 69, no. 1 (April 2015), 185–211.

21. James Tong, "The New Religious Policy in China: Catching Up with Systemic Reforms," *Asian Survey* 50, no. 5, (September/October 2010), 859–87.

22. Ibid.

23. Vala, *The Politics of Protestant Churches and the Party-State in China,* 176–177. In particular, it was rejected because its pastor was not ordained by the government.

24. Karrie J. Koesel, *Religion and Authoritarianism: Cooperation, Conflict, and the Consequences* (New York: Cambridge University Press, 2014), 132–36.

25. Karrie J. Koesel, "China's Patriotic Pentecostals," *Review of Religion and Chinese Society* 1, no. 1 (April 2014), 131–55.

26. Ian Johnson, *The Souls of China: The Return of Religion after Mao* (New York: Vintage, 2017).

27. This depiction of the Nanputuo temple is based on Ashiwa and Wank, "The Politics of Reviving a Buddhist Temple."

28. Robert Weller and Sun Yanfei, "Religion: The Dynamics of Religious Growth and Change," in Joseph Fewsmith, ed., *China Today, China Tomorrow: Domestic Politics, Economy, and Society* (Lanham, MD: Rowman & Littlefield Publishers, 2010).

29. Karrie J. Koesel, "Religion and the Regime: Cooperation and Conflict in Contemporary Russia and China," *World Politics* 69, no. 4 (October 2017), 676–712.

30. Koesel, *Religion and Authoritarianism*, 107–109.

31. Koesel, "The Political Economy of Religious Revival"; Nanlai Cao, *Constructing China's Jerusalem: Christians, Power, and Place in Contemporary Wenzhou* (Stanford: Stanford University Press, 2010).

32. Koesel, *Religion and Authoritarianism*.

33. Koesel, "The Political Economy of Religious Revival."

34. Laliberté, "The Politicization of Religion by the CCP"; Kuei-min Chang, "New Wine in Old Bottles: Sinicisation and State Regulation of Religion in China," *China Perspectives* 1/2 (January 2018), 37–44.

35. Chang, "New Wine in Old Bottles," 42. For the full document, see http://www.china.org .cn/government/whitepaper/node_8004087.htm.

36. Ibid., 43.

37. Koesel, "The Political Economy of Religious Revival," 216.

38. Weller and Sun, "Religion," 41.

39. Cao, *Constructing China's Jerusalem*.

40. Ian Buruma, *Bad Elements: Chinese Rebels from Los Angeles to Beijing* (New York: Random House, 2001); Hualing Fu and Richard Cullen, "Weiquan (Rights Protection) Lawyering in an Authoritarian State: Building a Culture of Public-Interest Lawyering," *China Journal*, no. 59 (January 2008), 111–27.

41. Chai Ling, *A Heart for Freedom: The Remarkable Journey of a Young Dissident, Her Daring Escape, and Her Quest to Free China's Daughters* (Carol Stream, IL: Tyndale House Publishers, 2011).

42. Carsten T. Vala and and Kevin O'Brien, "Attraction without Networks: Recruiting Strangers to Unregistered Protestantism in China," *Mobilization: An International Quarterly* 12, no. 1 (March 2007), 79–94.

43. Vala, "Protestant Christianity and Civil Society in Authoritarian China."

44. Reny, *Authoritarian Containment*. Her study is specifically limited to urban Protestant churches and does not address rural churches or Catholic churches. For similar treatments of the CCP's policy toward unregistered Protestant churches, see Jason Kindopp, "Fragmented yet Defiant: Protestant Resilience under Chinese Communist Party Rule," in Jason Kindopp and Carol Hamrin, eds., *God and Caesar in China: Policy Implications of Church-State Tensions* (Washington, DC: Brookings Institution Press, 2004), 122–145; and Vala, *The Politics of Protestant Churches and the Party-State in China*.

45. Dickson, *Red Capitalists in China*; Kellee Tsai, *Capitalism without Democracy: The Private Sector in Contemporary China* (Ithaca, NY: Cornell University Press, 2007); Yue Hou, *The Private Sector in Public Office: Selective Property Rights in China* (New York: Cambridge University Press, 2019).

46. Reny, *Authoritarian Containment*; Vala, "Protestant Christianity and Civil Society in Authoritarian China."

47. Koesel, "Religion and the Regime."

48. Taoism has not received enough scholarly attention to draw conclusions about its treatment by the CCP or local officials.

49. Vala, *The Politics of Protestant Churches and the Party-State in China.*

50. As noted in chapter 5, major events likes visiting heads of state are often preceded by increased political repression.

51. The head pastors at Shouwang and Wanbang were both ethnic Koreans with extensive ties to South Korean and other international organizations. This also violates the conditions of the containment strategy, but do not appear to be primary factors for explaining why Beijing and Shanghai cracked down on them.

52. Christian Shepherd, "China Outlaws Large Underground Protestant Church in Beijing," *Reuters*, September 9, 2018, https://www.reuters.com/article/us-china-religion/china-outlaws-large-underground-protestant-church-in-beijing-idUSKCN1LQ07W, accessed April 1, 2019.

53. Koesel, "The Rise of a Chinese House Church."

54. Elizabeth J. Perry, *Anyuan: Mining China's Revolutionary Tradition* (Berkeley: University of California Press, 2012).

55. See https://bitterwinter.org/150-pastors-arrested-at-year-end-gathering/, accessed April 1, 2019.

56. Cao, *Constructing China's Jerusalem.*

57. Ibid.

58. Reny, *Authoritarian Containment*, 149.

59. This same concern led to anti-Catholic bias in the United States. As candidate for the presidency, John Kennedy gave a speech on his religious views to reassure voters he was not beholden to the pope for his policy preferences. More recently, Senator Dianne Feinstein was criticized for asking about the religious views of judicial nominee Amy Coney Barrett, who in the past had written that Catholic judges should be guided by their faith when deciding cases.

60. "Shanghai Bishop Ma's Open Repentance Shocks Catholics," *UCAnews.com*, June 22, 2016, https://www.ucanews.com/news/shanghai-bishop-mas-open-repentance-shocks-catholics/76313, accessed September 7, 2019.

61. Jason Horowitz and Ian Johnson, "China and Vatican Reach Deal on Appointment of New Bishops," *New York Times*, September 22, 2018, https://www.nytimes.com/2018/09/22/world/asia/china-vatican-bishops.html, accessed April 12, 2019.

62. Ian Johnson, "In Landmark Ceremony, a Catholic Bishop Is Installed in China," *New York Times*, August 28, 2019, https://www.nytimes.com/2019/08/28/world/asia/catholic-bishop-china.html, accessed September 7, 2019.

63. Leah MarieAnn Klett, "Two Chinese Catholic Bishops Ordained under Landmark China-Vatican Agreement," *Christian Post*, August 29, 2019, https://www.christianpost.com/news/two-chinese-catholic-bishops-ordained-under-landmark-china-vatican-agreement.html, accessed September 7, 2019.

64. "China Mosque Demolition Sparks Standoff in Ningxia," *BBC News*, August 10, 2018, https://www.bbc.com/news/world-asia-china-45140551, accessed September 11, 2019; Gerry Shih, "China Tightens Its Grip on Ethnic Hui," *Washington Post*, September 21, 2019, https://www.washingtonpost.com/world/asia_pacific/boiling-us-like-frogs-chinas-clampdown-on-muslims-creeps-into-the-heartland-finds-new-targets/2019/09/20/25c8bb08-ba94-11e9-aeb2-a101a1fb27a7_story.html, accessed September 21, 2019.

65. Mimi Lau, "Chinese Arabic school to close as areas with Muslim populations are urged to study the Xinjiang way," *South China Morning Post*, December 9, 2018, https://www.scmp.com /news/china/politics/article/2177037/chinese-arabic-school-close-areas-muslim-populations -are-urged, accessed September 11, 2019.

66. This does not hold true for Tibetan Buddhism. Ironically, one of the themes in the patriotic education curriculum in Tibet is that Buddhism was not originally part of Tibetan culture. It tries—with very limited success—to separate Tibetan culture from the form of Buddhism practiced there. See Catriona Bass, "Learning to Love the Motherland: Education Tibetans in China," *Journal of Moral Education* 34, no. 4 (December 2005), 433–49.

67. Laliberté, "Buddhist Revival under State Watch."

68. Ashiwa and Wank, "The Politics of Reviving a Buddhist Temple," 353.

69. Ibid., 351.

70. Laliberté, "Buddhist Revival under State Watch," 110.

71. Laliberté also notes that entrepreneurial efforts by Buddhist temples are criticized as inappropriate by the laity, but the charitable work mitigates the criticism. Laliberté, "Buddhist Revival under State Watch," 113.

72. Tom Hancock, "China Clears Shaolin Temple's 'CEO Monk' of Corruption," *Financial Times*, February 6, 2017, https://www.ft.com/content/b2fe493c-ecee-11e6-930f-061b01e23655, accessed April 8, 2019.

73. For many years, he was also the political leader of the Tibetans in exile, but resigned from that post in 2011, at which point a president was elected.

74. Guobin Zhu, "Prosecuting 'Evil Cults:' A Critical Examination of Law Regarding Freedom of Religious Belief in Mainland China," *Human Rights Quarterly* 32, no. 3 (2010), 471–501.

75. David Ownby, *Falun Gong and the Future of China* (New York: Oxford University Press, 2008).

76. Vivienne Shue, "Legitimacy Crisis in China?" in Peter Hays Gries and Stanley Rosen, eds., *State and Society in 21st Century China: Crisis, Contention and Legitimation* (New York: Routledge, 2004), 41–68.

77. While no longer visible in China, Falun Gong remains active abroad. It is also behind the *Epoch Times* newspaper, the New Tang Dynasty cable television station, and the Shen Yun performance group. Its media empire has become an influential right-wing voice in American politics. See Kevin Roose, "How the *Epoch Times* Created a Giant Influence Machine," *New York Times*, October 24, 2020, https://www.nytimes.com/2020/10/24/technology/epoch-times -influence-falun-gong.html?referringSource=articleShare, accessed October 24, 2020.

78. Tim Hume, "'Eastern Lightning': The Banned Religious Group That Has China Worried," CNN, February 2, 2015, https://www.cnn.com/2014/06/06/world/asia/china-eastern -lightning-killing/index.html, accessed September 14, 2019.

Chapter 7: How Nationalistic Is China?

1. Barbara Demick and Julie Makinen, "China Government's Hand Seen in Anti-Japan Protests," *Los Angeles Times*, September 20, 2012, https://www.latimes.com/archives/la-xpm-2012 -sep-20-la-fg-china-japan-protests-20120921-story.html, accessed May 2, 2019.

2. Bo was eventually convicted of accepting bribes, embezzlement, and covering up his wife's murder of Neil Heywood. He was expelled from the CCP and sentenced to life in prison. His wife received a suspended death sentence, later reduce to life in prison. During the anticorruption campaign that begin in 2012, many of those linked to Bo were similarly punished. This fueled the belief that the campaign was at least partially intended to eliminate Xi Jinping's rivals.

3. Wenfang Tang and Benjamin Darr, "Chinese Nationalism and Its Political and Social Origins," *Journal of Contemporary China* 21, no. 77 (2012), 811–26.

4. Evan Osnos, "Angry Youth: The New Generation's Neo-Con Nationalists," *New Yorker* (July 28, 2008). Two Chinese graduate students in my seminar on Chinese politics once told me that they had been part of the angry youth while they were studying computer science in China, but after taking their first class in political science, they developed a different perspective on nationalism and decided to pursue degrees in international affairs in the United States.

5. Alastair Iain Johnston, "Is Chinese Nationalism Rising? Evidence from Beijing," *International Security* 41, no. 3 (2017), 7–43.

6. Tang and Darr, "Chinese Nationalism and Its Political and Social Origins"; Yongshin Kim, Doo Hwan Kim, and Seokho Kim, "Who Is Nationalist Now in China?: Some Findings from the 2008 East Asian Social Survey," *China: An International Journal* 14, no. 4 (November 2016), 131–43.

7. Jackson S. Woods and Bruce J. Dickson, "Victims and Patriots: Disaggregating Nationalism in Urban China," *Journal of Contemporary China* 26, no. 104 (2017), 167–82.

8. Alastair Iain Johnston, "How New and Assertive Is China's New Assertiveness?" *International Security* 37, no. 4 (Spring 2013), 7–48.

9. Andrew J. Nathan and Andrew Scobell, *China's Search for Security* (New York: Columbia University Press, 2012).

10. Kevin J. O'Brien and Lianjiang Li, "Campaign Nostalgia in the Chinese Countryside," *Asian Survey* 39, no. 3 (May–June, 1999), 375–93; Iza Ding and Jeffrey Javed, "Red Memory: Nostalgia, Trauma, and Political Attitudes in China," paper presented at the 2016 annual conference of the American Political Science Association.

11. Suisheng Zhao, "A State-Led Nationalism: The Patriotic Education Campaign in Post-Tiananmen China," *Communist and Post-Communist Studies* 31, no. 3 (September 1998), 287–302; Susan Shirk, *China: Fragile Superpower: How China's Internal Politics Could Derail Its Peaceful Rise* (New York: Oxford University Press, 2007); Zheng Wang, *Never Forget National Humiliation: Historical Memory in Chinese Politics* (New York: Columbia University Press, 2012).

12. Peter Hays Gries, *China's New Nationalism: Pride, Politics, and Diplomacy* (Berkeley: University of California Press, 2004), 48, citing Paul Cohen, "Remembering and Forgetting: National Humiliation in Twentieth Century China," *Twentieth-Century China* 27, no. 2 (2002), 1–39. See also Jonathan Unger, ed., *Using the Past to Serve the Present: Historiography and Politics in Contemporary China* (Armonk, NY: M. E. Sharpe, 1993).

13. The statements were "Unless China becomes modern, foreign countries will try to exploit it," "China's early modern encounter with Western imperial powers was a history of humiliation in which the motherland was subjected to the insult of being beaten because we were backwards," and "The 'century of humiliation' not only describes China's past history, it also describes foreigners' actions toward China today." See Woods and Dickson, "Victims and Patriots," 174.

14. Licheng Qian, Bin Xu, and Dingding Chen, "Does History Education Promote Nationalism in China? A 'Limited Effect' Explanation," *Journal of Contemporary China* 26, no. 104 (2017), 199–212.

15. After a public talk at my university, a Chinese student told me she hoped her boyfriend would take my class because he completely believed all he learned in the Patriotic Education Campaign. And yet somehow she had managed to be exposed to the same messages without absorbing them.

16. James Reilly, *Strong Society, Smart State: The Rise of Public Opinion in China's Japan Policy* (New York: Columbia University Press, 2012), 125.

17. Respondents were given the option of totally foreign, mostly foreign, mostly domestic, and totally domestic. Less than 10 percent of respondents answered either totally foreign or totally domestic, so the four original options have been condensed into two.

18. Enze Han, *Contestation and Adaptation: The Politics of National Identity in China* (New York: Oxford University Press, 2013). Han's argument is based on international factors: Tibetans have more international support for their cause, although they may overestimate the amount of that support and willingness of other countries to promote their cause. The Uighurs have less international support than the Tibetans, but more than other minorities in China. Moreover, they have ethnic kin across the border in Central Asian countries and Turkey. Because their ethnic kin enjoy a higher standard of living than do Uighurs in Xinjiang, the Uighurs are incentivized to seek more autonomy and even outright independence in order to improve their economic and political situations. Other minorities in China do not have cross-border kin with better situations.

19. Catriona Bass, "Learning to Love the Motherland: Educating Tibetans in China," *The Journal of Moral Education* 34, no. 4 (December 2005), 433–49; John Powers, *The Buddha Party: How the People's Republic of China Works to Define and Control Tibetan Buddhism* (New York: Oxford, 2017).

20. Bass, "Learning to Love the Motherland," 436–37.

21. Powers, *The Buddha Party*, 71ff.

22. Ibid., 51.

23. International Campaign for Tibet, https://www.savetibet.org/resources/fact-sheets/self-immolations-by-tibetans/ (updated December 2, 2019), accessed April 10, 2020.

24. Deng and O'Brien, "Relational Repression in China," 533–52.

25. Timothy Grose, "(Re)Embracing Islam in *Neidi*: The 'Xinjiang Class' and the Dynamics of Uighur Ethno-national Identity," *Journal of Contemporary China* 24, no. 91 (2015): 112.

26. "Life Inside China's Total Surveillance State," *Wall Street Journal* (December 19, 2017), https://www.wsj.com/video/life-inside-chinas-total-surveillance-state/CE86DA19-D55D-4F12-AC6A-3B2A573492CF.html, accessed October 14, 2018.

27. Paul Mozur, Jonah M. Kessel and Melissa Chan, "Made in China, Exported to the World: The Surveillance State," *New York Times* (April 24, 2019), https://www.nytimes.com/2019/04/24/technology/ecuador-surveillance-cameras-police-government.html, accessed May 6, 2019.

28. Gerry Shih and Emily Rauhala, "Angry over Campus Speech by Uighur Activist, Chinese Students in Canada Contact Their Consulate, Film Presentation," *Washington Post* (February 14, 2019), https://www.washingtonpost.com/world/angry-over-campus-speech-by-uighur

-activist-students-in-canada-contact-chinese-consulate-film-presentation/2019/02/14
/a442fbe4-306d-11e9-ac6c-14eea99d5e24_story.html?utm_term=.a29f9a462783, accessed February 14, 2019.

29. Han, *Contestation and Adaptation*, 50.

30. Sonny Shiu-Hing Lo, "Hong Kong," in William A. Joseph, ed., *Politics in China*, 3rd ed. (New York: Oxford University Press, 2019), 517–37.

31. Sebastian Veg, "The Rise of 'Localism' and Civic Identity in Post-handover Hong Kong: Questioning the Chinese Nation-state," *China Quarterly*, no. 230 (June 2017), 323–47; H. Christoph Steinhardt, Linda Chelan Li, and Yihong Jiang, "The Identity Shift in Hong Kong since 1997: Measurement and Explanation," *Journal of Contemporary China* 27, no. 110 (2018), 261–76.

32. Victoria Tin-bor Hui, "Hong Kong's Umbrella Movement: The Protests and Beyond," *Journal of Democracy* 26, no. 2 (April 2015), 111–21.

33. Paul Mozur, "In Hong Kong Protests, Faces Become Weapons," *New York Times* (July 27, 2019), https://www.nytimes.com/2019/07/26/technology/hong-kong-protests-facial-recognition-surveillance.html, accessed July 27, 2019; Gerry Shih and Anna Kam, "Without Heroes or Martyrs: Hong Kong's Protest Movement Faces Its Defining Moment," *Washington Post*, August 16, 2019, https://www.washingtonpost.com/world/asia_pacific/without-heroes-or-martyrs-hong-kongs-protest-movement-faces-its-defining-moment/2019/08/16/d460ce74-bfe1-11e9-a8b0-7ed8aod5dc5d_story.html, accessed August 20, 2019.

34. Tiffany May and Amy Qin, "The High School Course Beijing Accuses of Radicalizing Hong Kong," *New York Times*, September 1, 2019, https://www.nytimes.com/2019/09/01/world/asia/hong-kong-protests-education-china.html, accessed September 16, 2019. Earlier proposals by the Hong Kong government to introduce a national education curriculum emphasizing Chinese history and culture met fierce resistance and were eventually withdrawn.

35. Zhang was demoted in February 2020 as part of a shakeup of Beijing's officials handling Hong Kong affairs.

36. Andreas Fulda, "Beijing Is Weaponizing Nationalism against Hong Kongers," *Foreign Policy*, July 19, 2019, https://foreignpolicy.com/2019/07/29/beijing-is-weaponizing-nationalism-against-hong-kongers/, accessed April 13, 2020.

37. Shibani Mahtani, "A Student in Boston Wrote 'I am from Hong Kong.' An Onslaught of Chinese Anger Followed," *Washington Post* (May 25, 2019), https://www.washingtonpost.com/world/asia_pacific/a-student-in-boston-wrote-i-am-from-hong-kong-an-onslaught-of-chinese-anger-followed/2019/05/24/298ea3ee-719a-11e9-9331-30bc5836f48e_story.html, accessed May 25, 2019.

38. Sopan Deb and Marc Klein, "N.B.A. Executive's Hong Kong Tweet Starts Firestorm in China," *New York Times*, October 6, 2019, https://www.nytimes.com/2019/10/06/sports/daryl-morey-rockets-china.html, accessed April 17, 2020.

39. Keith Bradsher, Austin Ramzy, and Tiffany May, "Hong Kong Election Results Give Democracy Backers Big Win," *New York Times*, November 24, 2019, https://www.nytimes.com/2019/11/24/world/asia/hong-kong-election-results.html, accessed April 20, 2020.

40. Elaine Yu and Austin Ramzy, "Amid Pandemic, Hong Kong Arrests Major Pro-Democracy Figures," *New York Times*, April 18, 2020, https://www.nytimes.com/2020/04/18/world/asia/hong-kong-arrests.html, accessed April 20, 2020.

41. Chris Buckley, Keith Bradsher, and Tiffany May, "New Security Law Gives China Sweeping Powers over Hong Kong," *New York Times*, June 29, 2020, https://www.nytimes.com/2020/06/29/world/asia/china-hong-kong-security-law-rules.html?referringSource=articleShare, accessed August 13, 2020.

42. Article 38 of the NSL states that "This Law shall apply to offences under this Law committed against the Hong Kong Special Administrative Region from outside the Region by a person who is not a permanent resident of the Region." This article was presumably intended for people who leave Hong Kong and continue to criticize its government, but as written it could also apply to people who are not from Hong Kong.

43. Edward Wong, "China's Global Message: We Are Tough but Not Threatening," *New York Times*, October 2, 2019, https://www.nytimes.com/2019/10/02/world/asia/china-world-parade-military.html?smid=nytcore-ios-share, accessed October 3, 2019.

44. It was later revealed that this building had been selected by the CIA, the first time the CIA had selected a target for a missile strike. It was also the last time the CIA selected a target during the Kosovo crisis.

45. Gries, *China's New Nationalism*, 20; Joseph Fewsmith, *China since Tiananmen* (New York: Cambridge University Press, 2001).

46. As an interesting footnote to this episode, the American and Chinese governments quietly agreed to pay for damages to each other's embassies, with the United States paying $28 million for repairs to the Chinese embassy in Belgrade, and China paying $2.87 million for damages to the US embassy in Beijing and consulates in Chengdu and Guangzhou. The United States also paid $4.5 million in compensation for the three people killed in the bombing. In other words, each government took responsibility for damages done to the other's embassy. See Michael Laris, "U.S., China Reach Deal on Embassy Payments," *Washington Post*, December 16, 1999, https://www.washingtonpost.com/archive/politics/1999/12/16/us-china-reach-deal-on-embassy-payments/690c1ec6-b118-487a-a086-fc850ef67a67/?utm_term=.f5ff5cf06337, accessed May 2, 2019.

47. Fewsmith, *China since Tiananmen*.

48. Simon Denyer and Congcong Zhang, "A Chinese Student Praised the 'Fresh Air of Free Speech' at a U.S. College. Then Came the Backlash," *Washington Post* (May 23, 2017), https://www.washingtonpost.com/news/worldviews/wp/2017/05/23/a-chinese-student-praised-the-fresh-air-of-free-speech-at-a-u-s-college-then-came-the-backlash/?utm_term=.7d73332c3bd4, accessed May 9, 2019.

49. Brook Larmer, "Li Na, China's Tennis Rebel," *New York Times* (August 23, 2013), https://www.nytimes.com/2013/08/25/magazine/li-na-chinas-tennis-rebel.html, accessed May 9, 2019.

50. Jessica Chen Weiss, "How Hawkish Is the Chinese Public? Another Look at 'Rising Nationalism' and Chinese Foreign Policy," *Journal of Contemporary China* 28, no. 119 (2019), 679–95.

51. The German legacy in Qingdao lives on in Tsingtao (an alternative transliteration of Qingdao) beer. German settlers set up a brewery in Qingdao and named the beer after the city.

52. James Reilly, "A Wave to Worry About? Public Opinion, Foreign Policy and China's Anti-Japanese Protests," *Journal of Contemporary China* 23, no. 86 (2014), 202; Jessica Chen

Weiss, *Powerful Patriots: Nationalist Protest in China's Foreign Relations* (New York: Oxford University Press, 2014), 161.

53. Reilly, *Strong Society, Smart State*, 31.

54. Jianwei Wang and Xiaojie Wang, "Media and Chinese Foreign Policy," *Journal of Contemporary China* 23, no. 86 (March 2014), 216–35.

55. Jack L. Snyder, *From Voting to Violence: Democratization and Nationalist Conflict* (New York: W. W. Norton, 2000); Jack L. Snyder and Edward D. Mansfield, *Electing to Fight: Why Emerging Democracies Go to War* (Cambridge, MA: MIT Press, 2007).

56. Jessica Chen Weiss, "Autocratic Signaling, Mass Audiences and Nationalist Protest in China," *International Organization* 67, no. 1 (January 2013), 1–35.

57. Ibid., 24.

58. Their release came after the US government delivered a letter to the Chinese saying it was sorry for the death of the Chinese pilot and sorry the US plane entered Chinese air space without prior authorization. The wording of the letter was deliberately ambiguous, allowing the United States to characterize it as an expression of regret and the Chinese government to describe it as an apology. The EP-3 plane was eventually returned to the United States, but not before it was thoroughly disassembled and its technology examined. The United States had to send a cargo ship to retrieve the parts.

59. Iris Chang, *The Rape of Nanking* (New York: Perseus Books, 1997); Rana Mitter, *China's War with Japan 1937–1945: The Struggle for Survival* (New York: Penguin Books, 2013).

60. Weiss, *Powerful Patriots*, 82–83.

61. Jeremy L. Wallace and Jessica Chen Weiss, "The Political Geography of Nationalist Protest in China," *China Quarterly*, no. 222 (June 2015), 403–29.

62. Peter Hays Gries, Derek Steiger, and Tao Wang, "Popular Nationalism and China's Japan Policy: The Diaoyu Islands Protests, 2012–2013," *Journal of Contemporary China* 25, no. 98 (2016), 264–76.

63. Wallace and Weiss, "The Political Geography of Nationalist Protest in China," 404.

64. Reilly, *Strong Society, Smart State*, 211.

Chapter 8: Will China Become Democratic?

1. Ronald Inglehart and Christian Welzel, "How Development Leads to Democracy: What We Know About Modernization," *Foreign Affairs* 88, no. 2 (March/April 2009), 33–48.

2. Henry S. Rowen, "When Will the Chinese People Be Free?" *Journal of Democracy* 18, no. 3 (July 2007), 38–62.

3. Ronald Inglehart and Christian Welzel, *Modernization, Cultural Change, and Democracy* (New York: Cambridge University Press, 2005), 190–91.

4. Andrew Nathan, "The Puzzle of the Chinese Middle Class," *Journal of Democracy* 27, no. 2 (April 2016), 5–19.

5. Minxin Pei, *China's Trapped Transition: The Limits of Developmental Autocracy* (Harvard University Press, 2006); Shambaugh, *China's Future?*

6. Francis Fukuyama, *The End of History and the Last Man* (New York: The Free Press, 1992).

7. Fukuyama himself later partially recanted after the US interventions in Iraq and Afghanistan after 9/11 showed that overthrowing authoritarian regimes was just the beginning of a difficult process of state building. Instead of recommending that states limit their reach, Fukuyama called for building strong institutions as the basis for economic and political development. Simply replacing dictators did not automatically or inevitably lead to political stability and economic growth. Without effective institutions, even democracies will fail to deliver. See his "The Imperative of State-Building," *Journal of Democracy* 15, no. 2 (2004), 17–31.

8. Scott Kennedy, "The Myth of the Beijing Consensus," *Journal of Contemporary China* 19, no. 65 (June 2010), 461–477.

9. James Mann, *The China Fantasy: How Our Leaders Explain Away Chinese Repression* (New York: Viking, 2007).

10. Kurt M. Campbell and Ely Ratner, "The China Reckoning: How Beijing Defied American Expectations," *Foreign Affairs* 97, no. 2 (March/April 2018), 60–70.

11. Robert D. Putnam, *Bowling Alone: The Collapse and Revival of American Community* (New York: Simon and Schuster, 2001); Pippa Norris, *Democratic Deficit: Critical Citizens Revisited* (New York: Cambridge University Press, 2011).

12. Bruce Russett, *Grasping the Democratic Peace: Principles for a Post-Cold War World* (Princeton, NJ: Princeton University Press, 1993).

13. Barbara Geddes, "What Do We Know about Democratization after Twenty Years?" *Annual Review of Political Science* (1999), 115–144. At the time Geddes wrote, one-party regimes lasted an average of 22.7 years, compared to 15.1 years for personalist dictatorships and only 8.8 years for military dictatorships. A more recent study finds a similar pattern: twenty-six years for one-party regimes, eleven years for personalist regimes, and seven years for military dictatorships. See Erica Frantz, *Authoritarianism: What Everyone Needs to Know* (New York: Oxford University Press, 2018), 127–28.

14. Jude Blanchette, "What If? Short-term Implications of Xi Jinping's Death or Illness," *China Executive Intelligence*, September 2018.

15. Yue Hou, *The Private Sector in Public Office: Selective Property Rights in China* (New York: Cambridge University Press, 2019); Dickson, *Red Capitalists in China*.

16. Bruce J. Dickson, "Who Wants to Be a Communist? Career Incentives and Mobilized Loyalty in Contemporary China," *China Quarterly*, no. 217 (March 2014), 42–68.

17. Dan Slater, *Ordering Power: Contentious Politics and Authoritarian Leviathans in Southeast Asia* (New York: Cambridge University Press, 2010).

18. Martin K. Dimitrov, "Understanding Communist Collapse and Resilience," in Dimitrov, ed., *Why Communism Did Not Collapse: Understanding Authoritarian Regime Resilience in Asia and Europe* (New York: Cambridge University Press, 2013), 3–39.

19. Gordon Chang, *The Coming Collapse of China* (New York: Random House, 2001); Bruce Gilley, *China's Democratic Future: How It Will Happen and Where It Will Lead* (New York: Columbia University Press, 2004); Cheng Li, "The End of the CCP's Authoritarian Resilience? A Tripartite Assessment of Shifting Power in China," *China Quarterly*, no. 211 (September 2012), 595–623; Shambaugh, *China's Future?*; Minxin Pei, "China's Coming Upheaval: Competition, the Coronavirus, and the Weakness of Xi Jinping," *Foreign Affairs* 99, no. 3 (May/June 2020), 82–95.

20. Lardy, *The State Strikes Back.*

21. Jeremy L. Wallace, *Cities and Stability: Urbanization, Redistribution and Regime Survival in China* (New York: Oxford University Press, 2014).

22. One exception was a short-lived "cake debate," in which Chongqing Party Secretary Bo Xilai argued it was most important to cut the cake correctly (so as to ensure the equitable distribution of wealth even at the expense of economic growth) and Guangdong Party Secretary Wang Yang argued it was more important to enlarge the cake (by promoting economic growth even at the expense of equity). Ironically, Wang had previously served in Chongqing where he prioritized equity over growth, the very thing he was arguing against in his new post. See Chunhua Chen and Bruce J. Dickson, "Coping with Growth in China: Comparing Models of Development in Guangdong and Chongqing," *Journal of Chinese Governance* 3 (2018).

23. Shambaugh, *China's Communist Party.*

24. China's poverty rate as reported by the World Bank's World Development Indicators, using the standard of $1.90 per day in 2011 PPP dollars.

25. Leslie T. Chang, *Factory Girls: From Village to City in a Changing China* (New York: Random House, 2009).

26. Dickson, *The Dictator's Dilemma*, chapter 5.

27. Michelson, "Public Goods and State-Society Relations," 131–57; Dickson et al., "Public Goods and Regime Support in Urban China," 859–80; Jude Howell and Jane Duckett, "Re-Assessing the Hu-Wen Era: A Golden Age or Lost Decade for Social Policy in China," *China Quarterly* no. 237 (March 2019), 1–14.

28. Teresa Wright, *Accepting Authoritarianism: State-Society Relations in China's Reform Era* (Stanford: Stanford University Press, 2010).

29. Adam Przeworski and Fernando Limongi, "Modernization: Theories and Facts," *World Politics* 49, no. 2 (January 1997), 155–83.

30. Zheng Wang, *Never Forget National Humiliation: Historical Memory in Chinese Politics* (New York: Columbia University Press, 2012).

31. Rongbin Han, *Contesting Cyberspace in China: Online Expression and Authoritarian Resilience* (New York: Columbia University Press, 2018).

32. Shi, *The Cultural Logic of Politics in Mainland China and Taiwan*; Dickson, "Defining Democracy," chapter 6 in *Dictator's Dilemma.*

33. Shi, *The Cultural Logic of Politics in Mainland China and Taiwan*, 197–201. The original meaning of *minzhu* was "rule the people," a far cry from rule by and for the people.

34. Harry Harding, *China's Second Revolution: Reform after Mao* (Washington, DC: Brookings, 1987).

35. Wu Bangguo, "Full Text: Work Report of NPC Standing Committee (2011)," *GOV.cn*, last modified March 18, 2011, accessed October 29, 2013, http://english.gov.cn/official/2011-03/18/content_1827230_6.htm.

36. Clifford Coonan, "Democracy Not for China, Says Xi Jinping," *Irish Times*, April 24, 2014, https://www.irishtimes.com/news/world/asia-pacific/democracy-not-for-china-says-xi-jinping-1.1747853, accessed October 12, 2019.

37. Samuel P. Huntington, *The Third Wave: Democratization in the Late Twentieth Century* (Norman: University of Oklahoma Press, 1991).

286 NOTES TO PAGES 246-253

38. Freedom House, "Freedom in the World 2020," https://freedomhouse.org/report /freedom-world, accessed April 28, 2020.

39. Larry Diamond, *Ill Winds: Saving Democracy from Russian Rage, Chinese Ambition, and American Complacency* (New York: Penguin, 2019); Pippa Norris and Ronald Inglehart, *Cultural Backlash: Trump, Brexit, and Authoritarian Populism* (New York: Cambridge University Press, 2019); Sheri Berman and Maria Snegovaya, "Populism and the Decline of Social Democracy," *Journal of Democracy* 30, no. 3 (July 2019), 5–19; Milan Svolik, "Polarization versus Democracy," *Journal of Democracy* 30, no. 3 (July 2019), 20–32.

40. Huntington, *The Third Wave*; Stephan Haggard and Robert R. Kaufman, *Dictators and Democrats: Masses, Elites, and Regime Change* (Princeton, NJ: Princeton University Press, 2016).

41. Although de Klerk was not seen as a reformer before becoming president in 1989, he and Mandela shared the Nobel Peace Prize in 1993 for their negotiated end to apartheid in South Africa.

42. Graham Allison, *Destined for War: Can America and China Escape Thucydides's Trap?* (New York: Houghton Mifflin Harcourt, 2017).

43. Anna Fifield, "Battered by Coronavirus, China Maps Out an Economic Reality Check for a New Era," *Washington Post*, May 22, 2020, https://www.washingtonpost.com/world/as -coronavirus-exacts-a-heavy-economic-toll-china-declines-to-set-growth-target/2020/05/22 /4826bd6e-9985-11ea-ad79-eef7cd734641_story.html, accessed June 17, 2020.

44. Timur Kuran, "Now out of Never: The Element of Surprise in the East European Revolution of 1989," *World Politics* 44, no. 1 (October 1991), 7–48.

45. Philippe C. Schmitter and Terry Lynn Karl, "What Democracy Is . . . and Is Not," *Journal of Democracy* 2, no. 1 (Summer 1991), 75–88.

46. Yu-tzung Chang, Yun-han Chu, and Chong-Min Park, "Authoritarian Nostalgia in Asia," *Journal of Democracy* 18 no. 3 (July 2007), 66–80; Sarah E. Mendelson and Theodore P. Gerber, "Soviet Nostalgia: An Impediment to Russian Democratization," *Washington Quarterly* 29, no. 1 (2005), 83–96.

47. Mansfield and Snyder, *Electing to Fight: Why Emerging Democracies Go to War.*

BIBLIOGRAPHY

Alkon, Meir, and Eric H. Wang. "Pollution Lowers Support for China's Regime: Quasi-Experimental Evidence from Beijing." *Journal of Politics* 80, no. 1 (January 2018): 327–31.

Allison, Graham. *Destined for War: Can America and China Escape Thucydides's Trap?* New York: Houghton Mifflin Harcourt, 2017.

An Evaluation of and Recommendations on the Reforms of the Health System in China: Executive Summary. Beijing: State Council Development Research Council, 2005.

Ashiwa, Yoshiko, and David L. Wank. "The Politics of Reviving a Buddhist Temple: State, Association, and Religion in Southeast China." *Journal of Asian Studies* 65, no. 2 (May 2006).

Balla, Steven J. "Information Technology, Political Participation, and the Evolution of Chinese Policymaking." *Journal of Contemporary China* 21, no. 76 (2012): 655–73.

Balla, Steven J., and Zhou Liao. "Online Consultation and Citizen Feedback in Chinese Policymaking." *Journal of Current Chinese Affairs* 42, no. 3 (2013): 101–20.

Balla, Steven J., and Zhoudan Xie. "Online Consultation and the Institutionalization of Transparency and Participation in Chinese Policymaking." *China Quarterly*, forthcoming.

Bass, Catriona. "Learning to Love the Motherland: Educating Tibetans in China." *Journal of Moral Education* 34, no. 4 (December 2005): 433–49.

Batke, Jessica. "'The New Normal' for Foreign NGOs in 2020." *ChinaFile*, January 3, 2020. https://www.chinafile.com/ngo/analysis/new-normal-foreign-ngos-2020, accessed January 7, 2020.

Berman, Sheri, and Maria Snegovaya. "Populism and the Decline of Social Democracy." *Journal of Democracy* 30, no. 3 (July 2019): 5–19.

Bernstein, Thomas, and Xiaobo Lu. "Taxation without Representation: Peasants, the Central and the Local States in Reform China." *China Quarterly*, no. 163 (September 2000): 742–63.

Blanchette, Jude. "What If? Short-term Implications of Xi Jinping's Death or Illness." *China Executive Intelligence* (September 2018).

Blecher, Marc. "Hegemony and Workers' Politics in China." *China Quarterly*, no. 170 (June 2002): 283–303.

Bo, Zhiyue. *China's Elite Politics: Political Transition and Power Balancing.* Singapore: World Scientific Publishing Company, 2007.

Bradsher, Keith, Austin Ramzy, and Tiffany May. "Hong Kong Election Results Give Democracy Backers Big Win." *New York Times*, November 24, 2019. https://www.nytimes.com/2019/11/24/world/asia/hong-kong-election-results.html, accessed April 20, 2020.

Brady, Anne-Marie. *Marketing Dictatorship: Propaganda and Thought Work in Contemporary China*. Lanham, MD: Rowman & Littlefield, 2009.

Brødsgaard, Kjeld Erik. "Management of Party Cadres in China." In Kjeld Erik Brødsgaard and Zheng Yongnian, eds., *Bringing the Party Back In: How China Is Governed*. Singapore: Eastern Universities Press, 2004.

———. "Politics and Business Group Formation in China: The Party in Control?" *China Quarterly*, no. 211 (September 2012): 624–48.

———, ed. *Chinese Politics as Fragmented Authoritarianism: Earthquakes, Energy, and Environment*. New York: Routledge, 2017.

Brown, Kerry. 2012. *Hu Jintao: China's Silent Ruler*. Singapore: World Scientific Publishing Company.

Buckley, Chris. "A Chinese Law Professor Criticized Xi. Now He's Been Suspended." *New York Times*, March 26, 2019. https://www.nytimes.com/2019/03/26/world/asia/chinese-law-professor-xi.html, accessed July 5, 2019.

———. "As China's Woes Mounts, Xi Jinping Faces a Rare Rebuke at Home." *New York Times*, July 31, 2018. https://www.nytimes.com/2018/07/31/world/asia/xi-jinping-internal-dissent.html, accessed August 1, 2018.

Burns, John P. "Strengthening Central CCP Control of Leadership Selection: The 1990 Nomenklatura." *China Quarterly*, no. 138 (1994): 458–91.

Buruma, Ian. *Bad Elements: Chinese Rebels from Los Angeles to Beijing*. New York: Random House, 2001.

Cabestan, Jean-Pierre. 2012. "Is Xi Jinping the Reformist Leader China Needs?" *China Perspectives* 3: 69–76.

Cai, Meina, and Xin Sun. "Institutional Bindingness, Power Structure, and Land Expropriation in China." *World Development* 109 (September 2018): 172–86.

Cai, Yongshun. "Power Structure and Regime Resilience: Contentious Politics in China." *British Journal of Political Science* 38, no. 3 (July 2008): 411–32.

Campbell, Kurt M., and Ely Ratner. "The China Reckoning: How Beijing Defied American Expectations." *Foreign Affairs* 97, no. 2 (March/April 2018): 60–70.

Campbell, Matthew, and Peter Martin. "China's Latest Crackdown Target Is Liberal Economists." *Bloomberg Businessweek*, May 11, 2019. https://www.bloomberg.com/news/features/2019-05-11/china-s-latest-crackdown-target-is-liberal-economists, accessed May 5, 2019.

Cao, Nanlai. *Constructing China's Jerusalem: Christians, Power, and Place in Contemporary Wenzhou*. Stanford: Stanford University Press, 2010.

Chai Ling. *A Heart for Freedom: The Remarkable Journey of a Young Dissident, Her Daring Escape, and Her Quest to Free China's Daughters*. Carol Stream, IL: Tyndale House Publishers, 2011.

Chan, Anita. "Revolution or Corporatism? Workers in Search of a Solution." In David S. G. Goodman and Beverly Hooper, eds., *China's Quiet Revolution: New Interactions between State and Society*. New York: St. Martin's Press, 1994.

Chan, Tara Francis. "China Released a Uyghur Mother to Silence Her U.S. Son—Then Sent Her Back to Detention the Next Day." *Newsweek*, May 25, 2019. https://www.newsweek.com/xinjiang-uyghur-release-threaten-us-citizen-1435984, accessed May 25, 2019.

Chang, Gordon. *The Coming Collapse of China.* New York: Random House, 2001.

Chang, Iris. *The Rape of Nanking.* New York: Perseus Books, 1997.

Chang, Kuei-min. "New Wine in Old Bottles: Sinicisation and State Regulation of Religion in China." *China Perspectives* 1–2 (January 2018): 37–44.

Chang, Leslie T. *Factory Girls: From Village to City in a Changing China.* New York: Random House, 2009.

Chang, Yu-tzung, Yun-han Chu, and Chong-Min Park. "Authoritarian Nostalgia in Asia." *Journal of Democracy* 18, no. 3 (July 2007): 66–80.

Chen, Chunhua, and Bruce J. Dickson. "Coping with Growth in China: Comparing Models of Development in Guangdong and Chongqing." *Journal of Chinese Governance* 3 (2018).

Chen, Feng, and Mengxiao Tang. "Labor Conflicts in China: Typologies and Their Implications." *Asian Survey* 53, no. 3 (May/June 2013): 559–83.

Chen, Jidong, Jennifer Pan, and Yiqing Xu. "Sources of Authoritarian Responsiveness: A Field Experiment in China." *American Journal of Political Science* 60, no. 2 (April 2016): 383–400.

Chen, Jidong, and Yiqing Xu. "Why Do Authoritarian Regimes Allow Citizens to Voice Opinions Publicly?" *Journal of Politics* 79, no. 3 (July 2017): 792–803.

Chen, Jie. *A Middle Class without Democracy: Economic Growth and the Prospects for Democratization in China.* New York: Oxford University Press, 2013.

Chen, Xi. "Elitism and Exclusion in Mass Protest: Privatization, Resistance, and State Domination in China." *Comparative Political Studies* 50, no. 7 (June 2017): 908–34.

———. "The Logic of Fragmented Activism among Chinese State-Owned Enterprise Workers." *China Journal* 81 (January 2019): 58–80.

———. "Origins of Informal Coercion in China." *Politics and Society* 45, no. 1 (March 2017): 67–89.

———. *Social Protest and Contentious Politics in China.* New York: Cambridge University Press, 2012.

"China Mosque Demolition Sparks Standoff in Ningxia." *BBC News*, August 10, 2018. https://www.bbc.com/news/world-asia-china-45140551, accessed September 11, 2019.

Coonan, Clifford. "Democracy Not for China, Says Xi Jinping." *Irish Times*, April 24, 2014. https://www.irishtimes.com/news/world/asia-pacific/democracy-not-for-china-says-xi-jinping-1.1747853, accessed October 12, 2019.

Davies, James C. "Towards a Theory of Revolution." *American Sociological Review* 27, no. 1 (February 1962): 5–19.

Dean, Kenneth. "Local Communal Religion in Contemporary South-East China." *China Quarterly*, no. 174 (June 2003): 338–58.

Deb, Sopan, and Marc Klein. "N.B.A. Executive's Hong Kong Tweet Starts Firestorm in China." *New York Times*, October 6, 2019. https://www.nytimes.com/2019/10/06/sports/daryl-morey-rockets-china.html, accessed April 17, 2020.

Demick, Barbara, and Julie Makinen. "China Government's Hand Seen in Anti-Japan Protests." *Los Angeles Times*, September 20, 2012. https://www.latimes.com/archives/la-xpm-2012-sep-20-la-fg-china-japan-protests-20120921-story.html, accessed May 2, 2019.

Deng, Yanhua, and Kevin J. O'Brien. "Relational Repression in China: Using Social Ties to Demobilize Protesters." *China Quarterly*, no. 215 (September 2013): 533–52.

Denyer, Simon, and Congcong Zhang. "A Chinese Student Praised the 'Fresh Air of Free Speech' at a U.S. College. Then Came the Backlash." *Washington Post*, May 23, 2017. https://www.washingtonpost.com/news/worldviews/wp/2017/05/23/a-chinese-student-praised-the-fresh-air-of-free-speech-at-a-u-s-college-then-came-the-backlash/?utm_term=.7d73332c3bd4, accessed May 9, 2019.

Diamant, Neil J. *Embattled Glory: Veterans, Military Families, and the Politics of Patriotism in China, 1949–2007.* Lanham, MD: Rowman & Littlefield, 2009.

Diamond, Larry. *Ill Winds: Saving Democracy from Russian Rage, Chinese Ambition, and American Complacency.* New York: Penguin, 2019.

———. "Rethinking Civil Society: Toward Democratic Consolidation." *Journal of Democracy* 5, no. 3 (July 1994): 4–17.

Dickson, Bruce J. *The Dictator's Dilemma: The Chinese Communist Party's Strategy for Survival.* New York: Oxford University Press, 2016.

———. *Red Capitalists in China: The Party, Private Entrepreneurs, and Prospects for Political Change.* New York and London: Cambridge University Press, 2003.

———. *Wealth into Power: The Communist Party's Embrace of China's Private Sector.* New York and London: Cambridge University Press, 2008.

———. "Who Wants to Be a Communist? Career Incentives and Mobilized Loyalty in Contemporary China." *China Quarterly*, no. 217 (March 2014): 42–68.

Dickson, Bruce J., Pierre Landry, Mingming Shen, and Jie Yan. "Public Goods and Regime Support in Urban China." *China Quarterly*, no. 228 (December 2016): 859–80.

Dimitrov, Martin K. "Understanding Communist Collapse and Resilience." In Dimitrov, ed., *Why Communism Did Not Collapse: Understanding Authoritarian Regime Resilience in Asia and Europe.* New York: Cambridge University Press, 2013.

———. "Vertical Accountability in Communist Regimes: The Role of Citizen Complaints in Bulgaria and China." In Dimitrov, ed., *Why Communism Did Not Collapse: Understanding Authoritarian Regime Resilience in Asia and Europe.* New York: Cambridge University Press, 2013.

Ding, Iza, and Jeffrey Javed. "Red Memory: Nostalgia, Trauma, and Political Attitudes in China." Paper presented at the 2016 annual conference of the American Political Science Association.

Distelhorst, Greg. "The Power of Empty Promises: Quasi-Democratic Institutions and Activism in China." *Comparative Political Studies* 50, no. 4 (2017): 464–94.

Distelhorst, Greg, and Yue Hou. "Constituency Service under Nondemocratic Rule: Evidence from China." *Journal of Politics* 79, no. 3 (July 2017): 1024–40.

Donaldson, John A. *Small Works: Poverty and Economic Development in Southwest China.* Ithaca, NY: Cornell University Press, 2011.

Economy, Elizabeth C. *The River Runs Black: The Environmental Challenge to China's Future.* Ithaca, NY: Cornell University Press, 2004.

———. *The Third Revolution: Xi Jinping and the New Chinese State.* New York: Oxford University Press, 2018.

Edin, Maria. "State Capacity and Local Agent Control in China: CCP Cadre Management from a Township Perspective." *China Quarterly*, no. 173 (March 2003): 35–52.

Elfstrom, Manfred. "Two Steps Forward, One Step Back? Chinese State Reactions to Labour Unrest." *China Quarterly*, no. 240 (December 2019): 255–79.

Ewing, Richard Daniel. "Hu Jintao: The Making of a Chinese General Secretary." *China Quarterly* 173 (2003): 17–34.

Feng, Yuqing, and Xin He. "From Law to Politics: Petitioners' Framing of Disputes in Chinese Courts." *China Journal* 80 (July 2018): 130–49.

Fewsmith, Joseph. *China since Tiananmen*. New York: Cambridge University Press, 2001.

———. *The Logic and Limits of Political Reform in China*. New York: Cambridge University Press, 2013.

Fifield, Anna. "Battered by Coronavirus, China Maps Out an Economic Reality Check for a New Era." *Washington Post*, May 22, 2020. https://www.washingtonpost.com/world/as-coronavirus-exacts-a-heavy-economic-toll-china-declines-to-set-growth-target/2020/05/22/4826bd6e-9985-11ea-ad79-eef7cd734641_story.html, accessed June 17, 2020.

———. "Chinese App on Xi's Ideology Allows Data Access to Users' Phones, Report Says." *Washington Post*, October 16, 2019. https://www.washingtonpost.com/world/asia_pacific/chinese-app-on-xis-ideology-allows-data-access-to-100-million-users-phones-report-says/2019/10/11/2d53bbae-eb4d-11e9-bafb-da248f8d5734_story.html, accessed October 16, 2019.

———. "China's Conspicuously Absent Leader Reemerges—For an Audience with a Friendly Autocrat." *Washington Post*, February 5, 2020. https://www.washingtonpost.com/world/chinas-conspicuously-absent-leader-reemerges--for-an-audience-with-a-friendly-autocrat/2020/02/05/507e6d02-47de-11ea-91ab-ce439aa5c7c1_story.html, accessed February 6, 2020.

Fishkin, James S., Baogang He, Robert C. Luskin, and Alice Siu. "Deliberative Democracy in an Unlikely Place: Deliberative Polling in China." *British Journal of Political Science* 40, no. 2 (April 2010): 435–48.

Foley, Michael W., and Bob Edwards. "The Paradox of Civil Society." *Journal of Democracy* 7, no. 3 (July 1996): 38–52.

Franceschini, Ivan, and Elisa Nesossi, "State Repression of Chinese Labor NGOs: A Chilling Effect?" *China Journal* 80 (July 2018): 111–29.

Frantz, Erica. *Authoritarianism: What Everyone Needs to Know*. New York: Oxford University Press, 2018.

Fu, Diana. "Fragmented Control: Governing Contentious Labor Organizations in China." *Governance* 30, no. 3 (July 2017): 445–62.

———. *Mobilizing without the Masses: Control and Contention in China*. Cambridge: Cambridge University Press, 2017.

Fu, Diana, and Greg Distelhorst. "Grassroots Participation and Repression under Hu Jintao and Xi Jinping." *China Journal*, no. 79 (January 2018): 100–22.

Fu, Hualing, and Richard Cullen. "Weiquan (Rights Protection) Lawyering in an Authoritarian State: Building a Culture of Public-Interest Lawyering." *China Journal*, no. 59 (January 2008): 111–27.

Fukuyama, Francis. *The End of History and the Last Man*. New York: The Free Press, 1992.

———. "The Imperative of State-Building." *Journal of Democracy* 15, no. 2 (2004): 17–31.

Fulda, Andreas. "Beijing Is Weaponizing Nationalism against Hong Kongers." *Foreign Policy,* July 19, 2019. https://foreignpolicy.com/2019/07/29/beijing-is-weaponizing-nationalism -against-hong-kongers/, accessed April 13, 2020.

Gallagher, Mary E. *Authoritarian Legality in China: Law, Workers, and the State.* New York: Cambridge University Press, 2017.

Geddes, Barbara. "What Do We Know about Democratization after Twenty Years?" *Annual Review of Political Science* (1999): 115–44.

Gilley, Bruce. *Tiger on the Brink: Jiang Zemin and China's New Elite.* Berkeley: University of California Press, 1998.

———. *China's Democratic Future: How It Will Happen and Where It Will Lead.* New York: Columbia University Press, 2004.

Greitens, Sheena. "Rethinking China's Coercive Capacity: An Examination of PRC Domestic Security Spending, 1992–2012." *China Quarterly,* no. 232 (December 2017): 1002–25.

Gries, Peter Hays. *China's New Nationalism: Pride, Politics, and Diplomacy.* Berkeley: University of California Press, 2004.

Gries, Peter Hays, Derek Steiger, and Tao Wang. "Popular Nationalism and China's Japan Policy: The Diaoyu Islands Protests, 2012–2013." *Journal of Contemporary China* 25, no. 98 (2016): 264–76.

Groot, Gerry. *Managing Transitions: The Chinese Communist Party, United Front Work, Corporatism, and Hegemony.* New York and London: Routledge, 2004.

Grose, Timothy. "(Re)Embracing Islam in *Neidi*: The 'Xinjiang Class' and the Dynamics of Uighur Ethno-national Identity." *Journal of Contemporary China* 24, no. 91 (2015): 101–18.

Gueorguiev, Dimitar, and Edmund Malesky. "Consultation and Selective Censorship in China." *Journal of Politics* 81, no. 4 (October 2019).

Haggard, Stephan, and Robert R. Kaufman. *Dictators and Democrats: Masses, Elites, and Regime Change.* Princeton, NJ: Princeton University Press, 2016.

Han, Enze. *Contestation and Adaptation: The Politics of National Identity in China.* New York: Oxford University Press, 2013.

Han, Rongbin. *Contesting Cyberspace in China: Online Expression and Authoritarian Resilience.* New York: Columbia University Press, 2018.

Hancock, Tom. "China Clears Shaolin Temple's 'CEO Monk' of Corruption." *Financial Times,* February 6, 2017. https://www.ft.com/content/b2fe493c-ecee-11e6-930f-061b01e23655, accessed April 8, 2019.

Hao, Feng. "Green Peafowl Lawsuit Exposes Dam Damage." *China Dialogue,* November 19, 2018. https://www.chinadialogue.net/article/show/single/en/10939-Green-peafowl-lawsuit -exposes-dam-damage, accessed July 17, 2019.

Harding, Harry. *China's Second Revolution: Reform after Mao.* Washington, DC: Brookings, 1987.

———. "The Chinese State in Crisis." In Roderick MacFarquhar, ed., *The Politics of China,* 3rd ed. New York: Cambridge University Press, 2011.

Hasmath, Reza, Timothy Hildebrandt, and Jennifer Y. J. Hsu. "Conceptualizing Government-Organized Non-Governmental Organizations." *Journal of Civil Society* 15, no. 3 (2019): 267–84.

Hasmath, Reza, and Jennifer Y. J. Hsu. "Isomorphic Pressures, Epistemic Communities and State-NGO Collaboration in China." *China Quarterly*, no. 220 (December 2014): 936–54.

———. "Communities of Practice and the NGO Sector in China." Forthcoming.

He, Baogang. *Rural Democracy in China: The Role of Village Elections.* New York: Palgrave, 2007.

———. "Reconciling Deliberation and Representation: Chinese Challenges to Deliberative Democracy." *Representation* 51, no. 1 (2015): 35–50.

He, Baogang, and Mark Warren. "Authoritarian Deliberation: The Deliberative Turn in Chinese Political Development." *Perspectives on Politics* 9, no. 2 (Summer 2011), 269–89.

———. "Authoritarian Deliberation in China." *Daedalus* 146, no. 3 (Summer 2017): 159.

Heilmann, Sebastian. "From Local Experiments to National Policy: The Origins of China's Distinctive Policy Process." *China Journal*, no. 59 (January 2008): 1–30.

———, ed. *China's Political System.* Lanham, MD: Rowman & Littlefield, 2017.

Heilmann, Sebastian, and Elizabeth J. Perry, eds. *Mao's Invisible Hand: The Political Foundations of Adaptive Governance in China.* Cambridge, MA: Harvard University Asia Center, 2011.

Hernandez, Javier. "She's on a #MeToo Mission in China, Battling Censors and Lawsuits." *New York Times*, January 4, 2019. https://www.nytimes.com/2019/01/04/world/asia/china-zhou -xiaoxuan-metoo.html?_ga=2.50293414.1022361453.1549433306-1393789027.1549433306, ac- cessed March 18, 2019.

Heurlin, Christopher. *Responsive Authoritarianism in China: Land, Protests, and Policy-Making.* New York: Cambridge University Press, 2016.

Hildebrandt, Timothy. *Social Organizations and the Authoritarian State in China.* New York: Cambridge University Press, 2013.

Hirschman, Alfred. *Exit, Voice and Loyalty: Responses to Decline in Firms, Organizations, and States.* Cambridge, MA: Harvard University Press, 1970.

Hong Fincher, Leta. *Betraying Big Brother: The Feminist Awakening in China?* London: Verso, 2018.

Horowitz, Jason, and Ian Johnson. "China and Vatican Reach Deal on Appointment of New Bishops." *New York Times*, September 22, 2018. https://www.nytimes.com/2018/09/22 /world/asia/china-vatican-bishops.html, accessed April 12, 2019.

Horsley, Jamie. "China's Orwellian Social Credit Score Isn't Real." *Foreign Policy*, November 16, 2018; https://foreignpolicy.com/2018/11/16/chinas-orwellian-social-credit-score-isnt-real /, accessed September 2, 2020.

———. "Public Participation in the People's Republic: Developing a More Participatory Gov- ernance Model in China." *Yale Law School*, 2009. https://law.yale.edu/system/files /documents/pdf/Intellectual_Life/CL-PP-PP_in_the__PRC_FINAL_91609.pdf, ac- cessed August 21, 2019.

Hou, Yue. *The Private Sector in Public Service: Selective Property Rights in China.* New York: Cam- bridge University Press, 2019.

Howell, Jude. "All-China Federation of Trade Unions beyond Reform? The Slow March of Di- rect Elections." *China Quarterly*, no. 196 (December 2008): 845–63.

———. "Shall We Dance? Welfarist Incorporation and the Politics of State-Labour NGO Rela- tions." *China Quarterly*, no. 223 (September 2015): 702–23.

Howell, Jude. "NGOs and Civil Society: The Politics of Crafting a Civic Welfare Infrastructure in the Hu-Wen Period." *China Quarterly*, no. 237 (March 2019): 58–81.

Howell, Jude, and Jane Duckett. "Re-assessing the Hu-Wen Era: A Golden Age or Lost Decade for Social Policy in China." *China Quarterly*, no. 237 (March 2019): 1–14.

Hsu, Carolyn L., and Yuzhou Jiang. "An Institutional Approach to Chinese NGOs: State Alliance versus State Avoidance Strategies." *China Quarterly*, no. 221 (March 2015): 100–122.

Hsu, Carolyn L., and Jessica C. Teets, "Is China's New Overseas NGO Management Law Sounding the Death Knell for Civil Society? Maybe Not." *Asia-Pacific Journal* 14, issue 4, no. 3 (February 15, 2016).

Hsu, Jennifer Y. J., Carolyn L. Hsu, and Reza Hasmath. "NGO Strategies in an Authoritarian Context, and Their Implications for Citizenship: The Case of the People's Republic of China." *Voluntas* 28, no. 3 (June 2017): 1157–79.

Hsu, Jennifer Y. J., Timothy Hildebrandt, and Reza Hasmath. "'Going Out' or Staying In? The Expansion of Chinese NGOs in Africa." *Development Policy Review* 34, no. 3 (May 2016): 423–39.

Hui, Victoria Tin-bor. "Hong Kong's Umbrella Movement: The Protests and Beyond." *Journal of Democracy* 26, no. 2 (April 2015): 111–21.

Human Rights Watch. "China's Algorithms of Repression: Reverse Engineering a Xinjiang Police Mass Surveillance App." May 1, 2019. https://www.hrw.org/report/2019/05/02/chinas -algorithms-repression/reverse-engineering-xinjiang-police-mass, accessed May 9, 2019.

Hume, Tim. "'Eastern Lightning': The Banned Religious Group That Has China Worried." *CNN*, February 2, 2015. https://www.cnn.com/2014/06/06/world/asia/china-eastern -lightning-killing/index.html, accessed September 14, 2019.

Huntington, Samuel P. *Political Order in Changing Societies*. New Haven, CT: Yale University Press, 1970.

———. *The Third Wave: Democratization in the Late Twentieth Century*. Norman: University of Oklahoma Press, 1991.

Inglehart, Ronald. *Modernization and Postmodernization: Cultural, Economic, and Political Change in 43 Societies*. Princeton, NJ: Princeton University Press, 1997.

Inglehart, Ronald, and Christian Welzel. *Modernization, Cultural Change, and Democracy*. New York: Cambridge University Press, 2005.

———. "How Development Leads to Democracy: What We Know about Modernization." *Foreign Affairs* 88, no. 2 (March/April 2009): 33–48.

Jacobs, Andrew, and Chris Buckley. "Chinese Activists Test New Leader and Are Crushed." *New York Times*, January 14, 2014. https://www.nytimes.com/2014/01/16/world/asia/chinese -activists-test-new-leader-and-are-crushed.html, accessed September 19, 2019.

Johnson, Chris K., Scott Kennedy, and Mingda Qiu. "Xi's Signature Governance Innovation: The Rise of Leading Small Groups." Washington, DC: Center for Strategic and International Studies, October 17, 2017, https://www.csis.org/analysis/xis-signature-governance -innovation-rise-leading-small-groups, accessed August 21, 2019.

Johnson, Ian. "In Landmark Ceremony, a Catholic Bishop Is Installed in China." *New York Times*, August 28, 2019. https://www.nytimes.com/2019/08/28/world/asia/catholic-bishop -china.html, accessed September 7, 2019.

———. *The Souls of China: The Return of Religion after Mao*. New York: Vintage, 2017.

Johnston, Alastair Iain. "How New and Assertive Is China's New Assertiveness?" *International Security* 37, no. 4 (Spring 2013): 7–48.

———. "Is Chinese Nationalism Rising? Evidence from Beijing." *International Security* 41, no. 3 (2017): 7–43.

Kelliher, Daniel. "The Chinese Debate over Village Self-government." *China Journal* 37 (January 1997): 63–86.

Kennedy, John James. "The Price of Democracy: Vote Buying and Village Elections in China." *Asian Politics and Policy* 2, no. 4 (2010): 617–31.

Kennedy, Scott. "The Myth of the Beijing Consensus." *Journal of Contemporary China* 19, no. 65 (June 2010): 461–77.

Kim, Yongshin, Doo Hwan Kim, and Seokho Kim. "Who Is Nationalist Now in China?: Some Findings from the 2008 East Asian Social Survey." *China: An International Journal* 14, no. 4 (November 2016): 131–43.

Kindopp, Jason. "Fragmented yet Defiant: Protestant Resilience under Chinese Communist Party Rule." In Jason Kindopp and Carol Hamrin, eds., *God and Caesar in China: Policy Implications of Church-State Tensions*. Washington, DC: Brookings Institution Press, 2004.

King, Gary, Jennifer Pan, and Margaret E. Roberts. "How Censorship in China Allows Government Criticism but Silences Collective Expression," *American Political Science Review* 107, no. 2 (2013): 326–43.

Klett, Leah MarieAnn. "Two Chinese Catholic Bishops Ordained under Landmark China-Vatican Agreement." *Christian Post*, August 29, 2019. https://www.christianpost.com/news/two-chinese-catholic-bishops-ordained-under-landmark-china-vatican-agreement.html, accessed September 7, 2019.

Koesel, Karrie J. "China's Patriotic Pentecostals." *Review of Religion and Chinese Society* 1 no. 1, (April 2014): 131–55.

———. "The Political Economy of Religious Revival." *Politics and Religion* 8, no. 2 (June 2015): 211–35.

———. *Religion and Authoritarianism: Cooperation, Conflict, and the Consequences*. New York: Cambridge University Press, 2014.

———. "Religion and the Regime: Cooperation and Conflict in Contemporary Russia and China." *World Politics* 69, no. 4 (October 2017): 676–712.

Kornreich, Yoel, Ilan Vertinsky, and Pitman B. Potter. "Consultation and Deliberation in China: The Making of China's Health-Care Reform." *China Journal*, no. 68 (July 2012): 176–203.

Kostka, Genia. "What Do People in China Think about 'Social Credit' Monitoring?" *Washington Post*, March 21, 2019. https://www.washingtonpost.com/politics/2019/03/21/what-do-people-china-think-about-social-credit-monitoring/?utm_term=.b90e91139d44, accessed March 21, 2019.

Kostka, Genia, and Xiaofan Yu. "Career Backgrounds of Municipal Party Secretaries in China: Why Do So Few Municipal Party Secretaries Rise from the County Level?" *Modern China* 41, no. 5 (September 2015): 467–505.

Kou, Chien-Wen, and Wen-Hsuan Tsai. "'Sprinting with Small Steps' Towards Promotion: Solutions for the Age Dilemma in the CCP Cadre Appointment System," *China Journal*, no. 71 (January 2014): 153–71.

Kroeber, Arthur R. *China's Economy: What Everyone Needs to Know*. New York: Oxford University Press, 2016.

Kuhn, Robert Lawrence. *The Man Who Changed China: The Life and Legacy of Jiang Zemin*. New York: Crown Publishers, 2004.

Kuran, Timur. "Now Out of Never: The Element of Surprise in the East European Revolution of 1989." *World Politics* 44, no. 1 (October 1991): 7–48.

Laliberté, André. "Buddhist Revival under State Watch." *Journal of Current Chinese Affairs* 40, no. 2 (June 2011): 110.

———. "Managing Religious Diversity in China: Contradictions of Imperial and Foreign Legacies." *Studies in Religion* 45, no. 4 (December 2016): 495–519.

———. "The Politicization of Religion by the CCP: A Selective Retrieval." *Asiatische Studien—Études Asiatiques* 69, no. 1 (April 2015): 185–211.

Lam, Willy Wo-Lap. *Chinese Politics in the Hu Jintao Era: New Leaders, New Challenges*. Armonk, NY: M. E. Sharpe, 2006.

———. *Chinese Politics in the Era of Xi Jinping: Renaissance, Reform, or Retrogression?* New York: Routledge, 2015.

Landry, Pierre F., Xiaobo Lü, and Haiyan Duan. "Does Performance Matter? Evaluating Political Selection Along the Chinese Administrative Ladder." *Comparative Political Studies* 51, no. 8 (July 2018): 1074–1105.

Lardy, Nicholas. *The State Strikes Back: The End of Economic Reform in China?* Washington, DC: Peterson Institute for International Economics, 2019.

Laris, Michael. "U.S., China Reach Deal on Embassy Payments." *Washington Post*, December 16, 1999. https://www.washingtonpost.com/archive/politics/1999/12/16/us-china-reach-deal-on-embassy-payments/690c1ec6-b118-487a-a086-fc850ef67a67/?utm_term=.f5ff5cf06337, accessed May 2, 2019.

Larmer, Brook. "Li Na, China's Tennis Rebel." *New York Times*, August 23, 2013. https://www.nytimes.com/2013/08/25/magazine/li-na-chinas-tennis-rebel.html, accessed May 9, 2019.

Lau, Mimi. "Chinese Arabic School to Close as Areas with Muslim Populations Are Urged to Study the Xinjiang Way." *South China Morning Post*, December 9, 2018. https://www.scmp.com/news/china/politics/article/2177037/chinese-arabic-school-close-areas-muslim-populations-are-urged, accessed September 11, 2019.

Lee, Charlotte P. *Training the Party: Party Adaptation and Elite Training on Reform-Era China*. New York: Cambridge University Press, 2015.

Lee, Ching Kwan. *Against the Law: Labor Protests in China's Rustbelt and Sunbelt*. Berkeley: University of California Press, 2007.

Lee, Ching Kwan, and Yonghong Zhang. "The Power of Instability: Unraveling the Microfoundations of Bargained Authoritarianism in China." *American Journal of Sociology* 118, no. 6 (May 2013): 1475–1508.

Lee, Sing, and Arthur Kleinman. "Suicide as Resistance in Chinese Society." In Elizabeth J. Perry and Mark Selden, eds., *Chinese Society: Change, Conflict, and Resistance*. London and New York: Routledge, 2000.

Levitsky, Steven, and Lucan Way. "The Durability of Revolutionary Regimes." *Journal of Democracy* 24, no. 3 (July 2013): 5–17.

Li, Cheng. *China's Leaders: The Next Generation*. New York, NY: Rowman & Littlefield. 2001.

———. *Chinese Politics in the Xi Jinping Era: Reassessing Collective Leadership*. Washington, DC: Brookings Institution Press, 2016.

———. "The End of the CCP's Authoritarian Resilience? A Tripartite Assessment of Shifting Power in China." *China Quarterly*, no. 211 (September 2012): 595–623.

———. "The New Bipartisanship within the Chinese Communist Party." *Orbis* 49, no. 3 (Summer 2005): 387–400.

Li, Cheng, and Lynn White. "The Fifteenth Central Committee of the Chinese Communist Party: Full-Fledged Technocratic Leadership with Partial Control by Jiang Zemin." *Asian Survey* 38, no. 3 (March 1998): 231–64.

Li, Hongbin, and Li-An Zhou. "Political Turnover and Economic Performance: The Incentive Role of Personnel Control in China." *Journal of Public Economics* 89, nos. 9/10 (2005): 1743–62.

Li, Lianjiang. "Political Trust and Petitioning in the Chinese Countryside." *Comparative Politics* 40, no. 2 (January 2008): 209–26.

———. "The Politics of Introducing Direct Township Elections in China." *China Quarterly*, no. 171 (September 2002): 704–23.

Lieberthal, Kenneth G., and Michel Oksenberg. *Policy Making in China: Leaders, Structures, and Processes*. Princeton, NJ: Princeton University Press, 1988.

Lieberthal, Kenneth G., and David M. Lampton, eds. *Bureaucracy, Politics, and Decision Making in Post-Mao China*. Berkeley: University of California Press, 1992.

"Life Inside China's Total Surveillance State." *Wall Street Journal*, December 19, 2017. https://www.wsj.com/video/life-inside-chinas-total-surveillance-state/CE86DA19-D55D-4F12-AC6A-3B2A573492CF.html, accessed October 14, 2018.

Lo, Sonny Shiu-Hing. "Hong Kong." In William A. Joseph, ed., *Politics in China*, 3rd ed. New York: Oxford University Press, 2019.

Lorentzen, Peter L. "Designing Contentious Politics in Post-1989 China." *Modern China* 43, no. 5 (September 2017): 459–93.

———. "Regularizing Rioting: Permitting Public Protest in an Authoritarian Regime." *Quarterly Journal of Political Science* 8, no. 2 (2013): 127–58.

Lorentzen, Peter L., Pierre Landry, and John Yasuda. "Undermining Authoritarian Innovation: The Power of China's Industrial Giants." *Journal of Politics* 76, no. 1 (January 2014): 182–94.

Lu, Jie. *Varieties of Governance in China: Migration and Institutional Change in Chinese Villages*. New York: Oxford University Press, 2014.

Lü, Xiaobo, and Pierre F. Landry. "Show Me the Money: Interjurisdiction Political Competition and Fiscal Extraction in China." *American Political Science Review* 108, no. 3 (August 2014): 706–22.

Lynch, Marc. "After Egypt: The Promise and Limitations of the Online Challenge to the Authoritarian Arab State." *Perspectives on Politics* 9, no. 2 (June 2011): 301–18.

Ma, Deyong, and Szu-chien Hsu, "The Political Consequences of Deliberative Democracy and Electoral Democracy in China: An Empirical Comparative Analysis from Four Counties." *China Review* 18, no. 2 (May 2018): 21.

Ma, Josephine, Linda Lew, and Lee Jeong-ho. "A Third of Coronavirus Cases May Be 'Silent Carriers,' Classified Chinese Data Suggests." *South China Morning Post*, March 22, 2020. https://www.scmp.com/news/china/society/article/3076323/third-coronavirus-cases-may-be-silent-carriers-classified, accessed March 31, 2020.

MacFarquhar, Roderick, ed. *The Politics of China*, 3rd ed. New York: Cambridge University Press, 2011.

MacFarquhar, Roderick, and Michael Schoenhals. *Mao's Last Revolution*. Cambridge, MA: Harvard University Press, 2006.

Mahtani, Shibani. "A Student in Boston Wrote 'I am from Hong Kong.' An Onslaught of Chinese Anger Followed." *Washington Post*, May 25, 2019. https://www.washingtonpost.com/world/asia_pacific/a-student-in-boston-wrote-i-am-from-hong-kong-an-onslaught-of-chinese-anger-followed/2019/05/24/298ea3ee-719a-11e9-9331-30bc5836f48e_story.html, accessed May 25, 2019.

Manion, Melanie. "The Cadre Management System, Post-Mao: The Appointment, Promotion, Transfer and Removal of Party and State Leaders." *China Quarterly*, no. 102 (June 1985): 212–19.

———. "The Electoral Connection in the Chinese Countryside." *American Political Science Review* 90, no. 4 (December 1996): 736–48.

———. "How to Assess Village Elections in China." *Journal of Contemporary China* 18, no. 60 (June 2009): 379–83.

———. *Information for Autocrats: Representation in Chinese Local Congresses*. New York: Cambridge University Press, 2015.

———. "When Communist Party Candidates Can Lose, Who Wins?" *China Quarterly*, no. 195 (September 2008): 607–30.

Mann, James. *The China Fantasy: How Our Leaders Explain Away Chinese Repression*. New York: Viking, 2007.

Mansfield, Edward, and Jack Snyder. *Electing to Fight: Why Emerging Democracies Go to War*. Cambridge, MA: MIT Press, 2007.

Mao Zedong, "Some Questions Concerning Methods of Leadership," *Selected Works of Mao Tse-Tung*, vol. 3 (Beijing: Foreign Languages Press, 1967).

Martin, Peter. "Is Xi Jinping's Power Grab Starting to Backfire?" *Bloomberg Businessweek*, August 7, 2018. https://www.bloomberg.com/news/articles/2018-08-07/is-xi-jinping-s-bold-china-power-grab-starting-to-backfire, accessed August 7, 2018.

May, Tiffany, and Amy Qin. "The High School Course Beijing Accuses of Radicalizing Hong Kong." *New York Times*, September 1, 2019. https://www.nytimes.com/2019/09/01/world/asia/hong-kong-protests-education-china.html, accessed September 16, 2019.

Mendelson, Sarah E., and Theodore P. Gerber. "Soviet Nostalgia: An Impediment to Russian Democratization." *Washington Quarterly* 29, no. 1 (2005): 83–96.

Mertha, Andrew C. *China's Water Warriors: Citizen Action and Policy Change*. Ithaca, NY: Cornell University Press, 2008.

———. "'Fragmented Authoritarianism 2.0': Political Pluralization in the Chinese Policy Process." *China Quarterly*, no. 200 (December 2009): 995–1012.

Michelson, Ethan. "Public Goods and State-Society Relations: An Impact Study of China's Rural Stimulus." In Dali L. Yang, ed., *The Global Recession and China's Political Economy*. New York: Palgrave Macmillan, 2012.

Miller, Alice. "Who Does Xi Jinping Know and How Does He Know Them?" *China Leadership Monitor*, no. 32 (Spring 2010): 1–8.

———. "The Succession of Hu Jintao." *China Leadership Monitor*, no. 2 (Spring 2012): 1–8.

Minzner, Carl. *End of an Era: How China's Authoritarian Revival Is Undermining Its Rise*. New York: Oxford University Press, 2018.

Mitter, Rana. *China's War with Japan 1937–1945: The Struggle for Survival*. New York: Penguin Books, 2013.

Moore, Barrington. *Social Origins of Dictatorship and Democracy: Lord and Peasant in the Making of the Modern World*. Boston: Beacon Press, 1966.

Mozur, Paul. "In Hong Kong Protests, Faces Become Weapons." *New York Times*, July 27, 2019. https://www.nytimes.com/2019/07/26/technology/hong-kong-protests-facial-recognition-surveillance.html, accessed July 27, 2019.

Mozur, Paul, Jonah M. Kessel, and Melissa Chan. "Made in China, Exported to the World: The Surveillance State." *New York Times*, April 24, 2019. https://www.nytimes.com/2019/04/24/technology/ecuador-surveillance-cameras-police-government.html, accessed May 6, 2019.

Nathan, Andrew J. "Authoritarian Resilience." *Journal of Democracy* 14, no. 1 (January 2003): 6–17.

———. "The Puzzle of the Chinese Middle Class." *Journal of Democracy* 27, no. 2 (April 2016): 5–19.

Nathan, Andrew J., and Perry Link, eds. *The Tiananmen Papers*. New York: Public Affairs, 2001.

Nathan, Andrew J., and Andrew Scobell. *China's Search for Security*. New York: Columbia University Press, 2012.

Naughton, Barry. *Growing out of the Plan: Chinese Economic Reform, 1978–1993*. New York: Cambridge University Press, 1995.

Norris, Pippa. *Democratic Deficit: Critical Citizens Revisited*. New York: Cambridge University Press, 2011.

Norris, Pippa, and Ronald Inglehart. *Cultural Backlash: Trump, Brexit, and Authoritarian Populism*. New York: Cambridge University Press, 2019.

O'Brien, Kevin J. "Implementing Political Reform in China's Villages." *Australian Journal of Chinese Affairs*, no. 32 (July 1994): 33–59.

———. "Rightful Resistance." *World Politics* 49, no. 1 (October 1996): 31–55.

———. "Rightful Resistance Revisited." *Journal of Peasant Studies* 40, no. 6 (2013): 1051–62.

O'Brien, Kevin J., and Yanhua Deng. "The Reach of the State: Work Units, Family Ties and 'Harmonious Demolition.'" *China Journal* 74 (July 2015): 1–17.

———. "Repression Backfires: Tactical Radicalization and Protest Spectacle in Rural China." *Journal of Contemporary China* 24, no. 93 (2015): 457–70.

O'Brien, Kevin J., and Rongbin Han. "Path to Democracy? Assessing Village Elections in China." *Journal of Contemporary China* 18, no. 60 (June 2009): 359–78.

O'Brien, Kevin J., and Lianjiang Li. "Accommodating 'Democracy' in a One-Party State: Introducing Village Elections in China." *China Quarterly*, no. 162 (June 2000): 465–89.

———. "Campaign Nostalgia in the Chinese Countryside." *Asian Survey* 39, no. 3 (May/June, 1999): 375–93.

———. *Rightful Resistance in Rural China*. New York: Cambridge University Press, 2006.

———. "Selective Policy Implementation in Rural China." *Comparative Politics* 31, no. 2 (January 1999): 167–86.

Ong, Lynette H. "Thugs and Outsourcing of State Repression in China." *China Journal* 80 (July 2018): 94–110.

Ong, Lynette H. "'Thugs-for-Hire': Subcontracting of State Coercion and State Capacity in China." *Perspectives on Politics* 16, no. 3 (September 2018): 680–95.

Osnos, Evan. "Angry Youth: The New Generation's Neo-Con Nationalists." *New Yorker*, July 28, 2008.

Ownby, David. *Falun Gong and the Future of China*. New York: Oxford University Press, 2008.

Pan, Philip P. *Out of Mao's Shadow: The Struggle for the Soul of a New China*. New York: Simon and Schuster, 2008.

Pei, Minxin. "China's Coming Upheaval: Competition, the Coronavirus, and the Weakness of Xi Jinping," *Foreign Affairs* 99, no. 3 (May/June 2020): 82–95.

———. *China's Crony Capitalism: The Dynamics of Regime Decay*. Cambridge, MA: Harvard University Press, 2016.

———. *China's Trapped Transition: The Limits of Developmental Autocracy*. Cambridge, MA: Harvard University Press, 2006.

———. "'Creeping Democratization' in China." *Journal of Democracy* 6, no. 4 (October 1995): 65–79.

Perry, Elizabeth J. Anyuan: *Mining China's Revolutionary Tradition*. Berkeley: University of California Press, 2012.

———. "Chinese Conceptions of 'Rights': From Mencius to Mao—and Now." *Perspectives on Politics* 6, no. 1 (March 2008): 37–50.

———. "Labor Divided: Sources of State Formation in Modern China." In Joel Migdal, Atul Kohli, and Vivienne Shue, eds., *State Power and Social Forces: Domination and Transformation in the Third World*. New York: Cambridge University Press, 1994.

Phillips, Tom. "Joy as China Shelves Plans to Dam 'Angry River.'" *Guardian*, December 2, 2016. https://www.theguardian.com/world/2016/dec/02/joy-as-china-shelves-plans-to-dam-angry-river, accessed August 19, 2019.

"Plagiarism and Xi Jinping." *AsiaSentinel*, September 24, 2013. https://www.asiasentinel.com/politics/plagiarism-and-xi-jinping/, accessed July 17, 2018.

Plumer, Brad. "Coal Pollution in China Is Cutting Life Expectancy by 5.5 Years." *Washington Post*, July 8, 2013. http://www.washingtonpost.com/blogs/wonkblog/wp/2013/07/08/chinas-coal-pollution-is-much-deadlier-than-anyone-realized/, accessed May 19, 2020.

Powers, John. *The Buddha Party: How the People's Republic of China Works to Define and Control Tibetan Buddhism*. New York: Oxford, 2017.

"Professor Jia Xijin: Two Years of the Overseas NGO Law." *China Development Brief: NGOnews*, December 12, 2018. https://mp.weixin.qq.com/s/jQggzCN-5TpG9NeTWImbBw, accessed July 15, 2019.

Przeworski, Adam, and Fernando Limongi. "Modernization: Theories and Facts," *World Politics* 49, no. 2 (January 1997): 155–83.

Putnam, Robert D. *Bowling Alone: The Collapse and Revival of American Community*. New York: Simon and Schuster, 2001.

———. *Making Democracy Work: Civic Traditions in Italy*. Princeton, NJ: Princeton University Press, 1993.

Qian, Licheng, Bin Xu, and Dingding Chen. "Does History Education Promote Nationalism in China? A 'Limited Effect' Explanation." *Journal of Contemporary China* 26, no. 104 (2017): 199–212.

Qin, Amy, and Cao Li, "China Pushes for Quiet Burials as Coronavirus Death Toll Is Questioned," *New York Times*, April 3, 2020. https://www.nytimes.com/2020/04/03/world/asia/coronavirus-china-grief-deaths.html, accessed April 4, 2020.

"Rare Release of Xi's Speech on Virus Puzzles Top China Watchers." *Bloomberg News*, February 17, 2020. https://www.bloomberg.com/news/articles/2020-02-17/rare-release-of-xi-s-speech-on-virus-puzzles-top-china-watchers, accessed February 17, 2020.

Rauhala, Emily. "China's Claim of Coronavirus Victory in Wuhan Brings Hope, but Experts Worry It Is Premature." *Washington Post*, March 25, 2020. https://www.washingtonpost.com/world/asia_pacific/china-wuhan-coronavirus-zero-cases/2020/03/25/19bdbbc2-6d15-11ea-a156-0048b62cdb51_story.html, accessed March 25, 2020.

Reilly, James. *Strong Society, Smart State: The Rise of Public Opinion in China's Japan Policy*. New York: Columbia University Press, 2012.

———. "A Wave to Worry About? Public Opinion, Foreign Policy and China's Anti-Japanese Protests." *Journal of Contemporary China* 23, no. 86 (2014): 197–215.

Roberts, Margaret E. *Censored: Distraction and Diversion inside China's Great Firewall*. Princeton, NJ: Princeton University Press, 2018.

Rowen, Henry S. "When Will the Chinese People Be Free?" *Journal of Democracy* 18, no. 3 (July 2007): 38–62.

Russett, Bruce. *Grasping the Democratic Peace: Principles for a Post-Cold War World*. Princeton, NJ: Princeton University Press, 1993.

Saich, Tony. "Negotiating the State: The Development of Social Organizations in China." *China Quarterly*, no. 161 (March 2000): 124–41.

———. *Providing Public Goods in Transitional China*. New York: Palgrave Macmillan, 2008.

Saunders, Phillip C., Arthur S. Ding, Andrew Scobell, Andrew N. D. Yang, and Joel Wuthnow, eds. *Chairman Xi Remakes the PLA: Assessing Chinese Military Reforms*. Washington, DC: National Defense University Press, 2018.

Schell, Orville, and John Delury. *Wealth and Power: China's Long March to the 21st Century*. New York: Random House, 2014.

Schmitter, Philippe C., and Terry Lynn Karl. "What Democracy Is . . . and Is Not." *Journal of Democracy* 2, no. 1 (Summer 1991): 75–88.

Schwartz, Jonathan, and Shawn Shieh, eds. *State and Society Responses to Social Welfare Needs in China: Serving the People*. New York and London: Routledge, 2009.

Shambaugh, David. *China's Communist Party: Atrophy and Adaptation*. Berkeley and Washington, DC: University of California Press and Woodrow Wilson Center Press, 2009.

———. *China's Future?* Cambridge and Malden, MA: Polity, 2016.

———. "The Dynamics of Elite Politics during the Jiang Era." *China Journal*, no. 45 (January 2001): 101–11.

"Shanghai Bishop Ma's Open Repentance Shocks Catholics." *UCAnews.com*, June 22, 2016. https://www.ucanews.com/news/shanghai-bishop-mas-open-repentance-shocks-catholics/76313, accessed September 7, 2019.

Shepherd, Christian. "China Outlaws Large Underground Protestant Church in Beijing." *Reuters*, September 9, 2018. https://www.reuters.com/article/us-china-religion/china -outlaws-large-underground-protestant-church-in-beijing-idUSKCN1LQ07W, accessed April 1, 2019.

Shi, Tianjian. *The Cultural Logic of Politics in Mainland China and Taiwan*. New York: Cambridge University Press, 2015.

———. "Village Committee Elections in China: Institutional Tactics for Democracy." *World Politics* 51, no. 3 (April 1999): 385–412.

Shieh, Shawn. "Remaking China's Civil Society in the Xi Jinping Era." *ChinaFile*, August 2, 2018, https://www.chinafile.com/reporting-opinion/viewpoint/remaking-chinas-civil-society-xi -jinping-era, accessed June 22, 2020.

Shieh, Shawn, and Guosheng Deng. "An Emerging Civil Society: The Impact of the 2008 Sichuan Earthquake on Grass-roots Associations in China." *China Journal*, no. 65 (January 2011): 181–94.

Shih, Gerry. "China Tightens Its Grip on Ethnic Hui." *Washington Post*, September 21, 2019. https://www.washingtonpost.com/world/asia_pacific/boiling-us-like-frogs-chinas -clampdown-on-muslims-creeps-into-the-heartland-finds-new-targets/2019/09/20 /25c8bb08-ba94-11e9-aeb2-a101a1fb27a7_story.html, accessed September 21, 2019.

———. "'If I Disappear': Chinese Students Make Farewell Messages amid Crackdowns over Labor Activism." *Washington Post*, May 25, 2019. https://www.washingtonpost.com/world /asia_pacific/if-i-disappear-chinese-students-make-farewell-messages-amid-crackdowns -over-labor-activism-/2019/05/25/6fc949c0-727d-11e9-9331-30bc5836f48e_story.html?utm _term=.e5cce0288eeb, accessed May 25, 2019.

Shih, Victor, Christopher Adolph, and Mingxing Liu. "Getting Ahead in the Communist Party: Explaining the Advancement of Central Committee Members in China." *American Political Science Review* 106, no. 1 (February 2012): 166–87.

Shih, Gerry, and Anna Kam. "Without Heroes or Martyrs: Hong Kong's Protest Movement Faces Its Defining Moment." *Washington Post*, August 16, 2019. https://www.washingtonpost .com/world/asia_pacific/without-heroes-or-martyrs-hong-kongs-protest-movement-faces -its-defining-moment/2019/08/16/d460ce74-bfe1-11e9-a8b0-7ed8a0d5dc5d_story.html, accessed August 20, 2019.

Shih, Gerry, and Emily Rauhala. "Angry over Campus Speech by Uighur Activist, Chinese Students in Canada Contact Their Consulate, Film Presentation." *Washington Post*, February 14, 2019. https://www.washingtonpost.com/world/angry-over-campus-speech-by-uighur -activist-students-in-canada-contact-chinese-consulate-film-presentation/2019/02/14 /a442fbe4-306d-11e9-ac6c-14eea99d5e24_story.html?utm_term=.a29f9a462783, accessed February 14, 2019.

Shirk, Susan L. *China: Fragile Superpower: How China's Internal Politics Could Derail Its Peaceful Rise*. New York: Oxford University Press, 2007.

———, ed. *Changing Media, Changing China*. New York: Oxford University Press, 2010.

Shue, Vivienne. "Legitimacy Crisis in China?" In Peter Hays Gries and Stanley Rosen, eds., *State and Society in 21st-Century China: Crisis, Contention and Legitimation*. New York: Routledge, 2004.

Simon, Karla. *Civil Society in China: The Legal Framework from Ancient Times to the "New Reform Era."* New York: Oxford University Press, 2013.

Slater, Dan. *Ordering Power: Contentious Politics and Authoritarian Leviathans in Southeast Asia.* New York: Cambridge University Press, 2010.

Smith, Graeme. "The Hollow State: Rural Governance in China." *China Quarterly*, no. 203 (September 2010): 601–18.

Smith, Tony. *Thinking Like a Communist: State and Legitimacy in the Soviet Union, China, and Cuba.* New York: W. W. Norton, 1987.

Snyder, Jack L. *From Voting to Violence: Democratization and Nationalist Conflict.* New York: W. W. Norton, 2000.

Snyder, Jack L., and Edward D. Mansfield. *Electing to Fight: Why Emerging Democracies Go to War.* Cambridge, MA: MIT Press, 2007.

Spires, Anthony J. "Lessons from Abroad: Foreign Influences on China's Emerging Civil Society." *China Journal*, no. 68 (July 2012): 125–46.

Spires, Anthony J., Lin Tao, and Kin-man Chan. "Societal Support for China's Grass-Roots NGOs: Evidence from Yunnan, Guangdong and Beijing." *China Journal*, no. 71 (January 2014), 65–90.

Steinhardt, H. Christoph, Linda Chelan Li, and Yihong Jiang. "The Identity Shift in Hong Kong since 1997: Measurement and Explanation." *Journal of Contemporary China* 27, no. 110 (2018): 261–76.

Stockmann, Daniela. *Media Commercialization and Authoritarian Rule in China.* New York: Cambridge University Press, 2012.

Stromseth, Jonathan R., Edmund J. Malesky, and Dimitar D. Gueorguiev. *China's Governance Puzzle: Enabling Transparency and Participation in a Single-Party State.* New York: Cambridge University Press, 2017.

Svolik, Milan. "Polarization versus Democracy." *Journal of Democracy* 30, no. 3 (July 2019): 20–32.

Tang, Wenfang. *Populist Authoritarianism: Chinese Political Culture and Regime Sustainability.* New York: Oxford University Press, 2016.

———. "The Worshipping Atheist: Institutional and Diffused Religiosities in China." *China: An International Journal* 12, no. 3 (December 2014): 1–26.

Tang, Wenfang, and Benjamin Darr. "Chinese Nationalism and Its Political and Social Origins." *Journal of Contemporary China* 21, no. 77 (2012), pp. 811–26.

Teets, Jessica C. *Civil Society under Authoritarianism: The China Model.* New York: Cambridge University Press, 2014.

———. "The Evolution of Civil Society in Yunnan Province: Contending Models of Civil Society Management in China." *Journal of Contemporary China* 24, no. 91 (2015): 158–75.

———. "Post-Earthquake Relief and Reconstruction Efforts: The Emergence of Civil Society in China?" *China Quarterly*, no. 198 (June 2009): 330–47.

Teets, Jessica C., and Oscar Almen. "Advocacy under Xi: NPO Strategies to Influence Policy Change." *Nonprofit Policy Forum*, 2018.

Teets, Jessica C., and Shawn Shieh, "CSOs as Social Entrepreneurs in China: Strategic Rebranding or Evolution?" forthcoming.

Teiwes, Frederick C. "The Politics of Succession: Previous Patterns and a New Process." In Wong, John and Yongnian Zheng, eds. *China's Post-Jiang Leadership Succession: Problems and Perspectives*, 21–58. Singapore: Singapore University Press and World Scientific Publishing, 2002.

Thornton, Patricia M. "The New Life of the Party: Party-Building and Social Engineering in Greater Shanghai." *China Journal*, no. 68 (July 2012): 58–78.

Tong, James. "The Devil Is in the Local: Provincial Religious Legislation in China, 2005–2012." *Religion, State and Society* 42, no. 1 (March 2014): 66–88.

———. "The New Religious Policy in China: Catching Up with Systemic Reforms." *Asian Survey* 50, no. 5, (September/October 2010): 859–87.

Tong, Yanqi. "State, Society, and Political Change in China and Hungary." *Comparative Politics* 26, no. 3 (April 1994): 333–53.

Truex, Rory. *Making Autocracy Work: Representation and Responsiveness in Modern China.* New York: Cambridge University Press, 2016.

———. "Focal Points, Dissident Calendars, and Preemptive Repression." *Journal of Conflict Resolution* 63, no. 4 (April 2019): 1032–52.

Tsai, Kellee S. *Capitalism without Democracy: The Private Sector in Contemporary China.* Ithaca, NY: Cornell University Press, 2007.

Tsai, Lily Lee. *Accountability without Democracy: Solidary Groups and Public Goods Provision in Rural China.* New York: Cambridge University Press, 2007.

Unger, Jonathan, ed. *Using the Past to Serve the Present: Historiography and Politics in Contemporary China.* Armonk, NY: M. E. Sharpe, 1993.

Unger, Jonathan, and Anita Chan. "China, Corporatism, and the East Asian Model." *The Australian Journal of Chinese Affairs*, no. 33 (January 1995): 29–53.

Uretsky, Elanah. *Occupational Hazards: Sex, Business, and HIV in Post-Mao China.* Stanford: Stanford University Press, 2016.

Vala, Carsten T. *The Politics of Protestant Churches and the Party-State in China: God above Party?* London and New York: Routledge, 2017.

———. "Protestant Christianity and Civil Society in Authoritarian China: The Impact of Official Churches and Unregistered 'Urban Churches' on Civil Society Development in the 2000s." *China Perspectives*, no. 3 (July 2012): 43–52.

Vala, Carsten T., and Kevin O'Brien. "Attraction without Networks: Recruiting Strangers to Unregistered Protestantism in China." *Mobilization: An International Quarterly* 12, no. 1 (March 2007): 79–94.

Van der Kamp, Denise, Peter Lorentzen, and Daniel Mattingly. "Racing to the Bottom or to the Top? Decentralization, Revenue Pressures, and Governance Reform in China." *World Development* 95 (July 2017): 164–76.

Veg, Sebastian. "'The Rise of 'Localism' and Civic Identity in Post-Handover Hong Kong: Questioning the Chinese Nation-State." *China Quarterly*, no. 230 (June 2017): 323–47.

Walder, Andrew G. "The Decline of Communist Power: Elements of a Theory of Institutional Change." *Theory and Society* 23, no. 2 (April 1994): 297–323.

Wallace, Jeremy L. *Cities and Stability: Urbanization, Redistribution and Regime Survival in China.* New York: Oxford University Press, 2014.

Wallace, Jeremy L., and Jessica Chen Weiss. "The Political Geography of Nationalist Protest in China." *China Quarterly*, no. 222 (June 2015): 403–29.

Wang, Jianwei, and Xiaojie Wang. "Media and Chinese Foreign Policy." *Journal of Contemporary China* 23, no. 86, (March 2014): 216–35.

Wang, Shaoguang. "Changing Models of China's Policy Agenda Setting." *Modern China* 34, no. 1 (January 2008): 56–87.

———. "Money and Autonomy: Patterns of Civil Society Finance and Their Implications." *Studies in Comparative International Development* 40, no. 4 (Winter 2006): 3–29.

Wang, Yuhua. *Tying the Autocrat's Hand: The Rise of the Rule of Law in China.* New York: Cambridge University Press, 2015.

Wang, Yuhua, and Carl Minzner. "The Rise of the Chinese Security State." *China Quarterly*, no. 222 (June 2015): 339–59.

Wang, Zheng. *Never Forget National Humiliation: Historical Memory in Chinese Politics.* New York: Columbia University Press, 2012.

Wang, Zhengxu, and Anastas Vangeli. "The Rules and Norms of Leadership Succession in China: From Deng Xiaoping to Xi Jinping and Beyond." *China Journal*, no. 76 (July 2016): 24–40.

Wedeman, Andrew. *Double Paradox: Rapid Growth and Rising Corruption in China.* Ithaca, NY: Cornell University Press, 2012.

Wee, Sui-Lee, and Paul Mozur. "China Uses DNA to Map Faces, with Help from the West." *New York Times*, December 10, 2019. https://www.nytimes.com/2019/12/03/business/china-dna-uighurs-xinjiang.html?smid=nytcore-ios-share, accessed December 20, 2019.

Wee, Sui-Lee, and Vivian Wang. "Here's How Wuhan Plans to Test All 11 Million of Its People for Coronavirus." *New York Times*, May 15, 2020. https://www.nytimes.com/2020/05/14/world/asia/coronavirus-testing-china-wuhan.html?referringSource=articleShare, accessed May 15, 2020.

Weiss, Jessica Chen. "Autocratic Signaling, Mass Audiences and Nationalist Protest in China." *International Organization* 67, no. 1 (January 2013): 1–35.

———. "How Hawkish Is the Chinese Public? Another Look at 'Rising Nationalism' and Chinese Foreign Policy." *Journal of Contemporary China* 28, no. 119 (2019): 679–95.

———. *Powerful Patriots: Nationalist Protest in China's Foreign Relations.* New York: Oxford University Press, 2014.

Weller, Robert, and Sun Yanfei. "Religion: The Dynamics of Religious Growth and Change." In Joseph Fewsmith, ed., *China Today, China Tomorrow: Domestic Politics, Economy, and Society.* Lanham, MD: Rowman & Littlefield Publishers, 2010.

White, Gordon, Jude Howell, and Shang Xiaoyuan. *In Search of Civil Society: Market Reform and Social Change in Contemporary China.* Oxford: Oxford University Press, 1996.

Whiting, Susan. "The Cadre Evaluation System at the Grass Roots: The Paradox of Party Rule." In Barry Naughton and Dali Yang, eds. *Holding China Together: Diversity and National Integration in the Post-Deng Era.* New York: Cambridge University Press, 2004.

Wines, Michael. "Liang Congjie, Chinese Environmental Pioneer, Dies at 78." *New York Times*, October 10, 2010. https://www.nytimes.com/2010/10/30/world/asia/30liang.html, accessed July 17, 2019.

Wong, Edward. "China's Global Message: We Are Tough but Not Threatening." *New York Times*, October 2, 2019. https://www.nytimes.com/2019/10/02/world/asia/china-world-parade -military.html?smid=nytcore-ios-share, accessed October 3, 2019.

Woods, Jackson S., and Bruce J. Dickson. "Victims and Patriots: Disaggregating Nationalism in Urban China." *Journal of Contemporary China* 26, no. 104 (2017): 167–82.

Wright, Daniel B. *The Promise of the Revolution: Stories of Fulfillment and Struggle in China's Hinterland*. Lanham, MD: Rowman & Littlefield, 2003.

Wright, Teresa. *Accepting Authoritarianism: State-Society Relations in China's Reform Era*. Stanford: Stanford University Press, 2010.

———. *Popular Protest in China*. Medford, MA: Polity Press, 2018.

Yan, Xiaojun, and Kai Zhou. "Fighting the Prairie Fire: Why Do Local Party-States in China Respond to Contentious Challengers Differently?" *China: An International Journal* 15, no. 4 (November 2017): 43–68.

Yang, Fenggang. *Religion in China: Survival and Renewal under Communist Rule*. New York: Oxford University Press, 2012.

Yang, Guobin. *The Power of the Internet in China: Citizen Activism Online*. New York, NY: Columbia University Press, 2009.

Yang, Yuan. "Inside China's Crackdown on Young Marxists." *Financial Times*, February 13, 2019. https://www.ft.com/content/fd087484-2f23-11e9-8744-e7016697f225, accessed March 28, 2019.

Yu, Elaine, and Austin Ramzy. "Amid Pandemic, Hong Kong Arrests Major Pro-Democracy Figures." *New York Times*, April 18, 2020. https://www.nytimes.com/2020/04/18/world/asia /hong-kong-arrests.html, accessed April 20, 2020.

Zhao, Ziyang. *Prisoner of the State: The Secret Journal of Premier Zhao Ziyang*. New York: Simon and Schuster, 2009.

Zhao, Suisheng. "A State-Led Nationalism: The Patriotic Education Campaign in Post-Tiananmen China." *Communist and Post-Communist Studies* 31, no. 3 (September 1998): 287–302.

———. "Xi Jinping's Maoist Revival." *Journal of Democracy* 27, no. 3 (July 2016): 83–97.

Zhao, Tan. "Vote Buying and Land Takings in China's Village Elections." *Journal of Contemporary China* 27, no. 110 (2018): 277–94.

Zheng, Yongnian, and Gang Chen. "Xi Jinping's Rise and Political Implications." *China: An International Journal* 7, no. 1 (2009): 1–30.

Zhong, Raymond, and Paul Mazur. "Tech Giants Feel the Squeeze as Xi Jinping Tightens His Grip." *New York Times*, May 2, 2018. https://www.nytimes.com/2018/05/02/technology /china-xi-jinping-technology-innovation.html, accessed August 17, 2018.

Zhu, Guobin. "Prosecuting 'Evil Cults:' a Critical Examination of Law Regarding Freedom of Religious Belief in Mainland China." *Human Rights Quarterly* 32, no. 3 (2010): 471–501.

Zhu, Jiangnan, and Dong Zhang. "Weapons of the Powerful: Authoritarian Elite Competition and Politicized Anticorruption in China." *Comparative Political Studies* 50, no. 9 (August 2017): 1186–1220.

Zhu, Zi. "Backfired Government Action and the Spillover Effect of Contention: A Case Study of the Anti-PX Protests in Maoming, China." *Journal of Contemporary China* 26, no. 106 (2017): 521–35.

INDEX

Page numbers in *italics* refer to figures.

Soviet Union, 12, 161; breakup of, 32, 176, 212, 229, 237, 246, 247, 251; Eastern European regimes backed by, 252; longevity of, 234; *nomenklatura* system in, 33, 74
special economic zones (SEZs), 19, 21, 60, 79, 94
stability maintenance funds, 144
Standing Committee, of Politburo, 26, 37, 50, 52, 57, 60, 68, 153, 237; appointments to, 30, 48, 63; membership of, 32, 33; power of, 31; Xi's membership in, 61–62
State Administration for Religious Affairs (SARA), 167
State Council, 33, 167
state-owned enterprises (SOEs), 23–24, 46, 78, 134, 147, 189
strikes, 134, 136
strongman (personalist) regimes, 232
student activists: crackdown on (1986), 244; Hong Kong protests denounced by, 212; Japan denounced by, 222, 223; Marxist groups formed by, 151–52; nationalist, 197–98; Uighurs denounced by, 208; in umbrella movement, 211; US bombing protested by, 215, 216, 221; after World War I, 217–18
suicide, 136
Sun Liping, 129
surveillance, 17–18; during COVID-19 epidemic, 70; on historical anniversaries, 148; of NGOs, 109; through party cells, 12, 22, 33–34, 35, 100, 109, 234, 254; of private sector, 22; of religious groups, 167–68, 180; technological advances in, 142–43; under Xi, 28

Taiping Rebellion (1850–64), 165
Taiwan, 165, 212, 233, 245, 247, 251
Tajikistan, 231
Taoism, 164, 166, 169
taxation, 39, 78; leadership promotion linked to, 44–45
technocrats, 21, 23, 54

temple associations, 96–97
Tencent (technology company), 155, 156
term limits, 27, 37, 43, 48–50, 64, 244; Xi's elimination of, 38, 52–53, 118, 232
terrorism, 208
Thatcher, Margaret, 210
Three Gorges Dam, 74–76
Three Represents theory, 22, 26
thugs, 140, 150, 213–14
Tianjin, 76, 175
Tiananmen Square protests (1989), 10, 22, 25, 171, 187, 222; commemorations of, 148; crackdown on, 20, 35, 55, 57, 104, 127–28, 178, 188, 198; democratization dampened by, 241; goals of, 104, 126–27; political careers shaped by, 54–55, 57, 237; strategic response to, 139; suppressed discussion of, 127–28
Tibet, 7, 109, 168, 188, 204, 253; patriotic education in, 9, 205, 209, 224; protests in, 57, 93, 204–6
Tibetan Buddhism, 164, 168, 176, 186, 188, 204
Tojo, Hideki, 222
torture, 140
tourism, 81, 113, 173, 174–75, 187, 190, 199
trade unions, 115
Treaty of Versailles (1919), 218
Trump, Donald, 69, 230
Tunisia, 101, 159, 246, 247
Turkey, 140

Uighurs, 142, 168, 186, 203–4, 206–9, 253
Ukraine, 101
UNESCO, 77
Unirule, 117–18
United Front Work Department, 167, 183
United Kingdom, 208, 212
United Nations, 220, 223
United States, 85, 199, 208; China policy of, 229, 249, 251–52; Chinese trade war with, 240; Chinese views of, 192, 193, 212, 216; civil society in, 124; COVID-19 pandemic in, 71; internet use in, 154; participatory

democracy in, 5, 66, 86, 88; religious practice
in, 170; surveillance flights by, 221; term
limits in, 50
urbanization, 3, 41, 81, 132, 177–78, 228, 235

Vatican, 184–85
Vietnam, 231, 251
village elections, 38–42, 130–31
voluntarism, 121–22
VPNs (virtual private networks), 143, 154–55

Wanbang (All Nations Missionary Church),
181–82
Wang, Yuhua, 260n26
Wang Lijun, 238
Wang Qishan, 52
Wang Yang, 2, 285n22
Wan Li, 257n25
water pollution, 80, 82, 85
Weber, Max, 183
WeChat, 155
Welzel, Christian, 228
Wen Jiabao, 77, 237
Wenling, 94, 95
Wenzhou, 178, 183–84
Winnie the Pooh, 155, 156
women's rights, 4, 150–51
World Bank, 65
World Health Organization, 65, 69
World Trade Organization, 84, 253n8
World War I, 217
World War II, 199, 219, 222, 229
Wu Bangguo, 245
Wuhan, 69–70, 71
Wukan (village), 1–2, 5, 41, 128, 147

Xiamen, 61, 145, 173
Xi Jinping, 3, 7, 12, 14, 156, 192–93, 216; career
path of, 37, 50, 52, 53, 54, 59–63, 232, 238;
civil society under, 104, 107, 112, 125;
corruption battled by, 26, 52, 60, 61, 78, 123,
236, 238–39; COVID-19 response by, 69,
71–72; decision making centralized by,

67, 78; environmental policies of, 83, 112;
nationalistic rhetoric of, 215; as Olympic
Games administrator, 152–53; party
exclusivity under, 34; party strengthened
by, 27–28, 33; power consolidated by,
26–27, 51–53, 64, 98, 226, 232–33, 235–36;
protests under, 139, 150–53, 158, 160; public
consultation backed by, 87; religious
policies of, 163–64, 176–77, 179, 186, 188, 190;
repressiveness of, 4, 6, 9, 36, 96, 99–100,
107, 129, 144, 150–52, 160, 176–77, 179, 230,
234, 236, 241, 245, 254; term limits eliminated
by, 38, 52–53, 118, 232
Xi Lihua, 116
Xinjiang, 7, 93, 185–86, 253; detention camps
in, 142, 143, 186, 206, 207, 208–9; patriotic
education in, 9, 204, 206–9; surveillance
in, 143, 168, 207
Xi Zhongxun, 60
Xue Jinbo, 1
Xu Zhangrun, 118
Xu Zhiyong, 99

Yangtze River, 74, 75
Yao Yilin, 257n25
Yasukuni Shrine, 222
Yeltsin, Boris, 247
Youth League Faction, 56, 59, 61–63
YouTube, 154, 155
Yugoslavia, 251
Yunnan Province, 77, 112, 113, 120

Zeng Qinghong, 58, 63
Zeng Qinghuai, 261n41
Zhang Xiaoming, 212
Zhao Ziyang, 54, 127, 237, 257n25
Zhejiang Province, 61, 94, 135
Zhengding County, 61
Zhongnanhai, 189, 238
Zhu Rongji, 21, 255n8
Zimbabwe, 208
Zion Church, 182
Zoom, 128